FRAMING A CONVENTION COMMUNITY

The European Convention on Human Rights (ECHR) has evolved from an international agreement into an integrated legal community with an ever more pervasive effect on domestic law and individuals. The supranational authority of the European Court of Human Rights bypasses the nation state in a growing number of areas. Understanding the evolution of the ECHR and its Court may help in explaining and contextualising growing resistance against the Court, and in developing possible responses. Examining the Convention system through the prism of supranationality, Cedric Marti offers a fresh, comprehensive and interdisciplinary perspective on the expanding adjudicatory powers of the Court, including law-making. Marti addresses the growing literature of institutional studies on human rights enforcement to ascertain the particularities of the ECHR and its relationship to domestic legal systems. This study will be of great value to both scholars of international law and human rights practitioners.

Cedric Marti is Attorney at Law in Zurich, Switzerland. He holds a doctorate from the University of Zurich and was a visiting fellow at the Amsterdam Center for International Law.

Framing a Convention Community

SUPRANATIONAL ASPECTS OF THE EUROPEAN CONVENTION ON HUMAN RIGHTS

CEDRIC MARTI
University of Zurich

CAMBRIDGE
UNIVERSITY PRESS

CAMBRIDGE
UNIVERSITY PRESS

University Printing House, Cambridge CB2 8BS, United Kingdom

One Liberty Plaza, 20th Floor, New York, NY 10006, USA

477 Williamstown Road, Port Melbourne, VIC 3207, Australia

314–321, 3rd Floor, Plot 3, Splendor Forum, Jasola District Centre, New Delhi – 110025, India

103 Penang Road, #05–06/07, Visioncrest Commercial, Singapore 238467

Cambridge University Press is part of the University of Cambridge.

It furthers the University's mission by disseminating knowledge in the pursuit of education, learning, and research at the highest international levels of excellence.

www.cambridge.org
Information on this title: www.cambridge.org/9781108830119
DOI: 10.1017/9781108909075

First published 2021

A catalogue record for this publication is available from the British Library.

Library of Congress Cataloging-in-Publication Data
NAMES: Marti, Cedric, 1986– author.
TITLE: Framing a convention community : supranational aspects of the European Convention on Human Rights / Cedric Marti, University of Zurich.
DESCRIPTION: Cambridge, United Kingdom ; New York, NY : Cambridge University Press, 2021. | Includes bibliographical references and index.
IDENTIFIERS: LCCN 2021005082 | ISBN 9781108830119 (hardback) | ISBN 9781108821636 (paperback) | ISBN 9781108909075 (ebook)
SUBJECTS: LCSH: Convention for the Protection of Human Rights and Fundamental Freedoms (1950 November 5) | Human rights – Europe. | European Court of Human Rights.
CLASSIFICATION: LCC KJC5132.A4195 M37 2021 | DDC 341.4/8094–dc23
LC record available at https://lccn.loc.gov/2021005082

ISBN 978-1-108-83011-9 Hardback

To my parents and Marlene

Contents

Preface and Acknowledgments *page* ix
Table of Cases xi
Table of International Instruments xxiii
List of Abbreviations xxvi

Introduction 1

Aim of the Study: The Convention through the Prism of Supranationality 1
Added Value and Place of the Study in Scholarship 3
Layout and Methodology 9

1 **Supranationality: Sources, Evolution, and Conceptions** 11

1.1 Polysemic Nature of Supranationality 11
1.2 International Law Origins 12
1.3 From a Political toward a Legal and Scholarly Notion of European Integration 18
1.4 Quintessential Concept of EU Law Scholarship 22
1.5 Notion of International Institutional Law 29
1.6 Conclusion 32

2 **Rediscovering Supranationality** 35

2.1 Supranationality for the Purpose of the Present Study 35
2.2 Toward a General Framework for Law Beyond the State 35
2.3 A Functional Approach: Legal Integration 39
2.4 Contextualization 51
2.5 Conclusion 59

3 **From International toward Supranational Adjudication** 60
3.1 The Evolution of the Convention System: A Process of Supranationalization 60
3.2 The Establishment of a Human Rights Protection System in Europe 61
3.3 Pull toward Supranational Adjudication 67
3.4 Protocol 11: Establishment of a Supranational Court 81
3.5 Conclusion 83

4 **Sites of Judicial Integration and Their Transformation** 85
4.1 Judicial Integration 85
4.2 External Judicial Review 88
4.3 Extending Judicial Integration to the Area of Remedies and Enforcement 108
4.4 Emergence of Compliance Review 117
4.5 The Court's New Advisory Jurisdiction 122
4.6 Conclusion 129

5 **Supranational Lawmaking** 132
5.1 Beyond the Individual Dispute: The Court's Lawmaking Function 132
5.2 Expansive Nature of ECHR Lawmaking 134
5.3 The ECtHR as a Community Court 137
5.4 Establishing a Pan-European Human Rights Standard 142
5.5 (Re-)Imposing the European Protection Standard 152
5.6 Third-Party Interventions 159
5.7 Conclusion 161

6 **From Supranational Adjudication to Supranational Law?** 163
6.1 Supranationalization of Convention Law 163
6.2 Beyond Implementation Freedom: Supranationality Lite 164
6.3 Vertical Integration *qua* Domestic Law 181
6.4 Conclusion 195

Conclusion | Framing a Convention Community 198
Supranational Aspects of the Convention 198
A Narrative of Supranationalization 199
The Convention Community 204

Bibliography 213
Index 234

Preface and Acknowledgments

When my doctoral supervisor approached me with the idea of researching supranational aspects of the ECHR, I was immediately intrigued by the proposal, but also concerned that some could take issue with the ambitious premise of such undertaking. As I agreed to the topic, my supervisor smiled and answered: "It's a tricky one, but one that allows for creative thinking." As it turned out, "tricky" was a slight understatement. Yet, writing this book has indeed been a creative process and one that has left me inspired in many ways.

I am greatly indebted to my doctoral supervisor Professor Helen Keller, who has promoted and supported my research and career continuously. The foundations for the present study were laid at the University of Zurich during my time as a research associate at her Chair. Working for and with her on many projects has been a truly formative experience on both an academic and practical level, for which I am immensely thankful. I am also grateful to the second reader of my PhD thesis, Professor Matthias Oesch, as well as Professor Sebastian Heselhaus for supporting my research and requests for funding. I am further obliged to Professor Samantha Besson, organizer of the Prodoc doctoral colloquium at the University of Fribourg in 2015, which helped me flesh out some of my conceptual ideas more clearly. Much of the writing process I conducted during a research stay at the University of Amsterdam, which was made possible by the generous funding of the Swiss National Science Foundation. I wish to thank the members of the Amsterdam Center for International Law, in particular Professors André Nollkaemper, Ingo Venzke and Yvonne Donders for their hospitality and interest in my research. Heartfelt thanks go to my family, friends and colleagues, who inspired and supported me during this project.

Finally, I am grateful to Cambridge University Press for accepting my book proposal and allowing me to rework my PhD thesis into the present monograph. In particular, I wish to thank Tom Randall and Gemma Smith for their excellent assistance and guidance throughout the publishing process.

Table of Cases

EUROPEAN COURT AND EUROPEAN COMMISSION OF HUMAN RIGHTS

A, B and C v. *Ireland*, no. 25579/05, Grand Chamber Judgment of December 16, 2010, ECHR 2010-VI. 92, 143

A. *and Others* v. *the United Kingdom*, no. 3455/05, Grand Chamber Judgment of February 19, 2009. 104

A. v. *the United Kingdom*, no. 25599/94, Judgment of September 23, 1998, Reports 1998-VI. 171

Abdullazhon Mamadzhanovich Isakov v. *Russia*, no. 52286/14, Decision of July 5, 2016. 91

Ahmet Sadik v. *Greece*, no. 18877/91, Judgment of November 15, 1996, Reports 1996-V. 167

Airey v. *Ireland*, no. 6289/73, Judgment of October 9, 1979, Series A no.32. 76, 172

Akdivar and Others v. *Turkey (former Art. 50)*, no. 21893/93, Grand Chamber Judgment of September 16, 1996, Reports 1998-II. 92

Al-Adsani v. *the United Kingdom*, no. 35763/97, Grand Chamber Judgment of November 21, 2001, ECHR 2001-XI. 148

Al-Dulimi and Montana Management Inc. v. *Switzerland*, no. 5809/08, Grand Chamber Judgment of June 21, 2016, ECHR 2016-III. 154, 160, 169, 170

Al Nashiri v. *Poland*, no. 28761/11, Judgment of July 24, 2014. 100

Aleksanyan v. *Russia*, no. 46468/06, Judgment of December 22, 2008. 112

Amuur v. *France*, no. 19776/92, Judgment of June 25, 1996, Reports, 1996-III. 176

Ananyev and Others v. *Russia*, nos. 42525/07 and 60800/08, Judgment of January 10, 2012. 113

Anchugov and Gladkov v. *Russia*, nos. 11157/04 and 15162/05, Judgment of July 4, 2013. 192

Andrejeva v. *Latvia*, no. 55707/00, Grand Chamber Judgment of February 18, 2009, ECHR 2009-II. 165

Animal Defenders International v. *the United Kingdom*, no. 48876/08, Grand Chamber Judgment of April 22, 2013, 2013-II (extracts). 170
Ashingdane v. *the United Kingdom*, no. 8225/78, Judgment of May 28, 1985, Series A no. 93. 104
Assanidze v. *Georgia*, no. 71503/01, Grand Chamber Judgment of April 8, 2004, ECHR 2004-II. 111, 165
Association for the Defence of Human Rights in Romania – Helsinki Committee on Behalf of Ionel Garcea v. *Romania*, no. 2959/11, Grand Chamber Judgment of March 24, 2015. 91
Austria v. *Italy*, no. 788/60, Decision of January 11, 1961, DR 7. 67, 70
B v. *the United Kingdom*, no. 9840/82, Judgment of July 8, 1987, Series A no. 121-B. 172
Banković and Others v. Belgium and Others, no. 52207/99, Grand Chamber Decision of December 12, 2001, ECHR 2001-XII. 144
Barberà, Messegué and Jabardo v. *Spain (former Art. 50)*, nos. 10588/83, 10589/83 and 10590/83, Judgment of June 13, 1994, Series A no. 285-C. 119
Bayatyan v. *Armenia*, no. 23459/03, Grand Chamber Judgment of July 7, 2011, ECHR 2011-IV. 106, 145
Beaumartin v. *France*, no. 15287/89, Judgment of November 24, 1994, Series A no. 296-B. 174
Bekirski v. *Bulgaria*, no. 71420/01, Judgment of September 2, 2010. 99
Belilos v. *Switzerland*, no. 10328/83, Judgment of April 29, 1988, Series A no. 132. 72
Bhuyian v. *Sweden*, no. 26516/95, Plenary Decision of September 14, 1995. 96
Boyle and Rice v. *the United Kingdom*, nos. 9659/82 and 9658/82, Plenary Judgment of April 27, 1988, Series A no. 131. 176
Broniowski v. *Poland*, no. 31443/96, Grand Chamber Judgment of June 22, 2004, ECHR 2004-V. 113, 114
Bulgarian Helsinki Committee v. *Bulgaria*, nos. 35653/12 and 66172/12, Decision of June 28, 2016. 91
Burden v. *the United Kingdom*, no. 13378/05, Grand Chamber Judgment of April 29, 2008, ECHR 2008-III. 89
Burdov v. *Russia (No. 2)*, no. 33509/04, Judgment of January 15, 2009, ECHR 2009-I. 113, 115
Burmych and Others v. *Ukraine*, nos. 46852/13 etc., Grand Chamber Judgment of October 12, 2017, ECHR 2017 (extracts). 120
Campbell and Cosans v. *the United Kingdom*, nos. 7511/76 and 7743/76, Judgment of February 25, 1982, Series A no. 48. 172
Case 'Relating to certain aspects of the laws on the use of languages in education in Belgium' v. *Belgium*, nos. 1474/62 etc., Plenary Judgment of February 9, 1967, Series A no. 5. 68, 89, 102, 104, 171
Centre for Legal Resources on behalf of Valentin Câmpeanu v. *Romania*, no. 47848/08, Grand Chamber Judgment of July 17, 2014, ECHR 2014-V. 90

Certain legal questions concerning the lists of candidates submitted with a view to the election of judges to the ECtHR, Advisory Opinion of the Grand Chamber of February 12, 2008. 122
Certain legal questions concerning the lists of candidates submitted with a view to the election of judges to the ECtHR (No. 2), Advisory Opinion of the Grand Chamber of January 22, 2010. 122
Christine Goodwin v. *the United Kingdom*, no. 28957/95, Grand Chamber Judgment of Court July 11, 2002, ECHR 2002-VI. 148
Chrysostomos, Papachrysostomou and Loizidou v. *Turkey*, no. 15299/89, 15300/89 and 15318/89, Decision of March 4, 1991. 70
Cossey v. *the United Kingdom*, no. 10843/84, Plenary Judgment of September 27, 1990, Series A no. 184. 104
Cruz Varas and Others v. *Sweden*, no. 15576/89, Judgment of March 20, 1991, Series A no. 201. 97
Cyprus v. *Turkey*, no. 25781/94, Grand Chamber Judgment of May 12, 2014, ECHR 2014-II. 119
Damir Sibgatullin v. *Russia*, no. 1413/05, Judgment of April 24, 2012. 99
Danderyds Kommun v. *Sweden*, no. 525591/99, Decision of June 7, 2001. 165
De Becker v. *Belgium*, no. 214/56, Judgment of March 27, 1962, Series A no. 4. 70
De Cubber v. *Belgium (former Art. 50)*, no. 9186/80, Judgment of September 14, 1987, Series A no. 124-B. 119
De Souza Ribeiro v. *France*, no. 22689/07, Grand Chamber Judgment of December 13, 2012, ECHR 2012-VI. 177
De Wilde, Ooms and Versyp ("Vagrancy") v. *Belgium (Questions of Procedure)*, nos. 2832/66, 2835/66, and 2899/66, Judgment of November 18, 1970, Series A no. 12. 78
Denmark, Norway, Sweden and the Netherlands v. *Greece*, nos. 3321/67 etc., Report of November 5, 1969, Yearbook 12. 97
Di Trizio v. *Switzerland*, no. 7186/09, Judgment of February 2, 2016. 136
Diennet v. *France*, no. 18160/91, Judgment of September 26, 1995, Series A no. 325-A. 174
Dimitrov and Hamanov v. *Bulgaria*, nos. 48059/06 and 2708/09, Judgment of May 10, 2011. 113
Dudgeon v. *the United Kingdom*, no. 7525/76, Judgment of September 23, 1981, Series A no. 45. 77
Dybeku v. *Albania*, no. 41153/06, Judgment of December 18, 2007. 113
Egmez v. *Cyprus*, no. 12214/07, Decision of September 18, 2012. 118
Emre v. *Switzerland (No. 2)*, no. 5056/10, Judgment of October 11, 2011. 95, 119
Engel and Others v. *the Netherlands*, nos. 5100/71, 5101/71 and 5102/71, Judgment of June 8, 1976, Series A no. 22. 75
Enukidze and Girgvliani v. *Georgia*, no. 25091/07, Judgment of April 26, 2011. 99

Firth and Others v. *the United Kingdom*, nos. 47784/09, 47806/09 and 47812/09, Judgment of August 12, 2014. 191
García Ruiz v. *Spain*, no. 30544/96, Grand Chamber Judgment of January 21, 1999, ECHR 1999-I. 105
Gençel v. *Turkey*, no. 53431/99, Judgment of October 23, 2003. 111
Golder v. *the United Kingdom*, no. 4451/70, Judgment of February 21, 1975, Series A no. 18. 76, 77, 136, 143, 147, 177
Golder v. *the United Kingdom*, no. 4451/70, Report of June 1, 1973, Series B no. 16. 76
Gorraiz Lizarraga and Others v. *Spain*, no. 62543/00, Judgment of April 27, 2004, ECHR 2004-III. 89
Gorou v. *Greece (No. 2)*, no. 12686/03, Grand Chamber Judgment of March 20, 2009. 140
Greens and M.T. v. *the United Kingdom*, nos. 60041/08 and 60054/08, Judgment of November 23, 2010, ECHR 2010-VI (extracts). 109, 113, 116, 118, 191
Gross v. *Switzerland*, no. 67810/10, Grand Chamber Judgment of September 30, 2014, ECHR 2014-IV. 100
Guerra and Others v. *Italy*, no. 14967/89, Grand Chamber Judgment of February 19, 1998, Reports 1998-I. 172
Guiso-Gallisay v. *Italy (Just Satisfaction)*, no. 58858/00, Grand Chamber Judgment of December 22, 2009. 108
H.C.W. Schilder v. *the Netherlands*, no. 2158/12, Decision of October 16, 2012. 172
Haase and Others v. *Germany*, no. 34499/04, Decision of February 12, 2008. 118
Handyside v. *the United Kingdom*, no. 5493/72, Plenary Judgment of December 7, 1976, Series A no. 24. 104, 105, 108
Hassan v. *the United Kingdom*, Grand Chamber Judgment of September 16, 2014, no. 29750/09, ECHR 2014-VI. 148
Hatton and Others v. *the United Kingdom*, no. 36022/97, Grand Chamber Judgment of July 8, 2003, 2003-VII. 171, 173
Hirst v. *the United Kingdom (No. 2)*, no. 74025/01, Grand Chamber Judgment of October 6, 2005, ECHR 2005-IX. 116, 191
Hun v. *Turkey*, no. 5142/04, Judgment of November 10, 2005. 100
Hutten-Czapska v. *Poland (Friendly Settlement)*, no. 35014/97, Grand Chamber Judgment of April 28, 2008. 119
Immobiliare Saffi v. *Italy*, no. 22774/93, Grand Chamber Judgment of July 28, 1999, ECHR 1999-V. 173
Ireland v. *the United Kingdom*, no. 5310/71, Plenary Judgment of January 18, 1978, Series A no. 25. 69–71, 89, 91, 138–140, 165
Iwanczuk v. *Poland*, no. 25196/94, Judgment of November 15, 2001. 105
Jalloh v. *Germany*, no. 54810/00, Grand Chamber Judgment of July 11, 2006, ECHR, 2006-IX. 110

James and Others v. *the United Kingdom*, no. 8793/79, Plenary Judgment of February 21, 1986, Series A no. 98. 166, 177
Janowiec and Others v. *Russia*, nos. 55508/07 and 29520/09, Grand Chamber Judgment of October 21, 2013, ECHR 2013-V. 99, 100
Johnston and Others v. *Ireland*, no. 9697/82, Plenary Judgment of December 18, 1986, Series A no. 12. 136
Karner v. *Austria*, no. 40016/98, Judgment of July 24, 2003, ECHR 2003-IX. 89, 138–140, 162
Keegan v. *Ireland*, no. 28867/03, Judgment of July 18, 2006, 2006-X. 171
Khurshid Mustafa and Tarzibachi v. *Sweden*, no. 23883/06, Judgment of December 16, 2008. 178, 179
Klass and Others v. *Germany*, no. 5029/71, Plenary Judgment of September 6, 1978, Series A no. 28. 89, 90, 176, 177
Kleyn and Others v. *the Netherlands*, nos. 39343/98, 39651/98 and 43147/98, Grand Chamber Judgment of May 6, 2003, ECHR 2003-VI. 141
Klyakhin v. *Russia*, no. 46082/99, Judgment of November 30, 2004. 94
König v. *Germany*, no. 6232/73, Judgment of June 28, 1978, Series A no. 27. 75
Konstantin Markin v. *Russia*, no. 30078/06, Judgment of March 22, 2012, ECHR 2012-III (extracts). 8, 138–139, 205, 206
Kornakovs v. *Latvia*, no. 61005/00, Judgment of June 15, 2006. 94
Kozacioğlu v. *Turkey*, no. 2334/03, Grand Chamber Judgment of February 19, 2009. 92
Kübler v. *Germany*, no. 32715/06, Judgement of January 13, 2011. 110
Kurić and Others v. *Slovenia (Just Satisfaction)*, no. 26828/06, Judgment of March 12, 2014. 118
Kurić and Others v. *Slovenia*, no. 26828/06, Grand Chamber Judgment of June 26, 2012, ECHR 2012-IV (extracts). 113
Ladet Tromso and Stensaas v. *Norway*, no. 21980/93, Grand Chamber Judgment of May 20, 1999, 1999-III. 86
Lalmahomed v. *the Netherlands*, no. 26036/08, Judgment of February 22, 2011. 107
Lambert and Others v. *France*, no. 46043/14, Grand Chamber Judgment of June 5, 2015, 2015-III (extracts). 90
Lautsi v. *Italy*, no. 30814/06, Grand Chamber Judgment of 18 March 2011, ECHR 2011-III (extracts). 160
Lawless v. *Ireland (No. 1) (Preliminary Objections)*, no. 332/57, Judgment of November 14, 1960, Series A no. 1. 78
Le Compte, Van Leuven and De Meyere (former Article 50), nos. 6878/75 and 7238/75, Judgment of October 18, 1982, Series A no. 54. 108
Leyla Şahin v. *Turkey*, no. 44774/98, Grand Chamber Judgment of November 10, 2005, ECHR 2005-XI. 106
Loizidou v. *Turkey (Preliminary Objections)*, no. 15318/89, Judgment of March 23, 1995, Series no. A 310. 70, 71, 72, 74, 169

Loizidou v. *Turkey (Merits)*, no. 15318/89, Grand Chamber Judgment of December 18, 1996, Reports 1996-VI. 142, 147
López Ostra v. *Spain*, no. 16798/90, Judgment of December 9, 1994, Series A no. 303-C. 136
Lucà v. *Italy*, no. 33354/96, Judgment of February 27, 2001, ECHR 2001-II. 109
Lukenda v. *Slovenia*, no. 23032/02, Judgment of October 6, 2005, ECHR 2005-X. 113
Lungoci v. *Romania*, no. 62710/00, Judgment of January 26, 2006. 111
Lyons and Others v. *the United Kingdom*, no. 15227/03, Decision of July 8, 2003, ECHR 2003-IX. 118
M.S.S. v. *Belgium and Greece*, no. 30696/09, Grand Chamber Judgment of January 21, 2011, ECHR 2011-I. 160
Maestri v. *Italy*, no. 39748/98, Grand Chamber Judgment of February 17, 2004, ECHR 2004-I. 166
Mamatkulov and Abdurasulovic v. *Turkey*, nos. 46827/99 and 46951/99, Judgment of February 6, 2003. 5, 83
Mamatkulov and Askarov v. *Turkey*, nos. 46827/99 and 46951/99, Grand Chamber Judgment of February 4, 2005, ECHR 2005-I. 96, 97–98
Marckx v. *Belgium*, no. 6833/74, Judgment of June 13, 1979, Series A no. 31. 76, 77, 89, 109, 147, 171
Matko v. *Slovenia*, no. 43393/98, Judgment of November 2, 2006. 105
Mennesson v. *France*, no. 65192/11, Judgment of June 26, 2014. 125
Mürüvvet Küçük v. *Turkey*, no. 21784/04, Judgment of November 10, 2005. 100
N. and M. v. *Russia*, nos. 39496/14 and 39727/14, Decision of April 26, 2016. 91
Nachova and Others v. *Bulgaria*, nos. 43577/98 and 43579/98, Grand Chamber Judgment of July 6, 2005, ECHR 2005-VII. 172
Neumeister v. *Austria*, no. 1936/63, Judgment of June 27, 1968, Series A no. 8. 75
Nolan and K. v. *Russia*, no. 2512/04, Judgment of February 12, 2009. 99
Nowicka v. *Poland*, no. 30218/96, Judgment of December 3, 2002. 174
Oao Neftyanaya Kompaniya Yukos v. *Russia*. no. 14902/04, Judgment of July 31, 2014. 192
Öcalan v. *Turkey*, no. 46221/99, Grand Chamber Judgment of May 12, 2005, 2005-IV. 5, 136
Olaru and Others v. *Moldavia*, nos. 476/07 etc., Grand Chamber Judgment of July 28, 2009. 114
Oleksandr Volkov v. *Ukraine*, no. 21722/11, January 9, 2013, ECHR 2013-I. 111
Olsson v. *Sweden (No. 1)*, no. 10465/83, Judgment of March 24, 1988, Series A no. 130. 172
Olsson v. *Sweden (No. 2)*, no. 13441/87, Judgment of November 27, 1992, Series A no. 250. 118
Opuz v. *Turkey*, no. 33401/02, Judgment of June 9, 2009, ECHR 2009-III. 153–154, 156, 157

Osman v. *the United Kingdom*, no. 23452/94, Grand Chamber Judgment of October 28, 1998, Reports 1998-VIII. 172
Papamichalopoulos and Others v. *Greece (former Article 50)*, no. 14556/89, October 31, 1995, Series A no. 330-B. 108, 109
Paulic v. *Croatia*, no. 3572/06, Judgment of October 22, 2009. 178
Pavlović and Others v. *Croatia*, no. 13274/11, Judgment of April 2, 2015. 105
Pelipenko v. *Russia*, no. 69037/10, Judgment of January 16, 2014. 112, 119
Pla and Puncernau v. *Andorra*, no. 69498/01, Judgment of July 13, 2004, ECHR 2004-VIII. 105, 178
Plattform "Ärzte für das Leben" v. *Austria*, no. 10126/82, Judgment of June 21, 1988, Series A no. 139. 171
Pretty v. *the United Kingdom*, no. 2346/02, Judgment of April 29, 2002, ECHR 2002-III. 105, 137
Rantsev v. *Cyprus and Russia*, no. 25965/04, Judgment of January 7, 2010, ECHR 2010-I (extract). 136, 149–150, 151–152, 172
Rappaz v. *Switzerland*, no. 73175/10, Decision of March 26, 2013. 157
Recognition in domestic law of a legal parent-child relationship between a child born through a gestational surrogacy arrangement abroad and the intended mother, no. P16-2018–001, Advisory Opinion (Protocol 16) of April 10, 2019. 124
Ressegatti v. *Switzerland*, no. 17671/02, Judgment of July 13, 2006. 90
Riener v. *Bulgaria*, no. 46343/99, Judgment of May 23, 2006. 177
Rumpf v. *Germany*, no. 46344/06, Judgment of September 2, 2010. 113
S.A.S. v. *France*, no. 43835/11, Grand Chamber Judgment of July 1, 2014, ECHR 2014-III. 106, 107, 108
Sahin v. *Germany*, no. 30943/96, Grand Chamber Judgment of July 8, 2003, ECHR 2003-VIII. 116
Sanles Sanles v. *Spain*, no. 48335/99, Decision of October 26, 2000, ECHR 2000-XI. 90
Savriddin Dzhurayev v. *Russia*, no. 71386/10, Judgment of April 25, 2013, ECHR 2013-III (extracts). 96
Schalk and Kopf v. *Austria*, no. 30141/04, Judgment of July 24, 2010, ECHR 2010-IV. 136, 144, 145
Schenk v. *Switzerland*, no. 10862/84, Judgment of July 12, 1988, Series A no. 140. 102
Scoppola v. *Italy (No. 2)*, no. 10249/03, Grand Chamber Judgment of September 17, 2009. 150, 151
Scordino and Others v. *Italy (No. 1)*, no. 36813/97, Decision of March 27, 2003, ECHR 2003-IV. 156, 178
Scordino v. *Italy (No. 1)*, no. 36813/97, Grand Chamber Judgment of March 29, 2006, ECHR 2006-V. 158, 180
Scozzari and Giunta v. *Italy*, nos. 39221/98 and 41963/98, ECHR 2000-VIII. 108
Sejdić and Finci v. *Bosnia and Herzegovina*, nos. 27996/06 and 34836/06, Grand Chamber Judgment of December 22, 2009, ECHR 2009-VI. 165, 166, 169

Selmouni v. *France*, no. 25803/94, Grand Chamber Judgment of July 28, 1999, Reports 1999-V. 92, 176
Senator Lines GmbH v. *Fifteen Member States of the European Union*, no. 56672/00, Grand Chamber Decision of March 10, 2004, ECHR 2004-IV. 90
Shamayev and Others v. *Georgia and Russia*, no. 36378/02, Judgment of April 12, 2005, ECHR 2005-III. 101
Sheffield and Horsham v. *the United Kingdom*, nos. 22985/93 and 23390/94, Judgment of July 30, 1998, ECHR 1998-V. 148
Sidabras and Others v. *Lithuania*, nos. 50421/08 and 56213/08, Judgment of June 23, 2015. 119
Silver and Others v. *the United Kingdom*, nos. 5947/72 etc., Judgment of March 25, 1983, Series A no. 61. 177
Sisojeva and Others v. *Latvia*, no. 60654/00, Grand Chamber Judgment of January 15, 2007. 105
Sławomir Musiał v. *Poland*, no. 28300/06, Judgment of January 20, 2009. 112
Smith and Grady v. *the United Kingdom*, nos. 33985/96 and 33986/96, Judgment of September 27, 1999, ECHR 1999-VI. 174
Soering v. *the United Kingdom*, no. 14038/88, Plenary Judgment of July 7, 1989, Series A no. 161. 140
Stankova v. *Slovakia*, no. 7205/02, Judgment of October 9, 2007. 179
Storck v. *Germany*, no. 61603/00, Judgment of June 16, 2005, ECHR 2005-V. 178
Süheyla Aydin v. *Turkey*, no. 25660/94, Judgment of May 24, 2005. 101
Sunday Times v. *the United Kingdom (No. 1)*, no. 6538/74, Judgment of April 26, 1979, Series A no. 30. 78, 104
Suso Musa v. *Malta*, no. 42337/12, Judgment of July 23, 2013. 174
Swedish Engine Drivers' Union v. *Sweden*, no. 5614/72, Judgment of February 6, 1976, Series A no. 20. 166
T. v. *the United Kingdom*, no. 24724/94, Grand Chamber Judgment of December 16, 1999. 145
Tahsin Acar v. *Turkey*, no. 26307/95, Grand Chamber Judgment of April 8, 2004. 99, 100
Tarakhel v. *Switzerland*, no. 29217/12, Grand Chamber Judgment of November 4, 2014, ECHR 2014-VI (extracts). 160
Tigran Ayrapetyan v. *Russia*, no. 75472/01, Judgment of September 16, 2010. 99
Times Newspaper Ltd., Giles, Knightley and Potter v. *the United Kingdom*, no. 10243/83, Decision of March 6, 1985, DR 41. 118
Torreggiani and Others v. *Italy*, nos. 43517/09 etc., Judgment of January 8, 2013. 113
Tyrer v. *the United Kingdom*, no. 5856/72, Judgment of April 25, 1978, Series A no. 26. 70, 76, 80, 135, 143, 144
United Communist Party of Turkey v. *Turkey*, no. 19392/92, Grand Chamber Judgment of January 30, 1998, ECHR 1998-I. 168, 169

United Macedonian Organisation Ilinden – PIRIN and Others v. *Bulgaria (No. 2)*, nos. 41561/07 and 20972/08, Judgment of October 18, 2011. 119
Vallianatos and Others v. *Greece*, nos. 29381/09 and 32684/09, Grand Chamber Judgment of November 7, 2013, ECHR 2013-VI (extracts). 89
Van Droogenbroeck v. *Belgium*, no. 7906/77, Plenary Judgment of June 24, 1982, Series A no. 50. 177, 180
Varnava and Others v. *Turkey*, no. 16064/90 etc., Grand Chamber Judgment of September 18, 2009, ECHR 2009-V. 89, 90
Verein gegen Tierfabriken Schweiz (VgT) v. *Switzerland (No. 2)*, no. 32772/02, Grand Chamber Judgment of June 30, 2009. 108, 118, 168
Verein gegen Tierfabriken Schweiz (VgT) v. *Switzerland*, no. 24699/94, Judgment of June 28, 2001, ECHR 2001-VI. 166
Vermeire v. *Belgium*, no. 12849/87, Judgment of November 29, 1991, Series A no. 214-C. 179
Vinter and Others v. *the United Kingdom*, nos. 6069/09 and 130/10 3896/10, Grand Chamber Judgment of July 9, 2013, ECHR 2013-III (extracts). 144, 145
Von Hannover v. *Germany (No. 2)*, nos. 40660/08 and 60641/08, Grand Chamber Judgment of February 7, 2012, ECHR 2012-I. 194
Wagner and J.M.W.L. v. *Luxembourg*, no. 76240/01, Judgment of June 28, 2007. 106
Wemhoff v. *Germany*, no. 2122/64, Judgment (Merits) of June 27, 1968, Series A no. 7. 73, 135
Windisch v. *Austria (former Article 50)*, no. 12489/86, Judgment of June 28, 1993, Series A no. 255-D. 110
Winterwerp v. *the Netherlands*, no. 6301/73, Judgment of October 24, 1979, Series A no. 33. 80
Women on Waves and Others v. *Portugal*, no. 31276/05, Judgment of February 3, 2009. 173
X v. *Switzerland*, nos. 8778/79 etc., Decision of July 8, 1980, DR 20 240. 95
Young, James and Webster v. *the United Kingdom*, no. 7601/76 and 7806/77, Judgment of August 13, 1981, Series A no. 44. 80, 136
Yuriy Nikolayevich Ivanov v. *Ukraine*, no. 40450/04, Judgment of October 15, 2009. 120
Z v. *the United Kingdom*, no. 29392/95, Grand Chamber Judgment of May 10, 2001. 176
Zimmermann and Steiner v. *Switzerland*, no. 8737/79, Judgment of July 13, 1983, Series A no. 66. 172

COURT OF JUSTICE OF THE EUROPEAN UNION (PREVIOUSLY EUROPEAN COURT OF JUSTICE OF THE EUROPEAN COMMUNITIES)

Case 105/03, Criminal proceedings against Maria Pupino [2005] ECR I-5285. 26
Case 6/64, *Flaminio Costa* v. *E.N.E.L.* [1964] ECR 1141. 25

Case 11/70, *Internationale Handelsgesellschaft mbH* v. *Einfuhr- und Vorratsstelle für Getreide und Futtermittel* [1970] ECR 1125. 25
Case 57/65, *Alfons Lütticke GmbH* v. *Hauptzollamt Saarlouis* [1966] ECR 205. 24
Case 26/62, *NV Algemene Transporten Expeditie Onderneming van Gend & Loos* v. *Netherlands Inland Revenue Administration* [1963] ECR 1. 24
Opinion 1/91 [1991] ECR I-6079. 28
Opinion 2/13 ECLI:EU:C:2014:2454. 129
Case 106/77, *Staatliche Finanzverwaltung* v. *S.p.A. Simmenthal* [1978] ECR 629. 25
Case 14/83, *Sabine von Colson and Elisabeth Kamann* v. *Land Nordrhein-Westfalen* [1984] ECR 1891. 179

INTER-AMERICAN COURT OF HUMAN RIGHTS

Almonacid-Arellano et al v. *Chile*, Judgment of September 26, 2006, Series C no. 154. 47
Barrios Altos v. *Peru*, Judgment of March 14, 2001, Series C no. 75. 47
The Effect of Reservations on the Entry into Force of the American Convention on Human Rights, Advisory Opinion of September 24, 1982, OC-2/82, Series A no. 2. 74

INTERNATIONAL COURT OF JUSTICE

Accordance with International Law of the Unilateral Declaration of Independence in Respect of Kosovo, Advisory Opinion of July 22, 2010, I.C.J. Reports 2010 403. 42
Kasikili/Sedudu Island (Botswana v. *Namibia)*, Judgment of December 13, 1999, I.C.J. Reports 1999 1045. 144
LaGrand (Germany v. *United States of America)*, Judgment of June 27, 2001, I.C.J. Reports 2001 466. 45
Request for Interpretation of the Judgment of 31 March 2004 in the Case concerning Avena and Other Mexican Nationals (Mexico v. *United States of America)*, Judgment of January 19, 2009, I.C.J. Reports 2009 3. 46
Reservations to the Convention on Genocide, Advisory Opinion of May 28, 1951, I.C.J. Reports 1951 23. 74

PERMANENT COURT OF INTERNATIONAL JUSTICE

Case Concerning the Factory at Chorzów (Claim for Indemnity) (Merits), Judgment of September 13, 1928, P.C.I.J. (1928) Series A no. 17. 108
Jurisdiction of the Courts of Danzig, Advisory Opinion of March 3, 1928, P.C.I.J. (1928) Series B no. 15. 46
Treatment of Polish Nationals and Other Persons of Polish Origin or Speech in Danzig Territory, Advisory Opinion of February 4, 1932, P.C.I.J. (1932) Series A/B no. 24. 48

ANDEAN TRIBUNAL OF JUSTICE (COURT OF JUSTICE OF THE ANDEAN COMMUNITY)

Acción de incumplimiento interpuesta por la Junta del Acuerdo de Cartagena contra la República de Venezuela, 3-NaN-96. 47
Preliminary Ruling 1-IP-87. 48

CENTRAL AMERICAN COURT OF JUSTICE

Judgment 09–04–08–1996. 47, 48

EFTA COURT

Case E-4/01 *Karl K Karlsson hf* v. *the Icelandic State*, Advisory Opinion of May 30, 2002. 47

NATIONAL CASE LAW

Italian Constitutional Court

Judgment nos. 348–349/2007 of October 22 and 24, 2007. 189
Judgment no. 311/2009 of November 16, 2009. 186
Judgment no. 264/2012 of November 19, 2012. 186
Judgment no. 49/2015 of March 26, 2015. 192–193

Federal Supreme Court of Switzerland

125 II 417 *(PKK)*. 190
130 II 113. 184

Austrian Constitutional Court

Miltner, Judgment of October 14, 1987, VfSlg 11500/1987. 186

United Kingdom Supreme Court

Brigid McCaughey and another for Judicial Review (Northern Ireland) [2011] UKSC 20; [2012] 1 AC 725; [2011] 2 WLR 1279. 184
R v. Horncastle and Others [2009] UKSC 14; [2010] 2 AC 373; [2009] WLR (D) 358. 186, 187

United Kingdom House of Lords

Ghaidan v. *Godin-Mendoza* [2004] UKHL 30; [2004] 2 AC 557; [2004] 3 WLR 113. 186

Regina v. *Secretary of State for Transport Ex Parte Factortame Ltd* (No. 2) [1990] UKHL 13. 188
Re P and Others (Ap) (Appellants) (Northern Ireland) [2008] UKHL 38; [2009] 1 AC 173; [2008] 3 WLR 76. 183

Federal Constitutional Court of Germany

Unschuldsvermutung I, BVerfGE 74. 185
Gorgulu, BVerfGE 111. 184, 185, 186, 187
Sicherungsverwahrung I, BVerfGE 128. 185
Sicherungsverwahrung II, BVerfGE 131. 185

Russian Constitutional Court

Judgment no. 27-P/2013 of December 6, 2013. 191
Judgment no. 21-P/2015 of July 14, 2015. 186, 191
Judgment no. 12-P/2016 of April 19, 2016. 192
Judgment no. 1-P/2017 of January 19, 2017. 192

French State Council

Bitouzet, 3 July 1998, no. 1585929. 187

Table of International Instruments

INTERNATIONAL TREATIES

American Convention on Human Rights "Pact of San Jose" (adopted November 22, 1969, entered into force July 18, 1978), OAS Treaty Series No. 36, 1144 UNTS 123. (ACHR), 47, 49, 150
Charter of the United Nations (adopted June 26, 1945, entered into force October 24, 1945), 1 UNTS XVI. (UN Charter), 20, 66
Charter of Fundamental Rights of the European Union, OJ C 202 June 7, 2016. (EU Fundamental Rights Charter), 145
Consolidated Version of the Treaty on European Union, OJ C 202 June 7, 2016. (TEU), 190
Consolidated Version and the Treaty on the Functioning of the European Union, OJ C 202 June 7, 2016. (TFEU), 124, 128
Convention (XII) relative to the Creation of an International Prize Court (adopted October 18, 1907). (IPCC), 12, 13
Convention for the Protection of Human Rights and Fundamental Freedoms (adopted November 4, 1950, entered into force September 3, 1953) ETS 5 (as amended by Protocols No. 11 and No. 14). (ECHR), 97, 121, 201
Council of Europe Convention on Action against Trafficking in Human Beings (adopted on May 6, 2005, entered into force on February 1, 2008), CETS 197. (CoE Anti-Trafficking Convention), 149
Draft European Convention on Human Rights (adopted July 12, 1949 by the European Movement). (European Movement Draft Convention), 61–63, 64
Draft Treaty Embodying the Statute of the European Community (March 10, 1953). (EPC Draft Statute), 21
European Convention on Mutual Assistance in Criminal Matters (adopted April 20, 1959, entered into force June 12, 1962), ETS 30. 150
Merger Treaty (adopted April 8, 1965, entered into force July 1, 1967), OJ 152 of July 13, 1967. (Merger Treaty), 22

North American Free Trade Agreement (adopted December 17, 1992, entered into force January 1, 1994), 32 ILM 289, 605. (NAFTA), 44

Single European Act (adopted February 28, 1986, entered into force July 1, 1987), OJ L June 29, 1987. (Single European Act), 25

Statute of the Council of Europe (adopted May 5, 1949, entered into force August 3, 1949), ETS 1. (CoE Statute), 37, 117

Treaty Creating the Court of Justice of the Andean Community (adopted May 28, 1979, entered into force May 19, 1983) (as amended), 18 ILM 1203. (Treaty Creating the Andean Court of Justice), 47

Treaty Establishing the European Coal and Steel Community (adopted April 18, 1951, entered into force July 23, 1952) (not published). (ECSC Treaty), 22, 26, 33, 42, 63

Treaty Establishing the European Defense Community (adopted May 27, 1952) (EDC Draft Treaty), 21

Treaty of Lisbon Amending the Treaty on European Union and the Treaty Establishing the European Community (adopted December 13, 2007, entered into force December 1, 2009), OJ C 306 of December 17, 2007. (Lisbon Treaty), 26

Treaty Establishing the European Economic Community (adopted March 25, 1957, entered into force January 1, 1958) (not published). (EEC Treaty), 22, 46

Treaty Establishing the European Atomic Energy Community (adopted March 25, 1957, entered into force January 1, 1958) (not published). (Euratom Treaty), 22, 24

United Nations Convention on the Law of the Sea (adopted October 12, 1982, entered into force on November 16, 1994), 1833 UNTS 3. (UNCLOS), 42

COUNCIL OF EUROPE

Committee of Ministers

Recommendation (2000)2 on the re-examination or reopening of certain cases at domestic level following judgments of the European Court of Human Rights, January 19, 2000, 111, 116

Recommendation (2002)13 on the publication and dissemination in the member states of the text of the European Convention on Human Rights and of the case-law of the European Court of Human Rights, December 18, 2002, 158

Recommendation (2004)5 on the verification of the compatibility of draft laws, existing laws and administrative practice with the standards laid down in the European Convention on Human Rights, May 12, 2004, 158

Recommendation (2004)6 on the improvement of domestic remedies, May 12, 2004, 111, 116

Resolution (2004)3 on judgments revealing an underlying systemic problem, May 12, 2004, 112

Resolution DH (2006)45, States' obligation to co-operate with the European Court of Human Rights, July 4, 2006, 99
Resolution DH (2018)467, Execution of the judgments of the European Court of Human Rights: Five cases against the United Kingdom, December 6, 2018, 191
Interim Resolution (2017)379, Execution of the judgment of the European Court of Human Rights, Ilgar Mammadov against Azerbaijan, October 25, 2017, 121
Interim Resolution (2017)429, Execution of the judgment of the European Court of Human Rights, Ilgar Mammadov against Azerbaijan, December 5, 2017, 121

PARLIAMENTARY ASSEMBLY

Resolution 1226 (2000), Execution of judgments of the European Court of Human Rights, September 28, 2000, 155
Recommendation 1606 (2003), Areas where the European Convention on Human Rights cannot be implemented, June 23, 2003, 89
Recommendation 1809 (2007), Member states' duty to co-operate with the European Court of Human Rights, October 2, 2007, 99
Recommendation 2079 (2015), Implementation of judgments of the European Court of Human Rights, September 30, 2015, 121
Resolution 1571 (2007), Member states' duty to co-operate with the European Court of Human Rights, October 2, 2007, 99
Resolution 1856 (2012), Guaranteeing the authority and effectiveness of the European Convention on Human Rights, January 24, 2012, 158

UNITED NATIONS

ILC, Draft Articles on Responsibility of States for Internationally Wrongful Acts, UN Doc A/56/83, August 3, 2001. (ILC Draft Articles on State Responsibility), 56, 108, 165
UN General Assembly, Protocol to Prevent, Suppress and Punish Trafficking in Persons, Especially Women and Children, Supplementing the United Nations Convention against Transnational Organized Crime, November 15, 2000. (Palermo Protocol), 149
Security Council, Resolution 1244 (1999), 42

Abbreviations

ACHR	American Convention on Human Rights
ATJ	Andean Tribunal of Justice (Court of Justice of the Andean Community)
BVerfGE	Entscheidungen des Bundesverfassungsgerichts
CACJ	Central American Court of Justice
CARICOM	Caribbean Community and Common Market
CCJ	Caribbean Court of Justice
CDDH	Steering Committee for Human Rights (Council of Europe)
CJEU	Court of Justice of the European Union
CoE	Council of Europe
CoM	Committee of Ministers of the Council of Europe
ECHR	Convention for the Protection of Human Rights and Fundamental Freedoms
ECtHR	European Court of Human Rights
ECommHR	European Commission of Human Rights
ECJ	European Court of Justice (now Court of Justice of the European Union)
ECLI	European Case Law Identifier
ECR	European Court Reports
ECSC	European Coal and Steel Community
EDC	European Defense Community
EEA	European Economic Area
EEC	European Economic Community
EFTA	European Free Trade Association
EPC	European Political Community
ETS	European Treaty Series
EU	European Union
HA	High Authority (of the European Coal and Steel Community)

HRA	Human Rights Act 1998
IACtHR	Inter-American Court of Human Rights
IACommHR	Inter-American Commission on Human Rights
ICs	International Courts
ICC	International Criminal Court
ICJ	International Court of Justice
ICTY	International Criminal Tribunal for the former Yugoslavia
IHRL	International Human Rights Law
ILC	International Law Commission
ILM	International Legal Materials
IOs	International Organizations
IPCC	International Prize Court Convention
NAFTA	North American Free Trade Agreement
NGO	Non-governmental Organization
OJ	Official Journal (of the European Union)
PACE	Parliamentary Assembly of the Council of Europe
PCIJ	Permanent Court of International Justice
SICA	Central American Integration System
TEU	Treaty on European Union
TFEU	Treaty on the Functioning of the European Union
UKHL	United Kingdom House of Lords
UKSC	United Kingdom Supreme Court
UN	United Nations
UNCLOS	United Nations Convention on the Law of the Sea
UNESCO	United Nations Educational, Scientific and Cultural Organization
UNTS	United Nations Treaty Series
VCLT	Vienna Convention on the Law of Treaties
WTO	World Trade Organization

Introduction

AIM OF THE STUDY: THE CONVENTION THROUGH THE PRISM OF SUPRANATIONALITY

The European Convention on Human Rights (ECHR) has emancipated from an international agreement with a relatively weak enforcement structure into a highly sophisticated legal system with ever more pervasive effect on domestic law and individuals. At its center looms the world's most productive and successful international court. The European Court of Human Rights (ECtHR), directly accessible to over 800 million citizens across Europe, is the final interpreter of the Convention and final arbiter of disputes arising thereunder.

> The European Court of Human Rights is the nerve center of a system of human rights protection which radiates out through the domestic legal orders of virtually all European States. It sets common legal standards which permeate the legal orders of the Contracting States, standards which influence and shape domestic law and practice in areas such as criminal law, the administration of justice in criminal, civil and administrative matters, family law, aliens' law, media law, property law. Over the years and through its case law, the European Convention on Human Rights has become deeply entrenched in the legal and moral fabric of the societies of the older Council of Europe States and this same process is well under way in newer State Parties. Its crucial role in securing the peaceful development of greater Europe is a model for a system of strong and effective international justice.[1]

The ECtHR transformed and continues to transform the pan-European legal space through exercising direct, far-reaching and multifaceted public authority over states and individuals alike. This development has led to the scholarly assessment that "[m]ore than a typical international treaty, the ECHR corresponds to an idiosyncratic regime," which "serves as a regional 'quasi-Constitution', delimiting

[1] Report of the Evaluation Group to the Committee of Ministers on the ECHR, September 27, 2001, printed in Council of Europe, *Reforming the European Convention on Human Rights: A Work in Progress. A Compilation of Publications and Documents Relevant to the Ongoing Reform of the ECHR* (Strasbourg: Council of Europe Publishing 2009) pp. 561ff, 562.

an increasingly integrated public order that aims at protecting certain common values within a very specific geographic, cultural, historical, social, political and economic milieu, i.e., Europe."[2] In fact, already in the 1980s it was written that "although constructed upon tenets of traditional treaty law, the Convention law transcends the traditional boundaries drawn between international and domestic law."[3] Indeed, one observes a high degree of overlap both in terms of substance and functions between the Convention system and domestic legal orders. Concurrently, Convention law has gradually become an integral part of domestic legal orders. As a matter of domestic law, individuals can usually rely directly on Convention law. The result is a twofold legal integration which this book seeks to examine in more detail.

Unlike typical constitution-based systems, the emancipation of the ECtHR and the ECHR has largely occurred in an "apolitical" or legal context. The ECtHR remains an international court in the sense that it is not an appeals court formally embedded in domestic judicial systems. Neither form the Court nor the Convention part of some larger constitutional, political ordering (such as the EU), which would justify describing them as federal or constitutional, at least not in a narrow or formal sense. While the ECtHR operates under the auspices of the Council of Europe, it very much remains a treaty organ of the Convention, and the Council of Europe itself is a classical intergovernmental, international organization.

The aim of the book is to go deeper in the descriptive, analytical and conceptual analysis of legal integration under the ECHR. To this end, the study proposes to rediscover supranationality as a descriptive-analytical tool beyond EU law and investigate whether, and to what extent, elements denoted supranational can be found in the ECHR. Although usually reserved to the realm of EU law, the term supranational has, in fact, in different instances been associated with the collective enforcement system of the ECHR. Supranationality is understood as a relational concept to refer to law beyond the state that seeks to achieve a form of legal integration, either horizontally, through international institutions which can bypass states in their ability to determine the legal position of individuals, or vertically, in that law beyond the state is entrenched in the domestic legal order in a way that allows individuals to effectively rely thereon. More specifically, the book examines the ECHR system's particular autonomy, integrative force, and penetrating effect from different angles: the establishment of an autonomous and permanent Court with compulsory jurisdiction to deal with complaints from individuals (Chapter 3), the different judicial functions of the ECtHR (Chapter 4), lawmaking under the ECHR (Chapter 5), as well as the domestic effect and status of Convention law

[2] Stella-Eirini Vetsika and Vassilis P. Tzevelekos, "In Integration We Trust? The Reception of Supranational Law in the Greek Legal Order: 'A Tale of Love and Darkness'" (2010) 5 *Stals Research Paper* www.stals.sssup.it/files/stals_Vassilis_052010.pdf (accessed July 23, 2020) 1–24 at 4.

[3] Andrew Drzemczewski, "The Sui Generis Nature of the European Convention on Human Rights" (1980) 29 *International and Comparative Law Quarterly* 54–63 at 54.

(Chapter 6). For each of these areas, it is submitted that the concept of supranationality has particular analytical force to capture the authority of the ECtHR as well as the effect of Convention law both over and in contracting states.

The main claim put forward in this book is that one can distinguish between a horizontal and vertical process of supranationalization under the Convention system. Horizontally, the ECHR has become a site of deepening judicial integration. The Court exercises supranational authority that bypasses the nation state, and it does so in an ever-growing number of areas. Vertically, Convention law is today to a particular degree integrated into domestic law, rendering its (domestic) normativity unique. It is submitted that supranationalization is an incremental process, which unfolds over the entire lifespan of the ECHR system and continues up to date. It is a multifaceted and complex process dependent on and controlled by a number of different factors, some of which the book brings to light. The book further proposes to give meaning to the term Convention community, which today, could offer a more compelling description of the Convention (in the widest sense) than the term Convention system. Indeed, the claims that the Convention and the ECtHR have yielded a process of supranationalization fit the notion of community. In short, this book aims at offering an empirical deconstruction of the ECtHR's and ECHR's authority, the results of which should serve to frame a Convention community.

ADDED VALUE AND PLACE OF THE STUDY IN SCHOLARSHIP

The added value of this book lies in the fact that it is one of the first comprehensive studies on legal integration in the ECHR context. The book traces the incremental process of supranationalization of adjudication under the ECHR and Convention law as such. Theoretical or conceptual monographs on the ECHR and the ECtHR are in fact still fairly limited.[4] There are an abundant number of doctrinal treatises in the form of commentaries, articles, or books, either of general nature or devoted to specific ECHR rights. Also, there exists an overwhelming amount of literature on the evolution and the reform process of the Convention system. Even the body of theoretical and conceptual works on specific ECHR topics such as interpretation, subsidiarity, or the margin of appreciation doctrine is constantly growing. However, the observation that we lack "general studies on the construction of the ECtHR's authority" still holds largely true.[5] Against this background, looking at the Convention system through the prism of supranationality can offer a fresh conceptual perspective on the European human rights protection system and further our legal and institutional understanding of the Convention system. Supranationality is

4 For a notable exception, see for example, Jonas Christoffersen, *Fair Balance: Proportionality, Subsidiarity and Primarity in the European Convention on Human Rights* (Leiden: Martinus Nijhoff 2009).

5 Nico Krisch, *Beyond Constitutionalism – The Pluralist Structure of Postnational Law* (Oxford: Oxford University Press 2010), p. 128 (at fn. 101); see also Christoffersen, *Fair Balance*, p. 6.

a relational concept[6] and allows to build on what was described as a "systemic turn" in institutional ECHR literature.[7] This means that the framework adopted offers a comprehensive approach taking into account a broad variety of issues and relationships between different actors in the Convention system. It may be used to assess (inter alia):

- the evolution of the enforcement system under the Convention and its differentiation from traditional international adjudication;
- the quality and breadth of authority exercised by the Court over states and individuals alike (as a form of judicial governance and including the Court's lawmaking function);
- the authority and effect of the Court's case-law on and within states, particularly vis-à-vis individuals and state authorities;
- the relationship between the Court and states, but also other organs of the Council of Europe (e.g., the Committee of Ministers);
- and the relationship between domestic law and the ECHR more generally.

The author does not claim to put forward a general theory on the ECHR, which, in a normative sense, should guide the ECtHR in discharging its (judicial) role with respect to specific substantive issues. Admittedly, any conceptual analysis or narrative implies a degree of normativity and the choice of conception matters in grasping the object.[8] But the aim here is not to develop a normative program or, to borrow Çali's words, a thick conceptual theory.[9] Also, the author does not seek to promote supranationalization of the ECHR, rather to make the claim that such process actually exists, contribute to its understanding and thereby enhance critical reflection thereof. It is in this sense that the overall approach of this study is descriptive rather than normative. The aim is to go deeper in the descriptive stage of analysis and expose both the Court's powers and the effect of Convention law, which, in turn, can enhance conceptual clarity. In particular, revealing and discussing the supranational elements of the ECHR can make a contribution to unfolding legitimacy problems and provide a new starting point for future research and the perpetuating debate about the reform of the Convention system, which seems far from being settled.[10]

6 Peter Hay, *Federalism and Supranational Organizations: Patterns for New Legal Structures* (Urbana: University of Illinois Press 1966), p. 42.

7 Robert Harmsen, "The Reform of the Convention System: Institutional Restructuring and the (Geo-) Politics of Human Rights" in Jonas Christoffersen and Mikael Rask Madsen (eds.), *The European Court of Human Rights between Law and Politics* (Oxford: Oxford University Press 2011), p. 132.

8 Armin von Bogdandy and Ingo Venzke, *In Whose Name?: A Public Law Theory of International Adjudication* (Oxford: Oxford University Press 2014), p. 28.

9 Başak Çali, *The Authority of International Law* (Oxford: Oxford University Press 2015), p. 51.

10 Jonas Christoffersen and Mikael Rask Madsen (eds.), "Introduction: The European Court of Human Rights between Law and Politics," *The European Court of Human Rights between Law and Politics* (Oxford: Oxford University Press 2011), p. 13.

Admittedly, supranationality is not a very fashionable term these days. In scholarship, constitutionalism, legal pluralism, or constitutional pluralism seem to be the notions of today. Also, in times of Brexit and the rise of populism in Europe and beyond, one may encounter criticism for ignoring political realities, when taking supranationality as a conceptual starting point of any study. Indeed, the idea of backlash against international courts, including the ECtHR, has gained traction and increased scholarly attention.[11] Nonetheless, it is argued that examining supranationality under the ECHR is worthwhile for two reasons. First, the notion of supranationality has in fact on several occasions been invoked in the context of the ECHR. Already in May 1948 during the Congress of Europe, it was considered essential for safeguarding fundamental rights in Europe "that there should be established a Supreme Court with *supra-state* jurisdiction to which citizens and groups can appeal."[12] In scholarship, Helfer and Slaughter came up with the term of "supranational adjudication" to describe the jurisdiction of the ECtHR.[13] Since the jurisdiction of the Court became compulsory and every person within the Council of Europe enjoys the right to individual application, the Court itself found that "individuals now enjoy at the *supranational* level a real right of action to assert the rights and freedoms to which they are directly entitled under the Convention."[14] Similarly, in a partly dissenting opinion of the *Öcalan* case, a number of judges, including two former presidents of the Court, referred to the Court as a "supranational judicial body."[15] Besson also took up Helfer's and Slaughter's notion of supranational adjudication and assessed the legitimacy of supranational judicial review by the ECtHR.[16] Other well-known (ECHR) scholars have used the term supranational in the context of the Convention.[17] Moreover, the Convention as such

[11] To an extent, the narrative of backlash and resistance is a competing conceptualization or counter-trend to the one of supranationalization proposed by the present book. Yet, it is argued that in the case of the ECtHR, occasional resistance has always existed and can (still) be accommodated within the framework adopted. For more on this see subsequently pp. 8f.

[12] Congress of Europe, Cultural Resolution of May 7–10, 1948, Section 5 (emphasis added).

[13] Laurence R. Helfer and Anne-Marie Slaughter, "Toward a Theory of Effective Supranational Adjudication" (1997) 107 The Yale Law Journal 273–391.

[14] ECtHR, *Mamatkulov and Abdurasulovic* v. *Turkey*, nos. 46827/99 and 46951/99, Judgment of February 6, 2003, § 106 (emphasis added).

[15] ECtHR, *Öcalan* v. *Turkey*, no. 46221/99, Grand Chamber Judgment of May 12, 2005, 2005-IV, Joint Partly Dissenting Opinion of Judges Wildhaber, Costa, Caflisch, Türmen, Garlicki, and Borrego Borrego, § 9.

[16] Samantha Besson, "European Human Rights, Supranational Judicial Review and Democracy. Thinking Outside the Judicial Box" in Patricia Popelier, Catherine J. Van de Heyning, and Piet Van Nuffel (eds.), *Human Rights Protection in the European Legal Order: The Interaction between the European and the National Courts* (Cambridge: Intersentia 2011), pp. 97ff.

[17] These include Başak Çali, "The Logics of Supranational Human Rights Litigation, Official Acknowledgment, and Human Rights Reform: The Southeast Turkey Cases before the European Court of Human Rights, 1996–2006" (2010) 35 *Law and Social Inquiry* 311–337; Philip Leach and Alice Donald, *Parliaments and the European Court of Human Rights* (Oxford: Oxford University Press 2016), pp. 130ff; Janneke Gerards, "Judicial Deliberations in the European Court of Human Rights" in Nick Huls, Jacco Bomhoff, and Maurice Adams (eds.), *The Legitimacy of Highest Courts' Rulings – Judicial Deliberations and Beyond* (The Hague: T.M.C. Asser Press 2009), pp. 408f; Catherine J. Van de Heyning, "The Natural 'Home' of Fundamental Rights Adjudication: Constitutional Challenges

has been termed supranational law and has been compared to EU law in terms of its validity, effect, and rank within the domestic legal order.[18] What does it mean exactly to refer to the ECtHR as a supranational body or court? And what makes the ECHR, if anything, supranational? This book seeks to answer these questions.

Second, it is argued that the notion of supranationality is particularly suited to capture the essence of the Convention system in a descriptive sense. Today, the Court is often couched within a constitutionalist[19] and/or pluralist[20] framework (both in a descriptive and normative sense). Pluralist approaches usually have a narrower focus in that they deal with competing claims over final authority on fundamental rights issues. Constitutionalist approaches, however, overlap in many respects with this book in terms of their focus of inquiry. Elements denoted supranational are often regarded as hallmarks of constitutionalization too.[21] Yet, constitutional strands normally contrast the ECtHR's constitutional role with its function to deliver justice to individuals on a case-by-case basis while focussing on the former. Supranationality accommodates both of these functions. Also, as supranationality is, arguably, normatively less loaded and renounces thorny domestic analogies,[22] it may be well suited to express that the ECHR and the ECtHR are precisely not embedded within a larger political framework beyond the state.

This book also carries forward two important strands of ECHR scholarship and research. On the one hand, the book builds on research on the far-reaching effect of Convention law within domestic legal orders described as domestification[23] and

to the European Court of Human Rights" (2012) 31 *Yearbook of European Law* 128–161 at 138; Joshua L. Jackson, "Broniowski v. Poland: A Recipe for Increased Legitimacy of the European Court of Human Rights as a Supranational Constitutional Court" (2006) 39 *Connecticut Law Review* 759–806 at 769.

18 Giuseppe Martinico and Oreste Pollicino, *The Interaction between Europe's Legal Systems: Judicial Dialogue and the Creation of Supranational Laws* (Cheltenham: Edward Elgar 2012); Giuseppe Martinico, "Is the European Convention Going to Be 'Supreme'? A Comparative-Constitutional Overview of ECHR and EU Law before National Courts" (2012) 23 *European Journal of International Law* 401–424; Oreste Pollicino, "The New Relationship between National and the European Courts after the Enlargement of Europe: Towards a Unitary Theory of Jurisprudential Supranational Law?" (2010) 29 *Yearbook of European Law* 65–111; Carl Lebeck, "Supranational Law in a Cold Climate: European Law in Scandinavia" (2010) 4 *Stals Research Paper* www.stals.sssup.it/files/stals_Lebeck_042010.pdf (accessed July 23, 2020).

19 Instead of many Steven Greer and Luzius Wildhaber, "Revisiting the Debate about 'Constitutionalising' the European Court of Human Rights" (2012) 12 *Human Rights Law Review* 655–687; Alec Stone Sweet, "On the Constitutionalization of the Convention: The European Court of Human Rights as a Constitutional Court" (2009) 80 *Revue trimestrielle des droits de l'homme* 1–14.

20 For example, Krisch, *Beyond Constitutionalism*, pp. 109ff.

21 Chapter 2, Section 2.4.

22 Armin von Bogdandy, *Supranationaler Föderalismus als Wirklichkeit und Idee einer neuen Herrschaftsform* (Baden-Baden: Nomos 1999), p. 62.

23 Helen Keller and Alec Stone Sweet (eds.), "Assessing the Impact of the ECHR on National Legal Systems," *A Europe of Rights: The Impact of the ECHR on National Legal Systems* (Oxford: Oxford University Press 2008), pp. 677–712.

embeddedness[24] of the ECHR or loyalty[25] to the ECtHR.[26] Existing research in this area primarily focuses on the national plane investigating how the different contracting states implement the Convention, usually along the lines of the classical distinction between validity, applicability, and the rank of international law within domestic law.[27] This approach is based on the finding that the Convention leaves its implementation to contracting states and that the ECtHR, unlike the Court of Justice of the European Union, did not develop any top-down claim of direct effect or supremacy. The book questions this view and argues that the ECtHR has, even though only in subtle form, established certain important principles when it comes to giving effect to Convention law domestically.

On the other hand, the book builds on the systemic turn in ECHR scholarship. It has been widely acknowledged that the ECHR system is made up of a multitude of actors and levels sharing the responsibility of protecting human rights (so-called shared responsibility).[28] This has called into question a monolithic conception of contracting states under the ECHR. For instance, according to a particular reading of the subsidiarity principle, domestic institutions themselves are conceived of as Convention organs insofar as they are entrusted with the primary responsibility to ensure the substantive protection of Convention rights.[29] Based on Kantian theory, Stone Sweet even spoke of a (European) cosmopolitan legal order in which each state official bears a duty to protect Convention rights.[30] By framing a Convention community, the present book carries on said approaches. To be sure, the term community has been used before by eminent ECHR scholars[31] and the Court

24 Laurence R. Helfer, "Redesigning the European Court of Human Rights: Embeddedness as a Deep Structural Principle of the European Human Rights Regime" (2008) 19 *European Journal of International Law* 125–159.

25 Eirik Bjorge, *Domestic Application of the ECHR – Courts as Faithful Trustees* (Oxford: Oxford University Press 2015).

26 See further the volume edited by Janneke Gerards and Joseph Fleuren, *Implementation of the European Convention on Human Rights and of the Judgments of the ECtHR in National Case-law* (Cambridge: Intersentia 2014).

27 For example, Bjorge, *Domestic Application of the ECHR*, pp. 68ff. For an exception see Jörg Polakiewicz, "The Status of the Convention in National Law" in Robert Blackburn and Jörg Polakiewicz (eds.), *Fundamental Rights in Europe: The European Convention on Human Rights and Its Member States, 1950–2000* (Oxford: Oxford University Press 2001).

28 Janneke Gerards, "The European Court of Human Rights and the National Courts: Giving Shape to the Notion of 'Shared Responsibility'" in Janneke H. Gerards and Joseph Fleuren (eds.), *Implementation of the European Convention on Human Rights and of the Judgments of the ECtHR in National Case-law* (Cambridge: Intersentia 2014), pp. 13ff.

29 Christoffersen, *Fair Balance*, pp. 359ff; Harmsen, "Reform of the Convention System", p. 136.

30 Alec Stone Sweet, "A Cosmopolitan Legal Order: Constitutional Pluralism and Rights Adjudication in Europe" (2012) 1 *Global Constitutionalism* 53–90.

31 Paul Mahoney, "New Challenges for the European Court of Human Rights Resulting from the Expanding Case Load and Membership" (2002) 21 *Penn State International Law Review* 101–114 at 104; Luzius Wildhaber, "The Place of the European Court of Human Rights in the European Constitutional Landscape," *Conference of European Constitutional Courts XIIth Congress* (2002) p. 4.

itself[32]. Yet, the findings of this book, it is submitted, enable to give the notion a more specific meaning. Especially when drawing on constructivist insights, the existence of a community may be viewed as both a precondition and product of the ECHR's supranational dimension. A communitarian perspective underscores the importance of ECHR rights as community interest norms, the dialogical nature of their interpretation as well as the status and role of natural and legal persons and domestic authorities as community members.

Finally, it is submitted that understanding legal integration under the ECHR can, at least to some extent, help in explaining and putting into context the phenomenon of growing resistance against the ECtHR as well as map possible responses thereto.[33] Admittedly, backlash, which has become somewhat of a buzzword also in the ECHR context, especially in the wake of the Brighton Declaration,[34] could question the narrative of supranationalization.[35] However, when engaging with the growing body of literature on the topic, it is important to recognize that backlash or resistance may be used to refer to many different forms of negative reactions vis-à-vis the ECtHR stemming from various actors.[36] Important for the purpose of this book will be (i) to appreciate whether resistance is fundamental enough to go beyond the built-in contestation,[37] which is pedigree of the dialogical character of any international legal regime and even more so of human rights interpretation, and (ii) in how far resistance actually translates into relevant institutional or judicial reversals such as the curtailment of the Court's competences and powers.[38] It will be argued

32 ECtHR, *Konstantin Markin* v. *Russia*, no. 30078/06, Judgment of March 22, 2012, ECHR 2012-III (extracts), § 89.

33 On resistance against international courts in general see, for instance, Mikael Rask Madsen, Pola Cebulak, and Micha Wiebusch, "Backlash Against International Courts: Explaining the Forms and Patterns of Resistance to International Courts" (2018) 14 *International Journal of Law in Context* 197–220.

34 Mikael Rask Madsen, "Rebalancing European Human Rights: Has the Brighton Declaration Engendered a New Deal on Human Rights in Europe?" (2018) 9 *Journal of International Dispute Settlement* 199–222.

35 On resistance in the ECHR context see, for instance, Marten Breuer (ed.), "'Principled Resistance' to ECtHR Judgments: An Appraisal," *Principled Resistance to ECtHR Judgments – A New Paradigm?* (Berlin/Heidelberg: Springer, 2019), pp. 323–350; Sarah Lambrecht, "Assessing the Existence of Criticism of the European Court of Human Rights" in Patricia Popelier, Sarah Lambrecht, and Koen Lemmens (eds.), *Criticism of the European Court of Human Rights: Shifting the Convention System: Counter-dynamics at the National and EU Level* (Cambridge: Intersentia 2016), pp. 505–554; Øyvind Stiansen and Erik Voeten, "Backlash and Judicial Restraint: Evidence from the European Court of Human Rights" (2020) 64 *International Studies Quarterly* 770–784.

36 Madsen, Cebulak, and Wiebusch, "Backlash Against International Courts," 199ff.

37 Termed pushback or ordinary resistance by Madsen, Cebulak, and Wiebusch, "Backlash Against International Courts," 197ff. For similar reasons, Lemmens distinguishes between criticism regarding the Court's existence and its practice/functioning (Koen Lemmens, "Criticising the European Court of Human Rights or Misunderstanding the Dynamics of Human Rights Protection?" in Patricia Popelier, Sarah Lambrecht, and Koen Lemmens (eds.), *Criticism of the European Court of Human Rights: Shifting the Convention System: Counter-dynamics at the National and EU Level* (Cambridge: Intersentia 2016), pp. 26ff).

38 Madsen, Cebulak, and Wiebusch, "Backlash Against International Courts", 201.

that so far studies on resistance challenge the narrative of this book only parochially, but rather support a supranational as well as communitarian perspective on the ECHR.

LAYOUT AND METHODOLOGY

The present thesis comprises six chapters. Each chapter contains a separate introductory part which lays out the specific line of argument and the methodology adopted. The following overview remains, therefore, general in nature.

Chapters 1 and 2 are the conceptual and theoretical foundation of the book. Indeed, assessing supranational aspects of the ECHR requires to clarify what precisely is meant by this polysemic term to begin with. Chapter 1 aims at providing a survey of the sources, the evolution and the different – partly competing – conceptions of the notion of supranationality within (legal) discipline(s). It discusses the origins of the notion and contrasts the different contexts and ways in which the term supranational was used in the past and is used today. Chapter 2 then develops the book's conceptual framework. It proposes to rediscover supranationality as a notion that can apply outside the realm of EU law as an analytical and doctrinal catchword for international regimes possessing a number of specific attributes. The terminology developed in Chapter 2 includes a working definition of supranationality which approximates the concept from a functional perspective and distinguishes between vertical and horizontal legal integration. Chapter 2 also discusses the notion of community as used in international legal discourse and draws on constructivist regime theorists to better understand the (inter-)subjective character of common values and community interest norms.

Based on this conceptual framework developed in Chapter 2, Chapters 3 to 6 contain a two-pronged empirical study. Chapter 3 takes a legal-historical approach and traces the evolution towards supranational adjudication under the ECHR. Chapter 4 deconstructs judicial integration through the ECtHR. It disentangles the different dimensions of the Court's authority and discusses how the ECtHR exercises supranational authority bypassing states in an ever-growing number of areas. Whereas Chapter 4 discusses the Court's judicial role(s) strictu sensu, Chapter 5 contains a separate treatise on lawmaking and the effect of Strasbourg case-law beyond the individual case. Under the Convention system, judicial lawmaking is particularly extensive both in quality and quantity. Today, the text of the ECHR and its Protocols is merely the basis of a much larger notion of Convention law, which has grown over time into an autonomous body of law infused by Strasbourg jurisprudence. It is submitted that lawmaking by the ECtHR has supranational traits in two respects. On the one hand, the Court resorts to a particularly autonomous methodology in developing a common European human rights standard. On the other hand, the generalizable result of its jurisgenerative function must be observed throughout the community of Convention states (*res interpretata* effect). Chapter 6 then moves the inquiry into the vertical sphere and takes a closer look at the general effects of Convention law within domestic legal orders. The hypothesis is tested whether the ECHR in terms of its effects in domestic legal systems could be termed supranational law. The hypothesis is tested from the perspective of the Court but also from the perspective of national legal orders. As a methodological disclaimer, it must be stressed that Chapter 6 does not and cannot aim at providing an in-depth comparative study. Instead, the author relies on a very rich body of existing literature on the ECHR's domestic effect, while discussing a number of illustrative examples. Developments discussed under the heading of backlash or resistance are analyzed throughout Chapters 4–6 as a crossover topic. Indeed, distinguishing extraordinary from ordinary resistance as well as tracing the actual judicial or institutional consequences of resistance require a context-specific approach.

Finally, the conclusion sums up the findings of the study and proposes to give shape to the notion of Convention community.

Two general delimitations regarding the scope of this study are in order. First, the study does not aim at providing an (in-depth) comparison between EU law and the ECHR. EU law will be discussed as a source of the concept of supranationality. In the subsequent chapters, however, and as stressed earlier, the study adopts a general understanding of the notion which is to be viewed independently from EU law. Of course, EU law remains an archetype of supranationality and drawing parallels to the ECHR may be indicated to this extent. Also, EU law and the ECHR overlap both substantively and geographically and their respective impact onto domestic law is, therefore, often intertwined. As second delimitation, it must be stressed that the present study is not a general inquiry into states' compliance with Convention law. While supranationality may presuppose general acceptance of the binding force of ECtHR judgments, for instance, it is not examined in how far states comply with their specific primary or secondary obligations in a given area of Convention law.

1

Supranationality

Sources, Evolution, and Conceptions

1.1 POLYSEMIC NATURE OF SUPRANATIONALITY

Supranationality is a polysemic concept. The term appears in hundreds of titles of publications in legal and political science. Despite its frequent use – or maybe precisely because of it – it is said to lack an agreed definition and described as an amorphous concept.[1] Supranationality is first and foremost a scholarly notion whose understanding has evolved over time, feeding on many different conceptual sources. What exactly is regarded supranational varies greatly across different disciplines, fields of research, and (historical) contexts. Many use the term without further explaining it, and very few have devoted an entire article or monograph to the notion.[2]

This chapter seeks to lay the foundations for developing the conceptual framework of the study in more detail. In an attempt to simplify and synthesize, the chapter contrasts different conceptualizations of supranationality that exist(ed) at different points in time within and across different disciplines. The focus lies on legal writings, but scholarship in political science is selectively considered insofar it has impacted legal thinking. The approach adopted may leave many details obscure, but should provide a general idea of the different meanings of supranationality, their evolution as well as the contexts through and in which the concept is construed and used. The narrative adopted attempts to refrain from normative assessment, the latter being reserved for Chapter 2. The different understandings of supranationality

[1] Werner Schroeder and Andreas Th. Müller, "Elements of Supranationality in the Law of International Organizations" in Ulrich Fastenrath et al. (eds.), *From Bilateralism to Community Interest: Essays in Honour of Judge Bruno Simma* (Oxford: Oxford University Press 2011), p. 366; Joseph H. H. Weiler, "The Community System: The Dual Character of Supranationalism" (1981) 1 *Yearbook of European Law* 267–306 at 268.

[2] Notable exceptions being Hay, *Federalism, and Supranational Organizations*; Klaus von Lindeiner-Wildau, *La supranationalité en tant que principe de droit* (Leiden: A. W. Sijthoff 1970); Weiler, "Community System"; Schroeder and Müller, "Elements of Supranationality"; Cédric Chapuis, *Die Übertragung von Hoheitsrechten auf supranationale Organisationen* (Basel: Helbing & Lichtenhahn 1993).

should be contrasted on equal footing, shedding light on the political, normative, and doctrinal assumptions behind them.

An in-depth historical account on supranationality exceeds the scope of this chapter. Nevertheless, it seems worthwhile to explore the emergence of the term as follows. Section 1.2 looks at the international law origins of the notion. Although supranationality is today regularly and sometimes exclusively associated with the EU, the term originated in legal scholarship of the early twentieth century. Section 1.3 recalls how supranationality first became a political and later a legal notion during and following the establishment of the European Communities. Section 1.4 discusses the significance of supranationality as a quintessential or even idiosyncratic concept of EU law scholarship. Section 1.5 then turns to the law of international organizations (IOs) and international law literature operating mostly with in the category of supranational organizations. As a conclusion, Section 1.6 contrasts competing conceptions by identifying a number of reference points. It also discusses existing overlaps and offers explanations for the polysemic nature of supranationality.

1.2 INTERNATIONAL LAW ORIGINS

1.2.1 *Legal Scholarship of the Early Twentieth Century*

A closer look at the notion's genealogy reveals that supranationality is not the neologism of the European integration process it is generally believed to be.[3] In fact, different authors traced back the term *supranational* (*überstaatlich*) to German philosopher Nietzsche,[4] and international lawyers had begun using the notion already in the early twentieth century when international law was in a state of flux. The adjective supranational was first used with reference to international institutions, mostly courts. German scholar Franz von Liszt, for instance, referred to the project of an International Prize Court[5] agreed upon during the Second Hague Peace Conference in 1907 as a "supranational empire".[6] If established, the International Prize Court would have had compulsory jurisdiction to deal with

[3] Lindeiner-Wildau provides an in-depth survey of the early use of the notion (Lindeiner-Wildau, *Supranationalité*, pp. 1–38).

[4] Lindeiner-Wildau, *Supranationalité*, p. 12; Dusan Sidjanski, *Le principe supranational et le processus d'intégration dans les Communautés européennes* (Paris: Association des études internationales 1962), p. 5.

[5] The creation of the International Prize Court was agreed upon in the Convention relative to the Creation of an International Prize Court (IPCC). Although it never came into existence, the ambitious project attracted considerable attention in scholarship (see, for instance, Henry B. Brown, "The Proposed International Prize Court" [1908] 2 *American Journal of International Law* 476–489).

[6] Franz von Liszt, "Das Wesen des völkerrechtlichen Staatenverbandes und der Internationale Prisenhof," *Festgabe der Berliner juristischen Fakultät für Otto Gierke zum Doktorjubiläum 21. August 1910*, vol. III (Breslau: M & H Marcus 1910), p. 38.

prize matters, that is, the capturing of enemy ships and cargo at sea during wartime. It would have heard appeals from states and individuals against national judgments and could have annulled domestic acts of capture at issue.[7] Von Liszt emphasized that the envisaged Court would stand *above* domestic prize courts and appraised it as one of the greatest advances of international law, as the first step from a cooperative toward an authoritative organization of the associations of states (*Staatenverband*).[8] Few years later, the term supranational appeared in reference to the mixed arbitral tribunals established by the peace treaties of World War I.[9] Individuals were granted access to an international court for the first time.[10] The judges' position at the Permanent Court of International Justice created in 1922 was equally denoted supranational.[11]

In parallel, certain scholars began using the term in a more general manner – irrespective of particular international institutions.[12] As early as 1899, Kaufman used the term *jus supra partes* to express his view that certain international norms, such as the prohibition of piracy, create immediate rights and obligations for individuals.[13] Hull, on the other hand, distinguished between law *between* nations and a law *over* or *above* nations. The latter, he found, could also be termed *supranational law*.[14] While Hull's distinction remains somewhat elusive, Snow, another American lawyer, advocated a few years later in favor of replacing the term international law with supranational law altogether.[15] Both Hull and Snow shared the common assumption of an emerging world society or polity.[16] Snow defended the view that only the term supranational could accurately express the idea of a law governing the nations.[17] Dutch public lawyer Krabbe put forward a similar argument. In his book *Die moderne Staatsidee*, Krabbe considered international law a misleading notion. He also favored to speak of supranational law instead as it conveyed more clearly his

7 Liszt, "Wesen des Staatenverbandes," pp. 33ff. Arts. 3, 4, and 7 IPCC.

8 Liszt, "Wesen des Staatenverbandes," pp. 41ff.

9 Josef Kohler, "Völkerrechtliche Studien" (1912) 6 *Zeitschrift für Völkerrecht und Bundesstaatsrecht* 89–124 at 106.

10 Hermann Mosler, "Supra-National Judicial Decisions" (1981) 4 *Hastings International and Comparative Law Review* 425–472 at 429.

11 Lindeiner-Wildau, *Supranationalité*, p. 13.

12 With further references, Fritz Münch, "Die Abgrenzung des Rechtsbereiches der supranationalen Gemeinschaft gegenüber dem innerstaatlichen Recht" (1958) 2 *Verhandlungen der Tagung der Deutschen Gesellschaft für Völkerrecht* 73–93 at fn. 9; Lindeiner-Wildau, *Supranationalité*, p. 12.

13 Willhelm Kaufmann, *Die Rechtskraft des internationalen Rechtes und das Verhältniss der Staatsgesetzgebungen und der Staatsorgane zu demselben* (Stuttgart: F Enke 1899), pp. 27 and 30.

14 William Isaac Hull, "The Primary Sources of International Obligations" (1911) 5 *American Society of International Law Proceedings* 257–288 at 280ff, in particular 282f.

15 Alpheus Henry Snow, "The Law of Nations" (1912) 6 *American Journal of International Law* 890–900.

16 Snow speaks of a "federal body politic," whereas Hull refers to a "new political entity." Interestingly, Snow even defended such a claim in the absence of common organs.

17 Snow, "Law of Nations," 892.

view, according to which the community of individuals, rather than states, should be the main subject of the international legal order.[18]

1.2.2 *Scellian Theory*

Supranationality also became an important notion in the terminology of French legal theorist Scelle. He not only used the notion of supranationality for an empirical or descriptive account of the state of international law, but, more importantly perhaps, as a normative concept encapsulating what the international legal order ought to look like.[19] Scelle characterized the international society by distinguishing between interstate and supra-state societies (*sociétés interétatiques* and *sociétés superétatiques*).[20] In contrast to the former, supra-state societies are vested with their proper organs performing social functions on behalf of the society (such as lawmaking, adjudication, or enforcement).[21] Scelle regarded international institutions or organizations, including the aforementioned International Prize Court, the League of Nations, or the International Labour Organization as supra-state phenomena.[22] However, these sites of institutionalization were an exception in the international legal order otherwise dominated by interstate relations.[23] To remedy this general lack of institutionalization, Scelle developed his theory on role splitting (*dédoublement fonctionnel*): The organs of the state are required to operate in a dual capacity; they must act not only on behalf of the state but also on behalf of the international society given that the latter is devoid of its own organs and representatives.[24] As Schroeder and Mueller put it, *dédoublement fonctionnel* was for Scelle a "makeshift" toward a genuine supranational legal order.[25]

18 Hugo Krabbe, *Die moderne Staatsidee*, 2nd ed. (Leiden: Martinus Nijhoff 1919), p. 278.

19 Lindeiner-Wildau arguably overlooked this fact in his treatise.

20 There is, in fact, much to suggest that Scelle employed the terms super- and supra- interchangeably. Whereas, for instance, he described the League of Nations as an organization *superétatique*, he referred to its organs as institutions *supra-étatique* (Georges Scelle, *Précis de droit des gens. Principes et systématique* [Paris: Recueil Sirey 1932], p. 256; Lindeiner-Wildau, *Supranationalité*, p. 12 and fn. 40). This is probably why the term *superétatique* is commonly translated into English as supra-state (see, for instance, Martti Koskenniemi, *The Gentle Civilizer of Nations* [Cambridge: Cambridge University Press 2001], p. 332).

21 Scelle, *Précis de droit des gens*, pp. 49ff, 57.

22 Ibid., pp. 57, 268f and 270.

23 Georges Scelle, *Manuel élémentaire de droit international public* (Paris: Domat-Montchrestien 1943), pp. 21ff.

24 Scelle, *Précis de droit des gens*, pp. 57, 270; Scelle, *Manuel élémentaire*, pp. 22f; Antonio Cassese, "Remarks on Scelle's Theory of 'Role Splitting' (dédoublement fonctionnel) in International Law" (1990) 1 *European Journal of International Law* 210–231; Oliver Diggelmann, "Georges Scelle (1878–1961)" in Bardo Fassbender and Anne Peters (eds.), *The Oxford Handbook of the History of International Law* (Oxford: Oxford University Press 2012), pp. 1164f.

25 Schroeder and Müller, "Elements of Supranationality," p. 364.

Scellian theory combined a federalist and anthropocentric[26] vision of international law.[27] For Scelle, law was "objective" in that it corresponds to the social reality. Different societies coexist through bonds of solidarity among people, leading to a plurality of different legal orders with the world community at the very top.[28] As objective law is always of the same origin, there is unity of law and consequently legal monism.[29] Societies and legal orders are organized hierarchically along federal lines: The more inclusive society always prevails.[30] International law thus overrides domestic law (normative federalism) in analogy to the principle of *Bundesrecht bricht Landesrecht* in a federal state.[31] Scelle regarded federalism as a constant in the evolution of human society because it allowed for the reconciliation of two seemingly contradictory needs: autonomy and liberty of different societies on the one hand and peace and security among those societies on the other.[32] The superimposition of different societies and the gradual social integration through solidarity would ultimately lead to world federalism.[33] At the same time, Scelle's theory was radically anthropocentric. The individual is the immediate and exclusive subject of (international) law, hence the term "law of people" (*droits des gens*).[34] One of the last references to supranationality Scelle made as a member of the ILC.[35] Commenting on the Draft Declaration on Rights and Duties of States of 1949, Scelle referred to the third social function of organs proper to the supra-state society, which is enforcement:

> While there had been no possibility of enforcement under classic international law, new international law could be enforced by organs created for that purpose, thus making possible the eventual establishment of a supranational authority.[36]

26 Diggelmann, "Georges Scelle," p. 1162.
27 Scelle, *Précis de droit des gens*, pp. 189ff.
28 Cassese, "Scelle's Theory," 211.
29 Scelle, *Précis de droit des gens*, p. 32.
30 Koskenniemi, *Gentle Civilizer of Nations*, p. 332.
31 Scelle, *Manuel élémentaire*, p. 191.
32 Scelle, *Précis de droit des gens*, p. 188; Hubert Thierry, "The European Tradition in International Law: Georges Scelle" (1990) 1 *European Journal of International Law* 193–209 at 202.
33 Scelle, *Précis de droit des gens*, p. 32.
34 Thierry, "European Tradition," 202ff; Koskenniemi, *Gentle Civilizer of Nations*, p. 332.
35 Insofar one is inclined to partly disagree with Cassese, who, regarding the concept of supra-state societies, pointed out that "this part of Scelle's scientific contribution has been subject to fluctuations and a great deal of uncertainty," not least because Scelle "either dropped or at least muted [it] in his writings published after 1945" (Cassese, "Scelle's Theory," 213f).
36 *Yearbook of the ILC* (1949) 155 n 64. It has therefore been pointed out that supranationality in this context corresponds to international institutions guaranteeing and enforcing the respect for international law. Later, in 1954, Scelle provided an interesting definition of the term of institutional federalism. Though he did not refer to supranationality in this context, Scelle's demands overlap with some of the elements with reference to which the concept would later be defined: "Elle consiste essentiellement à créer, pour l'exercice des fonctions juridiques essentielles de l'ordre international, des organes dont les membres sont *ex officio* denationalisés, c'est-à-dire independants des gouvemants étatiques pour lesquels leurs décisions deviennent obligatoires" (Georges Scelle, "Quelques réflexions sur l'abolition de la competence de guerre" [1954] 58 *Revue générale de droit international public* 5–22 at 9).

1.2.3 Congress of Europe

Of particular interest to the present study is the fact that the notion of supranationality appeared in a resolution adopted by the Congress of Europe in May 1948 in reference to what would later become the European Court of Human Rights.[37] Held in The Hague in the wake of World War II, the Congress brought together over 700 delegates from civil and political society to discuss the future of a united Europe.[38] It opposed transnational groups such as the Union of European Federalists, which pursued a federalist vision and the creation of the "Estates General of Europe," to the Unionists under the lead of Winston Churchill, who advocated for intergovernmental cooperation in Europe.[39] The Congress recognized in a resolution that "(. . .) human rights are the essential bases (. . .) for a United Europe" and must be secured in a legally binding charter.[40] Moreover, it was considered "essential for the safeguarding of these rights that there should be established a Supreme Court with *supra-state* jurisdiction to which citizens and groups can appeal, and which is capable of assuring the implementation of the Charter."[41]

The resolution went back to a draft of French philosopher and lawyer Marc.[42] Marc was one of the leading figures of the federalist camp.[43] He stressed that the proposal for a Supreme Court must be viewed within a federalist framework[44] and that protecting people effectively from abuse of power would require safeguarding the independence of the supra-national tribunal vis-à-vis states and granting individuals direct access to it.[45] While both Scelle and Marc employed a federalist vocabulary, their underlying conceptions of federalism were different. Contrary to Scelle, Marc did not believe in the creation of a global superstate but rather in federalism by segregation.[46]

37 Lindeiner-Wildau, *Supranationalité*, pp. 1ff.

38 Congress of Europe, Verbatim Report I, 4; Jean-Michel Guieu, "Introduction. Le Congrès de La Haye (7–10 Mai 1948), Porte-parole de l'Europe?" in Jean-Michel Guieu and Christophe Le Dréau (eds.), *Le Congrès de l'Europe à La Haye (1948–2008)* (Bruxelles: Peter Lang 2009), pp. 15ff, 21, 26ff; Wilfried Loth, *Building Europe: A History of European Unification* (Berlin: De Gruyter Oldenbourg 2015), pp. 13ff.

39 Birte Wassenberg, *History of the Council of Europe* (Strasbourg: Council of Europe 2013); Loth, *Building Europe*, pp. 8ff; Dusan Sidjanski, *The Federal Future of Europe* (Ann Arbor: University of Michigan Press 2000), pp. 18ff.

40 Congress of Europe, Cultural Resolution of May 7–10, 1948, Section 4.

41 Ibid., Section 5 (emphasis added). Though the outcome of the Congress was generally perceived as a victory for the Unionists, this particular resolution amounted to a success for the Federalists (Guieu, "Congrès de La Haye," p. 87).

42 Congress of Europe, Verbatim Report IV, 45ff. Marc was founding member and General-Secretary of the Union of European Federalists ("Alexandre Marc" [*Historical Archives of the European Union*, 2006] http://archives.eui.eu/en/files/inventories/15209?d=inline accessed July 23, 2020).

43 Sidjanski, *Federal Future of Europe*, p. 19.

44 Ibid., pp. 49f.

45 Ibid.; Lindeiner-Wildau, *Supranationalité*, pp. 2f.

46 Antonio Cassese, *Five Masters of International Law: Conversations with R-J Dupuy, E Jimenez de Arechaga, R Jennings, L Henkin and O Schachter* (Oxford: Hart 2011), p. 17; see also Claude Nigoul,

1.2.4 *Commonalities in the Early Use of the Notion*

While brief and somewhat episodic, the preceding survey illustrates how in the early twentieth century international lawyers sporadically began using the adjective supranational. It also shows that the notion "was not born out of vacuum,"[47] but emerged as a result of profound structural changes in international law, which so far had been dominated by voluntarist positivism and (absolute) state sovereignty.[48] From the beginning, the notion was therefore associated with a certain idea of progress. On an institutional level, the term supranational served to capture a shift from a horizontal toward a more vertically organized international legal order featuring international institutions, which could take decisions binding on states. A crucial aspect was the demand for international adjudication and the peaceful settlement of international disputes. All three courts that prompted the use of supranationality were the result of a peace conference.[49] States were considered to represent a danger for both international peace and the individual, and supranationality reflected the idea that institutions and legal rules must function independently from states, above them so to speak, to secure peace effectively. Also, supranationality spoke to a trend of individualistic conceptions of international law among scholars during the 1920s and 1930s, which sought to protect the individual from the rising totalitarianism in Europe.[50] Scelle, Münch but also von Liszt and Krabbe acknowledged the individual as a (or the only) subject of international law, whereas both von Liszt and Marc used supranational in connection with the idea of guaranteeing the individual a direct right of access to an international court.

Another common denominator lies in the federalist vision or reading of the institutionalization of international law.[51] Against the background of American federalism, Hull transposed a federalist framework beyond the state onto the international legal system. Federalism was also crucial to Scelle's theory and after World War II it became a proper popular movement and central to Marc's vision for a United Europe. What is more, the increasing interdependence between states and their citizens led scholars such as Hull, Snow, and Scelle to speak of the

"René-Jean Dupuy et le fédéralisme: de Georges Scelle à Alexandre Marc," *Humanité et droit international. Mélanges René-Jean Dupuy* (Paris: A. Pédone 1991).

47 Schroeder and Müller, "Elements of Supranationality," p. 363.

48 On this "Classical International Law," see David Kennedy, "International Law and the Nineteenth Century: History of an Illusion" (1996) 65 *Nordic Journal of International Law* 385–420.

49 The Permanent Court of Arbitration was the result of the First Hague Peace Conference, whereas the International Prize Court was proposed at the Second Hague Peace Conference; the League of Nations and the Permanent Court of International Justice were the result of the Paris Peace Conference after World War I; what later was to become the European Court of Human Rights was proposed at the Congress of The Hague on a united Europe after World War II.

50 Anne Peters, *Beyond Human Rights* (Cambridge: Cambridge University Press 2016), pp. 16–20; Janne Nijman, *The Concept of International Legal Personality – An Inquiry into the History and Theory of International Law* (The Hague: T.M.C. Asser Press 2004), p. 126.

51 For a delineation of supranationality from current strands of federalism, see Chapter 2, Section 2.4.1.3.

emergence of a world society. The time after the Great War was seen as changing point of international law toward the law of peoples.[52] In this context, supranationality expressed the idea of a hierarchical ordering of norms. For Hull and Scelle, for instance, superiority followed from the fact that supranational law emanated or was addressed to a higher and more inclusive political body than that of one state. In sum, the term supranational emerged against the background of what was called the demystification or relativization of the nation-state.[53] The creation of independent international institutions, compulsory adjudication as well as recognizing the individual's subjectivity or a form of world polity all profoundly questioned the prevailing concept of state sovereignty.

1.3 FROM A POLITICAL TOWARD A LEGAL AND SCHOLARLY NOTION OF EUROPEAN INTEGRATION

1.3.1 *The Schuman Plan*

The more recent origins of the notion of supranationality lie in the particular political and historical context of postwar Europe. Schuman and Monnet, the "fathers" of European integration, are usually also considered to have coined the term supranational. While it was not until the negotiations on the establishment of the European Coal and Steel Community (ECSC) that supranationality became an important part of the vocabulary of Monnet and Schuman,[54] many have located its origins in the famous Schuman Declaration of May 9, 1950.[55] Supranationality is therefore closely linked to the political endeavor of securing the peaceful reconstruction of post-war Europe by unifying, in a limited sector, the war-stricken economies between France and Germany.[56] Like Marc, Schuman and Monnet were considered federalists,[57] although they followed a more pragmatic[58] and functional approach.[59] According to the Schuman Declaration, "the pooling of coal and steel production should immediately provide for the setting up of common foundations for economic development as

[52] Nicolas E. Politis, *Les nouvelles tendances du droit international* (Paris: Hachette 1927), p. 76; Peters, *Beyond Human Rights*, p. 19.
[53] Nijman, *International Legal Personality*, pp. 85ff.
[54] See subsequently Section 1.3.1.
[55] Sidjanski, *Principe supranational*, p. 30.
[56] Paul Reuter, "Le plan Schuman – La Communauté européenne du charbon et de l'acier," *Collected Courses of the Hague Academy of International Law*, vol. 81 (Leiden/Boston: Brill Nijhoff 1952), pp. 531–533; Alan S. Milward, *The Reconstruction of Western Europe, 1945–51* (Berkeley/Los Angeles: University of California Press 1984), p. 418.
[57] Sidjanski, *Principe supranational*, p. 31.
[58] Ibid.
[59] Reuter, "Le plan Schuman," p. 527. On functionalism, see famously David Mitrany, *A Working Peace System* (Chicago: Quadrangle Books 1966); on the significance of functionalism for European integration, see Walter Mattli, *The Logic of Regional Integration: Europe and Beyond* (Cambridge: Cambridge University Press 1999), pp. 21ff.

a first step in the federation of Europe" and "will lead to the realization of the first concrete foundation of a European federation indispensable to the preservation of peace."[60] Reminiscent of supranationality's international law origins, the Schuman Plan embodied change and progress too. It "tapped a vein of hope and idealism" and came to be seen as nothing less than "the first date of a new historical epoch."[61] Politically, Schuman considered an autonomous and independent community necessary in order to secure peaceful relations among European nations. It was the insight that "the security of the world or of a particular region must be anchored in something more solid than voluntary co-operation and the good will of the members" which "led to the new idea of 'supra-national' organs."[62]

1.3.2 *Incorporation into Positive Law: The ECSC Treaty*

How exactly supranationality became a key notion of European integration remains contested. Reuter, for instance, asserted that the term emerged spontaneously during the negotiations on the ECSC in 1950–51.[63] Another hypothesis is that supranationality was the result of avoiding the term *federal*. One finds support for the latter view when contrasting the Schuman Declaration to a speech Schuman gave on the state of the ECSC negotiations before the French National Assembly in July 1950.[64] The term supranational figured prominently in the speech, whereas any reference to federalism still present in the Declaration was omitted.[65]

Different organs of the ECSC as well as their powers were denoted supranational during the negotiations.[66] The ECSC Treaty entered into force on July 23, 1952; it was a *traité-loi* providing for a comprehensive set of substantive rules regulating the functioning of the common coal and steel market.[67] As executive organ composed of independent experts, a High Authority was responsible for ensuring the fulfilment of the objectives formulated in the Treaty.[68] In addition, the ECSC also comprised a Council, an Assembly, and a Court.[69] The Council was composed of representatives of national governments and tasked to harmonise the action of the High Authority and that of the governments.[70] The Assembly, in which delegates from

[60] Declaration by Robert Schuman of May 9, 1950.
[61] Milward, *Reconstruction of Western Europe*, p. 398.
[62] Josef L. Kunz, "Supra-National Organs" (1952) 46 *American Journal of International Law* 690–698 at 697.
[63] Reuter, "Le plan Schuman," p. 543.
[64] Lindeiner-Wildau, *Supranationalité*, p. 3.
[65] Robert Schuman, Speech before the French National Assembly on the State of Negotiations concerning the Schuman Plan, July 25, 1960.
[66] Lindeiner-Wildau, *Supranationalité*, pp. 4–6.
[67] For a detailed and original account on the negotiations and the establishment of the ECSC, see Reuter, "Le plan Schuman."
[68] Art. 8 ECSC Treaty.
[69] Art. 7 ECSC Treaty.
[70] Arts. 26 and 27 ECSC Treaty.

national parliaments were sitting, had some supervisory powers,[71] as did the Court, ensuring the rule of law in the interpretation and application of the treaty and of its implementing regulations.[72] Ultimately, it was only in respect to the function of the members of the High Authority, that supranationality became a notion of positive law. Article 9 ECSC Treaty read:

> (. . .) The members of the High Authority shall exercise their functions in complete independence, in the general interest of the Community. In the fulfilment of their duties, they shall neither solicit nor accept instructions from any government or from any organization. They will abstain from all conduct incompatible with the *supranational* character of their functions.
>
> Each member State agrees to respect this *supranational* character and to make no effort to influence the members of the High Authority in the execution of their duties.[73]

1.3.3 *General Acceptance as a Legal Term*

The lack of a uniform understanding during the negotiations on the ECSC did not prevent supranationality from becoming a generally accepted legal term.[74] Against the backdrop of the Korean War and the growing military strength of the Soviet bloc, collective security became of particular concern in Europe.[75] In response to the US call for a remilitarization of Western Germany under the newly founded NATO, French premier Pleven proposed the creation of a European army and a Defence Community (EDC),[76] organized "along the lines of the supranational blueprint put forward in the Schuman Declaration."[77] Whereas the Schuman Plan laid the economic foundations for peace in Europe, the Pleven Plan aimed at preventing that Germany would re-acquire military capacity under its own sovereign control.[78] In parallel to the negotiations on the ECSC, the EDC was drafted and signed by the signatory states of the ECSC. At the same time, the need was felt to provide for a wider democratic and political framework, through which the new European army

71 Arts. 21 and 24 ECSC Treaty.

72 Art. 31 ECSC Treaty.

73 Art. 9(5) and (6) ECSC Treaty (emphasis added). As Lindeiner-Wildau pointed out, Art. 100 of the UN Charter is of a similar wording (Lindeiner-Wildau, *Supranationalité*, pp. 7f).

74 At least, this is what Lindeiner-Wildau inferred from the fact that he could not find any discussions as to the meaning of supranational in neither the *travaux* of the EDC nor the EPC (Lindeiner-Wildau, *Supranationalité*, p. 10).

75 Josef L. Kunz, "Treaty Establishing the European Defense Community" (1953) 47 *American Journal of International Law* 275–281 at 275.

76 Kunz, "European Defense Community," 275.

77 Memorandum to the President of the French Council of Ministers, September 18, 1950; René Pleven, Statement on the Establishment of a European Army before French National Assembly, October 24, 1950.

78 Kunz, "European Defense Community," 275.

was to be controlled.[79] Article 38 of the EDC Draft Treaty, therefore, foresaw that the Assembly of the EDC, once operative, should study the creation of an Assembly elected on a democratic basis. To speed up this process, the ECSC Assembly was tasked to draft a Treaty constituting a European Political Authority thereby anticipating the work of the EDC Assembly.[80] The result was a proposal to incorporate the ECSC and the EDC into a new framework organization, the European Political Community (EPC).[81]

Neither the EDC nor the EPC ever came into existence.[82] However, both draft treaties featured the term supranational in a much more prominent manner than was the case for the ECSC Treaty.[83] The preamble of the EDC Draft Treaty, for example, spoke of a "supranational European organization" and pursuant to Article 1 "a European Defense Community, *supranational* in character" should be instituted. The Draft Treaty embodying the Statute of the European Community foresaw similar provisions.[84] Hence, in contrast to the ECSC Treaty, in which supranationality only appeared with respect to the High Authority's members, both the EDC and EPC would have been supranational as such *qua* positive law. In addition to this generalization of the term,[85] supranationality was paralleled by the re-emergence of federalist vocabulary. Article 38(1) of the EDC Draft Treaty set the goal of moving toward a "Federal or confederal structure, based upon the principle of the separation of powers and including, particularly, a bicameral representative system."[86] The introductory report to the EPC Draft Statute confirms this (con-)federal finality.[87] It is also in the context of the EPC that supranationality was more explicitly contrasted with the term intergovernmental and conceptualized as a middle ground between the national and international.[88]

79 Art. 38 EDC Draft Treaty; Basil Karp, "The Draft Constitution for a European Political Community" (1954) 8 *International Organization* 181–202 at 182; Kunz, "European Defense Community," 280.
80 Karp, "Draft Constitution," 183; Günther Jaenicke, "Der übernationale Charakter der Europäischen Wirtschaftsgemeinschaft" (1958) 19 *Zeitschrift für ausländisches öffentliches Recht und Völkerrecht* 153–196 at 158.
81 EPC Draft Statute, in particular Art. 5.
82 With the refusal of the French national assembly to ratify the EDC Draft Treaty, the creation of a European Political Community was equally off the table.
83 Kunz, "European Defense Community," 277.
84 See Art. 1 of the EPC Draft Statute.
85 Lindeiner-Wildau, *Supranationalité*, p. 9.
86 In similar fashion, Art. 8(2) of the EDC Draft Treaty read: "Without prejudice to the provisions of Article 125 below, the structure of these institutions as established by the present Treaty shall remain in effect until it is replaced by a new one, resulting from the establishment of a federal or confederal organization as provided in Article 38 below."
87 Heinrich von Brentano, "Introductory Report," *Draft Treaty Embodying the Statute of the European Community, Information and Official Documents of the Constitutional Committee* (1953), n. 18f.
88 Paul-Henri Spaak, Speech by the President of the Ad Hoc Assembly Made When Handing Over the Draft Statute of the European Political Community to the Six Ministers for Foreign Affairs, March 9, 1953.

1.3.4 *Banishment to Scholarship*

After the EDC and EPC failed, plans to revive European integration focused on the economic sphere.[89] The Rome Treaties signed in March 1957 established the European Economic Community (EEC) and a European Atomic Energy Community (Euratom). Although the institutional structure of the two new Communities was largely drawn up after the model of the ECSC, any reference in their respective treaties to supranationality was deliberately omitted. Both the EEC and the Euratom Treaty, which each established a Commission, had taken over large parts of the wording of Article 9 ECSC except for the word supranational.[90] It was hoped that "sacrificing" the term would enhance acceptance of the new treaties by national parliaments.[91] With the Merger Treaty of 1965, the High Authority of the ECSC and the Commissions of the EEC and the Euratom were succeeded by one single Commission.[92] The Merger Treaty adopted the wording of the EEC and Euratom Treaty, which meant that the term supranational disappeared permanently from positive Community law and was banished, henceforth, to the realm of (legal) scholarship.[93]

1.4. QUINTESSENTIAL CONCEPT OF EU LAW SCHOLARSHIP

1.4.1 *The Community Model*

A statutory definition being equally absent as a uniform use of supranationality, it was up to legal scholars to give – after the establishment of the ECSC – a more precise meaning to the newly created term of positive law. The multifaceted use of supranationality during the negotiations of the ECSC (as well as the EDC and the EPC), however, carried over to legal scholarship,[94] and the term was mostly understood as the general blueprint underlying the Community model.

Early treatises concentrated on two different aspects in particular. On the one hand, supranationality was located in the high degree of independence or autonomy of the ECSC organs vis-à-vis member states.[95] At the institutional level, the HA was

89 Resolution 35 of the ECSC Common Assembly of May 14, 1955.

90 Art. 157(2) EEC Treaty; Art. 126(2) Euratom Treaty.

91 Jaenicke, "Europäische Wirtschaftsgemeinschaft," 154; Hans Peter Ipsen, "Über Supranationalität" in H. Ehmke (ed.), *Festschrift für Ulrich Scheuner zum 70. Geburtstag* (Berlin: Duncker & Humboldt 1973), p. 211; Schroeder and Müller, "Elements of Supranationality," p. 363.

92 Art. 9 Merger Treaty.

93 Compare Art. 10 Merger Treaty; Ipsen, "Über Supranationalität," p. 211.

94 This is shown by the international congress of scholars on the ECSC in 1957 in Milan and Stresa, during which many diverging views were expressed not only on how to define supranationality but also whether it should at all be accepted as a legal notion. Jan Verzijl, for instance, identified between fifteen and twenty different criteria of supranationality (*Actes officiels du Congrès international d'études sur la Communauté européenne du charbon et de l'acier* [*Milan and Stresa*, 31 *May* – 9 *June* 1957] [Milan: Giuffrè 1957], p. 398; for an in-depth account see Lindeiner-Wildau, *Supranationalité*, pp. 13–38).

95 Reuter, "Le plan Schuman," p. 551; Günther Jaenicke, "Die Sicherung des übernationalen Charakters der Organe internationaler Organisationen" (1951) 14 *Zeitschrift für ausländisches*

composed of independent members that were neither accountable to nor bound by instructions of the governments that appointed them,[96] whereas, in terms of decision-making, it could bind states.[97] The HA was only bound by the ECSC Treaty itself and entrusted with managing, pursuing, and enforcing the interests of the community.[98] Similar considerations applied to the Commissions of the EEC and the Euratom, the Court of Justice of the Communities, but also to the ECSC's Assembly, which was composed of national parliamentarians appointed by national parliaments.[99]

On the other hand, early treatises detected supranationality in the HA's capacity to take decisions and recommendations that took effect automatically upon notification and were directly binding on enterprises in the steel and coal market of the member states (also termed *Völkerrechtsunmittelbarkeit* or *Durchgriff* in German doctrine).[100] Robertson, for instance, regarded this "the essence of the supranational power,"[101] while it was for Hay, arguably, the only meaningful criterion to distinguish the supra- from the international.[102] Scholars agreed that both the EEC and

öffentliches Recht und Völkerrecht 46–117; Peter Hay, "International and Supranational Organizations: Some Problems of Conceptualization" (1965) *University of Illinois Law Forum* 733–770; Klaus Dieter Schwantes, *Die Supranationalität: Eine Untersuchung internationaler wirtschaftlicher Organisationen Europas im 19. und 20. Jahrhundert* (Cologne: Universität Köln 1962), pp. 21ff; Lindeiner-Wildau, *Supranationalité*, pp. 13–38; Willem Jan Marie van Eysinga, "Supranational" in Walter Schätzel and Hans Jürgen Schlochauer (eds.), *Rechtsfragen der internationalen Organisation: Festschrift für Hans Wehberg zu seinem 70. Geburtstag* (Frankfurt/Main: Klostermann 1956), pp. 130f; Mosler, "Supra-National Judicial Decisions," 435.

96 Art. 9 ECSC Treaty.

97 Art. 14 ECSC Treaty stipulated that the High Authority's decisions shall be binding in all their detail, whereas recommendations shall be binding with respect to the objectives, which they specify. Ipsen, "Über Supranationalität," pp. 216ff.

98 Louis Delvaux, "La notion de supranationalité dans le traité du 18 avril 1951, créant la Communauté européenne du chabron et de l'acier," *Actes officiels du Congrès international d'études sur la Communauté européenne du charbon et de l'acier (Milan and Stresa, 31 May – 9 June 1957)*, vol. II (Milan: Giuffrè 1957), p. 234.

99 Jaenicke, "Europäische Wirtschaftsgemeinschaft," 170f; Jaenicke, "Organe internationaler Organisationen," 71; Hay, "International and Supranational Organizations," 738.

100 As regards, for instance, production quotas (Art. 58 ECSC Treaty), the establishment of manufacturing programs (Art. 59 ECSC Treaty), or pricing (Art. 60 ECSC Treaty; Arts. 14 and 15 ECSC Treaty). Art. 15 ECSC Treaty stated that when the High Authority's decisions and recommendations are individual in character, they shall be binding on the interested party upon notification and that in other cases, they shall take effect automatically upon publication. The High Authority could also adopt pecuniary sanctions or fix daily penalty payments in respect of defiant companies (e.g. Arts. 47, 58(4) or 59(7) ECSC Treaty). Hay, "International and Supranational Organizations," 736; Jaenicke, "Organe internationaler Organisationen," 47, 109; Kunz, "Supra-National Organs," 696; Hugo J. Hahn, "International and Supranational Public Authorities" (1961) 26 *Law and Contemporary Problems* 638–665 at 640; Arthur Henry Robertson, "Legal Problems of European Integration," *Collected Courses of the Hague Academy of International Law*, vol. 91 (Leiden: Brill Nijhoff 1957), p. 145; Mosler, "Supra-National Judicial Decisions," 435; Reuter, "Le plan Schuman," pp. 547ff; Münch, "Abgrenzung des Rechtsbereiches der supranationalen Gemeinschaft," 76; Schwantes, *Supranationalität*, pp. 32ff; Lindeiner-Wildau, *Supranationalité*, p. 38.

101 Robertson, "European Integration," p. 158.

102 Hay, "International and Supranational Organizations," 736.

the Euratom Treaty took over this principle of direct binding effect.[103] Both treaties stated that regulations shall have a general application and be binding in every respect and directly applicable in each member state, whereas decisions shall be binding in every respect for the addressees named therein.[104]

In short, supranationality was defined in reference to the Community model.[105] Much was still to change in the legal and political landscape of deepening European integration after legal scholarship first received the notion of supranationality. Compared to the limited coal and steel sector, the establishment of a common market through the Rome Treaties introduced a new dimension of economic integration, which was to gradually "spill over" into other fields of policy. However, the initial supranational blueprint was largely upheld and remained, therefore, a referential constant.[106] At the same time, supranationality became equally important to political science and integration theory.[107] Neo-functionalists, for instance, argued that supranationality created the conditions for "spill over effects" and, as a consequence, self-propelling integration.[108]

1.4.2 *Community Law*

Two landmark judgments of the European Court of Justice (ECJ, now CJEU) handed down in the early and mid-1960s strongly impacted the concept of supranationality. In *Van Gend en Loos*, the ECJ broadened the direct effect of Community law by acknowledging that primary law, if clear and legally perfect, was directly applicable, granting rights for individuals, which they can immediately invoke before national courts.[109]

103 Ibid.

104 Art. 189 EEC Treaty; Art. 161 Euratom Treaty.

105 For a more detailed and critical reflection on this, see Schwantes, *Supranationalität*, pp. 28f and 35f; Hay, "International and Supranational Organizations," 737–738; Rudolf L. Bindschedler, "Internationale Organisation (Grundfragen)" in Hans-Jürgen Schlochauer and Karl Strupp (eds.), *Wörterbuch des Völkerrechts* (Berlin: de Gruyter 1961), p. 75; Jaenicke, "Organe internationaler Organisationen," 81; Reuter, "Le plan Schuman," pp. 549f.

106 See subsequently Section 1.4.2.

107 Famously Ernst B. Haas, *Beyond the Nation-State: Functionalism and International Organization* (Stanford: Stanford University Press 1964); Leon N. Lindberg, *The Political Dynamics of European Economic Integration* (Stanford: Stanford University Press 1963); more recently, Wayne Sandholtz and Alec Stone Sweet, "Neo-Functionalism and Supranational Governance" in Erik Jones, Anand Menon, and Stephen Weatherill (eds.), *The Oxford Handbook of the European Union* (Oxford: Oxford University Press 2012), pp. 18–33.

108 On spill-over effects see, e.g., Lindberg, *European Economic Integration*, p. 8.

109 CJEU, Case 26/62, NV *Algemene Transporten Expeditie Onderneming van Gend & Loos* v. *Netherlands Inland Revenue Administration* [1963] ECR 1. The Court gradually extended the scope of the doctrine into the foray of secondary legislation, including directives. To be granted direct effect, a provision must be clear and legally perfect, which meant that it had to be specific, unconditional and requiring no further measures, either domestic or European (CJEU, Case 57/65, *Alfons Lütticke GmbH* v. *Hauptzollamt Saarlouis* [1966] ECR 205; with further references Gerhard Bebr, "Directly Applicable Provisions of Community Law: The Development of a Community Concept" [1970] 19 *International and Comparative Law Quarterly* 257–298).

Shortly after, the ECJ held in *Costa E.N.E.L* that Community law forms not only integral part of the legal system of the member states but also takes precedence over national law.[110] The ECJ later also clarified that Community law prevails over municipal law of any nature, including constitutional norms,[111] and entails a duty to set aside conflicting national provisions.[112]

The emerging discipline of Community law[113] assimilated the new doctrines into the concept of supranationality. Ipsen, for instance, amended the notion by the principles of direct effect and supremacy, as did Weiler in his influential article on the "Dual Character of Supranationalism."[114] In Weiler's case, direct effect and supremacy constituted part of what he termed normative supranationalism.[115] Henceforth, Community law was regarded supranational law because of its direct effect in and supremacy over domestic law.

1.4.3 *Supranationalism versus Intergovernmentalism*

Supranationalism and intergovernmentalism developed into two popular antitheses for assessing developments of European integration.[116] The Single European Act, for instance, strengthened supranational decision-making within the Community as it introduced majority voting in the Council and the co-decision procedure. Similarly, the transition to direct popular elections as well as bolstering the role of the Parliament were labeled "democratic supranationalism."[117] More generally, the Community method – that is, the sole right of the Commission to initiate legislation, the co-decision power shared between the Council and the European Parliament, the use of qualified majority voting in the Council and the compulsory jurisdiction of the ECJ – became equivalent to supranationalism, while the second and the third pillar of the EU were regarded intergovernmental in contrast.[118] The distinction between the

110 CJEU, Case 6/64, *Flaminio Costa* v. *E.N.E.L.* [1964] ECR 1141. The supremacy doctrine is often considered the logical consequence of direct effect (Karen J. Alter, *Establishing the Supremacy of European Law* [Oxford: Oxford University Press 2003], p. 19).

111 CJEU, Case 11/70, *Internationale Handelsgesellschaft mbH* v. *Einfuhr- und Vorratsstelle für Getreide und Futtermittel* [1970] ECR 1125.

112 CJEU, Case 106/77, *Staatliche Finanzverwaltung* v. *S.p.A. Simmenthal* [1978] ECR 629.

113 Morten Rasmussen, "Revolutionizing European Law: A History of the Van Gend en Loos Judgment" (2014) 12 *International Journal of Constitutional Law* 136–163 at 148.

114 Ipsen, "Über Supranationalität," p. 213; Weiler, "Community System," 273ff.

115 Weiler, "Community System," 273ff.

116 One of the early and most prominent examples is Weiler's piece on the "Dual Character of Supranationalism" (Weiler, "Community System"). For an example in the field of political science, see George Tsebelis and Geoffrey Garrett, "The Institutional Foundations of Intergovernmentalism and Supranationalism in the European Union" (2001) 55 *International Organization* 357–390.

117 For example, Robert Schütze, *European Constitutional Law* (Cambridge: Cambridge University Press 2012), p. 31.

118 "Community and Intergovernmental Methods" in *EUR-lex Glossary of Summaries* http://eur-lex.europa.eu/summary/glossary/community_intergovernmental_methods.html (accessed July 23, 2020).

supranational Community and the EU's intergovernmental second and third pillar was, however, never fully clear-cut and became gradually blurred.[119] More recently, scholars argued that with the Lisbon Treaty and the de-pillarization of the Union "the two classical dynamics of European institutional integration – intergovernmental and supranational – are no longer sufficient to explain the new, more complex, Treaty structures."[120] The dichotomy survived, however, until today. It often serves as a benchmark in accounts on the genealogy of EU law,[121] and is still used to assess EU governance post-Lisbon.[122]

1.4.4 *The EU's Legal Nature*

A contentious aspect of supranationality as a notion of European integration pertained to its relationship to sovereignty. Commentators generally agreed that supranationality had important ramifications for state sovereignty. Those who accepted that sovereignty is divisible or adopted a federal perspective spoke of a transferal of sovereignty to the European Communities. In their view, supranationality not only entailed a limitation of state sovereignty, but an actual and partial relinquishment thereof.[123] Schuman himself used the expression of a "partial fusion of sovereignty" with respect to the ECSC and its HA.[124] For others, state sovereignty remained a unitary concept, which excluded transferring parts of it in the first place.[125] These

[119] The Amsterdam Treaty communitarized large parts of the former third pillar and the Court extended in *Pupino* the "first pillar doctrine" of consistent interpretation to a framework decision adopted under the third pillar (CJEU, Case 105/03, *Criminal proceedings against Maria Pupino* [2005] ECR I-5285). See also Eleanor Spaventa, "Opening Pandora's Box: Some Reflections on the Constitutional Effects of the Decision in Pupino" (2007) 3 *European Constitutional Law Review* 5–24. Supranationalization of intergovernmental matters became the catchword (Carl Lebeck, "Sliding Towards Supranationalism? The Constitutional Status of EU Framework Decisions after Pupino" [2007] 8 *German Law Journal* 501–531).

[120] David Edward and Joxerramon Bengoetxea, "The Status and Rights of Sub-State Entities in the Constitutional Order of the European Union" in Anthony Arnull et al. (eds.), *A Constitutional Order of States? Essays in EU Law in Honour of Alan Dashwood* (Oxford: Hart 2011), p. 32.

[121] Among others Schütze, *European Constitutional Law*, pp. 9ff.

[122] See, for instance, Adriaan Schout and Sarah Wolff, "The 'Paradox of Lisbon': Supranationalism-Intergovernmentalism as an Administrative Concept" in Finn Laursen (ed.), *The EU's Lisbon Treaty: Institutional Choices and Implementation* (Farnham: Ashgate 2012), pp. 21–39. Christopher J. Bickerton, Dermot Hodson, and Uwe Puetter, "The New Intergovernmentalism and the Study of European Integration" in Christopher J. Bickerton, Dermot Hodson, and Uwe Puetter (eds.), *The New Intergovernmentalism* (Oxford: Oxford University Press 2015), pp. 1–50.

[123] Kunz, "Supra-National Organs," 697; Reuter, "Le plan Schuman," pp. 543ff.

[124] Robert Schuman, Speech before the French National Assembly on the State of Negotiations concerning the Schuman Plan, July 25, 1960; Mosler, "Supra-National Judicial Decisions," 361.

[125] See, for example, Schwantes, *Supranationalität*, pp. 11f. For Rosenstiel, the unitary character of sovereignty as a political quality of the state led him to reject supranationality as a legal notion (Francis Rosenstiel, *Le principe de supranationalité: essai sur les rapports de la politique et du droit* [Paris: A. Pédone 1962], pp. 30ff, in particular p. 40). Bindschedler, "Internationale Organisation," pp. 69ff.

authors argued that far-reaching competences or sovereign rights[126] had been transferred to the supranational level instead.[127] The shared view was that supranationality entailed the exercise of some sort of public power or authority[128] by the Communities usually reserved to states.[129] The temporal and substantive scope of this authority, however, was equally contested as the modalities of the conferral. Certain authors regarded, for instance, a permanent or at least indeterminate conferral of public authority a necessary requirement of supranationality.[130] Also, it was sometimes argued that supranational organs must necessarily exercise powers in a certain field of subject-matter deemed to be politically significant.[131]

Whether and how sovereignty or sovereign rights had been transferred to the Communities also impacted the understanding of supranationality's legal nature. Early conceptions usually drew an analogy to the two known "judicial-political categories" in public international law, states, and IOs.[132] Being supranational in character, the Communities would lie somewhere in between,[133] beyond traditional IOs but below a federation or a federal state.[134] Others understood supranational law as pre-federal law,[135] which came with the particular (normative) assumption that supranationality was only transitional, ultimately leading to a federal state. It was Monaco who first described the supranational Community as a legal system *sui generis*.[136] The *sui generis* notion gained considerable traction in wake of the landmark cases *Van Gend en Loos* and *Costa E.N.E.L.*, in which the Court considered the EEC an autonomous and new legal order.[137] This dictum was deemed

126 German scholars often used the term *Hoheitsrechte*, arguably because it also figures in Art. 24(1) of the German Basic Law (Münch, "Abgrenzung des Rechtsbereiches der supranationalen Gemeinschaft," 78f; Schwantes, *Supranationalität*, p. 12).

127 Münch, "Abgrenzung des Rechtsbereiches der supranationalen Gemeinschaft," 78f; Schwantes, *Supranationalität*, pp. 11f; Jaenicke, "Organe internationaler Organisationen," 86; Hay, "International and Supranational Organizations," 735.

128 Hahn, "Public Authorities," 640.

129 Fritz Münch, "Délimitation du domaine du droit des Communautés supranationales par rapport au droit étatique," *Actes officiels du Congrès international d'études sur la Communauté européenne du charbon et de l'acier (Milan and Stresa, 31 May – 9 June 1957)*, vol. II (Milan: Giuffrè 1957), p. 276.

130 Schwantes, *Supranationalität*, pp. 17ff; Lindeiner-Wildau, *Supranationalité*, pp. 19ff.

131 With further references Lindeiner-Wildau, *Supranationalité*, pp. 16ff.

132 Weiler, "Community System," 268.

133 Kunz, "Supra-National Organs," 697.

134 Henry L. Mason, *The European Coal and Steel Community: Experiment in Supranationalism* (Leiden: Martinus Nijhoff 1955).

135 Carl Friedrich Ophüls, "Europas partieller Bundesstaat" (1951) 6 *Die Gegenwart* 25–29; Walter Hallstein, *Der unvollendete Bundesstaat: Europäische Erfahrungen und Erkenntnisse* (Düsseldorf: Econ 1969).

136 Ricardo Monaco, "La Communità sopranazionale nell'ordinamento internazionale" (1953) 8 *La Comunità Internazionale* 441–458; later also Delvaux, "Notion de supranationalité," p. 235.

137 In *Costa* v. *E.N.E.L.*, the Court considered the EEC Treaty "an independent source of law." In the French version of the judgment, the term autonomous was used (*"une source autonome"*). On the notion of autonomy see, e.g., René Barents, *The Autonomy of Community Law* (Alphen aan den Rijn: Kluwer Law International 2004).

revolutionary and a decisive turning point in the history of European law.[138] The Court had allegedly cut "the umbilical cord with classic international law."[139] Rasmussen recently asserted that *Van Gend en Loos* was grounded on the deliberate (political) choice of the Court "to differentiate European law from international public law and (...) address the perceived weaknesses of the latter, namely the lack of uniform interpretation (...)."[140] Internal autonomy was later complemented by external autonomy of the Community in respect to international law.[141] As a result, supranationality too, was increasingly conceptualized outside the international law framework and became an alternative for or synonymous to describing the Community and its law as autonomous or *sui generis*.[142] In part, this still holds true today. A leading textbook on EU law explains that supranationality "fits the *sui generis* nature of the European Communities/Union perfectly."[143]

However, recourse to supranationality in order to explain the legal nature of the EEC (and later the EU) had always been contested.[144] Qualifying the European Communities as supranational, if the very definition of that term was derived from the object it should describe, was criticized as circular.[145] Therefore, supranationality did not seem to offer anything new conceptually.[146] It became a proxy or placeholder for the contested legal nature of European integration, and it maybe even prevented a more in-depth debate on this issue for a while. In the further evolution of EU law, supranationality was gradually superseded by "thicker" theoretical concepts. Constitutionalism, constitutional pluralism, and federalism are used today to theorize EU law and the European legal order more generally.[147] It is not the place here to discuss whether these notions have been employed more successfully, but it is worth pointing out that many feel that we are still missing a sound theory on the legal nature of the EU.[148]

138 Recently, Rasmussen, "Revolutionizing European Law," 155.
139 Robert Schütze, *From Dual to Cooperative Federalism* (Oxford: Oxford University Press 2009), p. 58.
140 Rasmussen, "Revolutionizing European Law," 160.
141 CJEU, Opinion 1/91 [1991] I-6079.
142 Ipsen, for instance, saw the sole function of the notion of supranationality in distinguishing the Community and its law from traditional IOs (Ipsen, "Über Supranationalität," p. 223). See also Bruno De Witte, "The European Union as an International Legal Experiment" in Gráinne de Búrca and J. H. H. Weiler (eds.), *The Worlds of European Constitutionalism* (Cambridge: Cambridge University Press 2012), p. 50.
143 Koen Lenaerts et al., *European Union Law*, 3rd ed. (London: Sweet & Maxwell 2011), p. 17.
144 Barents, *Autonomy of Community Law*, pp. 54f.
145 Hay, "International and Supranational Organizations" 738; Barents, *Autonomy of Community Law*, pp. 54f.
146 Hay, "International and Supranational Organizations," 739.
147 On these concepts and how they relate to supranationality see Chapter 2, Section 2.4.
148 Regarding the EU's relationship to international law, see, for instance, Samantha Besson and Pola Cebulak, "Introduction" in Samantha Besson and Nicolas Levrat (eds.), *L'Union européenne et le droit international – The European Union and International Law* (Zurich/Paris: Schulthess/LDGJ 2015), pp. 5ff.

1.5 NOTION OF INTERNATIONAL INSTITUTIONAL LAW

1.5.1 *Supranational Organizations*

Concurrently to developing into a quintessential notion of emerging EU law scholarship, supranationality also became a standard term of the international law vocabulary, in particular within international institutional law.[149] The term supranational organization found its way into the taxonomy of IOs, denoting a particular type,[150] distinguishable from mere intergovernmental organizations. Though a new phenomenon with hybrid or quasi-federal features, supranational organizations were still considered part of the family of IOs and located within the international law framework.[151]

1.5.2 *Inductive versus Deductive Definitions*

As to defining the new category of supranational organizations, one can distinguish between inductive and deductive approaches in international legal scholarship. A majority of scholars followed an inductive reasoning and extrapolated a definition from the European Union or its predecessors. The elements constituting a supranational organization correspond to a succinct abstraction of the specific legal features of the European Communities and later the EU or their law. Hence, today, supranationality is often construed as an umbrella term for the following elements pertaining to the relationship between member states, the organization, and individuals: the independence or autonomy of the organization or its organs, the

[149] On the existence of a (sub-)discipline of the law of IOs or international institutional law see Jan Klabbers, "The Paradox of International Institutional Law" (2008) 5 *International Organizations Law Review* 151–173. "International Institutional Law" is usually used interchangeably with the law of IOs, although the former appears to be more inclusive in scope (on institutionalization below the threshold of formal IOs see Chapter 2, Section 2.2.2).

[150] Although there is no universally accepted definition of what constitutes an IO (Jan Klabbers, *An Introduction to International Organizations Law*, 3rd ed. [Cambridge: Cambridge University Press 2015], p. 6), there exists wide agreement on at least some constitutive elements by reference to which an international organization is to be defined in legal terms. An IO is as a form of cooperation based on an international agreement established under international law and vested with at least one organ capable of having a will of its own (Michel Virally, "Definition and Classification of International Organizations: A Legal Approach" in Georges Abi-Saab (ed.), *The Concept of International Organization* [Paris: UNESCO 1981], pp. 50ff; Henry G. Schermers and Niels M. Blokker, *International Institutional Law*, 5th ed. [Leiden/Boston: Brill Nijhoff 2011], pp. 36ff). Rather than a constituting element itself, scholars usually consider international legal personality as a presumed consequence of qualifying an organization as an IO (e.g., Klabbers, *International Organizations Law*, p. 46).

[151] Jaenicke, "Organe internationaler Organisationen," 50f; Hahn, "Public Authorities," 663; Kunz, "Supra-National Organs," 697; contra Chittharanjan F. Amerasinghe, *Principles of the Institutional Law of International Organizations*, 2nd ed. (Cambridge: Cambridge University Press 2005), p. 12. ILC, First Report on the Relations between States and Inter-Governmental Organizations by Abdullah A El-Erian, *Yearbook of the ILC* (vol. II) (1963) 169.

capacity of the organization to take decisions binding on its member states without their consent, the primacy and/or direct effect of law emanating from the organization, the existence of a parliament, and the existence of a judiciary with compulsory jurisdiction.[152]

In this context too, approaches defining supranationality with reference to the EU or its predecessors lent themselves to criticism of circular reasoning.[153] In turn, different scholars suggested a EU independent definition. Lindeiner-Wildau, for instance, adopted a purely etymological method.[154] Researching the meaning of the terms "supra" and "national," he concluded that the basis of supranationality is the principle of subordination.[155] Others such as Schlochauer or Wehberg, but also Blokker and Schermers, to take a more recent example, adopted a deductive method in defining supranationality. Of these, Blokker and Schermers' definition is probably the most influential, even if, in substance, it comes close to earlier, inductive definitions based on the EU. Blokker and Schermers define a supranational organization with respect to the following five characteristics: (1) the power to take decisions binding on the member states, (2) independence of the decision-making organs by allowing binding decisions to be adopted by majority vote or by composing them of independent individuals, (3) empowerment to make rules that directly bind the inhabitants of the member states, (4) power to enforce its decisions, even without the cooperation of the governments, and (5) some degree of financial autonomy.[156] Blokker and Schermers acknowledge that not even the EU fulfils all the previous requirements, which is why, one could compare their definition to a Weberian ideal type.[157] Similar to the first uses of supranationality in international legal scholarship in the early twentieth century, deductive approaches display a strong subjective element. It depends on the determination of the analyst which criteria are regarded decisive for defining the concept.[158]

[152] This list represents a synthesis of different definitions and therefore omits certain nuances. Francesco Capotorti, "Supranational Organizations" in Rudolf Bernhardt (ed.), *Encyclopedia of Public International Law*, vol. IV (Amsterdam: Elsevier 2000), pp. 737ff; Schroeder and Müller, "Elements of Supranationality," p. 361; Matthias Ruffert and Christian Walter, *Institutionalisiertes Völkerrecht*, 2nd ed. (Munich: C. H. Beck 2015), n. 16f; Kristen Schmalenbach, "International Organizations or Institutions, General Aspects" in Rüdiger Wolfrum (ed.), *Max Planck Encyclopedia of Public International Law*, online ed. (Oxford: Oxford University Press 2014), n. 16–19; Klabbers, *International Organizations Law*, pp. 26f.

[153] Hay, "International and Supranational Organizations," 739; Lindeiner-Wildau, *Supranationalité*, pp. 42ff; Weiler, "Community System," 268f.

[154] Lindeiner-Wildau, *Supranationalité*, pp. 39–41.

[155] Ibid., p. 44.

[156] Schermers and Blokker, *International Institutional Law*, pp. 56f.

[157] Max Weber, "Die 'Objektivität' sozialwissenschaftlicher und sozialpolitischer Erkenntnis" (1904) 19 *Archiv für Sozialwissenschaft und Sozialpolitik* 22–87; Richard Swedberg and Olga Agevall, *The Max Weber Dictionary: Key Words and Central Concepts*, 2nd ed. (Stanford: Stanford University Press 2016), pp. 156–158.

[158] Hay, "International and Supranational Organizations," 739.

1.5.3 *Relative versus Absolute Conceptualizations*

Another conceptual distinction becomes apparent, when studying the reception of supranationality in international (institutional) law. First, supranational organizations may be conceived of as an all or nothing concept. It is the cumulative presence of certain elements rendering an IO supranational. Put differently, "a quantitative aggregation of supranational elements" effects "a qualitative transformation from the mere international to the supranational character of an organization."[159] Under this view, supranationality may serve as a shorthand reference for the EU, to distinguish it from other IOs,[160] or to exclude the EU from the law of IOs altogether.[161] If at all, only regional economic integration organizations based on the EU model, such as the ECOWAS, SICA, CARICOM, or the Andean Community, could be denoted supranational.[162] This absolute conceptualization was criticized for its lack of utility for general systematization. If the purpose of classifying IOs was to reduce complexity, a category that only applies to one single organization appears not very helpful.[163]

The other way of conceptualizing supranationality is to understand it as a relative concept. Accordingly, an IO is not *either* supranational *or* intergovernmental. One or several elements of supranationality can be present in an IO. This flexible use means that supranationality is construed less as a quality of an IO, but rather of specific organs, their powers or law more generally.[164] Early treatises on supranationality mostly followed such a relative understanding.[165] Jaenicke, for example, analyzed the supranational character of many different international organs, concluding that the dividing line between international and supranational cannot be determined

[159] Schroeder and Müller, "Elements of Supranationality," fn. 36. Similar was the view that the preponderance of a supranational organ within an organization justifies the whole organization to be considered supranational (Hahn, "Public Authorities," 641).

[160] Ignaz Seidl-Hohenveldern and Gerhard Loibl, *Das Recht der internationalen Organisationen einschliesslich der supranationalen*, 6th ed. (Cologne/Berlin: Heymanns Verlag 2000), pp. 7f; Ruffert and Walter, *Institutionalisiertes Völkerrecht*, pp. 16f.

[161] Amerasinghe, *Institutional Law of International Organizations*, p. 12. Virally came to the same conclusion, distinguishing (intergovernmental) organizations which aim at cooperation from (supranational) organizations which aim at achieving integration (Virally, "International Organizations," pp. 54–56).

[162] Schmalenbach, "International Organizations," n. 17. In this context, the term supranational legal transplant has been used (see Karen J. Alter and Laurence R. Helfer, "Transplanting the European Court of Justice: The Experience of the Andean Tribunal of Justice" (2012) 60 *American Journal of Comparative Law* 629–664). Salvatore Caserta, "Regional Integration through Law and International Courts – the Interplay between De Jure and De Facto Supranationality in Central America and the Caribbean" (2017) 30 *Leiden Journal of International Law* 579–601 at 579.

[163] Schroeder and Müller, "Elements of Supranationality," p. 367.

[164] Jaenicke, "Organe internationaler Organisationen," 49f; Philippe Sands and Pierre Klein, *Bowett's Law of International Institutions*, 6th ed. (London: Sweet & Maxwell 2009), p. 19. For a broad understanding of the term "Supranational Law," see e.g., Münch, "Délimitation du domaine du droit des Communautés supranationales," 275.

[165] See, for instance, Jaenicke, "Organe internationaler Organisationen," 50ff and 64f.

in an abstract manner.[166] Partly, contemporary scholarship still relies on these early conceptualizations. Schermers and Blokker, for instance, suggest that the distinction supranational-intergovernmental "is a matter of degree; the view that it is so fundamental as to exclude supranational organizations from the study of international organizations must be rejected."[167] They define supranational organizations in abstract terms and, although not even the EU qualifies as truly supranational according to their definition, they use the term in a relative sense, to indicate that supranational elements prevail in a specific organization.[168] Following the same approach, Schroeder and Müller recently engaged in a search for elements of supranationality in the law of IOs.[169] They propose to use supranationality as a doctrinal catchword to indicate "a shift of the balance of power and control between member states and IOs in favor of the latter to the extent that is hard to reconcile with traditional sovereignty claims."[170] They submit that supranationality may serve for static and dynamic comparison: one can compare different IOs and their stages of development with each other but also unveil and investigate processes of supranationalization within one particular IO.[171] The latter is comparable to the function of supranationality within EU law and the supranational-intergovernmental dichotomy often used to assess the evolution of EU law.[172] The critique, however, put forward against a relative conceptualization is that supranationality becomes too broad of a notion and therefore loses (some of) its descriptive value.[173]

1.6 CONCLUSION

As Hay already formulated in 1966, supranationality is to a great extent a matter of approach and interpretation.[174] It has become a doctrinal notion that feeds on a lot of different conceptual sources[175] and is informed by differing assumptions on a variety of issues.[176] This chapter has tackled the concept by singling out four important contexts in which supranationality is or was used: the turn to modern international

166 Jaenicke, "Organe internationaler Organisationen," 51.
167 Schermers and Blokker, *International Institutional Law*, p. 51.
168 Ibid.
169 For similar approaches see Sands and Klein, *Bowett's Law*, p. 19; Eric De Brabandere, "The Impact of Supranationalism on State Sovereignty from the Perspective of the Legitimacy of International Organisations" in Duncan French (ed.), *Statehood and Self-Determination* (Cambridge: Cambridge University Press 2013), p. 450.
170 Schroeder and Müller, "Elements of Supranationality," p. 367.
171 Ibid., p. 359.
172 See earlier Section 1.4.3.
173 Hay, *Federalism and Supranational Organizations*, p. 36.
174 Hay, "International and Supranational Organizations," p. 738.
175 Schroeder and Müller, "Elements of Supranationality," pp. 360f.
176 On the implicit and explicit assumptions underlying the different understandings of supranationality, see Barents, *Autonomy of Community Law*, pp. 40ff.

law, the negotiations leading up to and the establishment of the European Communities, EU law scholarship and the law of IOs. Across these different contexts but also within each of them, there are competing conceptualizations of the notion. Four reference points may prove helpful in navigating and comparing them: the methodological approach in defining the concept (inductive, deductive, etymological, positive law?), the concept's object(s) (IOs, specific organs (of IOs), powers of either of them, law in general?) the concept's legal nature (international, federal, something in between, *sui generis*?) and the concept's function (descriptive, doctrinal, legal, normative?). To be sure, these four points are closely interlinked and mutually dependent. The interconnection is particularly apparent between the concept's function and definitional method. If the concept's purpose is to serve as a tailor-made descriptor of the EU or its law, then, for one, an inductive method based on the EU has to be adopted and, for another, to remain a notion of theoretical relevance, supranationality has to account for the evolution, complexification, and differentiation of the European integration process. Also, attributing supranationality as a term of IO law the sole function of distinguishing the Community model from traditional IOs meant that supranationality did not reside in one particular, but rather in the accumulation of a plurality of elements, considering that no feature of the ECSC alone was fundamentally novel.[177] In contrast, if supranationality is to serve as a general notion of international institutional law, it must exhibit a degree of generalization that actually allows applying it beyond the EU. Another linkage exists between the definitional method and the concept's nature. In particular, if supranationality is defined with reference to the EU, whatever assumption is held on the latter's legal nature usually predetermines the understanding of supranationality in this respect too. Lastly, the legal nature and the concept's function are closely intertwined. Locating supranationality can delimit its scope as a theoretical concept. The view, for instance, that anything supranational is categorically distinct to international public law bound the concept to EU law and isolated it from other disciplines.

There are also a number of notable overlaps however. First, two conceptions, in particular, mutually reinforce each other in a way that may explain why today many understand supranationality as something intrinsically linked to the EU. Supranationality as a quintessential notion of EU law scholarship capturing the legal essence of European integration and the absolute conception within the law of IOs highlighting the special (*sui generis* character) of the EU both suggest idiosyncrasy to the EU. It is not surprising, therefore, that the term supranational has become a simple shorthand reference for the EU or EU law that is used

[177] Hay, "International and Supranational Organizations," 739; Schwantes, *Supranationalität*, p. 37; Kunz, "Supra-National Organs," 697ff; Reuter, "Le plan Schuman," pp. 543ff. Even the faculty of the High Authority to adopt binding decisions vis-à-vis individuals could already be found in the Danube Commission (see Chapter 2, Section 2.3.2).

interchangeably with both of the latter.[178] Secondly and in contrast, the original use of supranationality in the early twentieth century actually lends support to relative conceptions still present in international institutional law today. Resisting the temptation to read present-day approaches back into earlier writings, one cannot deny that supranationality emerged before the European Communities did and had originally been used in a more flexible manner. Third, despite all divergences, there seems to be agreement over at least a number of elements that constitute supranationality. The different definitions referred to throughout this chapter are at times more similar to one another than one would initially expect.

In short, supranationality is today construed through both international law and EU law, which is one of the very reasons its meaning is difficult to pin down. Supranationality, as a doctrinal concept, appears to be somewhat trapped by the dilemma of whether EU law is still to be conceived of as being part of international law or not. Maybe, glossing over this intractable question is needed to achieve a less ambiguous conception of supranationality.

[178] Instead of many see Achilles Skordas, "Supranational Law" in Rüdiger Wolfrum (ed.), *Max Planck Encyclopedia of Public International Law*, online ed. (Oxford: Oxford University Press 2012); Peter L. Lindseth, "Supranational Organizations" in Ian Hurd, Ian Johnstone, and Jacob Katz Cogan (eds.), *Oxford Handbook of International Organizations* (Oxford: Oxford University Press 2016), pp. 152–170.

2

Rediscovering Supranationality

2.1 SUPRANATIONALITY FOR THE PURPOSE OF THE PRESENT STUDY

The survey in Chapter 1 demonstrated that using the notion of supranationality requires terminological and conceptual transparency. The polysemic nature of supranationality must not necessarily weaken its potential as a doctrinal concept, but using the term certainly requires a careful description of how it is understood. This chapter seeks to do exactly that. It lays out the conceptual and terminological basis for study and contextualizes the supranationality framework with regard to existing approaches in international legal scholarship.[1] More specifically, this chapter proposes to rediscover the notion of supranationality. It is argued that supranationality as defined in the following can serve as a useful descriptive-analytical framework for studying international law and, as such, help to expose legal phenomena, provide theoretical systematization, and reduce complexity.[2] The overall argument is developed in four steps. The first step is to provide a conceptual framework by spelling out methodological biases, shedding light on some general aspects, and providing terminological clarifications. In a second step, supranationality is defined by adopting a functional perspective. It is submitted that elements usually denoted supranational fulfil two integrative functions, a horizontal and vertical one. In a last step, the conceptual framework expounded is contextualized with respect to existing theoretical strands in legal scholarship as well as the notion of (international) community. As the present study proposes to give meaning to the term of Convention community, the community notion requires special attention.

2.2 TOWARD A GENERAL FRAMEWORK FOR LAW BEYOND THE STATE

2.2.1 *Beyond EU Law*

The particular inquiry of this study requires to construe supranationality in a way so it can be applied as an analytical framework beyond the EU. Supranationality is

[1] The idea is not, however, to assess and compare the scientific value of the different conceptions of supranationality in general.

[2] Hay, *Federalism and Supranational Organizations*, p. 74.

therefore not viewed as something categorically distinct from international law, but rather as a general phenomenon of law beyond the state, be it international or EU law. This is not to say that a broad definition of supranationality must omit any reference to EU law. The latter can be viewed as the context in which supranationality is most developed. But "freeing" supranationality from the EU as the concept's only source and object should allow a wider spectrum to come into view. The present understanding of supranationality is thus based on existing legal scholarship that advocates for a relative reading.[3] At the same, it is inspired by the work of political scientists, which often use the term more broadly than international lawyers do.[4] In order to function as a general analytical framework, the definition proposed must, on the one hand, exhibit a certain degree of generalization and abstraction. If the definition is too broad and inclusive, on the other hand, the concept's specificity is lost and therewith also much of its descriptive-analytical value.

2.2.2 *Beyond the Law of IOs*

Traditionally, supranationality is equated with supranational organizations, which have long been part of the common taxonomy of IOs. However, based on a relative understanding, the term supranationality is increasingly used outside the law of IOs *stricto sensu*. International courts or international criminal law, for instance, have been denoted supranational.[5] Despite this shift toward a more general use of supranationality across international law, conceptual approaches remain to an extent cleave to IOs. It is submitted that instead of formal IOs, international regimes would be the more appropriate concept to delineate the research object of supranationality. The notion of regime is understood here in a hybrid sense based on Krasner's classic definition in international relations theory[6] as well as on the use of the notion by international lawyers:[7] Regimes are thus sets of primary and secondary rules relating to a specific, functionally delimited subject matter and administered by international institutions. While international institutional law remains of relevance, operating with the notion of regime, it is argued, has advantages over approaches that stick to the formal category of IOs. First, it allows to account for institutions or institutionalizations below the threshold of formal IOs such as treaty bodies (in human rights law and international environmental law for instance) or international courts.[8] Institutionalized cooperation between states may fall

[3] See Chapter 1, Section 1.5.3.

[4] For example, Volker Rittberger, Bernhard Zangl, and Andreas Kruck, *Internationale Organisationen* (Berlin/Heidelberg: Springer 2013), pp. 23f.

[5] More on the latter Subsequently Section 2.3.2.

[6] Stephen D. Krasner, "Structural Causes and Regime Consequences: Regimes as Intervening Variables" (1982) 36 *International Organization* 185–205.

[7] ILC, Report of the Study Group on the Fragmentation of International Law finalized by Martti Koskenniemi, A/CN.4/L.682, April 13, 2006, 81.

[8] As their name suggests, treaty bodies are created by ordinary treaties and not a treaty establishing an IO or by an organ of such. Treaty bodies may vary as regards their structure, composition or function. In

short of presenting all the characteristics of an IO, but nevertheless present supranational features. This aspect is of particular importance to the present study. Admittedly, both the ECtHR and also the ECHR are firmly embedded within the Council of Europe,[9] which undoubtedly qualifies as a formal IO. At the same time, however, the ECtHR is not a statutory organ of the organization and the ECHR[10] is a treaty body tasked to monitor the ECHR. Second, the regime notion not only puts emphasis on institutional aspects but also substantive ones and includes international legal rules in a more general way. Third, the regime notion accounts for the phenomenon of functional specialization of law (beyond the state).[11] It was noted that "much of the action in international law shifted to specialized regimes."[12] Focusing on a specific regime allows delimiting the object of study to a certain interrelated area of substantive law (e.g., trade, environment, human rights) instead of focusing on a particular IO, whose competences may cover broad fields of subject matter. Often, substantive issues are closely linked to institutional ones and the former may explain the later or vice versa.

2.2.3 *Descriptive-Analytical Value*

For the purpose of the present study, the supranationality framework serves a descriptive-analytical function. For one, it is not argued that the act of qualifying something as supranational comes with particular legal ramifications – except for, maybe, where domestic constitutions refer to the term and attach specific legal

the field of human rights, they are usually composed of experts, set up to supervise treaty commitments and, in one form or another, embedded within the structure of an existing IO (Paul C. Szasz, "The Complexification of the United Nations System" (1999) 3 *Max Planck Yearbook of United Nations Law* 1–57 at 18). In the field of environmental or arms control law, treaty bodies are permanent and institutionalized conferences of the parties (COPs), which may even be vested with their own subsidiary bodies, a secretariat and the competence to adopt new binding commitments for the parties (Geir Ulfstein, "Treaty Bodies and Regimes" in Duncan B. Hollis (ed.), *The Oxford Guide to Treaties* [Oxford: Oxford University Press 2012], pp. 428ff). Szasz considered treaty bodies as "International Organizations Manquées," whereas Churchill and Ulfstein argued with respect to environmental treaty bodies that when assessing their powers, the law of treaties should be supplemented by international institutional law (Robin R. Churchill and Geir Ulfstein, "Autonomous Institutional Arrangements in Multilateral Environmental Agreements: A Little-Noticed Phenomenon in International Law" (2000) 94 *American Journal of International Law* 623–659 at 632f). Others rely on the distinct will criteria and the competence to stipulate new rules to qualify treaty bodies as IOs (Catherine Brölmann, *The Institutional Veil in Public International Law* [Oxford: Hart 2007], p. 24).

9 Among other aspects, the expenditure on the Court is borne by the CoE (Art. 50 ECHR), the judges are entitled to the privileges and immunities provided for in Article 40 of the CoE Statute (Art. 51), the Committee of Ministers of the CoE monitors the execution of the Court's judgments (Art. 46 ECHR), and the judges are elected by the Parliamentary Assembly of the CoE (Art. 22 ECHR).

10 Compare Art. 10 CoE Statute. Georg Ress, "The Effect of Decisions and Judgments of the European Court of Human Rights in the Domestic Legal Order" (2005) 40 *Texas International Law Journal* 359–382.

11 ILC, Report on the Fragmentation of International Law, 136f.

12 Daniel Bodansky and John R. Crook, "Symposium on the ILC's State Responsibility Articles: Introduction and Overview" (2002) 96 *American Journal of International Law* 773–791 at 774.

consequences to it.[13] Even in these instances, however, the term supranational is mostly reduced to cover the EU, which is why determining something as supranational, at least in the scope of this study, will most likely be devoid of any direct legal impact on the ground. In turn, it is not posited that employing the notion has nocausal force whatsoever. The aspiration of the study must be to provide a conceptual framework that has added value in descriptive-analytical terms. As such, it may inform the normative debate and feed back into concrete changes in legal practice. Also, as a legal notion, supranationality remains informed through law which necessarily links it to legal and normative consequences.[14]

For another, the present conceptualization does not include a normative program. It is true that any conceptual analysis or narrative implies a degree of normativity. Though supranationality has also been described as technocratic and normatively neutral,[15] one might argue that with it resonates the assumption of autonomous and effective international institutions being both positive and necessary (especially considering the notion's origins[16]). What is more, supranationality may sometimes be associated with the idea of political convergence between or even the overcoming of nation-states. While awareness about these normative biases seems important, it must be stressed that this study does not seek to promote supranationality. The framework should allow to empirically test whether and to what extent supranationality or supranationalization exists outside EU law, contribute to its understanding, and thereby enhance critical reflection.

2.2.4 *Formal Conception*

Another methodological aspect is that supranationality is construed here as a formal concept. It refers to certain effects or characteristics of law and institutions beyond the state that, at least in principle, may stem from any field or subject area of law (e.g., human rights law, economic law, investment law, the law of collective security, law of the sea, etc.). In other words, the concept is content-independent. However, it might well be that supranationality is more likely to occur in certain areas than others, or that the far-reaching effects usually described as supranational may result from the special moral or normative authority of the norms at play. In fact, researching supranationality may precisely uncover such relationships.

13 Art. 140 of the Swiss Constitution, for instance, requires a mandatory referendum for accession to organizations for collective security or to "supranational communities."

14 In a similar vein on the concept of IO, see Brölmann, *Institutional Veil*, p. 14.

15 Bogdandy, *Supranationaler Föderalismus*, p. 62.

16 Chapter 1, Section 1.2.

2.2.5 *Terminology*

Based on the preceding considerations, a threefold distinction can be made between the notion of supranationality as a legal reality or phenomenon, supranationalization as the process toward this reality, and supranationalism as the normative take on that reality. Contrasting supranationalism and supranationality is new in that existing scholarship often uses the terms interchangeably. Similar to the distinction between, for instance, legal plurality and legal pluralism, supranationalism versus supranationality can be used to distinguish between descriptive and normative approaches and avoid conflation of the two. Supranationalism would entail a normative claim, the desirability of supranationality so to speak. The distinction between supranationality and supranationalization reflects what Schroeder and Müller described as the static and dynamic aspects of the concept. Whereas supranationality provides a snapshot at a given point in time, supranationalization accounts for dynamism and becomes the keyword to analyze processes by which supranationality emerges or develops.[17]

2.3 A FUNCTIONAL APPROACH: LEGAL INTEGRATION

2.3.1 *Integrative Force of Supranationality*

The present study proposes to define supranationality by looking at what it seeks to achieve, which is, it is submitted, a form of legal integration.[18] Revealing the integrative force of supranationality should allow to find sufficiently precise benchmarks for meaningful descriptive-analytical purposes, while at the same time maintaining sufficient breadth to allow for generalization across different international regimes.[19]

The common denominator of the elements and traits usually denoted supranational is that they seek to achieve a form of legal integration,[20] either on a horizontal or a vertical plane (more on these two dimensions later). Following

[17] Schroeder and Müller, "Elements of Supranationality," p. 359. While the process of supranationalization has been researched extensively for the EU law, studies on supranationality in other international regimes have usually been limited to static comparisons so far.

[18] This functional perspective on supranationality as a legal phenomenon must be distinguished from (neo-)functionalism as a political theory of integration (see Chapter 1, Section 1.4.1), as a theory of IO law, as well as from the general functionality of international regimes or IOs, that is, their functionally delimited competences/subject matter (Brölmann, *Institutional Veil*, pp. 25f).

[19] Although it is probably not possible to fully avoid the criticism that the results were determined (beforehand) by the choice of elements to be compared.

[20] Peter Malanczuk, *Akehurst's Modern Introduction to International Law*, 7th ed. (London: Routledge 1997), p. 95. Therefore, De Brabandere is right in regarding supranationality a yardstick for integration (De Brabandere, "Impact of Supranationalism," pp. 452f).

Besson, legal integration means that the international and domestic legal orders overlap in terms of their objects and subjects,[21] in particular in their ability to not only formulate but also enforce legal rules directly vis-à-vis natural and legal persons (citizens[22]). Supranationality describes the effect of directly determining through law the position of individuals, overcoming state intermediation as well as the traditional de-coupling of the authority of international law from enforcement.[23] In this form, law beyond the state or its institutions subsume within a larger whole, supplant state structures,[24] and limit state sovereignty, understood as a state's supreme authority within its own territory,[25] to a particular extent.[26] This integrative dimension of supranationality may be further illustrated by distinguishing between horizontal and vertical integration. Although discussed separately in the following, the two dimensions may overlap or coincide.

2.3.2 *Horizontal Dimension*

The first integrative dimension of supranationality concerns the international level. Starting point is the observation that international institutions and regimes are allocated certain public functions and exercise dispersed public authority.[27] Supranationality connects, however, two additional elements, which together, achieve horizontal integration.

21 Samantha Besson, "How International Is the European Legal Order? Retracing Tuori's Steps in the Exploration of European Legal Pluralism" (2008) 5 *NoFo* 50–70 at 55f.

22 As a shorthand reference, the term refers to all persons within a state's jurisdiction (Samantha Besson, "The Authority of International Law – Lifting the State Veil" (2008) 31 *Sydney Law Review* 343–380 at fn. 41).

23 Federico Fabbrini, "The Constitutionalization of International Law: A Comparative Federal Perspective" (2013) 6 *European Journal of Legal Studies* 7–26 at 12; Çali, *Authority of International Law*, p. 31.

24 Ruffert and Walter, *Institutionalisiertes Völkerrecht*, p. 16. Supranationality in this sense has a sociological or psychological component, which goes beyond the term's legal definition. It may refer to those legal norms and institutions beyond the state whose authority and governing function become, similar to domestic rules and domestic public authority, perceptible for the individual (in day-to-day life). The more supranationality is distinct, the more this perception is shared collectively among groups of citizens.

25 Samantha Besson, "Sovereignty" in Rüdiger Wolfrum (ed.), *Max Planck Encyclopedia of Public International Law* (Oxford: Oxford University Press 2012).

26 Instead of many, see Hay, *Federalism and Supranational Organizations*, p. 69; Fabbrini, "Constitutionalization of International Law," 12.

27 This observation, of course, presupposes acceptance of the view that public authority is actually divisible. In a broad sense, it can be defined as "the competence of states and other entities to perform public tasks (to produce public goods) and to achieve compliance by cooperative means or by sanctions including physical enforcement as a last resort" (Jost Delbrück, "Transnational Federalism: Problems and Prospects of Allocating Public Authority Beyond the State" (2004) 11 *Indiana Journal of Global Legal Studies* 31–55 at 35f). Janne Nijman and André Nollkaemper (eds.), "Beyond the Divide," *New Perspectives on the Divide Between National and International Law* (Oxford: Oxford University Press 2007), p. 348.

The first element is independence or autonomy in legally binding decision-making.[28] Any IO is per definition required to have some sort of *volonté distinct* – that is, the capability of expressing or formulating a will of its own, distinct from that of its creators.[29] In Klabber's elucidating terms, the *volonté distinct* "swirls around in the midst of a tension between viewing the organization as a distinct entity (...) and seeing it as merely the vehicle of its member-states."[30] Supranationality describes the situation, in which this tension is resolved in favor of the former[31] through the capacity to take decisions binding on or within (member) states, either by a majority vote of state representatives or through a body composed of independent persons such as experts, international civil servants, judges, or even parliamentarians.[32] As a result, the organ or institution in question can not only formulate its own a will but also impose it on others. Such "de-coupling"[33] or shift from "consent to compulsion"[34] enables international institutions to exercise their functions independently from individual states' interests and pursue common interests or overcome collective action problems.[35]

The second element concerns the enforcement of law beyond the state and the effect of international decisions.[36] It lies in the fact that international regimes are vested with the power to operate directly against natural or legal persons.[37] Cassese described this as the "direct exercise of public authority by international institutions over individuals' affecting the latter's" legal position unilaterally[38] and Schermers and Blokker as the power "to perform governmental functions without the need or

[28] Decision-making is to be understood in a very broad sense, including adjudication.

[29] Schermers and Blokker, *International Institutional Law*, p. 44; Schmalenbach, "International Organizations," n. 8. For an in-depth treatise of the subject of autonomy of IOs, see Richard Collins and Nigel D. White (eds.), *International Organizations and the Idea of Autonomy: Institutional Independence in the International Legal Order* (London: Routledge 2011).

[30] Jan Klabbers, *An Introduction to International Institutional Law*, 1st ed. (Cambridge: Cambridge University Press 2009), p. 59.

[31] Supranationality may help navigate an area, which is characterized by the inherent tension between community interests and sovereignty and for which a convincing theory is said to be lacking (Klabbers, *International Organizations Law*, p. 5).

[32] The latter are sometimes also termed integrated organs (see, for example, Sascha Rolf Lüder, "The Legal Nature of the International Criminal Court and the Emergence of Supranational Elements in International Criminal Justice" (2002) 84 *International Review of the Red Cross* 79–92 at 85).

[33] Çali, *Authority of International Law*, p. 25.

[34] Stephen Gardbaum, "Human Rights as International Constitutional Rights" (2008) 19 *European Journal of International Law* 749–768 at 759.

[35] On IOs as community representatives and enforcers, see Kenneth W. Abbott and Duncan Snidal, "Why States Act through Formal International Organizations" (1998) 42 *The Journal of Conflict Resolution* 3–32 at 23ff.

[36] Hence, the view that it is sufficient for an institution to have a will of its own or enjoy legal personality in order to be considered supranational is rejected here. This would imply that any IO must be regarded supranational.

[37] W. Paul Gormley, *The Procedural Status of the Individual before International and Supranational Tribunals* (Leiden: Martinus Nijhoff 1966), p. 73.

[38] Sabino Cassese, "Is There a Global Administrative Law?" in Armin von Bogdandy et al. (eds.), *The Exercise of Public Authority by International Institutions* (Berlin/Heidelberg: Springer 2010), pp. 761, 763.

the possibility for national governments to transform the rules of the organization into domestic law."[39] Also, this is what had initially been termed direct effect under the ECSC and constituted "the essence" of the HA's supranational power.[40]

Together, these two elements (autonomy in decision-making and direct enforcement over individuals) make up horizontal integration. Rather than penetrating the domestic sphere, law beyond the state bypasses or circumvents the latter by lifting the natural or legal person onto the international plane, altering directly their (international) legal position. Today, there are still only few examples of international institutions (beyond the EU) enjoying such supranational authority: "the impermé-ability of the veil of sovereignty is still the default rule."[41] Exceptions include, for instance, the International Seabed Authority established under the UNCLOS[42] or the UN Security Council with its powers under Chapter VII.[43] Arguably, the most far-reaching example of horizontal integration in this form is the case of a territory placed under international administration such as the constitutional framework put into place for Kosovo under the United Nations Interim Administration Mission in Kosovo (UNMIK), which, according to the ICJ represents "a specific legal order" *in lieu* of domestic law.[44] Equally far-reaching – at least from the perspective of the individual concerned – is the power of international criminal tribunals to prosecute and try individual perpetrators.[45]

39 Schermers and Blokker, *International Institutional Law*, p. 56.

40 Robertson, "European Integration," p. 158. See also Mosler, "Supra-National Judicial Decisions," 435. As the European Danube Commission could already adopt decisions that were binding on individuals it is often considered a supranational forerunner. On the forerunners of supranationality in general Lindeiner-Wildau, *Supranationalité*, pp. 64–94.

41 Schroeder and Müller, "Elements of Supranationality," pp. 365f.

42 Arts. 160 and 162 UNCLOS; Schroeder and Müller, "Elements of Supranationality," p. 373; René-Jean Dupuy, "Images de Georges Scelle" (1990) 1 *European Journal of International Law* 235–239 at 239; Schermers and Blokker, *International Institutional Law*, p. 979.

43 Katja Schmitz, *Durchgriffswirkung von Massnahmen der UN und ihrer Sonderorganisationen unter besonderer Berücksichtigung von Resolutionen des UN-Sicherheitsrates: Die Entwicklung supranationaler Strukturen* (Frankfurt/Main: Peter Lang 2003). See also Michael W. Doyle, "The UN Charter – A Global Constitution?" in Jeffrey L. Dunoff and Joel P. Trachtman (eds.), *Ruling the World?* (Cambridge: Cambridge University Press 2012), p. 115. One must point out, though, that majority voting in the Council is, to an extent, offset by the veto power of the permanent members. Schroeder and Müller recently argued that the ICJ in its *Kosovo Advisory Opinion* has "authoritatively accepted the Security Council's capacity to impose binding obligations also on individuals" (ICJ, *Accordance with International Law of the Unilateral Declaration of Independence in Respect of Kosovo*, Advisory Opinion of July 22, 2010, I.C.J. Reports 2010 403, para. 116f; Schroeder and Müller, "Elements of Supranationality," pp. 374f.).

44 Security Council, Resolution 1244 (1999), in particular paras. 6, 10 and 11; ICJ, *Kosovo Advisory Opinion*, para. 88f; Laurence Boisson de Chazournes, "Functionalism! Functionalism! Do I Look like Functionalism?" (2015) 26 *European Journal of International* Law 951–956 at 953.

45 For a comprehensive analysis see Lüder, "Legal Nature of the ICC"; Cedric Marti, "Supranationality Beyond the EU?" in Samantha Besson and Nicolas Levrat (eds.), *L'Union européenne et le droit international – The European Union and International Law* (Zurich/Paris: Schulthess/LDGJ 2015), pp. 28ff.

A special category of horizontal integration or supranational authority exists in the area of adjudication. Adjudication may not be what is typically understood as part of global governance in a narrow sense, but it is, nevertheless, a form of exercising public authority.[46] Helfer and Slaughter coined the term supranational adjudication[47] to describe international courts having jurisdiction over cases involving non-state actors (individuals, companies) as opposed to ad hoc interstate and state-controlled adjudication.[48] Other scholars such as Mégret or Besson took up the notion but gave it a slightly modified meaning. While Mégret understands the term broadly as access of non-state actors to international courts/tribunals,[49] Besson adds compulsory jurisdiction[50] as an element to Helfer and Slaughter's definition.[51] In a similar vein, but maybe less discriminate De Baere, Chané, and Wouters use the term supranational courts relying on Schermers and Blokker's definition of supranational organizations[52].[53]

Supranational adjudication, too, is an instance of horizontal integration. While any system of (international) adjudication per definition requires autonomous or independent decision-making with binding effect on the parties, the shift here from consent to compulsion lies in compulsory jurisdiction and the possibility to bring a state (or its citizens) before an international court without continuous consent. In addition, supranational courts and tribunals have jurisdiction to directly apply and enforce law beyond the state with respect to individuals or enterprises.[54] Their jurisdiction thus overlaps with the state's judicial powers in respect of its citizens.[55] Today, one finds supranational adjudication in areas such as regional economic

46 Armin von Bogdandy and Ingo Venzke, "Beyond Dispute: International Judicial Institutions as Lawmakers," in Armin von Bogdandy and Ingo Venzke (eds.), *International Judicial Lawmaking* (Berlin/Heidelberg: Springer 2012), pp. 3ff.

47 Mosler already spoke of supranational judicial decisions (e.g., Mosler, "Supra-National Judicial Decisions," 435).

48 Laurence R. Helfer and Anne-Marie Slaughter, "Toward a Theory of Effective Supranational Adjudication" (1997) 107 *The Yale Law Journal* 273–391 at 289; Besson, "European Human Rights," p. 104; Mosler, "Supra-National Judicial Decisions," 435.

49 Frédéric Mégret, "Private Actor Litigation and the Evolving Legitimacy of Supranational Adjudication" (2012) *RSCAS Policy Papers – Courts, Social Change and Judicial Independence* 3–10.

50 Besson, "European Human Rights," p. 103. Comparable to supranational adjudication in the above sense is Alter's definition of "new style courts" (Karen J. Alter, *The New Terrain of International Law: Courts, Politics, Rights* [Princeton: Princeton University Press 2014], p. 18).

51 See also Jay Lawrence Westbrook, "Legal Integration of NAFTA Through Supranational Adjudication" (2008) 43 *Texas International Law Journal* 349–358.

52 Chapter 1, Section 1.5.2.

53 Geert De Baere, Anna-Luise Chané, and Jan Wouters, "The Contribution of International and Supranational Courts to the Rule of Law: A Framework for Analysis" in Geert De Baere and Jan Wouters (eds.), *The Contribution of International and Supranational Courts to the Rule of Law* (Cheltenham: Edward Elgar 2015), pp. 32ff.

54 Helfer and Slaughter, "Effective Supranational Adjudication," 288; Besson, "European Human Rights," p. 104.

55 Alter, *New Terrain of International Law*, p. 18.

integration,[56] human rights law,[57] international investment law,[58] or international criminal law.[59]

Horizontal integration in the sense described earlier – that is, overlapping levels of authority over the same issues as well as natural and legal persons – necessarily begs the question of how these different levels of authority interact and relate to each other. For Delbrück, for instance, the "interconnectedness of the different entities exercising public authority (. . .) structurally binds them together."[60] He goes as far as positing that "the constitutions of supranational organizations and their member states mutually supplement each other – the constitution of one is part of the constitution of the other."[61] While it is difficult to draw generalizations across different regimes, supranationality indeed usually calls for a particularly developed structural principle governing the interaction or allocation of powers between the international and domestic levels of authority, such as, for instance, the principle of subsidiarity[62] (particularly, but not only in human rights law[63]) or the principle of complementarity[64] in international criminal law.

2.3.3 *Vertical Dimension*

2.3.3.1 Penetration of Domestic Law

The other integrative effect of supranationality plays out at the domestic level. It relates to the penetration of the domestic legal order rather than its mere circumvention. Law beyond the state is being vertically integrated into or entrenched within the domestic legal system. Integration in this sense depends on the internal effect of law beyond the state, which, in turn, is the result of the complex interaction of international and municipal law. While law beyond the state can be more or less determinative with respect to its own effects in domestic law, the latter usually still claims to have the final say on the matter. This necessitates to look at both the international and domestic level. Within this integrative dimension of

[56] Beyond EU law, one can cite, for instance, the Court of Justice of the Andean Community or Chapter 11 of the NAFTA Agreement.

[57] For the example of the ECtHR, see the detailed analysis in Chapter 3.

[58] Bilateral investment treaties usually provide for compulsory investor–state arbitration.

[59] In contrast to Helfer and Slaughter, quasi-judicial bodies such as the Human Rights Committee are not regarded an example of supranational adjudication here as they lack the power to adjudicate disputes in a legally binding manner.

[60] Delbrück, "Transnational Federalism," 52.

[61] Ibid., 75.

[62] Ibid., 53.

[63] Samantha Besson, "Subsidiarity in International Human Rights Law – What Is Subsidiary about Human Rights?" (2016) 61 *American Journal of Jurisprudence* 69–107.

[64] Art. 17 ICC Statute; for an in-depth treatise, see Mohamed M. El Zeidy, *The Principle of Complementarity in International Criminal Law* (Leiden/Boston: Brill 2008).

supranationality, one can further distinguish between two different aspects: direct invocability of law beyond the state as well as its effectiveness within the domestic legal order.

2.3.3.2 Invocability

Law beyond the state is integrated into domestic law, if it is directly enforceable and invocable *within* national law.[65] This corresponds to the notions of direct effect or self-executing norms defined as domestic "enforcement of an international obligation without being dependent on implementing legislation."[66] As law beyond the state is directly invocable before domestic courts/authorities, individuals themselves become "enforcers" within domestic legal structures. In this context, enforcement is not only a decentralized but also a bottom-up process.

Direct effect in this sense is narrower than just the creation of individual rights or obligations by international law,[67] as it also comprises direct domestic enforceability.[68] It is also to be distinguished from (direct) validity. Validity refers to whether an international rule is recognized as law of the land and as a source of rights or obligations in the domestic legal order.[69] Validity depends on the mode of incorporation of international law into domestic law and direct effect not always requires direct validity. However, validity is usually a precondition for direct effect.[70] Indirect effect refers to the situation, where an international rule is enforced through a domestic provision that incorporates, implements, or overlaps with the former.[71] The concept of consistent interpretation, for instance, which is the interpretation of national law in conformity with international law, can be understood as a form of

65 On invocability and enforceability Mathias Forteau, "The Role of the International Rules of Interpretation for the Determination of Direct Effect of International Agreements" in Helmut Philipp Aust and Georg Nolte (eds.), *The Interpretation of International Law by Domestic Courts* (Oxford: Oxford University Press 2016), pp. 99f.

66 André Nollkaemper, *National Courts and the International Rule of Law* (Oxford: Oxford University Press 2011), p. 118. Shelton speaks of "direct application" (Dinah Shelton, "Introduction," in Dinah Shelton (ed.), *International Law and Domestic Legal Systems – Incorporation, Transformation, and Persuasion* [Oxford: Oxford University Press 2011], p. 12). On the origins and meaning(s) of the term "self-executing," see Yuji Iwasawa, "The Doctrine of Self-Executing Treaties in the United States: A Critical Analysis" (1985) 26 *Virginia Journal of International Law* 627–650; Carlos Manuel Vazquez, "The Four Doctrines of Self-Executing Treaties" (1995) 89 *American Journal of International Law* 695–723.

67 On this see ICJ, *LaGrand (Germany* v. *United States of America)*, Judgment of June 27, 2001, I. C. J. Reports 2001 466, 494.

68 Forteau, "International Rules of Interpretation," p. 100. Therefore, the ICJ judgments in the cases of *Avena* and *LaGrand* are not directly pertinent.

69 Nollkaemper, *National Courts*, p. 130.

70 Ibid., pp. 130ff.

71 Ibid., pp. 117–118. The distinction between direct and indirect effect may, however, sometimes also be used when referring to the conditions of validity, which gives it "an unfortunate double meaning" (Ingo Venzke and Li-ann Thio, *The Internal Effects of ASEAN External Relations* [Cambridge: Cambridge University Press 2016], p. 77).

indirect effect.[72] However, distinguishing between direct and indirect effect or between direct effect and consistent interpretation for that matter may sometimes be difficult. For one, direct effect may equally presuppose the existence of a rule of national law (written or unwritten) that allows courts to give effect to international law. Either a general constitutional rule incorporates the entire body of international law into the national legal order, or a rule of reference incorporates particular treaties or specific rules of international law. For another, direct and indirect effect may coincide in that a rule of international law is applied directly on the basis of a rule of reference, while the rule of reference itself is construed on the basis of the principle of consistent interpretation.[73]

Direct effect can either be granted by domestic law,[74] in which case it is usually construed as a domestic constitutional doctrine[75] or it can (concurrently) be imposed "top-down," in which case its origins are deemed international or European.[76] The standard rule in international law remains that international legal rules leave it to states to determine how to give effect to them, even where they directly create rights (or obligations) for individuals.[77] In other words, whether and under which conditions direct effect is granted remains a matter of domestic law.[78] The situation is different as regards EU law.[79] In *Van Gend en*

[72] Extensively on the notion of consistent interpretation, see Nollkaemper, *National Courts*, pp. 139ff.

[73] Gerrit Betlem and André Nollkaemper, "Giving Effect to Public International Law and European Community Law before Domestic Courts" (2003) 14 *European Journal of International Law* 569–589 at 572.

[74] Shelton, "Introduction," p. 12.

[75] Armin von Bogdandy, "Pluralism, Direct Effect, and the Ultimate Say: On the Relationship between International and Domestic Constitutional Law" (2008) 6 *International Journal of Constitutional Law* 397–413 at 402.

[76] André Nollkaemper, "The Duality of Direct Effect of International Law" (2014) 25 *European Journal of International Law* 105–125 at 106f.

[77] Thomas Buergenthal, "Self-Executing and Non-Self-Executing Treaties in National and International Law," *Collected Courses of the Hague Academy of International Law*, vol. 235 (Leiden/Boston: Brill Nijhoff 1992), p. 320. Buergenthal distinguishes the term of direct applicability (international obligation to make certain individual treaty rights enforceable), from the term self-executing, which refers to treaties deemed by national courts of usually monist states to create directly enforceable domestic rights. Others draw a similar distinction contrasting direct applicability with direct effect (Koen Lenaerts, "Direct Applicability and Direct Effect of International Law in the EU Legal Order" in Inge Govaere et al. (eds.), *The European Union in the World* [Leiden/Boston: Brill Nijhoff 2013], p. 45).

[78] States may exceptionally commit themselves to ensure that certain treaty provisions can be directly applied and enforced in domestic courts (PCIJ, *Jurisdiction of the Courts of Danzig*, Advisory Opinion of March 3, 1928, P. C. I. J. Series B no. 15, 17–18). However, such obligation doesn't exist as a matter of general international law (Sean D. Murphy, "Does International Law Obligate States to Open Their National Courts to Persons for the Invocation of Treaty Norms That Protect or Benefit Persons?" in David Sloss (ed.), *The Role of Domestic Courts in Treaty Enforcement* [Cambridge: Cambridge University Press 2009], pp. 85ff). See also ICJ, *Request for Interpretation of the Judgment of 31 March 2004 in the Case concerning Avena and Other Mexican Nationals (Mexico* v. *United States of America)*, Judgment of January 19, 2009, I. C. J. Reports 2009 3, 44).

[79] Mario Mendez, *The Legal Effects of EU Agreements* (Oxford: Oxford University Press 2013), p. 11; Buergenthal, "Treaties," p. 327.

Loos the CJEU not only asserted that the EEC Treaty contained rights, which must be enforceable before domestic courts, but that they are so immediately and *qua* Community law.[80] The same may hold true – at least in theory – for other regional integration frameworks such as, for instance, the Andean Community[81] and the SICA.[82] In reference to EU law, both the Court of Justice of the Andean Community[83] and the CACJ introduced the principle of direct effect to their respective Communities[84].[85] It is usually this form of imposed direct effect which is denoted supranational.[86]

The distinction between imposed and domestic direct effect is, however, not that clear cut. On the one hand, the conditions under which domestic law grants international norms direct effect often hinges on international factors. Determining direct effect is thus "an interactive process which supposes to analyze together the international provision and the domestic legal order to assess whether the said provision can be applied as it stands by domestic organs."[87] On the other hand, although the far-reaching claims of the CJEU were accepted in practice, a comparative analysis reveals that even in the EU, direct effect cannot exclusively be derived internationally as it for many states still depends on some sort of (prior) constitutional recognition.[88] Therefore, the view that only imposed direct effect *à la* EU law is to be regarded supranational is rejected here.[89] If supranationality were to be construed as a top-down

80 Chapter 1, Section 1.4.2.

81 For a detailed account see Karen J. Alter and Laurence R. Helfer, *Transplanting International Courts*, vol. I (Oxford: Oxford University Press 2017).

82 Caserta, "Regional Integration," 588ff.

83 Direct effect in the sense of direct applicability is provided for in Art. 3 of the Treaty creating the Court of Justice of the Andean Community.

84 ATJ, *Acción de incumplimiento interpuesta por la Junta del Acuerdo de Cartagena contra la República de Venezuela*, 3-NaN-96, 13ff. CACJ, Judgment of April 9, 1996. The CCJ of the CARICOM has been more hesitant in this respect (Caserta, "Regional Integration," 591f).

85 Similar far-reaching claims have so far *not* emerged within other regional economic integration regimes in South America (Forteau, "International Rules of Interpretation," p. 108), Africa (Richard Frimpong Oppong, *Legal Aspects of Economic Integration in Africa* [Cambridge: Cambridge University Press 2011], pp. 195ff) or Asia (Venzke and Thio, *ASEAN External Relations*). As regards Europe, the EFTA Court explicitly rejected the position that "individuals and economic operators can rely directly on non-implemented EEA rules before national courts" (EFTA Court, Case E-4/01, *Karl K Karlsson hf* v. *the Icelandic State*, Advisory Opinion of May 30, 2002). Under the ACHR, the situation is somewhat more difficult to ascertain (IACtHR, *Almonacid-Arellano et al* v. *Chile*, Judgment of September 26, 2006, Series C no. 154; *Barrios Altos* v. *Peru*, Judgment of March 14, 2001, Series C no. 75; compare Christina Binder, "The Prohibition of Amnesties by the Inter-American Court of Human Rights" in Armin von Bogdandy and Ingo Venzke (eds.), *International Judicial Lawmaking* [Berlin/Heidelberg: Springer 2012], p. 295; Ariel E. Dulitzky, "An Inter-American Constitutional Court? The Invention of the Conventionality Control by the Inter-American Court of Human Rights" (2015) 50 *Texas International Law Journal* 45–93 at 57).

86 Chapter 1, Section 1.4.2.

87 Forteau, "International Rules of Interpretation," p. 104 and 106. See also Nollkaemper, *National Courts*, p. 128.

88 Besson, "How International Is the European Legal Order?," 57.

89 For a similar understanding, see Mosler, "Supra-National Judicial Decisions," 435.

claim only, it would remain a notion hard to reconcile with legal reality.[90] What is decisive for the present conceptualization is that direct effect serves the same purpose irrespective of its source, which is to allow for the implementation and effectiveness of law beyond the state without further need of implementing measures by the domestic legislature.[91] At the same time, however, it would be too indiscriminate to treat every instance, in which an international provision may be directly relied upon before a domestic court or authority as supranational. Therefore, the view held here is that supranationality should become the catchword if a specific body of law beyond the state is generally and for the most part directly invocable by individuals within the domestic legal order as a result of the interplay of both domestic and international sources.

2.3.3.3 Supremacy?

The second aspect of vertical integration of law beyond the state concerns the rank of the latter within municipal law. At the international level, international law takes precedence over domestic law of any kind as reflected by the well-established principle that domestic law cannot be invoked as a justification for the non-observance of an international obligation.[92] If the principle of supremacy of international law were to be a criterion of supranationality, international law would be supranational in *toto*.[93] Unless one adheres to the Kelsian pyramid, however, international supremacy of international law does not easily translate into supremacy within domestic law. On the contrary, the prevailing classical and arguably dualist view asserts that international law is generally indifferent as to the question of what rank it is accorded in the domestic legal system.

The exceptions to this rule are, again, EU law, Andean Community law, or Central American Community law, which go as far as determining their own rank within the domestic legal order, claiming precedence over any conflicting rule of domestic law (even national constitutions).[94] The conventionality control which the IACtHR requires from domestic courts has also been interpreted as an obligation of the latter to set aside domestic law in conflict with the

90 For a similar view on direct effect, see Nollkaemper, "Direct Effect of International Law," 110. Nollkaemper aptly noted that "one cannot disassociate the rule as proclaimed from the rule as received." For this reason and from a sociological standpoint, it was distinguished between de facto and de jure supranationality: "RICs [Regional International Courts] can become engines of supranationality only to the extent to which they are supported by a set of institutional, political, and societal pre-conditions allowing for the concrete enforcement of the rulings of the RIC at the regional and national levels." (Caserta, "Regional Integration," 579).

91 As to direct effect, see Nollkaemper, "Direct Effect of International Law," 106f and 110.

92 PCIJ, *Treatment of Polish Nationals and Other Persons of Polish Origin or Speech in Danzig Territory*, Advisory Opinion of February 4, 1932, P. C. I. J. (1932) Series A/B no. 24. See also Art. 27 VCLT.

93 Kunz, "Supra-National Organs," 694.

94 CJEU, *Costa* v. *E.N.E.L.*; ATJ, *Preliminary Ruling* 1-IP-87; CACJ, Judgment of April 9, 1996.

ACHR (no matter its formal rank within municipal law).[95] More generally, one finds sometimes comparable claims in scholarship based on monist or natural law arguments, according to which the supremacy of international law is also to be effective within domestic law, at least as regards certain specific international norms such as *ius cogens* norms for example[96] or strong duties of international law.[97]

Like for the (direct) effect of law beyond the state, the latter's rank is thus above all determined by the national legal order. State practice in this regard is heterogenic, if not at times even schizophrenic.[98] Two generalizations can be made, however. First, virtually no state seems ready to accept full and unconditional supremacy of international law over domestic law. International law ranks in only very few states above or at the same level as the domestic constitution, which is usually supreme.[99] Second, the rank of international law within domestic law is increasingly perceived as a non-formal, content, or rule-based issue, allowing for or even demanding differentiation depending on the substance of the norm in question. As a consequence, from the domestic perspective, international law does not necessarily equal international law and certain international norms such as human rights or *ius cogens* rules, for instance, may rank higher in the domestic hierarchy of sources than others.[100] Both these aspects actually led international scholars to question whether the formal principle of international law supremacy should not be requalified at the international level in order to "bridge" the existing divide between the status of international law internationally and the status of international law domestically.[101]

Again, supranationality cannot alone hinge on a top-down claim of superiority considering that even in the EU, member states have rejected such assertion. Equally unrealistic would be to construe supremacy as absolute or unconditional, given that virtually all domestic legal systems place some sort of constitutional limit to the supremacy of law beyond the state. In fact, it might even be questionable if supremacy is to be regarded as an element of supranationality at all. Indeed, only EU law specific conceptualizations rely on supremacy, while scholars that provide an abstract definition mostly renounce to make supremacy a characteristic of supranationality.[102]

95 Dulitzky, "Invention of the Conventionality Control," 60.

96 With further references, Çali, *Authority of International Law*, pp. 39 and 40; Nijman and Nollkaemper, "Beyond the Divide," pp. 342ff.

97 Çali, *Authority of International Law*, pp. 77ff.

98 Anne Peters, "Supremacy Lost: International Law Meets Domestic Constitutional Law" (2009) 3 *Vienna Journal on International Constitutional Law* 170–198 at 194.

99 For a detailed comparative study, see Peters, "Supremacy Lost"; André Nollkaemper, "Rethinking the Supremacy of International Law" (2010) 65 *Zeitschrift für öffentliches Recht* 65–85.

100 Peters, "Supremacy Lost," 185.

101 Nollkaemper, "Supremacy of International Law." A recent proposal in this regard is Çali's reconstruction of the authority of international law, which distinguishes between different shades of authority, that is, strong, weak, and rebuttable duties (Çali, *Authority of International Law*, pp. 72, 75).

102 This holds true, for instance, for Schroeder and Müller, "Elements of Supranationality"; Schermers and Blokker, *International Institutional Law*.

Moreover, vertical integration as described earlier can also be achieved in the absence of a strict rule of hierarchy. It may well be that a norm of law beyond the state is rendered ineffective when set aside following a conflict with a domestic norm, but this does not necessarily put vertical integration as such into question. For all of these reasons, the view is taken here that supremacy can be perceived of as an element of supranationality, but not necessarily a constitutive one. Supremacy is less a formal rule of status or rank, but hinges primarily upon the competences as well as attitudes of those interpreting the law.[103] It follows that supremacy entails the faculty of domestic courts to review a domestic act for its compatibility with law beyond the state and in case of conflict accord, as a general rule, precedence to the latter.[104] As for direct effect, supremacy in this form is the result of the interaction of both international and domestic elements.

2.3.4 *Supranational Law*

Based on the functional approach adopted, a terminological clarification is necessary as regards the term of supranational law. The dual integrative force of supranationality identified earlier means that supranational law is understood in two ways here. On the one hand, supranational law may refer to when law beyond the state contains rights and/or obligations of natural or legal persons that can be enforced internationally in a compulsory manner. International criminal law or certain human rights treaties can be considered supranational law to the extent that these bodies of law are backed with institutions either to which individuals or legal persons have access to or which have jurisdiction over the latter. On the other hand, supranational law may refer to the particular effect of which law beyond the state benefits within domestic law; notably, the fact that it is integrated within the domestic legal order and can be directly enforced, sometimes even notwithstanding conflicting domestic law.

Supranational law has further to be delineated from transnational but also national law. Transnational law differs from supranational law – and from law beyond the state in general – in at least two ways. It is at the same time more and less inclusive. Transnational law is broader in that it is usually understood as including not only public law but also private law and sometimes even non-binding rules.[105] Within this hybrid paradigm, the classical and formal distinctions between public/private and

[103] For the ECHR context, see Keller and Stone Sweet, "Impact of the ECHR," pp. 683f.

[104] Peters, "Supremacy Lost," 186.

[105] Philip C. Jessup, *Transnational Law* (New Haven: Yale University Press 1956), p. 2; Carrie Menkel-Meadow, "Why and How to Study 'Transnational Law'" (2010) 1 *UC Irvine Law Review* 97–129 at 103ff. For some, transnational law does not include public international law as its sources and addressees are private actors (with further references Roger Cotterrell, "What Is Transnational Law?" (2012) 37 *Law & Social Inquiry* 500–524).

binding/non-binding collapses.[106] At the same time, transnational law is sometimes construed as having narrower scope. According to this view, transnational law is limited to regulating cross-border issues to the exclusion of internal situations (such as, for instance, human rights issues as long as they do not have an extraterritorial dimension).[107]

The delineation of supranational law vis-à-vis domestic law reveals to be more complex as this distinction might essentially be a formal one. Supranational law penetrates domestic law in ways that can make it difficult to distinguish between the two. Things become even more complicated when supranational norms overlap in terms of substance with domestic ones and are constituted through and by (their interaction) with domestic law. However, there remain important formal differences. First, in terms of sources, supranational law ultimately originates outside the domestic realm and is produced or consolidated according to international rules. Second, the scope of application of supranational law transcends one specific domestic legal system. And third, unlike national law, supranational law can often – though not always – be enforced and disputes over it be adjudicated at the international level.

2.4 CONTEXTUALIZATION

2.4.1 *Existing Theoretical Frameworks*

2.4.1.1 The Domestic-International Intersection

The present conceptualization of supranationality shares several assumptions and findings of existing theoretical (normative) strands. The idea of supranational law seems to align with monist and/or constitutionalist conceptions of the national-international interface. The origins of supranationality lie in international legal literature of mostly monist scholars.[108] Also, direct effect and supremacy as a matter of European law were equated with imposing strong monism,[109] and both direct effect and supremacy are considered to be constitutional doctrines.[110] Some constitutionalists further hold the view that certain

106 Kaarlo Tuori, "Transnational Law" in Miguel Maduro, Kaarlo Tuori, and Suvi Sankari (eds.), *Transnational Law: Rethinking European Law and Legal Thinking* (Cambridge: Cambridge University Press 2014), pp. 17ff.

107 Jessup, *Transnational Law*, p. 2. Such delineation, however, does not hold true if one, as Shaffer, takes a process-oriented perspective focusing on "the transnational production of legal norms and institutional forms in particular fields and their migration across borders, regardless of whether they address transnational activities or purely national ones" (Gregory C. Shaffer, "Transnational Legal Ordering and State Change," *Transnational Legal Ordering and State Change* [Cambridge: Cambridge University Press 2012], p. 6).

108 Chapter 1, Section 1.2.2.

109 Gerard Conway, *EU Law* (London: Routledge 2015), p. 217.

110 Eric Stein, "Lawyers, Judges, and the Making of a Transnational Constitution" (1981) 75 *American Journal of International Law* 1–27; Federico Mancini, "The Making of a Constitution for Europe"

"constitutional" norms of international law (*jus cogens*, universal values, human rights, etc.) enjoy special normative force and therefore automatically trump conflicting norms, also within the domestic realm.[111] Concurrently, the example of the EU has shown that supranationality and legal pluralism, which in its many facets has emerged as the prevailing approach,[112] are, at least in analytical terms, not mutually exclusive concepts: the EU as the paradigmatic example of supranationality is today regularly conceived of in pluralist terms in order to account for the merely conditional acceptance of the doctrines of direct effect and supremacy.[113] Supranational law and the hybrid nature of direct effect and supremacy seem to escape the classic monism/dualism paradigm,[114] and instead confirm the observation that "the system has become 'neomonistic', with new channels opening for the inter-penetration of international and domestic law through judicial decision, legislation, and executive action."[115] Both vertical and horizontal integration reflect that the divide between domestic and international increasingly collapses and is regularly circumvented. In short, supranationality, as construed here, has not necessarily to be viewed as a monist concept, but is compatible with the descriptively more powerful notion of legal pluralism.

2.4.1.2 Global Constitutionalism

The overlaps between supranationality and constitutionalism are not limited to the domestic–international intersection. A number of elements of horizontal integration are sometimes regarded hallmarks of global – at least sectoral or regime specific – constitutionalization in international law. Supranationality and constitutionalization may thus refer to the same legal reality. As Schroeder and Müller put it: "identifying processes of supranationalization may be seen as grist to the mill of the 'constitutionalists'."[116] For one, this holds true for the departure from consent-based decision-making beyond the state and the

(1989) 26 *Common Market Law Review* 595–614; Joseph H. H. Weiler, "The Transformation of Europe" (1991) 100 *Yale Law Journal* 2403–2483.

111 With further references Çali, *Authority of International Law*, p. 39.

112 Instead of many Krisch, *Beyond Constitutionalism*; Bogdandy, "Pluralism." For a juxtaposition see Çali, *Authority of International Law*, pp. 38–43. Besson is more critical toward an opposition of legal pluralism and constitutionalism in this area (Samantha Besson, "The Truth about Legal Pluralism" (2012) 8 *European Constitutional Law Review* 354–361 at 357ff).

113 Miguel Poiares Maduro, "Three Claims of Constitutional Pluralism" in Matej Avbelj and Jan Komárek (eds.), *Constitutional Pluralism in the European Union and Beyond* (Oxford: Hart 2012), pp. 67ff.

114 Nijman and Nollkaemper, "Beyond the Divide," pp. 341ff; Bogdandy, "Pluralism," 397f; Çali, *Authority of International Law*, pp. 130ff.

115 Nijman and Nollkaemper, "Beyond the Divide," p. 349.

116 Schroeder and Müller, "Elements of Supranationality," p. 377.

centralization within international regimes.[117] For another, constitutionalization, as supranationality, focuses on the anthropocentric dimension of international law and the growing participation and importance of the individual as (the ultimate) international legal subject.[118] To some extent, one could thus argue that supranationality captures the specific structural pedigree of the constitutionalization of international law.

Differences exist, however, in regard to "thicker" understandings of global constitutionalism concerned with keeping international institutions (and their law) in check based on principles such as democracy, separation of powers, human rights, or the rule of law. In so far as constitutionalism ties empowerment to control,[119] it can have an important complementary function to supranationality or supranationalism, which by themselves are less concerned with issues of legitimacy or checks and balances.[120] The same holds true for other normative approaches that seek to frame the legitimacy of international institutions or international governance, such as, for instance, public law approaches[121] or global administrative law[122].[123]

2.4.1.3 Federalism

Distinguishing supranationality from federalism reveals to be particularly difficult. Supranationality can be viewed as an offspring of federalist thought,[124] and it may

117 Stephen Gardbaum, "Human Rights and International Constitutionalism" in Jeffrey L. Dunoff and Joel P. Trachtman (eds.), *Ruling the World?: Constitutionalism, International Law, and Global Governance* (Cambridge: Cambridge University Press 2009), p. 246; Anne Peters, "Global Constitutionalism Revisited" (2005) 39 *International Legal Theory* 39–67 at 51 and 58; Jan Klabbers, "Setting the Scene" in Jan Klabbers, Anne Peters, and Geir Ulfstein (eds.), *The Constitutionalization of International Law* (Oxford: Oxford University Press 2009), p. 14.

118 Gardbaum, "Human Rights and International Constitutionalism," p. 249; Anne Peters, "Membership in the Global Constitutional Community" in Jan Klabbers, Anne Peters, and Geir Ulfstein (eds.), *The Constitutionalization of International Law* (Oxford: Oxford University Press 2009), pp. 157ff.

119 Geir Ulfstein, "Institutions and Competences" in Jan Klabbers, Anne Peters, and Geir Ulfstein (eds.), *The Constitutionalization of International Law* (Oxford: Oxford University Press 2009), pp. 55ff.

120 This has become particularly evident in case of the European Union.

121 Armin von Bogdandy et al. (eds.), *The Exercise of Public Authority by International Institutions* (Berlin/Heidelberg: Springer 2010).

122 Nico Krisch and Benedict Kingsbury, "Introduction: Global Governance and Global Administrative Law in the International Legal Order" (2006) 17 *European Journal of International Law* 1.

123 Both approaches share with one another – and also with the concept of supranationality – the observation that international institutions have transformed global governance and international law in ways that undermine states' sovereignty. In contrast to supranationality, however, they account to an extent for the de-formalization of international law, include private actors of international governance and are less concerned with the traditional opposition between binding/non-binding international instruments (Armin von Bogdandy Philipp Dann, and Matthias Goldmann, "Developing the Publicness of Public International Law: Towards a Legal Framework for Global Governance Activities" in A. von Bogdandy, et al. (eds.), *The Exercise of Public Authority by International Institutions* [Berlin/Heidelberg: Springer 2010], pp. 7–16; Krisch and Kingsbury, "Global Governance," 1, 2–5).

124 Chapter 1, Sections 1.2.1-1.2.4.

owe its existence as a notion of positive law to the very fact that the "F-word" was avoided in the ECSC Treaty.[125] Whether federal and supranational could indeed be used synonymously, as sometimes submitted in scholarly writings,[126] depends on how the term federal is construed. One can distinguish a state-centered approach from broader conceptions of federalism.[127] A state-centered[128] or statist[129] reading focuses on federalism as a particular form of national political organization, namely the federal state or a national federation (as opposed to mere confederations of sovereign states at the international level).[130] Especially with respect to the EU and its predecessors, supranationality was sometimes understood as a transitional concept that would ultimately or necessarily lead to the creation of a federal state.[131] Nowadays, the view that supranationality is a pre-federal concept in this narrow sense – a "halfway house" – is clearly to be rejected, not only in the light of the evolution of the EU,[132] but even more so considering international law more generally.[133] For the same reasons, I would also reject the view that certain elements of supranationality – such as direct effect or supremacy for instance – are comparable to the legal situation in a federal state. Whereas for the EU a tentative analogy with a federal state seems feasible,[134] this is arguably not the case for other international or regional regimes. But even in the EU, supremacy, for instance, operates in legal reality quite differently than the principle of supremacy known in federal states.[135]

125 Chapter 1, Section 1.3.2.

126 See, for instance, Alec Stone Sweet and Wayne Sandholtz, "European Integration and Supranational Governance" (1997) 4 *Journal of European Public Policy* 297–317 at 303: "We use the term 'supranational', in part, to emphasize that the EC is an international organization, and that EC politics is a form of international politics. And we have avoided using the term 'federal' here in order to avoid an argument about the precise nature of the EC polity and how it compares with other federal polities."

127 On the historic debate on federalism, see Daniel Halberstam, "Federalism: Theory, Policy, Law" in Michel Rosenfeld and András Sajó (eds.), *The Oxford Handbook of Comparative Constitutional Law* (Oxford: Oxford University Press 2012), pp. 578ff; Daniel J. Elazar, *Exploring Federalism* (Tuscaloosa/London: University of Alabama Press 1987), pp. 33ff.

128 Delbrück, "Transnational Federalism," 47.

129 Jean L. Cohen, *Globalization and Sovereignty* (Cambridge: Cambridge University Press 2012), p. 82.

130 On the classical, often sovereignty-based debate on the taxonomy and distinction between federation, federalism and confederation see Halberstam, "Federalism," pp. 578ff.

131 Chapter 1, Section 1.4.4.

132 Robert Howse and Kalypso Nicolaidis (eds.), "Introduction," *The Federal Vision* (Oxford: Oxford University Press 2001), p. 8.

133 Klabbers, "Setting the Scene," p. 32. For a comprehensive overview of proposals of a world or European federation since the end of World War I, see Ivan Bernier, *International Legal Aspects of Federalism* (London: Longman 1973), pp. 202ff.

134 With further references to early scholarship, Hay, *Federalism and Supranational Organizations*, pp. 60ff; Koen Lenaerts, "Federalism and the Rule of Law: Perspectives from the European Court of Justice" (2011) 33 *Fordham International Law Journal* 1338–1387.

135 Anne Peters, "Rechtsordnungen und Konstitutionalisierung: Zur Neubestimmung der Verhältnisse" (2010) 65 *Zeitschrift für öffentliches Recht* 3–63 at 49.

Nonetheless, supranationality remains closely connected to broader conceptions of federalism that transpose the federal idea to governance beyond the nation-state, be it European[136] or international[137] governance.[138] In as much as federalism is understood as a constitutional arrangement or as a constitutional theory, these approaches often overlap with[139] or complement[140] global and European constitutionalism or constitutional pluralism discussed earlier. Building on William Riker's classical definition, Halberstam recently (re-)defined federalism as "the coexistence within a compound polity of multiple levels of government each with constitutionally grounded claims to some degree of organizational autonomy and jurisdictional authority."[141] The jurisdiction of the central (federal) entity within the territory of member units and the former's direct reach over citizens[142] is what both supranationality and federalism share as defining elements.[143] That is why Hay, for instance, regarded supranational organizations as a form of "functional federalism"[144] and others stressed the hybrid character of supranationality oscillating between IOs and federal states.[145]

Federalism, however, goes beyond supranationality in at least three ways. First, by combining self-rule and shared rule, unity within diversity,[146] federalism may prescribe how (supranational) authority ought to be allocated among

136 See instead of many Koen Lenaerts, "Constitutionalism and the Many Faces of Federalism" (1990) 38 *American Journal of Comparative Law* 205–263; Schütze, *Dual to Cooperative Federalism*.

137 For an early account, see Scelle (Chapter 1, Section 1.2.2) or on the "impact of the federal model on international law," Bernier, *Legal Aspects of Federalism*, pp. 211ff. More recent examples in international law include Delbrück; with further references Halberstam, "Federalism," pp. 605ff; Cohen, *Globalization and Sovereignty*; Fabbrini, "Constitutionalization of International Law."

138 For a discussion of how federalism in this sense relates to the concept of sovereignty see Cohen, *Globalization and Sovereignty*, pp. 115–150. Starting point of such broader conceptions is often US federalism under the Articles of Confederation as well as under the US Constitution of 1787, which was described as "a hybrid system of governance that combined international with national modes of governance" (Halberstam, "Federalism," p. 578).

139 Daniel J. Elazar, *Constitutionalizing Globalization: The Postmodern Revival of Confederal Arrangements* (Lanham: Rowman & Littlefield 1998), p. 3. For Lenaerts "federalism proceeds from the very essence of constitutionalism, which is limited government operating under the rule of law" (Lenaerts, "Constitutionalism," 205).

140 Cohen, for instance, submitted that "federation as a type of union of states that is not itself a state, (...) may provide the missing concepts needed to theorize a mode of political integration (via extension) that is normatively attractive and analytically necessary to make the discourse of the constitutionalization of international law and of regional or global 'governance institutions' meaningful" (Cohen, *Globalization and Sovereignty*, p. 83).

141 Halberstam, "Federalism," p. 580.

142 Kenneth C. Wheare, *Federal Government* (Oxford: Oxford University Press 1946), p. 2.

143 Stone Sweet and Sandholtz, "European Integration," 303.

144 Hay, *Federalism and Supranational Organizations*, pp. 79–103, in particular 89ff.

145 Chapter 1, Sections 1.4.4 and 1.5.1. Therefore, Diggelmann, for instance, regards the Articles of Confederation as an early type of supranational association of states (Oliver Diggelmann, "Supranationalität in geschichtlicher Perspektive: Die 'Articles of Confederation' (1781–1789)" in Thomas Bruha (ed.), *Europäischer Föderalismus im Licht der Verfassungsgeschichte* [Schaan: Verlag der Liechtensteinischen Akademischen Gesellschaft 2011], p. 119).

146 Elazar, *Exploring Federalism*, pp. 5, 12, 16 and 38.

different levels of governance in order to achieve common goals while still maintaining autonomy of member units. Second, unlike supranationality, federalism is first and foremost a political theory and as such entails a particular conception of political form.[147] As Cohen argues federalism makes up for the "lack of political-theoretical precision" of "the proliferation of concepts like 'post-', 'supra-', or 'trans'national to refer to emergent political formations and talk of regional and global governance."[148] She goes as far as construing "a constitutional polity that is not itself a state,"[149] a federal "*demos of demoi*" so to speak.[150] This feeds directly into the third point that distinguishes supranationality from federalism. Like global constitutionalism or global administrative law, scholars applying federalism beyond the state usually seek to provide a certain normative (republican) framework including democratic standards, rule of law, human rights, or good governance.[151]

In short, as a "thin conceptual theory"[152] – if one dares to speak of a theory at all – which does not come with any broader normative vision, the supranationality framework may complement and inform more fully fledged theories rather than being perceived as mutually exclusive to them.

2.4.2 *The Notion of Community*

In the realm of EU law, supranationality had become synonymous with the specific Community model or Community law.[153] The notion of community is, of course, not one that is exclusive to EU law. "International community" is a widely used term in international law that has been codified in the VCLT as well as the ILC Draft Articles on State Responsibility.[154] In scholarship, the idea of an international community has remained contentious. Some scholars have stressed the ambiguity, even the potential danger of the concept.[155] They argue that speaking of an international community simply reflects a specific

147 Cohen, *Globalization and Sovereignty*, p. 85.

148 Ibid., p. 81. This is precisely why Bogdandy proposed the term "supranational *federalism*" for the EU (Bogdandy, *Supranationaler Föderalismus*). With respect to international law more generally and for the same reasons, Delbrück spoke of "transnational *federalism*" (Delbrück, "Transnational Federalism").

149 Cohen, *Globalization and Sovereignty*, p. 83.

150 Ibid., p. 146.

151 Delbrück, "Transnational Federalism," 519; Cohen, *Globalization and Sovereignty*, p. 82; Howse and Nicolaidis, "Introduction," pp. 2ff and 9.

152 This expression is borrowed from Çali (*Authority of International Law*, p. 51).

153 Chapter 1, Sections 1.4.1-1.4.2.

154 The term "international community as a whole" is used in the context of *jus cogens* and *erga omnes* norms (Draft Articles 25, 33, and 42 as well as Art. 53 VCLT).

155 Christian J. Tams, "The 'International Community' as a Legal Concept" in Jean d'Aspremont and Sahib Singh (eds.), *Concepts for International Law: Contributions to Disciplinary Thought* (Cheltenham: Edward Elgar 2019), pp. 505–523.

normative vision of or agenda for international law,[156] creating risk of abuse and exacerbating hegemony and inequality concerns.[157] Notwithstanding these reservations, Paulus' attempt of defining the term has found general acceptance.[158] According to him, the distinctive feature of a community in international law lies in a (inter-)subjective sense of belonging expressed through shared or common values: a minimum of cohesion to the social bond between its members.[159] Similar definitions refer to a collective identity[160] and common objectives[161], ethos,[162] or moral enterprise[163] making up a community. Put differently, a community is composed of members (as opposed to mere actors).[164] The term international community is often used universally, that is, in reference to the international legal order at large. Yet, regionally or functionally limited communities may also exist within the international community.[165] The crucial and contentious question is what level of belonging, collective identity or cohesion must be reached among members to justify speaking of a community and how this should be measured.[166] Here one's normative vision informs the analytical or conceptual approach the most.

Community in this sense intersects in different ways with supranationality and legal integration.[167] Interests determined and enforced through supranational decision-making[168] may be framed as community interests. As Besson observed, "the commonality of community interests usually translates into the collective identity of their holders and/or bearers, that is, a 'community' (. . .)."[169] However, even

156 Tams, "International Community," pp. 506ff.

157 For example, Prosper Weil, "Towards Relative Normativity in International Law?" (1983) 77 *The American Journal of International Law* 413–442 at 441; Santiago Villalpando, "The Legal Dimension of the International Community: How Community Interests Are Protected in International Law" (2010) 21 *European Journal of International* 387–419 at 388; Dino Kritsiotis, "Imagining the International Community" (2002) 13 *European Journal of International Law* 961–992 at 992; Martti Koskenniemi, "The Subjective Dangers of Projects of World Community," in Antonio Cassese (ed.), *Realizing Utopia: The Future of International Law* (Oxford: Oxford University Press 2012), pp. 9–11.

158 Andreas Paulus, "International Community," in Rüdiger Wolfrum (ed.), *Max Planck Encyclopedia of International Law*, online ed. (Oxford: Oxford University Press 2013).

159 Paulus, "International Community," n. 3.

160 Samantha Besson, "Community Interests in International Law: Whose Interests Are They and How Should We Best Identify Them?" in G. Nolte and E. Benvenisti (eds.), *Community Interests Across International Law* (Oxford: Oxford University Press 2018), p. 39.

161 Peters, "Global Constitutional Community," p. 153.

162 David C. Ellis, "On the Possibility of 'International Community'" (2009) 11 *International Studies Review* 1–26 at 6f.

163 Thomas M. Franck, *Fairness in International Law and Institutions* (Oxford: Oxford University Press 1998), p. 11.

164 Peters, "Global Constitutional Community," p. 153.

165 Franck, *Fairness in International Law*, p. 12.

166 Put differently: whether "there is a social and legal reality behin the expression" (Villalpando, "Legal Dimension of the International Community," 388).

167 Peters, "Global Constitutional Community," p. 153.

168 See earlier Section 2.3.2.

169 Besson, "Community Interests in International Law," p. 39.

in the (initial) absence of commonality, "community interests may also actually contribute to constituting their holders or bearers as a community in the first place."[170] The same could be said for vertical integration and the invocability of law beyond the state within domestic legal orders: it presumably requires acceptance of certain common underlying values, while, at the same time, it further socializes[171] domestic actors and thereby fosters a sense of belonging (to a community). In addition, direct invocability as well as direct enforcement of law beyond by international institutions vis-à-vis natural and legal persons validate the communitarian perspective that looks beyond states to include individuals, groups, or companies.[172]

Supranational authority, in particular, overlaps with domestic jurisdictions in the exercise of public authority over natural and individual legal persons and therefore calls for a developed structural principle.[173] It is under such structuring principle, that one may speak of members of a "discursive" or "rhetorical" community.[174] Insights of constructivist regime theorists may help in understanding the dialogical but also the intersubjective nature of communities.[175] Indeed, both of these aspects are central to constructivist regime theory:

> To endorse a norm not only expresses a belief, but also creates impetus for behavior consistent with the belief. While ideas are usually individualistic, norms have an explicit intersubjective quality because they are collective expectations. The very idea of "proper" behavior presupposes a community able to pass judgments on appropriateness.[176]

What is considered appropriate is neither exogenously given nor fixed: interest, identities but also norms are socially constructed, determined through deliberation and a process of mutual constitution. Regimes are, therefore, considered "inherently dialogical in character."[177] Constructivism, through its emphasis on the inter-subjective nature of shared understandings, norms, and practices, also elucidates the role and increased influence of non-state actors in international law.[178] It offers insights as to how shared values, and hence communities, are constituted in international law.

170 Ibid.

171 Thomas Risse and Kathnjn Sikkink, "The Socialization of International Human Rights Norms into Domestic Practices: Introduction" in Thomas Risse, Stephen C. Ropp, and Kathnjn Sikkink (eds.), *The Power of Human Rights: International Norms and Domestic Change* (Cambridge: Cambridge University Press 1999), p. 5.

172 Tams, "International Community."

173 See earlier Section 2.3.2.

174 Kritsiotis, "Imagining the International Community," 965ff; Franck, *Fairness in International Law*, pp. 25–26.

175 Krasner, "Structural Causes and Regime Consequences," 186.

176 Risse and Sikkink, "Socialization of International Human Rights Norms," p. 7.

177 John Gerard Ruggie, *Constructing the World Polity: Essays on International Institutionalization* (London: Routledge 2000), p. 100 (see also pp. 16, 33f and 43).

178 Margaret E. Keck and Kathryn Sikkink, *Activists beyond Borders: Advocacy Networks in International Politics* (Ithaca/London: Cornell University Press 1998); Jutta Brunnée and Stephen J. Toope,

To summarize, while supranationality refers to legal-institutional aspects of integration, community, especially when drawing on constructivist insights, could be viewed as both the latter's (social) precondition and product.

2.5 CONCLUSION

This chapter has proposed a rediscovery of supranationality as a general and analytical-descriptive notion of law beyond the state. It is not submitted that this is the only valid conceptualization of the notion, but one that can be useful for studying international regimes. In order to give the term a sufficiently precise meaning and define relevant benchmarks for the chapters to come, supranationality was defined from a functional perspective. The common denominator of the elements and traits usually denoted supranational are connected in that they achieve a form of legal integration, either horizontally, through international institutions which can bypass states in their ability to determine the legal position of individuals, or vertically, in that law beyond the state is entrenched in the domestic legal order in a way that allows individuals to rely on it directly. Drawing on constructivist insights, the constitution of a community in the sense of an intersubjective sense of belonging can be regarded as both the (social) precondition and product of this legal integration.

As an analytical framework, supranationality can contribute to our understanding of law beyond the state. It helps describe and compare and, hence, systematize international regimes.[179] More specifically, it captures conceptually and analytically the observations of scholars that, in certain regimes (i) binding decision-making power has shifted from states to independent institutions (ii) the structure of international rules is inward targeted, overlapping with domestic law in that individuals are the addressees and beneficiaries of international norms not (only) states,[180] certain rules enjoy (iii) a particular degree of normativity or authority[181], (iv) permeate the domestic legal order[182] and, as a result, (v) the voluntarist state-centered paradigm is increasingly side-lined in these instances. As a "thin conceptual theory"[183] – if one dares to speak of a theory at all – which does not come with any broader normative vision, the supranationality framework may complement and inform more fully fledged theories.

"Constructivism and International Law" in Jeffrey L. Dunoff and Marc. A. Pollack (eds.), *Interdisciplinary Perspectives on International Law and International Relations: The State of the Art* (Cambridge: Cambridge University Press 2012), pp. 119–145.

179 Virally, "International Organizations," p. 57.

180 For example, Peters, *Beyond Human Rights.*

181 Çali, *Authority of International Law*; Besson, "The Authority of International Law," 349.

182 Besson, "The Authority of International Law," 349.

183 Çali, *Authority of International Law*, p. 51.

3

From International toward Supranational Adjudication

3.1 THE EVOLUTION OF THE CONVENTION SYSTEM: A PROCESS OF SUPRANATIONALIZATION

This chapter introduces the two-pronged argument that the Convention system developed into a Convention community based on horizontal and vertical integration. Since the entry into force of Protocol 11, the ECtHR is often described as a supranational Court.[1] This chapter aims at giving preliminary answers as to what exactly this means. It discusses how the ECtHR transformed from an international into a supranational Court and identifies the pillars of supranational adjudication introduced with Protocol 11. According to Besson, "[t]he ECtHR started as an international court applying an international Convention in the framework of an international organization."[2] Indeed, adjudication under the ECHR started out rather modestly and transformed only gradually from an international into the supranational type of adjudication it is today.[3] In order to ascertain this transformation, a legal-historical perspective is adopted that analyzes the (institutional) developments and reforms of the Convention system. In this context, it is also necessary to revisit some of the well-known classics of early Strasbourg case-law. These cases will shed light on the conceptualization of the ECtHR as a supranational rather than an international court.

Tracing the transformation from international to supranational adjudication overlaps with and confirms existing narratives of the incremental de-politicization, judicialization, and individualization of the ECHR enforcement system.[4] However, this chapter

[1] Introduction, 6f.

[2] Besson, "European Human Rights," p. 120; Helfer and Slaughter, "Effective Supranational Adjudication," 293.

[3] Besson, "European Human Rights," p. 105.

[4] See, in particular, Ed Bates, *The Evolution of the European Convention on Human Rights* (Oxford: Oxford University Press 2010); Mikael Rask Madsen, "The Protracted Institutionalization of the Strasbourg Court: From Legal Diplomacy to Integrationist Jurisprudence" in Jonas Christoffersen and Mikael Rask Madsen (eds.), *The European Court of Human Rights between Law and Politics* (Oxford: Oxford University Press 2011), pp. 43–60. More technical approaches have focused on efficiency concerns and the question of how Strasbourg can deal more effectively with the growing workload, sometimes at the expense of discussing wider geopolitical realities and reflecting on the

offers a new approach in that it focuses on adjudication and connects existing accounts on the institutional evolution of the Convention system to an overall narrative and a broader conceptual framework. Retracing and researching the early stages of supranationalization of the Convention system should contribute to a better understanding of the structural but gradual transformation of the ECHR enforcement structure since its inception toward a horizontally integrated judicial mechanism. Against this background, the chapter starts by recalling the original enforcement system set up under the 1950 Convention and discusses a number of early jurisprudential developments concerning jurisdiction, institutional matters but also the interpretation of the ECHR, revealing a pull of the Convention toward supranational adjudication. In the subsequent sections, the focus lies on Protocol 11, on how it altered the protection machinery of the Convention fundamentally and in a way that justifies using the term supranational.

3.2 THE ESTABLISHMENT OF A HUMAN RIGHTS PROTECTION SYSTEM IN EUROPE

3.2.1 *The European Movement and Ambitions for a Supranational Court*

Without dwelling on the details of the Convention's drafting history, it seems important to briefly look at the origins of the Convention for there was at the very outset already the ambition to create a system of supranational adjudication. The impetus to create the ECHR goes back to the Congress of Europe held in 1948. In The Hague, both unionists and federalists agreed that the adoption of a Charter of Human Rights would be central to Europe's united future. The Congress also demanded a court with "supra-state jurisdiction" tasked to safeguard and protect the rights guaranteed in the Charter.[5] The Congress's "Message to Europeans" reiterated this powerfully. It spoke of a desire for "a Charter of Human Rights guaranteeing liberty of thought, assembly and expression as well as the right to form a political opposition" and for "a Court of Justice with adequate sanctions for the implementation of this."[6] Following the Congress, the European Movement, which advocated for a federal future of postwar Europe, put forward a draft of a European Convention on Human Rights, including a draft statute for a proposed European Court of Human Rights.[7] The European Movement Draft

actual purpose of the protection machinery (see the critique by Harmsen, "Reform of the Convention System," p. 121).

5 Chapter 1, Section 1.2.3. Alain Zysset, *The ECHR and Human Rights Theory: Reconciling the Moral and the Political Conceptions* (London: Routledge 2017), pp. 78f.

6 *Congress of Europe: The Hague, May 1948: Resolutions* (International Committee of the Movements for European Unity 1948) 15–16.

7 Draft European Convention on Human Rights, submitted by the European Movement to the Committee of Ministers of the Council of Europe, July 12, 1949 (hereinafter "European Movement Draft Convention"). See European Movement, *European Movement and the Council of Europe* (London: Hutchinson & Co 1950), pp. 114–115.

Convention foresaw the creation of a permanent Court, which was to be assisted by a Commission and to which state parties as well as every natural or legal person in the territory of a state party could complain about an infringement of the rights guaranteed in the Convention.[8] It also provided for the far-reaching remedial power of the Court to require the state concerned to repeal the offending act and take penal or administrative action (in regard to the persons responsible for the infringement).[9] The Preamble referred to three specific goals of the Convention: the preservation of moral and democratic values as Europe's common heritage, guaranteeing the rule of law, human rights, and fundamental freedoms, and ensuring the universal application of the UN Declaration of Human Rights of 1948. The Convention and its protection machinery should secure peace on the European continent and establish a "collective security system" against resurgences of tyranny and oppression.[10] In figurative terms, Bates described the purpose of the European Movement Draft Convention to set up an "alarm bell" for democratic Europe that would prevent backsliding into dictatorship.[11] In order to avoid encroaching upon the jurisdiction of national courts, the draft included a provision which stated the Court and the Commission can only deal with a complaint "when the internal, juridical processes of the State concerned have been exhausted."[12] As to substance, Article 1 of the European Movement Draft Convention contained an enumeration of eleven rights securing the "minimum essential," while Article 6 left more detailed protection up to negotiations through a supplementary agreement.[13] In the meantime and as an interim regime, the enumeration of rights in Article 1 should prevent abrogation or diminution to the extent that such rights were already secured by each country at the date of the signing of the Convention.[14] The European Movement thus alleviated concerns that the proposed Convention would imply a surrender of sovereignty by stressing that states would not have to concede anything they have not already pledged for.[15] It recalled that most Western states had already acknowledged the necessity of some form of "supranational authority to secure peace freedom and prosperity,"[16] and that the Convention's immediate aim was only to freeze, so to speak, the *status quo* of national human rights protection.[17] Both the proposed Court and Convention, however, had also to be seen as part of the broader

[8] Art. 7(a) and (b) European Movement Draft Convention; William A. Schabas, *The European Convention on Human Rights: A Commentary* (Oxford: Oxford University Press 2015), p. 635.

[9] Art. 13(b) European Movement Draft Convention.

[10] On the broader political context, the drafting history and the influence of the Nuremberg trials on the Draft Convention see European Movement, pp. 111–115, 124–125.

[11] Bates, *Evolution of the ECHR*, p. 54.

[12] Art. 7(c) European Movement Draft Convention; European Movement, p. 121.

[13] European Movement, pp. 120, 122f.

[14] Art. 6(a) European Movement Draft Convention.

[15] European Movement, p. 127.

[16] Ibid.

[17] *Collected Edition of the "Travaux Préparatoires" of the European Convention on Human Rights*, vol. I (Leiden: Martinus Nijhoff 1975), p. 278. Bates, *Evolution of the ECHR*, pp. 57, 66.

political vision of the European Movement for a federal Union among European states. The Court was considered the first step toward this Union, while the Convention could potentially develop into the Union's Bill of Rights.[18]

3.2.2 *Intergovernmental Trajectory of the Council of Europe and the Rejection of an Early Supranational Court*

Negotiations on and drafting of the 1950 Convention took place within the newly created Council of Europe (CoE). Contrary to the European Movement's aspirations, the CoE emerged as a traditional intergovernmental organization,[19] except maybe for its Consultative Assembly – later renamed Parliamentary Assembly – which was composed of national parliamentarians but lacked, for the greater part, meaningful decision-making capacity. To that extent, even the Assembly remained a forum of cooperation respectful of state sovereignty.[20] Generally, the idea of the pooling of sovereignty, which later came to prevail in the economic area and the smaller ECSC, did not gain momentum in the CoE context. Undoubtedly, this intergovernmental background had its bearing on the final version of the 1950 Convention text.

The Assembly of the CoE and its Consultative Committee on Legal and Administrative Questions discussed the endeavor of a European human rights treaty extensively. The Assembly passed a recommendation to the Committee of Ministers (CoM) of the CoE calling for a Court of Justice that should monitor the observance of the new human rights treaty. The recommendation was based on a dual enforcement structure consisting of a Court and a Commission. Unlike the European Movement Draft, the recommendation only foresaw an individual right to petition the Commission, whereas access to the Court would be indirect, through a referral by the Commission.[21] In the Assembly, Teitgen – one of the fathers of the European Movement Draft – insisted that "as conscience of Europe" a judicial organ was needed whose decisions, unlike those of political bodies, could not easily be disregarded.[22]

The elaboration of the 1950 Convention was then up for negotiation among experts and government officials under the auspices of the CoM. Although taking the recommendation of the Consultative Assembly as a starting point, the CoM decided to start from scratch and clarify whether concluding a Convention was

18 *Collected Edition of the "Travaux Préparatoires" of the European Convention on Human Rights*, vol. II (Leiden: Martinus Nijhoff 1975), pp. 178 and 180. Bates, *Evolution of the ECHR*, p. 74.

19 Apparently, many of those involved in The Hague Congress failed to realize the intergovernmental nature of the Council of Europe project. Robertson, "European Integration," p. 83.

20 Mikael Rask Madsen, "From Cold War Instrument to Supreme European Court: The European Court of Human Rights at the Crossroads of International and National Law and Politics" (2007) 32 *Law & Social Inquiry* 137–159 at 143.

21 Travaux Préparatoires ECHR, vol. II, p. 276.

22 Ibid., p. 174.

feasible in the first place. On the part of certain governments there was, in fact, opposition against a Convention and the intrusion it entailed into internal affairs. While these states could not elude the considerable pressure to conclude a human rights treaty, they were keen to make sure that the resulting loss of sovereignty would be minimal.[23] As a result, the idea of a Convention was endorsed, but two important "political issues" remained contentious: First, whether the Convention should consist of a catalogue of enumerated or clearly defined rights, and secondly, what kind of enforcement system should be put in place and who should have access to it. The two issues were connected in that the potential loss of sovereignty was considered greater in the case of a vaguely drafted Convention vested with organs tasked to interpret it. Interestingly, some states categorically opposed the establishment of a Court with compulsory jurisdiction because it would have entailed a "transfer of powers," which could "only be the last chapter of European integration."[24] During the negotiations, states retained the idea of a collective enforcement structure,[25] but did neither agree on the establishment of a Court nor on the recognition of even an indirect right of individual petition.[26] The time was not (yet) ripe for a system of supranational adjudication. Following the Schuman Declaration, European integration was to set off in a functionally limited area and the CoE in Strasbourg was not part of it.[27]

3.2.3 *Original State-Centric and Quasi-Judicial System*

The Convention adopted in November 1950 was in many ways a compromise.[28] In terms of rights enshrined, it overlapped with the European Movement Draft Convention.[29] However, the 1950 Convention provided for quite a different and complex enforcement regime. A Commission was tasked with the primary responsibility to supervise observance of the Convention while final decision-making power over the merits of an alleged violation remained with the intergovernmental CoM. The Commission only had compulsory jurisdiction with respect to interstate complaints,[30] while acceptance of the right to individual application before it was optional. As was acceptance of the jurisdiction of the Court, to which only states or

23 Bates, *Evolution of the ECHR*, pp. 76, 79.

24 *Collected Edition of the "Travaux Préparatoires" of the European Convention on Human Rights*, vol. IV (Leiden: Martinus Nijhoff 1977), p. 128.

25 Bates, *Evolution of the ECHR*, p. 54.

26 Schabas, *ECHR: A Commentary*, pp. 632 and 637. Zysset therefore distinguishes between "the initial political impetus for the ECHR," which was the supranational judicial protection of individual rights, and "the diplomatic impetus," which "clearly limited the normative scope of the ECHR to an interstate complaint and optional quasi-judicial mechanism" (Zysset, *ECHR and Human Rights Theory*, p. 83).

27 Chapter 1, Section 1.3.1.

28 Schabas, *ECHR: A Commentary*, p. 633.

29 Bates, *Evolution of the ECHR*, p. 54.

30 Former Art. 24 ECHR.

the Commission could refer a case that was already found admissible by the Commission and with respect to which conciliation had failed.[31] In the proceedings before the Court, the Commission as defender of the public interest argued the case on behalf of the applicant.[32] Both judges and commissioners were appointed part-time and some of them – if not officially, at least in practice – protected national interests.[33] The two optional clauses through which states could accept the right to individual petition and the jurisdiction of the Court were inspired by Article 36 of the ICJ Statute.[34] In regard to individual applications, submission to the protection system had to be made entirely voluntary for there to be consensus among states to set up a Court to begin with.[35]

In short, the original system was of hybrid design combining diplomatic-political and quasi-judicial elements, with compulsory jurisdiction of the Commission for interstate applications being the exception. For the most part and compared to the ambitions of the European Movement, adjudication under the ECHR remained largely state-controlled. The political nature of the system also transpired in early Strasbourg case-law, which Madsen described as a period of "legal diplomacy."[36] Moreover, "diplomatic constraints" continued to tie the attitude of states toward the Convention and its organs too. By and large, they were concerned with safeguarding national interests.[37]

In terms of substance, the option of fleshing out the content of rights had prevailed over a mere enumeration. Different provisions equally show the drafters' intentions to limit encroachments on national sovereignty and adhere to a classical international treaty law regime. The Convention contains broadly coached limitation provisions, allows for reservations (Article 64 EHCR) as well as for derogations (Article 15 ECHR), and even includes a colonial clause (Article 63 ECHR). Governments expected that they would only rarely be found in violation of the Convention, although there arguably must have been the fear – or the hope for some – that the Convention organs would come to play an active role.[38]

3.2.4 *Foundations for a Development Toward Supranational Adjudication*

Despite the generally low level of judicialization at the outset, the creation of a collective enforcement structure and the establishment of a Court in combination

31 See former Articles 19, 25, 28–32, and 48 ECHR.

32 Bates, *Evolution of the ECHR*, p. 402.

33 Anthony Lester, "The European Court of Human Rights after 50 Years" in Jonas Christoffersen and Mikael Rask Madsen (eds.), *The European Court of Human Rights between Law and Politics* (Oxford: Oxford University Press 2011), p. 102.

34 More on the significance of Article 36 of the ICJ Statute in Section 3.3.1.1.

35 Bates, *Evolution of the ECHR*, p. 404.

36 Madsen, "Protracted Institutionalization of the Strasbourg Court," p. 44.

37 Madsen, "Supreme European Court," 144ff, 148.

38 Bates, *Evolution of the ECHR*, p. 104.

with the two optional clauses laid the foundations for further development of the system toward supranational adjudication.[39] On the one hand, compulsory jurisdiction in respect of interstate applications provided for a "bold" exception to the consensus rule and the freedom of states to settle international disputes autonomously.[40] Admittedly, it was expected that states, for diplomatic reasons, would be very hesitant to make use of the interstate procedure and bring cases against each other before the Commission.[41] However, the agreement on a collective enforcement structure was notable. As Tomuschat put it, pursuant to former Article 24 ECHR, every state was "entitled – and politically even called upon – to act as a guardian of legality in instances where another State party is seen as breaching the provisions of the ECHR."[42] One may detect in the interstate procedure rudiments of a communitarian element. It expresses "the idea that the ECHR as a whole protects common goods, the preservation of which lies in the public interest of the community of States assembled under the roof of the ECHR."[43] Collective enforcement would later become a significant notion and reference point for Convention organs in construing their jurisdiction and competences.[44] On the other hand, even the optional right to individual application and the establishment of a Court with optional jurisdiction still represented a remarkable achievement.[45] It opened the door for an incremental development toward a more fully fledged and supranational judicial structure at a speed agreeable to all governments. The initially conservative diplomatic approach of the Strasbourg organs had a confidence-inspiring effect and contributed to contracting parties increasingly accepting the optional clauses during the following period.[46]

Finally, the election of judges to the Court as established under the 1950 Convention was always quite unique from an international law perspective. Instead of an intergovernmental body, the 1950 Convention tasked the Consultative Assembly composed of national parliamentarians with electing a judge in respect of each contracting party. To be sure, governments retained considerable influence by nominating three candidates for the election.[47] Nonetheless, the power to elect judges to the Court was an exception to the otherwise consultative function of the Assembly. It was argued that the election procedure – which should later essentially be retained also for the new Court

39 Madsen, "Supreme European Court," 140.

40 Article 33(1) UN Charter; Christian Tomuschat, *Human Rights: Between Idealism and Realism* (Oxford: Oxford University Press 2014), p. 4.

41 *Collected Edition of the "Travaux Préparatoires" of the European Convention on Human Rights*, vol. V (Leiden: Martinus Nijhoff 1979), p. 266.

42 Tomuschat, *Human Rights*, p. 4.

43 Ibid.

44 See subsequently Section 3.3.1.

45 Bates, *Evolution of the ECHR*, pp. 101f.

46 Madsen, "Protracted Institutionalization of the Strasbourg Court," p. 44. See also Keller and Stone Sweet, "Impact of the ECHR," p. 679.

47 See former Arts. 38 and 39 ECHR.

under Protocol 11 – reflects a "cautious expression" of a cosmopolitan approach of justifying public authority as citizens relate more or less directly to international institutions through "supranational parliamentary fora."[48]

3.3 PULL TOWARD SUPRANATIONAL ADJUDICATION

3.3.1 *Differentiation from Traditional International Adjudication*

3.3.1.1 Moving Beyond State-Controlled Adjudication

If the original enforcement architecture was modest, this did not prevent the Court and the Commission from conceptualizing adjudication under the Convention in a more progressive fashion.[49] Early case-law on jurisdiction revealed that contracting states would be unsuccessful in invoking state sovereignty or interstate arguments in Strasbourg. Despite of what was essentially an opt-in system of protection, Strasbourg organs distinguished the Convention system from traditional international and state-controlled adjudication. They did so, as will be discussed in the following sections, relying on the notion of collective enforcement and the objective nature of ECHR obligations.

In only the third interstate case brought to Strasbourg, Austria argued that Italy had violated Article 6 ECHR in respect of Italian nationals belonging to the German-speaking Upper Adige minority of South Tyrol.[50] At the time of the alleged violations, Austria itself was not yet a party to the Convention. Deciding on its jurisdiction *ratione temporis*, the Commission had thus to establish whether Austria was barred from exercising its right to bring an interstate application against Italy, in the absence of a reciprocal right of Italy to complain about matters arising within the jurisdiction of Austria for that same period of time.[51] The Commission responded in the negative. Referring to the Preamble of the Convention, it held that:

> [T]he purpose of the High Contracting parties in concluding the Convention was not to concede to each other reciprocal rights and obligations in pursuance of their individual national interests but to realise the aims and ideals of the Council of Europe, as expressed in its Statute, and to establish a common public order of the

48 Bogdandy and Venzke, *In Whose Name?*, p. 35.

49 In so far, the present account goes counter – or at least provides an exception – to Madsen's assessment that the Court's early case-law was particularly conservative and diplomatic. It should be stressed though that this qualification primarily pertains to the Court's practice with respect to procedural and institutional issues (as opposed to its case-law under substantive rights).

50 ECommHR, *Austria* v. *Italy*, no. 788/60, Decision of January 11, 1961, DR 7.

51 Ibid., § 17.

> free democracies of Europe with the object of safeguarding their common heritage of political traditions, ideals, freedom and the rule of law.[52]

The Commission highlighted the objective character of the Convention, which it essentially grounded in the specific nature of the Convention guarantees "being designed rather to protect the fundamental rights of individual human beings (…) than to create subjective and reciprocal rights for the High Contracting Parties themselves."[53] The Commission went on to stress that the objective character of the Convention was also reflected in the institutional setup to ensure observance of the ECHR. The very notion of collective enforcement was testament to that, as was the fact that the right to file an interstate complaint was unqualified, that is, any state party could complain about any alleged breach of the Convention regardless of whether the alleged victim was a national of that state or the latter's interests were affected in some way.[54] When resorting to the interstate procedure, states "vindicate" the public order of Europe, not rights of their own or of their nationals.[55] The Commission powerfully concluded that a

> High Contracting Party, when it refers an alleged breach of the Convention to the Commission under Art. 24 is not to be regarded as exercising a right of action for the purpose of enforcing its own rights, but rather as bringing before the *Commission an alleged violation of the public order of Europe*.[56]

A few years later, the Court handed down its first judgment in the *Belgian Linguistic Case* series.[57] The French-speaking applicants had seized the Commission alleging that the Belgian laws on the use of languages in education violated Articles 8 and 14 ECHR and Article 2 of the First Protocol. They complained that their children only had access to primary and intermediate education in Dutch. At the stage of preliminary objections, the Belgian government contested the Court's jurisdiction *ratione materiae*. It argued, inter alia, that the questions raised before the Court belonged to the state's *domaine réservé*.[58] The Court rejected this view. It stressed that its task, together with the Commission, was to ensure the observance of the engagements undertaken by the contracting parties (Article 19) and that it had, to this aim, jurisdiction over all cases concerning the interpretation and application of the Convention referred to it in accordance with (then) Article

52 Ibid., § 18 (emphasis added).

53 Ibid., § 19.

54 Ibid., §§ 19ff.

55 Schabas, *ECHR: A Commentary*, p. 835; Matthew Craven, "Legal Differentiation and the Concept of the Human Rights Treaty in International Law" (2000) 11 *European Journal of International Law* 489–519 at 512.

56 *Austria* v. *Italy*, § 20 (emphasis added).

57 ECtHR, *Case "Relating to certain aspects of the laws on the use of languages in education in Belgium"* v. *Belgium*, nos. 1474/62 etc., Plenary Judgment of February 9, 1967, Series A, no. 5.

58 Ibid., § 10.

48 ECHR.[59] Moreover, the Court alluded to the special nature of the Convention and human rights more generally:

> [T]he Convention and the Protocol, which relate to matters normally falling within the domestic legal order of the Contracting States, are international instruments whose main purpose is to lay down certain international standards to be observed by the Contracting States in their relations with persons under their jurisdiction (Article 1 of the Convention) (art. 1).[60]

As the Court found that the case indeed concerned the interpretation and application of the Convention and its Protocols, it rejected that the notion of reserved domain could be invoked as a preliminary objection of incompetence.[61] Even more to the point, the Commission submitted before the Court that "when a case, relates to the interpretation or application of the Convention, the idea of the reserved domain has in principle no place in the system of supervision set up by the Convention."[62] This was an early indication that the notion of state sovereignty would come to play a limited role within the Convention system.

The Court's judgment in its first interstate case of *Ireland* v. *the United Kingdom* was equally important for several reasons.[63] The case originated against the backdrop of the conflict in Northern Ireland and concerned the extrajudicial detention and interrogation of presumed IRA members. Before the Court, the United Kingdom conceded to breaches of Article 3 ECHR and therefore submitted, relying inter alia on the case-law of the ICJ, that the ECtHR should decline jurisdiction.[64] The Court, however, found that the case did not become moot:

> [T]he Court considers that the responsibilities assigned to it within the framework of the system under the Convention extend to pronouncing on the non-contested allegations of violation of Article 3 (art. 3). The Court's judgments in fact serve not only to decide those cases brought before the Court but, more generally, to *elucidate, safeguard and develop the rules instituted by the Convention*, thereby contributing to the observance by the States of the engagements undertaken by them as Contracting Parties (Article 19) (art. 19).[65]

With that statement, the Court not only further distinguished adjudication under the Convention from the consensual model, it also laid the basis for lawmaking under the ECHR.[66] *Ireland* v. *the United Kingdom* was also an opportunity for the

59 Ibid., §§ 13f.
60 Ibid., § 13.
61 Ibid., § 14.
62 Ibid., § 12.
63 ECtHR, *Ireland* v. *the United Kingdom*, no. 5310/71, Plenary Judgment of January 18, 1978, Series A, no. 25, § 154. See also David Bonner, "Ireland v. United Kingdom" (1978) 27 *International and Comparative Law Quarterly* 897–907.
64 *Ireland* v. *the United Kingdom*, § 152.
65 Ibid., § 154 (emphasis added).
66 Chapter 5, Sections 5.2-5.3.

Court to confirm the objective conception of the Convention developed in earlier cases such as *Austria* v. *Italy*. Reflecting on Article 1 ECHR and on the question of whether domestic legislation can be challenged in Strasbourg *in abstracto*, the Court made the following famous dictum:

> Unlike international treaties of the classic kind, the Convention comprises more than mere reciprocal engagements between contracting States. It creates, over and above a network of mutual, bilateral undertakings, objective obligations which, in the words of the Preamble, benefit from a "collective enforcement."[67]

Inversely to the constellation of *Ireland* v. *the United Kingdom*, the Court already held in 1962 that it may proceed to examining a case *ex-officio*, even though the applicant wished to withdraw his application.[68] In *Tyrer* v. *the United Kingdom*, for instance, the Court accepted the argument of the Commission's delegate according to which "the applicant's wishes must be subordinated to the general interest to ensure respect for human rights as defined in the Convention."[69] This confirmed, both ways so to speak, that adjudication under the Convention was more than mere dispute settlement and that parties, once Strasbourg organs had been seized, could not freely dispose over the proceedings anymore.

The case of *Loizidou* v. *Turkey* represented a further important step toward supranational adjudication. It originated as one of three applications lodged in 1991 with the Commission, which declared the applications in large parts admissible.[70] Cypriot citizens alleged violations of the ECHR following the 1974 invasion by Turkish troops. On request of Cyprus, the case of Mrs. Loizidou was referred to the Court, and Turkey contested the Court's jurisdiction relying, in particular, on restrictions it had attached to the declarations accepting the right to individual petition before the Commission (former Article 25 ECHR) and the Court's compulsory jurisdiction (former Article 46 ECHR).[71] The restrictions should limit the Commission's and Court's competence *ratione loci* "to the territory to which the Constitution of the Republic of Turkey is applicable,"[72] precisely to avoid that Strasbourg organs would deal with applications relating to Turkey's military presence in Northern Cyprus.[73] Before the Court, the Turkish government submitted that both optional clauses were modeled after Article 36 of the ICJ Statute, which indicated that the drafters of the Convention had intended to give

67 *Ireland* v. *the United Kingdom*, § 239.

68 ECtHR, *De Becker* v. *Belgium*, no. 214/56, Judgment of March 27, 1962, Series A, no. 4. Although the Court decided in the end to strike out the case.

69 ECtHR, *Tyrer* v. *the United Kingdom*, no. 5856/72, Judgment of April 25, 1978, Series A, no. 26, § 24.

70 ECHR, *Chrysostomos, Papachrysostomou and Loizidou* v. *Turkey*, nos. 15299/89, 15300/89 and 15318/89, Decision of March 4, 1991.

71 *Loizidou* v. *Turkey (Preliminary Objections)*, no. 15318/89, Judgment of March 23, 1995, Series A, no. 310, § 54.

72 Ibid., §§ 15, 25, and 27.

73 Bates, *Evolution of the ECHR*, p. 442.

states the same freedom to include restrictions as enjoyed with respect to the acceptance of the ICJ's jurisdiction.[74]

The Court decided the issue by firstly recalling *Ireland* v. *the United Kingdom* and "the special character of the Convention as a treaty for the collective enforcement of human rights and fundamental freedoms."[75] It then extended the scope of two interpretative doctrines developed within the realm of substantive rights to Convention provisions "governing the operation of the Convention's enforcement machinery."[76] It stressed that it must interpret former Articles 25 and 46 (and whether they allowed for restrictions) in the light of present-day conditions as well as in a way so as to make the Convention's safeguards practical and effective.[77] On the one hand, this approach allowed the Court to focus on the implications of Turkey's restrictions: if permitted, they "would not only seriously weaken the role of the Commission and Court in the discharge of their functions but would also diminish the effectiveness of the Convention as a constitutional instrument of European public order."[78] On the other hand, recurring to the living instrument doctrine allowed the Court to take into account present-day conditions and the evolution of the Convention system. At the time, almost all parties to the ECHR had accepted the Commission and the Court's competence without any restrictions *ratione loci* or *materiae*.[79] The fact that Cyprus and the United Kingdom had also attached restrictions to their declarations under former Article 25 ECHR did not, according to the Court, "disturb the evidence of a practice denoting practically universal agreement amongst Contracting Parties that Articles 25 and 46 (...) of the Convention do not permit territorial or substantive restrictions."[80] Finally, alluding, again, to the special character of the Convention, the Court further developed the distinctive nature of its adjudicatory role (compared to the ICJ):

> In the first place, the context within which the International Court of Justice operates is quite distinct from that of the Convention institutions. The International Court is called on inter alia to examine any legal dispute between States that might occur in any part of the globe with reference to principles of international law. The subject-matter of a dispute may relate to any area of international law. In the second place, unlike the Convention institutions, the role of the International Court is not exclusively limited to direct supervisory functions in respect of a lawmaking treaty such as the Convention.
>
> Such a fundamental difference in the role and purpose of the respective tribunals, coupled with the existence of a practice of unconditional acceptance under

74 *Loizidou* v. *Turkey (Preliminary Objections)*, § 67.
75 Ibid., § 70.
76 On these doctrines see subsequently Section 3.3.2.
77 *Loizidou* v. *Turkey (Preliminary Objections)*, §§ 71f.
78 Ibid.
79 *Loizidou* v. *Turkey (Preliminary Objections)*, § 79.
80 Ibid., § 80.

> Articles 25 and 46 (art. 25, art. 46), provides a compelling basis for distinguishing Convention practice from that of the International Court.[81]

As a result, the Court found Turkey's territorial restrictions to be invalid.[82] It also held that they could be separated from the remainder of the declaration, leaving, thus, intact Turkey's acceptance of the two optional clauses.[83] In so doing, the Grand Chamber rejected the position according to which the territorial restrictions formulated "were so essential that disregarding any of them would make the entire declaration void with the consequence that Turkey's acceptance of the right of individual petition would lapse."[84] Quite to the opposite, the Court held that, considering Strasbourg case-law – especially the *Belilos* case[85] – and subsequent state practice, Turkey had willingly accepted the risk that the Court could rule the restrictions to be invalid, while leaving the declarations themselves intact.[86]

As a result, the Court distanced itself and adjudication under the Convention quite remarkably from the state-centric, consensual, and voluntary character of the initial quasi-judicial enforcement system.[87] If the Convention itself was more than a mere contractual enterprise, acceptance of the supervisory system had to be too. *Loizidou* was decided by the Court at a time when all contracting states had accepted both optional clauses and, in fact, already agreed on reforming the system into one that features compulsory adjudication. In hindsight and as Bates stressed: "*Loizidou* helped to reinforce a position whereby in practice States either had to accept the right of individual petition unconditionally (other than temporal restrictions), or not at all."[88] *Loizidou* and the description of the ECHR as a constitutional instrument also brought to light more clearly what had already transpired in earlier case-law, which is the Court's individualistic conception of the Convention. The very nature of human rights as constitutional norms implied recognizing the individual as an international legal person in the European human rights system.[89]

81 Ibid., §§ 83–85.
82 Ibid., § 89.
83 Ibid., §§ 90–98.
84 Ibid., § 90. Turkey argued the same with respect to the jurisdiction of the Court.
85 In *Belilos*, the Court held that Switzerland remained fully bound by the ECHR after it had struck down a reservation to the Convention made by the Swiss government (ECtHR, *Belilos* v. *Switzerland*, no. 10328/83, Judgment of April 29, 1988, Series A, no. 132, § 60).
86 *Loizidou* v. *Turkey (Preliminary Objections)*, § 95.
87 Bates, *Evolution of the ECHR*, p. 443. This point is confirmed when looking at the reactions of international lawyers to the judgment. From the viewpoint of general international law, it was questioned whether the severability of the declaration could still be justified under the *lex specialis* principle (Jonathan I. Charney, "Is International Law Threatened by Multiple International Tribunals?," *Collected Courses of the Hague Academy of International Law*, vol. 271 [Leiden/Boston: Brill 1998], p. 163).
88 Bates, *Evolution of the ECHR*, p. 444.
89 Roland Portmann, *Legal Personality in International Law* (Cambridge: Cambridge University Press 2010), p. 172.

3.3.1.2 Squaring Adjudication with Substance

The Court's early case-law revealed two important aspects regarding the nature of the Convention. First, the ECHR is not simply a contractual or reciprocal enterprise.[90] As an objective treaty,[91] the ECHR does not (primarily) protect the interests of the contracting states, but rights of individuals.[92] To use the words of Simma, obligations under the ECHR are "essentially 'inward targeted,' turning 'States' insides out in an almost literal sense."[93] From the perspective of the law of treaties, the ECHR falls into the category of lawmaking treaties. In a domestic analogy, lawmaking treaties (*traités lois*) – sometimes also termed treaties of normative or integral/inherent character – denote that the substance of their norms is "statutory rather than contractual."[94] In contrast to synallagmatic treaties, lawmaking treaties contain self-existent obligations that do not require corresponding performance by the other parties and thereby also elude the compliance pull of reciprocity.[95] One can witness "a shift toward rule of law expectations of compliance with the rules regardless of what other states might be doing."[96] Considering that the ECHR is a lawmaking treaty, the Court regarded it "necessary to seek the interpretation that is most appropriate in order to realize the aim and achieve the object of the treaty, not that which would restrict to the greatest possible degree the obligations undertaken by the Parties."[97]

Second, the Convention does more than confer rights on individuals against states. The Convention organs conceptualized ECHR rights as collective values of CoE members and posited that there is a general or common interest in the

90 For a nuanced critique of the assumption of non-reciprocity in human rights treaties, see Craven, "Human Rights Treaty."

91 Interestingly, already Kaufmann, the work of which belongs to the origins of the notion of supranationality (Chapter 1, Section 1.2.1) used the term "objective treaty" (Kaufmann, *Rechtskraft des internationalen Rechtes*, p. 31). It must be stressed that the ECtHR's understanding of "objective" must not be confused with treaties establishing an objective regime, that is, treaties containing (*erga omnes*) obligations also for third parties (on the latter see Francesco Salerno, "Treaties Establishing Objective Regimes" in Enzo Cannizzaro (ed.), *The Law of Treaties Beyond the Vienna Convention* [Oxford: Oxford University Press 2011], pp. 225–243).

92 Lea Brilmayer, "From 'Contract' to 'Pledge': The Structure of International Human Rights Agreements" (2007) 77 *British Yearbook of International Law* 163–202 at 165.

93 Bruno Simma, "Reservations to Human Rights Treaties – Some Recent Developments" in Gerhard Hafner et al. (eds.), *Liber Amicorum Professor Ignaz Seidl-Hohenveldern: In Honour of His 80th Birthday* (The Hague: Kluwer Law International 1998), p. 660.

94 For a detailed account on the notion Catherine Brölmann, "Law-Making Treaties: Form and Function in International Law" (2005) 74 *Nordic Journal of International Law* 383–403 at 384.

95 Brölmann, "Law-Making Treaties," 388; Catherine Brölmann, "Typologies and the 'Essential Juridical Character' of Treaties" in Michael J. Bowman and Dino Kritsiotis (eds.), *Conceptual and Contextual Perspectives on the Modern Law of Treaties* (Cambridge: Cambridge University Press 2018), pp. 79–102. ILC, Second Report on the Law of Treaties by Sir Gerald Fitzmaurice, *Yearbook of the ILC* (vol. II) (1957), 31. Brilmayer therefore opposes human rights treaties as "pledges" to other treaties as "contracts" (Brilmayer, "Contract to Pledge," 163ff).

96 Alter, *New Terrain of International Law*, p. 18.

97 ECtHR, *Wemhoff* v. *Germany*, no. 2122/64, Judgment of June 27, 1968, Series A, no. 7, § 8.

protection thereof across the Convention system.[98] In reference to the Convention's Preamble, the Court even spoke of the establishment of a common public order.[99] The notion of collective enforcement is both justification and product of this view.

The special nature of the Convention and the recognition thereof through its organs created a pull toward supranational adjudication.[100] As Brölmann argued, lawmaking treaties suffer from an inherent gap between form and function. The contractual or consensual paradigm lying at the core of every treaty only fits squarely with the function that lawmaking treaties are set up to perform.[101] Lawmaking or normative treaties pull away from the consensual paradigm toward centralization, assuming a life of their own.[102] As demonstrated earlier, this holds particularly true for the Convention. Early on, Strasbourg organs sought to break free from concepts such as reciprocity or continuous state consent invoking the objective nature of the ECHR. What is more, based on the idea of collective enforcement, the Court and the Commission construed their task as one of upholding common values beyond settling disputes.[103] Bogdany and Venzke, therefore, rightly make the ECtHR out to be the prime example of an organ acting on behalf of a value-based (international) community.[104] Promoting community interests and values the ECtHR derives its legitimacy "from these functions, and not just from state consent."[105] A similar conception is that of viewing the ECtHR as a trustee court. According to this modification of the principal-agent theory, the ECtHR is a "super" agent of

98 This would correspond to what Craven referred to as a cognitivist approach (Craven, "Human Rights Treaty," 515f). See also Alexander Orakhelashvili, "Restrictive Interpretation of Human Rights Treaties in the Recent Jurisprudence of the European Court of Human Rights" (2003) 14 *European Journal of International Law* 529–568 at 533.

99 *Loizidou* v. *Turkey (Preliminary Objections)*, §§ 71f.

100 One could cite other examples of treaties which, in terms of their substance, nature, and structure are comparable to the ECHR, yet are devoid of any form of supranational adjudication. Other regional or universal human rights instruments, international labor rights conventions, or international humanitarian law (IHL) come to mind here. In IHL, however, a certain element of reciprocity is undoubtedly at play (Craven, "Human Rights Treaty," 499). See also ICJ, *Reservations to the Convention on Genocide*, Advisory Opinion of May 28, 1951, I.C.J. Reports 1951 23; IACtHR, *The Effect of Reservations on the Entry into Force of the American Convention on Human Rights*, Advisory Opinion of September 24, 1982, OC-2/82, Series A, no. 2, § 29.

101 Brölmann, "Law-Making Treaties," 387. This also goes back to the fact that the VCLT does not formally recognize such a special category of treaties (Craven, "Human Rights Treaty," 493).

102 Brölmann, "Law-Making Treaties," 402f.

103 Craven, "Human Rights Treaty," 511. Human rights treaties contain essentially self-binding commitments. This being said, adjudication under human rights treaties can also be other binding, in the sense that commitments are made for the future and hence will be imposed on "another," differently composed government or legislator (Andreas Føllesdal, "Subsidiarity and International Human-Rights Courts: Respecting Self-Governance and Protecting Human Rights – or Neither?" (2016) 79 *Law and Contemporary Problems* 147–163 at 151.

104 Bogdandy and Venzke, *In Whose Name?*, pp. 28ff, in particular 46ff.

105 Ibid., p. 47.

contracting states acting as a trustee of the Convention regime. As such, it discharges "fiduciary" duties and has an obligation to pursue the overarching values and objectives placed in trust by states on the establishment of the regime.[106]

3.3.2 *Establishing Autonomy through Special Interpretative Techniques*

That adjudication under the ECHR was different from traditional interstate adjudication did not only show in jurisdictional matters. It became apparent in the interpretation of substantive Convention law too. The (scholarly) debate on whether ECHR interpretation constitutes a self-contained regime confirms that the special character of the ECHR extends also to interpretation.[107] A brief look at some of the landmark cases suffices to highlight three special interpretative techniques and illustrate how they allowed Strasbourg organs to gain considerable autonomy over Convention states in setting a Europe-wide human rights standard.[108] While the Court did rely on the rules of interpretation codified in Articles 31–33 VCLT in some of the cases discussed subsequently, it did so primarily "to mould its own autonomous means of interpretation."[109]

The first important doctrine developed by Strasbourg organs is that of autonomous interpretation. In the case of *Engel* decided in 1976, the Court was confronted with the question whether sanctions classified as disciplinary in Dutch law could still fall under the criminal limb of Article 6 ECHR.[110] Relying on the approach developed by the Commission, the Court agreed that the notion of "criminal charge" is an autonomous concept in so far as its meaning cannot hinge upon domestic law alone but must be defined, instead, "within the meaning of the Convention."[111] Two years later, the Court held under the civil limb of Article 6 ECHR that the term "civil rights and obligations" is equally autonomous.[112] These

106 Alec Stone Sweet and Helen Keller (eds.), "Introduction: The Reception of the ECHR in National Legal Orders," A *Europe of Rights: The Impact of the ECHR on National Legal Systems* (Oxford: Oxford University Press 2008), pp. 8f; Alec Stone Sweet and Thomas L. Brunell, "Trustee Courts and the Judicialization of International Regimes" (2013) 1 *Journal of Law and Courts* 61–88.

107 For example, Bruno Simma and Dirk Pulkowski, "Of Planets and the Universe" (2006) 17 *European Journal of International Law* 483–530; Craven, "Human Rights Treaty"; Daniel Rietiker, "The Principle of 'Effectiveness' in the Recent Jurisprudence of the European Court of Human Rights: Its Different Dimensions and Its Consistency with Public International Law – No Need for the Concept of Treaty Sui Generis" (2010) 79 *Nordic Journal of International Law* 245–277; Magdalena Forowicz, *The Reception of International Law in the European Court of Human Rights* (Oxford: Oxford University Press 2010), pp. 23–71.

108 Instead of many, George Letsas, *A Theory of Interpretation of the European Convention on Human Rights* (Oxford: Oxford University Press 2007).

109 Forowicz, *Reception of International Law*, p. 25.

110 ECtHR, *Engel and Others* v. *the Netherlands*, nos. 5100/71, 5101/71 and 5102/71, Judgment of June 8, 1976, Series A, no. 22.

111 Ibid., § 81. The Court used the expression "within the meaning of the Convention" already earlier (ECtHR, *Neumeister* v. *Austria*, no. 1936/63, Judgment of June 27, 1968, Series A, no. 8, § 18).

112 ECtHR, *König* v. *Germany*, no. 6232/73, Judgment of June 28, 1978, Series A, no. 27, § 89.

cases built the basis for the doctrine of autonomous interpretation, according to which certain ECHR notions are semantically independent[113] and must be given a European sense[114] so to speak and, as a consequence, elude determination through contracting states (at least to a certain extent). In *Engel*, the Court reasoned:

> If the Contracting States were able at their discretion to classify an offence as disciplinary instead of criminal, or to prosecute the author of a "mixed" offence on the disciplinary rather than on the criminal plane, the operation of the fundamental clauses of Articles 6 and 7 (art. 6, art. 7) would be *subordinated to their sovereign will*.[115]

Another doctrine developed by the Court in that period held that the Convention safeguards must be interpreted in a way as to be practical and effective. References to the idea of effectiveness appeared as early as in *Marckx* v. *Belgium*, where the Court concluded that the effective respect for family life may, in addition to negative undertakings, include positive obligations on the part of states.[116] A few years later, the Court famously stated in *Airey* that "the Convention is intended to guarantee not rights that are theoretical or illusory but rights that are practical and effective."[117] The Court used the "practical and effective" doctrine to interpret (especially) procedural guarantees broadly, while construing corresponding exceptions narrowly.[118] In fact, one might argue that the Court already relied on the doctrine of effectiveness in the *Golder* case in 1975,[119] when it decided that the right to a fair trial in Article 6 ECHR implied a right to access domestic courts in the first place.[120] The UK government had no success in this case in invoking the *Lotus* principle of international law, according to which limitations on the free exercise of sovereignty are not to be presumed.[121] In short, the effectiveness principle allowed the Court to construe the ECHR "in favor of the individual and against state sovereignty (the *pro homine* principle)."[122]

The last doctrine to be mentioned is dynamic or evolutive interpretation. In *Tyrer*, the Court ruled that judicial corporal punishment of juveniles amounted to degrading punishment as prohibited by Article 3 ECHR. For the first time, the Court held that the ECHR was "a living instrument which, (. . .) must be interpreted in the light

113 George Letsas, "The Truth in Autonomous Concepts: How to Interpret the ECHR" (2004) 15 *European Journal of International Law* 279–305 at 282.

114 Eva Brems, *Human Rights: Universality and Diversity* (Leiden: Martinus Nijhoff 2001), p. 394.

115 *Engel and Others* v. *the Netherlands*, § 81 (emphasis added).

116 ECtHR, *Marckx* v. *Belgium*, no. 6833/74, Judgment of June 13, 1979, Series A, no. 31, § 31.

117 ECtHR, *Airey* v. *Ireland*, no. 6289/73, Judgment of October 9, 1979, Series A, no. 32, § 24.

118 For example, Alastair Mowbray, "The Creativity of the European Court of Human Rights," (2005) 5 *Human Rights Law Review* 57–79 at 72ff.

119 ECtHR, *Golder* v. *the United Kingdom*, no. 4451/70, Judgment of February 21, 1975, Series A, no. 18.

120 Ibid., §§ 26–36.

121 ECommHR, *Golder* v. *the United Kingdom*, no. 4451/70, Report of June 1, 1973, Series B, no. 16, § 15.

122 Luzius Wildhaber, "The European Convention on Human Rights and International Law," (2007) 56 *International and Comparative Law Quarterly* 217–232 at 223.

of present-day conditions,"[123] and that it "cannot but be influenced by the developments and commonly accepted standards in (...) the member states of the Council of Europe."[124] Evolutive or dynamic interpretation was crucial for the Court to do away with domestic legislation such as the discrimination of children born out of wedlock in Belgium (so-called "illegitimate children")[125] or the penalization of homosexuality in Northern Ireland.[126] It was a means to scrutinize public perception and legislation in a specific country with respect to the present-day standard shared among CoE member states.[127] In sum, it reflected that with respect to substantive issues too, the Court conceived of itself as a Community court tasked to identify and uphold a common and evolving European human rights standard.

The preceding survey illustrates how the Court embraced different innovative interpretative tools[128] through which it developed Convention rights and assumed significant interpretative autonomy vis-à-vis states. The critique by commentators and dissenting judges alike, that the Court's expansive interpretation had illegitimately bypassed the sovereign consent and initial intent of the contracting parties,[129] certainly confirms this point.[130] That interpretative autonomy was nonetheless generally accepted may be the result of the Court relying on novel judicial doctrines "free of prejudged conceptions about the scope of legitimate treaty interpretation."[131]

3.3.3 *Shifting the Focus on the Individual*

As a treaty guaranteeing individual rights, the ECHR naturally pulled toward supranational adjudication. Indeed, that the individual only had limited standing under the original enforcement system was difficult to reconcile with the system's very purpose of protecting individuals. As Mégret aptly observed, "the long-term logic of regional human rights courts has been that courts designed to protect

[123] *Tyrer* v. *the United Kingdom*, § 31.

[124] Ibid.

[125] *Marckx* v. *Belgium*.

[126] ECtHR, *Dudgeon* v. *the United Kingdom*, no. 7525/76, Judgment of September 23, 1981, Series A, no. 45.

[127] George Letsas, "The ECHR as a Living Instrument: Its Meaning and Legitimacy" in Andreas Føllesdal, Birgit Peters, and Geir Ulfstein (eds.), *Constituting Europe* (Cambridge: Cambridge University Press 2013), p. 112.

[128] Mowbray, "Creativity of the ECtHR." More on this in Chapter 5, Section 5.2.2.

[129] See, among others, the Separate Opinion of Judge Sir Gerald Fitzmaurice in the judgment in *Golder* v. *the United Kingdom*. For a more detailed treatise on this question, for example, Alastair Mowbray, "Between the Will of the Contracting Parties and the Needs of Today: Extending the Scope of Convention Rights and Freedoms beyond What Could Have Been Foreseen by the Drafters of the ECHR" in Eva Brems and Janneke Gerards (eds.), *Shaping Rights in the ECHR* (Cambridge: Cambridge University Press 2013), pp. 17–37.

[130] Bogdandy and Venzke, *In Whose Name?*, p. 65.

[131] Christoffersen, *Fair Balance*, p. 67f.

individuals ultimately cannot avoid the issue of individual agency, or run into deep contradictions."[132] Hence, it is at least partly owed to the Convention being a safeguard for individuals, that the status of the individual in Strasbourg gradually developed from "bystander" to becoming "the cornerstone of the system."[133]

Under the original system, the individual who seized the Commission was not a party in the proceedings before the Court once a case was referred to it by either the Commission or a contracting party.[134] Step by step, however, the applicant gained participatory rights before the Court. Already in its first judgment, the Court clarified that confidentiality concerns did not forbid the Commission to communicate to the applicant the report it had drawn up following an application.[135] In the same proceedings, the Court also allowed the Commission to present the applicant's observations on the case. The Court reasoned that the applicant was directly concerned and his point of view, therefore, necessarily had to be considered.[136] About ten years on, the Court further accepted that the applicant's representative, upon request of and assisting the Commission, could address the Court directly.[137] Subsequently, the applicant's counsel actually argued the case before the Court in place of the Commission.[138] By the early 1980s, the Court had revised its Rules of Court to expressly guarantee the applicant a right to present his or her own case before it.[139] The applicant was now in a position to request interim and evidentiary measures, file written submissions, appear before the Court or submit a claim for just satisfaction.[140] This was an important step toward supranational adjudication as the linkage between the Court and the individual became (more) direct.[141] The newly acquired rights in the proceedings before the Court stood in contrast to the applicant's standing or rather lack thereof before the CoM, which, in cases that were not referred to the Court, retained the actual decision-making power. However, the Commission's practice of referring cases was increasingly depoliticized leading to more cases ending up before Court instead of the CoM. Also, the CoM itself did

[132] Mégret, "Private Actor Litigation," 5f.

[133] Bates, *Evolution of the ECHR*, p. 167.

[134] See earlier Section 3.2.3.

[135] ECtHR, *Lawless* v. *Ireland (No. 1) (Preliminary Objections)*, no. 332/57, Judgment of November 14, 1960, Series A, no. 1, 514ff.

[136] Ibid., 512ff.

[137] ECtHR, *De Wilde, Ooms, and Versyp ("Vagrancy")* v. *Belgium (Questions of Procedure)*, nos. 2832/66, 2835/66 and 2899/66, Judgment of November 18, 1970, Series A, no. 12.

[138] ECtHR, *Sunday Times* v. *the United Kingdom (No. 1)*, no. 6538/74, Judgment of April 26, 1979, Series A, no. 30; Bates, *Evolution of the ECHR*, p. 402.

[139] Revised Rules of the Court 1982, in particular, Rule 30.

[140] Paul Mahoney, "Developments in the Procedure of the European Court of Human Rights: The Revised Rules of Court" (1983) 3 *Yearbook of European Law* 127–167 at 133f.

[141] Antônio Augusto Cançado Trindade, *The Access of Individuals to International Justice* (Oxford: Oxford University Press 2011), p. 33.

usually not question the findings of the Commission, simply endorsing the latter's report as it stood.[142]

Protocol 9 further strengthened the applicant's position substantially. It amended former Article 44 ECHR to also grant "persons, non-governmental organizations or groups of individuals" a right to refer a case to the Court.[143] Unlike than for states and the Commission, however, the referral by the applicant was not automatic. A panel of three judges had to consider the case sufficiently serious or otherwise important.[144] Not all states ratified Protocol 9 and soon after it entered into force, it was superseded by the fundamental overhaul of the protection system through Protocol 11.[145] Nonetheless, Protocol 9 was testament – this time on the part of contracting states – to the steadily closing gap between the Convention as an instrument securing individual rights and the limited standing of the individual in Strasbourg proceedings:

> The situation whereby the individual is granted rights but not given the possibility to exploit fully the control machinery provided for enforcing them, could today be regarded as inconsistent with the spirit of the Convention, not to mention compatibility with domestic-law procedures in States Parties.[146]

3.3.4 *Recognition of a Broader (Legal) Community*

Based on the idea of collective enforcement, the Strasbourg organs conceptualized ECHR rights and their protection as common interests.[147] Seizing the Strasbourg machinery of protection partly equals vindicating rights of the public order of Europe,[148] or, in more modern terms perhaps, enforcing the rule of law.[149] Emphasizing collectiveness and common interests echoed the construction of a community and the view that this community was impacted by Strasbourg case-law. This, in turn, presented another pull factor toward supranational adjudication. A communitarian perspective suggests inclusiveness,[150] and therefore raised the question as to whether other actors than the parties to the proceedings (or the applicant) should be granted access to Strasbourg. The Court's gradual practice to allow

142 For a detailed account on these practices, Bates, *Evolution of the ECHR*, pp. 409–415, 414 in particular.
143 See Art. 3 of Protocol 9. Preceding Protocol 9, Protocol 8 restructured the Commission into two Chambers and allowed it to sit in Committees of at least three judges to deal more effectively with the increasing number of (inadmissible) applications. Protocol 8 entered into force on January 1, 1990.
144 Art. 5(2) Protocol 9. If the panel refused, the CoM was competent to decide the case.
145 Protocol 9 was opened for signature in 1990 and entered into force in 1992.
146 Explanatory Report Protocol 9, para. 12.
147 In more detail Chapter 5, Section 5.3.
148 See earlier fn. 55 and 56.
149 Alter, *New Terrain of International Law*, pp. 18f.
150 Chapter 2, Section 2.4.2.

third-party interventions can therefore be seen as a formal recognition that it was part of a broader (legal) community.

In the *Tyrer* case in 1978, the Court denied the first *amicus curiae* request by an NGO.[151] One year later, however, it allowed the UK government to submit observations through the Commission in a case that concerned the Netherlands.[152] In *Young, James and Webster* v. *the United Kingdom*, the same possibility was for the first time granted to a non-state actor, namely the British Trades Union Congress. During the oral proceedings, the Court went on to hear a representative of the Congress.[153] Based on this practice, the Court formally introduced third-party status in its revised Rules of Court of 1982. A newly added provision prescribed that the President of the Court could, "in the interest of the proper administration of justice, invite any Contracting State which is not a Party to the proceedings to submit written comments" and "also extend such an invitation or grant leave to any person concerned other than the applicant."[154] The inclusion of the new provision reflected that adjudication under the ECHR had become judicialized and turned away from the diplomatic and interstate context. Admittedly, the provision did not entail a formal right to intervene, but it nevertheless enhanced access to the Court. Allowing wider participation also meant recognizing that Strasbourg case-law impacted states and individuals beyond the individual dispute, which may have an interest in conveying their standpoint to the Court and partake in the development of Convention law.[155] It acknowledged the idea of participatory legitimacy, conveying a sense of ownership to stakeholders.[156] Furthermore, interventions by NGOs, in particular, were considered crucial for ensuring representation of broader social interests, which neither the Commission nor the applicant were in a position to defend directly.[157] Overcoming the assumption that the state alone is entitled to represent the interests of its people at the international level, wider non-state actor access and the new form of immediate interaction between the Court and civil society revealed a particular supranational element.[158]

[151] Dinah Shelton, "The Participation of Nongovernmental Organizations in International Judicial Proceedings" (1994) 88 *American Journal of International Law* 611–642 at 630.

[152] ECtHR, *Winterwerp* v. *the Netherlands*, no. 6301/73, Judgment of October 24, 1979, Series A, no. 33, § 7.

[153] ECtHR, *Young, James, and Webster* v. *the United Kingdom*, nos. 7601/76 and 7806/77, Judgment of August 13, 1981, Series A, no. 44, §§ 8–10.

[154] Art. 37(2) Rules of Court 1982. For an overview of the practice following the adoption of the new provision Shelton, "Participation of Nongovernmental Organization," 632–638; Olivier De Schutter, "Sur l'émergence de la société civile en droit international: le rôle des associations devant la Cour européenne des droits de l'homme" (1996) 7 *European Journal of International Law* 372–410 at 381ff.

[155] Bogdandy and Venzke, *In Whose Name?*, p. 28. On the different types of interventions during that period, see De Schutter, "Émergence de la société civile," 387ff.

[156] Daniel Bodansky, "The Legitimacy of International Governance: A Coming Challenge for International Environmental Law" (1999) 93 *American Journal of International Law* 596–624 at 617.

[157] De Schutter, "Émergence de la société civile," 405.

[158] Ibid., 407f.

3.4 PROTOCOL 11: ESTABLISHMENT OF A SUPRANATIONAL COURT

If the development toward an adversarial and proper judicial procedure in Strasbourg was incremental and already ongoing, the adoption of Protocol 11 in 1994 arguably represented the most decisive step toward a system of supranational adjudication.[159] Officially, Protocol 11 aimed at tackling the increasing workload, streamlining the protection system, and strengthening its judicial elements.[160] In reality, however, the changes it introduced were more profound than the Protocol's *rationale* suggested.[161] The two-tier system was replaced by a single and permanent Court.[162] Not only was the quasi-judicial function of the CoM in dealing with individual applications abolished – the CoM did, however, retain its responsibilities of supervising the execution of judgments – but the new Court was endowed with compulsory jurisdiction. While a majority of states already favored a single Court system, the Stockholm compromise brought those states on board that still wished to maintain a dual structure.[163] As a concession, Protocol 11 provided for a two-tier element within the single Court system. In exceptional circumstances, a Chamber judgment can be reheard by the Grand Chamber on request of any party to the case and provided that a panel of five judges of the Grand Chamber grants the request.[164] Furthermore, after several failed attempts, there was finally agreement among contracting states that every individual should henceforth enjoy a right to directly petition the Court. As Bates put it: "Protocol 11 sealed an enduring right of access to the Court for all individuals who were subject to the 'jurisdiction' (Article 1 ECHR) of the member States, one that could not be taken away by any State unless it denounced the Convention itself."[165]

Protocol 11 codified the possibility of third-party interventions in the Convention (Article 36 ECHR) and introduced a new provision on judicial independence and impartiality of ECtHR judges (Article 21 ECHR). Yet, as to the Court's composition,

159 In contrast and because they also include quasi-judicial organs in their definition of supranational adjudication (Chapter 2, Section 2.3.2), Helfer and Slaughter assessed the ECHR adjudicatory system already pre-protocol 11 as supranational (Helfer and Slaughter, "Effective Supranational Adjudication," 293ff). If that view is not followed here, it must be acknowledged that it has its merits. By the 1990s all states had accepted both optional clauses and, hence, the right to individual petition before the Commission and the jurisdiction of the Court had become generally recognized.

160 Explanatory Report Protocol 11, para. 23; Bates, *Evolution of the ECHR*, p. 453; Schabas, *ECHR: A Commentary*, pp. 633f.

161 As Harmsen noted, the focus on efficiency concerns at the expense of a broader reflection on the purpose(s) of the Convention system appears to be somewhat a constant in the reform discussions (Harmsen, "Reform of the Convention System," p. 121).

162 The idea of a merger of the two Strasbourg institutions was already discussed in the 1980s but abandoned because of a "growing dissatisfaction with Strasbourg" (Bates, *Evolution of the ECHR*, pp. 423–430).

163 Bates, *Evolution of the ECHR*, pp. 456ff.

164 Art. 43 ECHR.

165 Bates, *Evolution of the ECHR*, p. 467.

the concept of the national judge was retained.[166] To date, the Strasbourg bench, therefore, has a strong intergovernmental dimension as the number of judges equals that of contracting parties. What is more, it was agreed upon as part of the Stockholm compromise that the national judge of the defending contracting party will always figure in the composition of the Grand Chamber, once the latter is seized following a relinquishment or to reconsider a Chamber judgment.[167] All in all, however, the national judge concept remained one of the few aspects protective of national sovereignty. It didn't detract from the overall unprecedented character of the reform through Protocol 11. Surprisingly, the far-reaching limitations Protocol 11 placed on national sovereignty were largely uncontroversial: "key aspects of the interstate bargain struck in 1950, viewed at the time as necessary safeguards of national sovereignty, had come to be widely perceived as anomalous relative to the evolution of a system which had successfully established its judicial credentials on the basis of a growing body of individual litigation."[168] The emergence around that time of a Convention-specific epistemic community certainly contributed to the reform being increasingly perceived of as a technical matter, to be dealt with by experts.[169] However, it is arguably also in part due to the Convention's pull and incremental development toward supranational adjudication that sovereignty concerns were only minor compared to the changes introduced by Protocol 11.

Scholars widely appreciated the important structural changes introduced by Protocol 11 as such.[170] The reform was regarded as the transformation of the original alarm bell of Europe into a fully fledged judicial system,[171] or as marking the "paradigmatic turn from 'interstate justice' to 'individual justice'."[172] From a comparative perspective of human rights regimes and international law more generally, the post-Protocol 11 era was nothing less than "revolutionary."[173] The unique element of the Court's new compulsory jurisdiction led Ress to speak of a "turning point" and "paradigm change."[174] The Convention had definitely overcome the (perceived) weakness of IHRL's authority associated with the general lack of obligatory and effective enforcement structures. Compulsory jurisdiction coupled with the individual right to access the Court provided the cornerstone for an effective enforcement machinery. The ECHR now benefited from judicial

166 Art. 20 ECHR.
167 Harmsen, "Reform of the Convention System," p. 123.
168 Ibid., p. 125.
169 Ibid., pp. 124f.
170 The literature on Protocol 11 is abundant. Instead of many see Andrew Drzemczewski, "A Major Overhaul of the European Human Rights Convention Control Mechanism: Protocol No. 11" (1995) IV *Collected Courses of the Academy of European Law* 121–244.
171 Bates, *Evolution of the ECHR*, pp. 36, 462.
172 Zysset, *ECHR and Human Rights Theory*, p. 86.
173 Ress, "Decisions and Judgments of the ECtHR."
174 Georg Ress, "Supranationaler Menschenrechtsschutz und der Wandel der Staatlichkeit" (2004) 64 *Zeitschrift für ausländisches öffentliches Recht und Völkerrecht* 621–639 at 636.

supremacy as individuals could drag states against their will to Strasbourg and obtain a final and binding ruling on their allegations.[175]

Only shortly after Protocol 11 entered into force, the Chamber of the First Section of the Court found that "individuals now enjoy at the *supranational* level a real right of action to assert the rights and freedoms to which they are directly entitled under the Convention."[176] Protocol 11 indeed amended the Convention to combine all three elements of supranational adjudication: Autonomous decision-making with binding effect, compulsory jurisdiction as well as access of and jurisdiction over natural and legal persons.[177] It established an independent and permanent Court (Article 19); through acceptance of the Court's compulsory jurisdiction (Article 32 ECHR) and the absolute right of individual application (Article 34 ECHR) contracting parties gave up control over the cases that can be brought to Strasbourg against them, yet they accept the outcome of proceedings as formally binding (Article 46 ECHR); and, finally, by adjudicating fundamental rights disputes, the Court directly determines the legal position of individuals vis-à-vis contracting states.[178] It is in this sense that the ECtHR exercises supranational authority and has rightly been termed a *supranational* Court.[179]

3.5 CONCLUSION

This chapter provided an introduction to investigating supranational aspects of the ECHR by tracing the ECtHR's evolution from an international into a supranational Court. It revealed that while the establishment of supranational adjudication is primarily the result of Protocol 11 and thus rests on a formal choice and commitment of contracting states, the special nature of the Convention as a human rights treaty, exercised, from the very beginning, a pull toward supranational adjudication. On the one hand, the Court and the Commission distinguished early on the collective protection system under the Convention from interstate and state-controlled adjudication. They conceptualized their task as one of being adjudicators of a community, upholding fundamental rules of the European public order, rather than serving state interests or settling disputes *strictu sensu*. This understanding was equally reflected in the area of interpretation, where the Court, by resorting to innovative and special interpretative tools, assumed increasing autonomy over contracting parties in setting a common European human rights standard. On the other hand, Strasbourg organs and states alike gradually recognized that the logic of

175 Stone Sweet and Brunell, "Trustee Courts," 62ff, 77.

176 *Mamatkulov and Abdurasulovic* v. *Turkey*, § 106 (emphasis added).

177 Chapter 2, Section 2.3.2.

178 Zysset's use of the term supranational to describe the ECtHR suggests that he relies on a similar definition of supranationality, although he seems to add a qualification, making the supranational quality of the ECtHR dependent on direct effect of its judgments (Zysset, *ECHR and Human Rights Theory*, compare pp. 85ff and 112).

179 See Introduction, fn. 6.

human rights *qua* individual rights demanded formal inclusion of the individual in the adjudicative process also at the international level. Moreover, by allowing third-party interventions, the ECtHR acknowledged that it was part of, and impacting, a broader community, whose members had a legitimate interest in entering into a more immediate exchange with Strasbourg. These developments paved the way for reform, including the fundamental one of Protocol 11, and for the formal commitment by contracting states to supranational adjudication.

Largely based on the model of a classical IO, member states of the CoE made sure that the organization would stay on an intergovernmental trajectory and remain respectful of state sovereignty. Yet, a couple of decades after the creation of the CoE, the ECHR, through its enforcement structure, emerged as a site of supranationalization and legal (not political) integration in Strasbourg, leading to "a slow but constant change of the sphere of sovereignty of the modern state" in Europe.[180] While the Strasbourg enforcement system long had a special supranational legitimation in the election of the Court's judges, its matching supranational authority was fully established with the entry into force of Protocol 11. Conceiving of the transformation culminating in Protocol 11 as a process of supranationalization provides the basis for the following chapters and the claim of horizontal and vertical legal integration under the Convention.

180 Ress, "Decisions and Judgments of the ECtHR," 364.

4

Sites of Judicial Integration and Their Transformation

4.1 JUDICIAL INTEGRATION

By adjudicating fundamental rights disputes the ECtHR performs a judicial function that has typically been domestic in nature and contrasts starkly with the settlement of conventional interstate disputes.[1] The Court's compulsory jurisdiction turned the ECHR into legal rights that are directly and unconditionally enforceable in Strasbourg, for every person in the CoE from Vladivostok to Reykjavik.[2] The Court exercises supranational public authority since it directly and autonomously determines, in manifold ways, the international legal relationship between states and the individual seizing the Court (and sometimes even beyond).[3] Lemmens described this integration by way of de-nationalization nicely:

> [T]he Court both creates a space that supersedes the nation, and diminishes the nation's claim of legal power over the citizen. In other words, when a person submits an argument to the Court, he or she in some sense transcends their status as a national to become a European citizen.[4]

[1] Besson, "European Human Rights," fn. 10; Alter, *New Terrain of International Law*, p. 18.

[2] Ress, "Supranationaler Menschenrechtsschutz," 633.

[3] In substance, the assertion of judicial integration appears to be shared by scholars researching the constitutionalization or cosmopolitan character of the ECHR (E.g., Regine Gerards, *Die Europäische Menschenrechtskonvention im Konstitutionalisierungsprozess einer gemeineuropäischen Grundrechtsordnung* [Frankfurt/Main: Peter Lang 2007]; Stone Sweet, "Constitutionalization of the Convention"; Stone Sweet, "Cosmopolitan Legal Order"; Wojciech Sadurski, "Partnering with Strasbourg: Constitutionalisation of the European Court of Human Rights, the Accession of Central and East European States to the Council of Europe, and the Idea of Pilot Judgments" [2009] 9 *Human Rights Law Review* 397–453).

[4] Lemmens, "Criticising or Misunderstanding?," p. 32. The statement can even be qualified as any person under the jurisdiction of a contracting state, regardless of citizenship or nationality, enjoys protection under the Convention and can thus be subjected to the Court's authority. See also Maria Iglesias Vila, "Subsidiarity, Margin of Appreciation and International Adjudication within a Cooperative Conception of Human Rights" (2017) 15 *International Journal of Constitutional Law* 393–413 at 412f.

Referring to integration, of course, should not imply that the ECtHR replaces domestic protection of human rights.[5] IHRL in general and the Convention in particular never aimed at substituting domestic human rights mechanisms – even though their function can get close to that of domestic human rights, especially with respect to states, which lack basic protection. In principle, however, each level performs its own function. This is expressed by the truism that the ECHR supervisory system is only "subsidiary" or – maybe more aptly put – "complementary."[6] Neither does the ECtHR seek to impose uniformity or harmonization of domestic human rights, although this may, to an extent, be the natural byproduct of its lawmaking function.[7] Also, the ECHR system remains sensibly different from more autonomous political, federal, or state-like entities such as the EU. This is what Besson refers to when stressing that subsidiarity in IHRL has a particular meaning that differs from that of subsidiarity in the EU:

> [T]he ECHR is not an autonomous legal system or order. Nor is there an independent polity (e.g., the Council of Europe's) constituted by it. To that extent, the context of human rights subsidiarity is not that of an encompassing legal or political system including different equivalent units albeit at different levels of decision-making. Human rights subsidiarity differs therefore in this fundamental respect from subsidiarity in EU law or in a federal entity or order.[8]

Besson's view is partly based on a note by the Jurisconsult of the Court submitted in the context of the Interlaken follow-up process:

> The concept of subsidiarity is not quite the same in the European Union and in the Convention, a fact which is hardly surprising if we consider the different nature of the two systems. The legal system of the European Union, which has a quasi-State institutional structure and rule-making powers reinforced by the direct effect and precedence of EU law, corresponds to an integration model. Accordingly, subsidiarity in the context of the European treaties implies above all a kind of "competitive subsidiarity," referring to the competing powers of the Union and the Member States. By contrast, as the Convention does not provide for any supranational decision-making powers, the Court's jurisdiction is strictly confined to supervising States' conduct. This is therefore an internationalist approach far removed from the quasi-State model, and the legal system established by the Convention is based on harmonisation. Consequently, subsidiarity in this context is a kind of "complementary subsidiarity": the Court's powers of intervention are confined to those cases where the domestic institutions

5 The ECtHR regularly reiterates that it is not its task to "take the place of domestic authorities." The French wording of that standard formula is even more on point: "*[L]a Cour n'a point pour tâche (. . .) de se substituer aux juridictions nationales*" (among others ECtHR, *Ladet Tromso and Stensaas v. Norway*, no. 21980/93, Grand Chamber Judgment of May 20, 1999, ECHR 1999-III, § 60).

6 Besson, "Subsidiarity," 77.

7 Conclusion, Community Interests, Collective Identity, and the Inalienable Core of Autonomy.

8 Besson, "Subsidiarity," 88.

are incapable of ensuring effective protection of the rights guaranteed by the Convention.[9]

Certainly, the ECHR system cannot be connected to a larger autonomous political unit, and subsidiarity between the Convention level and the domestic legal order may be a question of sequencing rather than competition.[10] Human rights treaties, in general, "unlike a constitution, are not meant to contain all the fundamental principles of a political community; they are not meant to constitute a system of political organization for a particular people."[11] The Court is embedded within the larger structure of the CoE, but the latter is a typical example of an intergovernmental, not a supranational IO and does not aim at political integration.[12] More importantly, the Court is not a formal organ of the CoE but a treaty body tasked to monitor observance of the ECHR. There is therefore no connection or separation of powers between the Court and the Council of Europe regarding a larger political ordering.[13] However, it does not necessarily follow from the complementary nature of the ECHR nor from the absence of a political and state-like structure that the Court does not exercise supranational public authority as explained earlier. Any assertion to the contrary, it is submitted, risks downplaying the role and powers of the ECtHR as well as the impact of Convention law. Partly, the contrasting viewpoints of the present conceptualization compared to the note of the Court's Jurisconsult have terminological reasons. On the one hand, the note appears to rely upon an absolute understanding of supranationality, according to which the latter is exclusive to the EU. On the other hand, the Jurisconsult uses the term integration with a clear political connotation that contrasts with the legal or judicial understanding of the term here. Moreover, it is important to stress that it is not posited that the ECtHR is to be conceptualized as an appellate jurisdiction of a larger integrated judicial system. The claim of horizontal integration is much more modest – namely that the Convention system provides for a complementary layer of public authority that directly operates on individuals alongside that of domestic legal systems.

It is submitted that the supranational authority of the Court can be divided into four distinctive "sites," which are addressed consecutively in this chapter. While they certainly overlap and depend on each other, they will be discussed separately in order to ascertain the areas, scope, and intensity of judicial integration under the Convention. Discussing and disentangling these different sites should also provide insights as to how and why the Court's (judicial) function and powers evolved and

9 ECtHR, "Principle of Subsidiarity" (Interlaken Follow-Up), Note by the Jurisconsult of July 8, 2010, para. 3.

10 Besson, "Subsidiarity," 104.

11 Letsas, "ECHR as a Living Instrument," p. 107.

12 Chapter 3, Section 3.2.2.

13 The ECHR itself delegates of course certain competences to the CoM and the PACE (e.g., Art. 22 ECHR or 46(2) ECHR).

continue to evolve since the establishment of supranational adjudication. The first site of judicial integration concerns the ECtHR's classical function of external judicial review. When seized by an applicant, the Court, insofar as the application is admissible, provides an independent, final, and binding review of whether a state has honored its obligations under the Convention (Section 4.2). The second site of judicial integration concerns remedies. In addition to authoritatively deciding whether or not the Convention has been violated, the Court may occasionally also rule on remedies and determine the legal consequences following an adverse judgment (Section 4.3). The third site discussed is an area in which the Court's role has only recently begun to evolve. While reviewing state compliance with ECtHR judgments has traditionally been placed under the political oversight of the CoM, the Court may under certain circumstances also address this question today (Section 4.4). The fifth and last site discussed in this chapter is the Court's new advisory jurisdiction to deliver preliminary rulings as introduced by Protocol 16 (Section 4.5). Finally, lawmaking by the ECtHR can equally be construed as a site of judicial integration. The breadth and general nature of this topic, however, justify treating it separately in the subsequent chapter.

4.2 EXTERNAL JUDICIAL REVIEW

4.2.1 *The Right to Access the Court: The Fragile Heart of Supranational Adjudication*

4.2.1.1 Locus Standi: Between Individual Grievance and Enforcement of the ECHR

The unconditional right of individual petition is enshrined in Article 34 ECHR and lies at the core of supranational adjudication. It negotiates state sovereignty in a way that empowers individuals to directly seize the Court and enables the latter to decide on the individual's legal position as a result. Free access of individuals to the Court through Article 34 ECHR is the heart of the supranational system; it not only places the individual onto the international level but also provides for a steady docket, which is crucial for establishing supranational authority.[14]

Standing before the ECtHR delimits the scope of access to supranational adjudication.[15] Article 34 ECHR provides that the Court may receive applications from any person, nongovernmental organization, or group of individuals claiming to be the victim of a violation of the Convention or its Protocols. In contrast to

[14] On the resulting "feedback loop" Keller and Stone Sweet, "Impact of the ECHR," p. 689.

[15] The case-law discussed in the following on Art. 34 ECHR builds on the earlier practice of Strasbourg organs (Commission and Court) on former Art. 25 ECHR (right to individual application to the Commission). For a general treatise see Julien Marquis, *La qualité pour agir devant la Cour européenne des droits de l'homme* (Zurich: Schulthess 2017).

interstate cases, a general interest in the observance of the Convention is not sufficient grounds to lodge an individual application. Already the old Court held that the ECHR does not provide for an *actio popularis* for individuals, "it does not permit individuals to complain against a law *in abstracto* simply because they feel that it contravenes the Convention."[16] The individual alleging a violation of the Convention must thus show that he or she has actually been personally affected.[17] This so-called victim requirement, however, is interpreted broadly because protection under the ECHR must be practical and effective,[18] but also because the right to individual application serves to an extent to ensure that Convention violations are not left unsanctioned.[19]

The Court asserted that the notion of victim must be understood autonomously – that is irrespective of whether a person has the capacity to take action in domestic law for instance[20] – and should never be applied in a rigid, mechanical, or inflexible fashion.[21] Victim status does not require actual prejudice[22] and an applicant can also be directly affected by domestic legislation in the absence of a concrete implementing measure by state authorities.[23] Furthermore, the Court grants standing to so-called indirect victims "to whom the violation would cause harm or who would have a valid and personal interest in seeing it brought to an end."[24] Broadening access to indirect victims empowers relatives or next-of-kin to petition Strasbourg where the direct victim has disappeared or deceased for instance.[25] In addition, the Court also recognized close relatives as indirect victims in cases brought under Articles 5, 6, or 8 ECHR to exonerate a late person of any finding of guilt, to protect their own reputation or that of their family or to protect

16 ECtHR, *Klass and Others* v. *Germany*, no. 5029/71, Plenary Judgment of September 6, 1978, Series A no. 28, § 33. Contracting states rejected the idea of the Parliamentary Assembly and the Human Rights Commissioner to introduce an *actio popularis* type of system in the form of a public prosecutor (PACE, Recommendation 1606 (2003), 10 ii and iii; Harmsen, "Reform of the Convention System," fn. 30).

17 *Ireland* v. *the United Kingdom*, §§ 239 and 240.

18 For an overview of the case-law see CoE/ECtHR, "Practical Guide on Admissibility Criteria" (2014), 14ff.

19 Following Mégret, "Private Actor Litigation," 9.

20 ECtHR, *Gorraiz Lizarraga and Others* v. *Spain*, no. 62543/00, Judgment of April 27, 2004, ECHR 2004-III, § 35.

21 ECtHR, *Karner* v. *Austria*, no. 40016/98, Judgment of July 24, 2003, ECHR 200-IX, § 25.

22 Ibid.

23 That is "if he is required either to modify his conduct or risks being prosecuted (. . .) or if he is a member of a class of people who risk being directly affected by the legislation (. . .)" (ECtHR, *Burden* v. *the United Kingdom*, no. 13378/05, Grand Chamber Judgment of April 29, 2008, ECHR 2008-III, § 34; *Case "Relating to certain aspects of the laws on the use of languages in education in Belgium"* v. *Belgium*; *Marckx* v. *Belgium*).

24 ECtHR, *Vallianatos and Others* v. *Greece*, nos. 29381/09 and 32684/09, Grand Chamber Judgment of November 7, 2013, ECHR 2013-VI (extracts), § 47.

25 For a leading case see ECtHR, *Varnava and Others* v. *Turkey*, nos. 16064/90 etc., Grand Chamber Judgment of September 18, 2009, ECHR 2009-V, § 112.

material interests in pecuniary rights.[26] While this practice is fairly limited in scope and requires a personal interest of the indirect victim,[27] it shows the Court's willingness to soften the individualized *locus standi* rule, especially in cases of an overriding and general interest to enforce the Convention considering the gravity of the alleged violations.[28]

Last but not least there is the category of potential victims in Strasbourg. As the name suggests, potential victims have not (yet) suffered a Convention violation but can put forward evidence that such will likely occur.[29] This category goes back to the *Klass* case, in which the applicants alleged that German law allowing for secret surveillance measures was contrary to Article 8 ECHR. As surveillance measures could be ordered and implemented in secret, the applicants were unable to know, let alone claim in Strasbourg, that they were directly affected. Referring to the purpose of the system of individual applications being the efficacious protection of individuals, the Court held that the applicants must nonetheless be treated as victims.[30] The constellation of potential victims stretches the substantive and temporal link between a specific state measure and the persons affected by it.

In certain exceptional circumstances, the Court can forego the victim requirement altogether. It conceded that an application can be lodged in the name and on behalf of a vulnerable person without the latter having issued a valid power of attorney or specific instructions to the person purporting to act for him or her.[31] In the case of *Câmpeanu* decided in 2014, the Grand Chamber further extended this case-law by allowing an NGO to act as a so-called de facto representative.[32] Although exceptional,[33] *Câmpeanu* was ground-breaking. The case concerned a young man of Roma ethnicity who suffered from HIV and severe intellectual disability. He died in the state's care after having been run through different care facilities that failed to provide him with even the most basic mental and physical care.[34] An NGO, which was never mandated by the victim (or anyone else for that matter), brought the case to

26 With further references "Practical Guide on Admissibility Criteria," para. 23.

27 ECtHR, *Sanles Sanles* v. *Spain*, no. 48335/99, Decision of October 26, 2000, ECHR 2000-XI.

28 See the Court's reasoning in *Varnava and Others* v. *Turkey* (§§ 111–113) or *Ressegatti* v. *Switzerland*, no. 17671/02, Judgment of July 13, 2006, § 26.

29 ECtHR, *Senator Lines GmbH* v. *Fifteen Member States of the European Union*, no. 56672/00, Grand Chamber Decision of March 10, 2004, ECHR 2004-IV.

30 *Klass and Others* v. *Germany*, §§ 30–38.

31 This case-law goes back to the Commission and is recapitulated in detail in ECtHR, *Lambert and Others* v. *France*, no. 46043/14, Grand Chamber Judgment of June 5, 2015, 2015-III (extracts), §§ 89–95. Rule 45(3) Rules of Court normally requires that the applicant's representative submits a power of attorney or written authority to act.

32 ECtHR, *Centre for Legal Resources on behalf of Valentin Câmpeanu* v. *Romania*, no. 47848/08, Grand Chamber Judgment of July 17, 2014, ECHR 2014-V.

33 Ibid., § 112.

34 On the merits, the Court found a violation of Art. 2 (under both its substantive and procedural heading) and a violation of Art. 13 in conjunction with Art. 2 ECHR.

Strasbourg.[35] The Romanian government argued that the Court should dismiss the case as an *actio popularis*.[36] The Court, however, recalled *Ireland* v. *the United Kingdom* and its broader role of enforcing ECHR rights.[37] It also stressed that the direct victim was deprived of any means to take care of his interests; initially because he was never appointed a (legal) guardian and later because his state of health had deteriorated leaving him incapable of expressing any instructions. These aspects, combined with the fact that the deceased victim had no next-of-kin, led the Court to conclude that the NGO must be allowed to act as his de facto representative.[38] Initially, *Câmpeanu* seemed to have paved the way for a more pronounced role of NGOs in (de facto) representing (extremely) vulnerable persons, which are not in a position (anymore) to defend their own interests or appoint a representative to that effect.[39] However, the Chamber of the Fifth Section qualified *Câmpeanu* in a subsequent decision in a way that barely leaves it any scope of application.[40] It remains to be seen whether the Grand Chamber will accept such a narrow interpretation of its judgment.[41]

This short purview on the scope of access to the Court under Article 34 ECHR illustrates that, although clearly guided by the idea of individual grievance and rejecting a system of *actio popularis*, the Court has interpreted *locus standi* rules with certain flexibility so as to allow the inclusion of generalized interests.

4.2.1.2 Procedural Subsidiarity

Locus standi is just one of several procedural requirements, which have to be met, for the Court to be competent to exercise judicial review (Articles 1, 34 and 35 ECHR). Respect for those requirements reflects the procedural facet of subsidiarity.[42] It must suffice here to mention the obligation to exhaust (effective)

35 *Câmpeanu* v. *Romania*, §§ 104 and 107.

36 Ibid., § 84.

37 Chapter 3, Section 3.3.1.1.

38 *Câmpeanu* v. *Romania*, §§ 112 and 114.

39 For a subsequent case in which an NGO was granted standing as de facto representative see ECtHR, *Association for the Defence of Human Rights in Romania – Helsinki Committee on Behalf of Ionel Garcea* v. *Romania*, no. 2959/11, Grand Chamber Judgment of March 24, 2015, §§ 39–46.

40 ECtHR, *Bulgarian Helsinki Committee* v. *Bulgaria*, nos. 35653/12 and 66172/12, Decision of June 28, 2016, § 52. In two other decisions, the Chamber of the Third Section refused to allow a non-mandated lawyer to de facto represent disappeared persons, which, however, still had next of kin (ECtHR, *Abdullazhon Mamadzhanovich Isakov* v. *Russia*, no. 52286/14, Decision of July 5, 2016, §§ 36–43; *N. and M.* v. *Russia*, nos. 39496/14 and 39727/14, Decision of April 26, 2016, §§ 56–63).

41 The qualification in *Bulgarian Helsinki Committee* v. *Bulgaria* also appears surprisingly restrictive and formalistic from the viewpoint of the Court's previous case-law on de facto representation through lawyers or other persons (compare fn 31). For a detailed analysis see Helen Keller and Aurore Garin, "Câmpeanu: quo vadis? – Le recours individuel en péril" (2017) 111 *Revue trimestrielle des droits de l'homme* 485–510.

42 Besson, "Subsidiarity," 79f.

domestic remedies. According to Article 35(1) ECHR, the Court may only deal with an application once all domestic remedies have been exhausted. As the Court explained in detail in *Selmouni* v. *France*, this rule embodies the subsidiary or complementary nature of the Court's competence:

> (...) States are dispensed from answering for their acts before an international body before they have had an opportunity to put matters right through their own legal system. That rule is based on the assumption, reflected in Article 13 of the Convention – with which it has close affinity – that there is an effective remedy available in respect of the alleged breach in the domestic system. In this way, it is an important aspect of the principle that the machinery of protection established by the Convention is subsidiary to the national systems safeguarding human rights (...). Thus, the complaint intended to be made subsequently to the Court must first have been made – at least in substance – to the appropriate domestic body, and in compliance with the formal requirements and time-limits laid down in domestic law (...).[43]

National courts must be given the opportunity to determine questions regarding the compatibility of domestic law with the Convention before the Court may engage in review.[44] Yet, procedural subsidiarity in this sense finds its limits in the requirement of effectiveness of domestic human rights protection. The Convention organs always stressed that the exhaustion rule is not an absolute one but must be applied in a flexible way, without excessive formalism.[45] Hence, they established an important qualification of the rule: applicants are only obliged to exhaust those domestic remedies that are accessible, capable of providing redress, and offer reasonable prospects of success.[46] This led to a waiver of the requirement to exhaust domestic remedies in an increasing number of cases and enables the Court to scrutinize the effectiveness of domestic remedies as a result.[47]

4.2.1.3 Article 34 ECHR under Pressure: Overload and Backlash

The preceding discussion should not obscure the fact that the realization of Article 34 ECHR has become increasingly difficult. If the unfettered right of every person in Europe to petition the Court can be described as the supranational heart of the Convention system, it equally is its Achilles heel. It was because of the major judicial effort, efficiency, and innovation that Strasbourg lawyers and judges saved

43 ECtHR, *Selmouni* v. *France*, no. 25803/94, Grand Chamber Judgment of July 28, 1999, Reports 1999-V, § 74.

44 ECtHR, *A, B and C* v. *Ireland*, no. 25579/05, Grand Chamber Judgment of December 16, 2010, ECHR 2000-VI, § 142.

45 ECtHR, *Kozacioğlu* v. *Turkey*, no. 2334/03, Grand Chamber Judgment of February 19, 2009, § 40.

46 ECtHR, *Akdivar and Others* v. *Turkey (former Art. 50)*, no. 21893/93, Grand Chamber Judgment of September 16, 1996, Reports 1998-II, § 68.

47 Besson, "European Human Rights," p. 107.

the Court from literally drowning in a flood of cases.[48] From a practical perspective, admissibility has become an issue of docket control playing a central role in the continuous reform of the Court. Protocol 14, for instance, introduced a new admissibility criterion according to which the Court may declare inadmissible any individual application if it considers that the applicant has not suffered a significant disadvantage (Article 35(3)(b) ECHR).[49] Similarly, Protocol 15 reduces the time limit to submit an application to Strasbourg from six to four months.[50] Meeting the admissibility criteria has become ever more difficult for applicants. Of 40,667 applications disposed of judicially in 2019, the Court declared inadmissible or struck out 38,480 applications.[51] Chances that the Court considers the merits of a case are thus only about 5 percent.

More fundamentally, the (debate on the) reform of the Court has shown that the unconditional right to individual application is not sacrosanct. For a while now, scholars in favor of a constitutional role of the ECtHR have argued that the Court should give up providing individual redress in each and every case and instead only hear cases which are of particular importance to the broader development of Convention law.[52] Access to the Court has, however, also become the target of political resistance. In the negotiations leading up to the Brighton Declaration, the UK government championed the idea of a fundamental circumcision of the right to individual application. It proposed, among other things, to allow the Court to consider only those cases in which either national courts made a clear error in applying Convention rights or which raise a serious interpretative question.[53] The British proposal can be regarded as an attempt at backlash in that it tried to fundamentally change the "rules of the game."[54] Although state parties ultimately rejected the British proposal and reaffirmed their attachment to the unconditional right of individual application as a cornerstone of the system,[55] Brighton and its

48 Much of the reform endeavors in recent years have focused on figuring out how to deal most effectively with inadmissible decisions, hence the introduction through Protocol 14 of single judge formations and Committees of three judges.

49 The provision, however, further qualifies: "(...) unless respect for human rights as defined in the Convention and the Protocols thereto requires an examination of the application on the merits and provided that no case may be rejected on this ground which has not been duly considered by a domestic tribunal." For a critical discussion see Dinah Shelton, "Significantly Disadvantaged? Shrinking Access to the European Court of Human Rights" (2016) 16 *Human Rights Law Review* 303–322.

50 Art. 4 Protocol 15.

51 See the ECtHR statistics of 2019, available at www.echr.coe.int/Documents/Stats_analysis_2019_ENG.pdf (accessed July 23, 2020).

52 Most prominently Luzius Wildhaber, "Rethinking the European Court of Human Rights" in Jonas Christoffersen and Mikael Rask Madsen (eds.), *The European Court of Human Rights between Law and Politics* (Oxford: Oxford University Press 2011), pp. 204ff.

53 Draft Brighton Declaration, para. 23(c).

54 Madsen, Cebulak, and Wiebusch, "Backlash against International Courts," 202f.

55 High Level Conference on the Future of the European Court of Human Rights, Brighton Declaration, April 20, 2012, para. 2. See also High Level Conference on the Implementation of the

follow-up process are a reminder that the right to individual application cannot be taken for granted.

Securing the effectiveness of the right to individual application may also encounter problems on the ground. Access may be seriously hampered when state authorities are exerting pressure on an applicant not to seize the Court.[56] In a number of cases, the Court was confronted with situations where an applicant was threatened, intimidated, or hindered otherwise in freely exercising his or her right to individual application. In response, the Court stressed that Article 34 ECHR guarantees an absolute right and that applicants must "be able to communicate freely with the Court without being subjected to any form of pressure from the authorities," be it "direct coercion and flagrant acts of intimidation" or "other improper indirect acts or contacts designed to dissuade or discourage applicants from using a Convention remedy."[57] If there is undue interference, the Court may find an autonomous violation of Article 34 ECHR, in addition to any eventual violation of the substantive provisions of the Convention.[58]

In brief, there are a number of challenges, both practical and normative, in realizing or safeguarding the effectiveness of the right enshrined in Article 34 ECHR. Figuratively speaking, the heart of the supranational system thus remains fragile.

4.2.2 *Binding Force of the Court's Rulings*

4.2.2.1 Article 46(1) ECHR: Binding Outcome of Judicial Review

In addition to individual access, an important tenant of supranational adjudication is that the outcome of the Court's judicial review is formally binding. It is what distinguishes the Court from the quasi-judicial procedures present in IHRL and constitutes the formal aspect of its autonomy vis-à-vis contracting states.[59] Under the heading "binding force," Article 46 ECHR states that the contracting parties undertake to abide by the final judgment of the Court in any case to which they are parties. The ECHR establishes a special regime of responsibility for invoking but also determining breaches of the Convention. When rendering a judgment, the Court decides – or declares, to use its own terms – with obligatory legal force whether or not the respondent state has breached the applicant's rights under the Convention.[60]

European Convention on Human Rights, Our Shared Responsibility, Brussels Declaration, March 27, 2015, para. 1.

56 Mégret, "Private Actor Litigation," 6.

57 ECtHR, *Klyakhin* v. *Russia*, no. 46082/99, Judgment of November 30, 2004, § 119.

58 E.g., ECtHR, *Kornakovs* v. *Latvia*, no. 61005/00, Judgment of June 15, 2006, §§ 163–167.

59 Compare, for instance, the "views" rendered by the UN Human Rights Committee pursuant to Art. 5(4) of the Optional Protocol to the ICCPR.

60 In so far as the judgment has become final (Arts. 42 and 44 ECHR).

In adjudicative terms, Article 46(1) ECHR embodies the principle of *res judicata inter partes.*[61] Formally, this means that contracting parties undertake to accept the outcome of the determination by the Court as final and definitive,[62] while in a substantive sense, they are to accept the content of the Court's finding as the truth.[63] The *res judicata* effect is limited in three ways. *Ratione personae*, it is limited *inter partes*, to the parties in the case. The wording of Article 46(1) ECHR may be misleading in this regard as it only refers to states, but the binding legal force also applies to the applicant.[64] He or she cannot bring the same case a second time to Strasbourg for instance.[65] *Ratione temporis*, the authority of the *res judicata* is limited to all legal and factual elements as they stood and were known before the delivery of the judgment.[66] *Ratione materiae*, the *res judicata* effect is limited to the matter in dispute and the operative provisions of the judgment.[67] The Court's reasoning, however, remains important to understand and contextualize the operative provisions. In fact, the Court insisted more broadly that Article 46(1) ECHR obliges the respondent state to abide by both the "conclusions and spirit" of a judgment.[68]

Whereas Article 46(1) ECHR only refers to "judgments," the Court's decisions on (in)admissibility are equally vested with binding force. Moreover, there are two additional areas (discussed subsequently) to which the Court extended its decision-making power. To secure its task of judicial review, the Court may adopt binding interim measures as well as requests for cooperation.

[61] Elisabeth Lambert-Abdelgawad, *The Execution of Judgments of the European Court of Human Rights*, 2nd ed. (Strasbourg: Council of Europe Publishing 2008), p. 7. Art. 46(1) ECHR is therefore also a reminder of the principle of *pacta sunt servanda* (Schabas, *ECHR: A Commentary*, p. 867).

[62] In this context, French or German speaking scholars often speak, in analogy to domestic law, of formal legal force (*force de la chose jugée* and *formelle Rechtsfkraft* respectively) (Xavier-Baptiste Ruedin, *Exécution des arrêts de la Cour européenne des droits de l'homme: procédure, obligations des Etats, pratique et réforme* [Basel: Helbing Lichtenhahn 2009], p. 98; Marten Breuer, "Artikel 46" in Ulrich Karpenstein and Franz C. Mayer (eds.), *EMRK Konvention zum Schutz der Menschenrechte und Grundfreiheiten Kommentar*, 2nd ed. [Munich: C. H. Beck 2015], n. 31).

[63] With regard to former Art. 53 ECHR the Commission held: "Cette disposition consacre l'effet relative de la chose jugeée à l'égard des seuls arrêts de la Cour europeéenne des Droits de l'Homme" (ECommHR, *X* v. *Switzerland*, nos. 8778/79 etc., Decision of July 8, 1980, DR 20 240, 241). Ruedin, *Exécution des arrêts*, pp. 107f.

[64] Breuer, "Artikel 46," p. 31.

[65] See Art. 35(2)(b) ECHR.

[66] Ruedin, *Exécution des arrêts*, pp. 119ff. According to Rule 80 Rules of Court a party may, in the event of the discovery of a fact which might by its nature have a decisive influence and which, when a judgment was delivered, was unknown to the Court and could not reasonably have been known to that party, request the Court, within a period of six months after that party acquired knowledge of the fact, to revise that judgment.

[67] Ruedin, *Exécution des arrêts*, pp. 110–119.

[68] ECtHR, *Emre* v. *Switzerland (No. 2)*, no. 5056/10, Judgment of October 11, 2011, §§ 68 and 75.

4.2.2.2 Interim Relief

The Court may, *pendis litis*, order interim measures based on Rule 39 Rules of Court. Rule 39 is interesting for present purposes for several reasons. It extends the scope of the Court's supranational authority in a temporal sense to the pre-judgment/decision phase, broadens access of individuals to the Court, and expands the Court's autonomous decision-making power over states and individuals.

Interim measures are a powerful tool to directly place individuals – usually the applicant – under immediate international protection and prevent harm that would not be reparable by a decision on the merits.[69] Interim measures thus secure that judicial review by the Court remains meaningful and is not frustrated through acts or omissions during the proceedings. The Court regularly reiterates that interim measures are only applied "in limited spheres"[70] or "in truly exceptional cases."[71] In other words, they require, in order to be granted, a situation of urgency in both a temporal and substantive sense. Yet, interim measures have been issued with respect to alleged violations under a number of different Convention provisions (e.g., Articles 2, 3, 5, 6, 8, 10 ECHR or 1 Protocol 1), including but not only limited to situations of risks for life and limb.[72] Addressees of interim measures are usually states and Rule 39 thus extends the Court's decision-making power to demanding specific action from the respondent government pending litigation. Interim measures may require state authorities to abstain from deportation or eviction, provide adequate medical treatment, transfer a detainee to a medical institution, or grant him or her access to a lawyer.[73] Exceptionally, the Court may also impose interim measures on the applicant.[74]

The Court endowed interim measures over time and through its case-law with obligatory force.[75] As part of the broader trend toward individualization and judicialization, interim measures were formally introduced in 1974 in the Commission's Rules of Procedure.[76] However, already before a formal legal basis existed, the

69 Interim measures have therefore been described as a procedural weapon in the arsenal of the adjudicator (Sandy Ghandhi, "The Human Rights Committee and Interim Measures of Relief" (2007) 13 *Canterbury Law Review* 203–226 at 203).

70 *Mamatkulov and Askarov* v. *Turkey*, nos. 46827/99 and 46951/99, Grand Chamber Judgment of February 4, 2005, ECHR 2005-I, § 104.

71 ECtHR, *Savriddin Dzhurayev* v. *Russia*, no. 71386/10, Judgment of April 25, 2013, ECHR 2013-III (extracts), § 213.

72 For a detailed account on the Court's practice and further references see Helen Keller and Cedric Marti, "Interim Relief Compared: Use of Interim Measures by the UN Human Rights Committee and the European Court of Human Rights" (2013) 73 *Heidelberg Journal of International Law* 325–372 at 346–360.

73 Keller and Marti, "Interim Measures," pp. 343f.

74 ECommHR, *Bhuyian* v. *Sweden*, no. 26516/95, Plenary Decision of September 14, 1995.

75 On this development, among many, Alastair Mowbray, "A New Strasbourg Approach to the Legal Consequences of Interim Measures" (2005) 5 *Human Rights Law Review* 377–386.

76 Rule 36 of the Rules of Procedure of the ECommHR 1974.

Commission was asking respondent Governments to stay the execution of measures, which would render the application pending before it devoid of purpose.[77] Under the pre-Protocol 11 system, the Court maintained that Convention organs lacked the authority to "order" interim measures that are binding on the parties.[78] It was the new (supranational) Court that took a different position on the issue and departed from earlier Strasbourg case-law. In the case of *Mamatkulov and Askarov* v. *Turkey* the Grand Chamber upheld a Chamber judgment of the First Section according to which a failure to comply with interim measures resulted in a breach of Article 34 ECHR:

> a failure by a Contracting State to comply with interim measures is to be regarded as preventing the Court from effectively examining the applicant's complaint and as hindering the effective exercise of his or her right of [individual application] and, accordingly, as a violation of Article 34.[79]

Whereas the Court primarily derives the binding effect of interim measures from Article 34 ECHR, it also referred to Article 46 ECHR. It stressed that "the effects of the indication of an interim measure to a Contracting State (. . .) must be examined in the light of the obligations which are imposed on the Contracting States by Articles 1 (. . .) and 46 of the Convention."[80] Both the right to individual application and the binding force of judgments would be frustrated, if interim measures could be disregarded. Interestingly, the supranationalization of the enforcement system[81] figured prominently in the Court's reasoning:

> [T]he Court would stress that although the Convention right to individual application was originally intended as an optional part of the system of protection, it has over the years become of high importance and is now a key component of the machinery for protecting the rights and freedoms set forth in the Convention. Under the system in force until 1 November 1998, the Commission only had jurisdiction to hear individual applications if the Contracting Party issued a formal declaration recognising its competence, which it could do for a fixed period. The system of protection as it now operates has, in that regard, been modified by Protocol No. 11, and the right of individual application is no longer dependent on a declaration by the Contracting States. Thus, individuals now enjoy at the international level a real right of action to assert the rights and freedoms to which they are directly entitled under the Convention.[82]

[77] For example, ECommHR, *Denmark, Norway, Sweden and the Netherlands* v. *Greece*, nos. 3321/67 etc., Report of November 5, 1969, Yearbook 12.

[78] ECtHR, *Cruz Varas and Others* v. *Sweden*, no. 15576/89, Judgment of March 20, 1991, Series A no. 201, §§ 94–105.

[79] *Mamatkulov and Askarov* v. *Turkey*, §§ 125 and 128.

[80] Ibid., § 126.

[81] Chapter 3, Sections 3.3 and 3.4.

[82] *Mamatkulov and Askarov* v. *Turkey*, § 122.

The Grand Chamber copy-pasted this entire paragraph from the Chamber judgment, replacing only the term "supranational" with "international" in the last sentence.[83] Admittedly, the Court had other important reasons to reach the finding that its Rule 39 orders were binding, such as evolving international legal practice for instance. By then, the ICJ, the IACtHR, and even the UN human rights treaty bodies had already established the binding effect of interim measures.[84] Nonetheless, the Chamber and Grand Chamber regarded the power to order binding interim relief to be a consequence of supranational adjudication. Contracting parties later expressly accepted this position in the Follow-up Plan to the Izmir Declaration, in which they emphasized the duty to comply with interim measures.[85]

4.2.2.3 Cooperation and Assistance

Cooperation is another area in which the Court enjoys autonomy to take binding decisions on states and individuals.[86] Because of the subsidiary nature of its review, the Court usually pays deference to the domestic level as regards factual questions.[87] The Court remains, however, formally responsible to establish the facts of a case and may deem it necessary to gather additional evidence or take investigative measures. Cooperation and assistance of the parties are crucial to ensure the Court access to relevant sources, documents, and information. Similar to interim measures, the Court's powers in the area of cooperation are judge-made rather than the result of an express conferral by contracting parties. The Court's stance on cooperation became noticeably more assertive following the enlargement of the CoE. Confronted with more serious failures to protect human rights at the domestic level, the Court's role in respect of the new contracting states resembled that of a first instance court, which had to establish and investigate the facts.[88]

83 Compare Chapter 3, Section 4.3.
84 *Mamatkulov and Askarov* v. *Turkey*, §§ 40–53, 113–117.
85 Izmir Declaration, Follow-up Plan, Section A., para. 3; see also CDDH, Report on interim measures under Rule 39 Rules of Court, CDDH(2013)R77 Addendum III, para. 2.
86 Apart from ECHR commentaries, there is surprisingly little literature on cooperation. For an exception see Helena De Vylder and Yves Haeck, "The Duty of Cooperation of the Respondent State during the Proceedings before the European Court of Human Rights" in Eva Brems and Yves Haeck (eds.), *Human Rights and Civil Liberties in the 21st Century* (Berlin/Heidelberg: Springer 2014), pp. 37–67; Olga Chernishova and Nina Vajic, "The Court's Evolving Response to the States' Failure to Cooperate" in D. Spielmann (ed.), *The European Convention on Human Rights: A Living and Dynamic Instrument – Liber Amicorum in Honour of Judge Rozakis* (Brussels: Bruylant 2011), pp. 47–79.
87 See subsequently Section 4.2.3.
88 Empirical research suggests that the lack of cooperation by states is a more recent problem of the Convention system. It was only after 1999 that the number of violations of Art. 38 ECHR had significantly increased, in large part due to either Turkish, Russian or (other) Eastern European cases pertaining to allegations of grave human rights violations (e.g., Arts 2 and 3 ECHR) (De Vylder

The Court grounds states' duty to cooperate in Article 38 ECHR,[89] although this provision deals primarily with the examination of a case and refers to assistance by states rather than cooperation.[90] Reflecting Strasbourg case-law, the Court codified in its Rules of Court a more explicit duty of both the parties to a case as well as other contracting states to cooperate "fully in the conduct of the proceedings" and take any action "the Court considers necessary for the proper administration of justice."[91] On this basis, the ECtHR can adopt a wide range of evidentiary requests and instructions, including the production of documents or witness statements.[92] The Court asserted that its requests for cooperation are immediately binding "from the moment such a request has been formulated, whether it be on initial communication of an application to the Government or at a subsequent stage in the proceedings."[93] Moreover, because Protocol 14 encouraged the Court to take joint decisions on the admissibility and merits of an application, states must cooperate already before a decision on admissibility has been taken.[94]

Any contracting state requested to cooperate must act in due diligence[95] and within the time limits provided by the Court.[96] Partial or non-performance entails a violation of Article 38 ECHR.[97] If governments invoke confidentiality or security considerations to justify failure to cooperate, the Court reviews whether there are indeed "reasonable and solid grounds for treating the documents in question as secret or confidential."[98] Even if the answer is positive, the Court further examines whether the government has taken all possible measures, such as redacting documents, for instance, that would still allow them to comply with the Court's request.[99]

and Haeck, "Duty of Cooperation," pp. 43ff). See also PACE, Resolution 1571(2007); Recommendation 1809(2007); CoM, Resolution DH (2006)45.

89 For example, ECtHR, *Damir Sibgatullin* v. *Russia*, no. 1413/05, Judgment of April 24, 2012, § 67.

90 Art. 38 ECHR goes back to Art. 28(1)(a) of the 1950 Convention. Entitled "examination of the case" Art. 38 ECHR provides that the Court shall examine the case together with the representatives of the parties and, if need be, undertake an investigation, for the effective conduct of which the contracting party concerned shall furnish all necessary facilities.

91 Rule 44A Rules of Court.

92 For example, ECtHR, *Tigran Ayrapetyan* v. *Russia*, no. 75472/01, Judgment of September 16, 2010, § 63.

93 ECtHR, *Janowiec and Others* v. *Russia*, nos. 55508/07 and 29520/09, Grand Chamber Judgment of October 21, 2013, ECHR 2013-V, § 203.

94 Explanatory Report Protocol 14, paras. 73 and 90.

95 ECtHR, *Tahsin Acar* v. *Turkey*, no. 26307/95, Grand Chamber Judgment of April 8, 2004, § 255.

96 ECtHR, *Enukidze and Girgvliani* v. *Georgia*, no. 25091/07, Judgment of April 26, 2011, § 297.

97 *Damir Sibgatullin* v. *Russia*, § 67; *Bekirski* v. *Bulgaria*, no. 71420/01, Judgment of September 2, 2010, § 115.

98 *Janowiec and Others* v. *Russia*, § 206 with reference to *Nolan and K.* v. *Russia*, no. 2512/04, Judgment of February 12, 2009, § 56.

99 Ibid. Also, the Court has pointed to the fact that legitimate national security concerns may be accommodated in Strasbourg proceedings (by restricting access to the document in question under Rule 33 Rules of Court or, *in extremis*, by holding a hearing behind closed doors) (*Janowiec and Others* v. *Russia*, § 215).

Article 38 ECHR is also closely linked to Article 34 ECHR.[100] It is in fact the "corollary" of the undertaking not to hinder the effective exercise of the right of individual application.[101] The obligation to cooperate seeks to prevent frustration of the right to individual application in situations, in which it would be impossible for the applicant to bring forward proof because only state authorities have access to information capable of corroborating or refuting his or her allegations:[102]

> Indeed, the effective exercise of this right may be thwarted by a Contracting Party's failure to assist the Court in conducting an examination of all circumstances relating to the case, including in particular by not producing evidence which the Court considers crucial for its task. Both provisions work together to guarantee the efficient conduct of the judicial proceedings and they relate to matters of procedure rather than to the merits of the applicants' grievances under the substantive provisions of the Convention or its Protocols.[103]

For this reason, failure to comply with evidentiary requests may not only violate Article 38 ECHR but can also soften the standard of evidence applied by the Court in favor of the applicant.[104] In *Janowiec and Others* v. *Russia*, the Court further confirmed that Article 38 ECHR, like Article 34 ECHR, contains a free-standing procedural obligation of states, which can be breached irrespectively of whether the Court finds a violation of any substantive right(s) guaranteed in the Convention.[105]

The obligation to cooperate also applies to the applicant and their representative. Unlike for states, of course, as far as the applicant is concerned, the Court cannot sanction a failure to cooperate by finding a violation of the Convention. However, according to the Rules of Court, it may draw "such inferences as it deems appropriate,"[106] which may go as far as striking out an application pursuant to Article 37 ECHR. The Court has done so, for instance, after an applicant failed to produce a medical report[107] or undergo a medical examination.[108] As the peculiar case of *Gross* v. *Switzerland* shows, a lack of cooperation may even constitute an abuse of the right of application within the meaning of Article 35(3)(a) ECHR. In this case concerning euthanasia, the Swiss applicant had deceased while her case was pending at the Court. Communicating with her counsel only through an intermediate, Mrs. Gross made sure that, in case of her death, the former would

100 De Vylder and Haeck consider the relationship to be one of *lex specialis* (Art. 38 ECHR) and *lex generalis* (Art. 34 ECHR) (De Vylder and Haeck, "Duty of Cooperation," p. 39). See also ECtHR, *Al Nashiri* v. *Poland*, no. 28761/11, Judgment of July 24, 2014, §§ 365ff.

101 *Janowiec and Others* v. *Russia*, § 209.

102 Ibid., § 254.

103 Ibid.

104 *Janowiec and Others* v. *Russia*, § 254; *Tahsin Acar* v. *Turkey*, § 253.

105 *Janowiec and Others* v. *Russia*, § 209 *in fine*. As indicated by the Court, this finding is in line with the Court's existing practice under Art. 34 ECHR.

106 Rule 44C(1) Rules of Court.

107 ECtHR, *Hun* v. *Turkey*, no. 5142/04, Judgment of November 10, 2005.

108 ECtHR, *Mürüvvet Küçük* v. *Turkey*, no. 21784/04, Judgment of November 10, 2005.

not be informed and, consequently, that proceedings in Strasbourg would not be discontinued. When the information about her death got public, the case had already reached the Grand Chamber. Referring, *inter alia*, to the applicant's duty to cooperate (Rule 44A Rules of Court) and divulge relevant information of their own motion (Rule 47(7) Rules of Court), the Grand Chamber concluded that the late applicant had intentionally misled the Court.[109]

In addition to producing evidence, parties must also assist the Court when it takes investigative measures itself.[110] For onsite visits by the Court, for example, Rule A2 Annex Rules of Court requires the state concerned to extend to the Court's delegation the facilities and cooperation necessary for the proper conduct of the proceedings including freedom of movement within the territory and provide for adequate security arrangements for the delegation, the applicant and all witnesses. Assistance in this sense is equally covered by Article 38 ECHR[111] and the Court found a violation of the same when, for instance, members of the Court were denied access to a detained applicant,[112] or a contracting state failed to identify or summon police officers in order for them to appear during a fact-finding mission.[113]

Rule A5(4) Annex Rules of Court and Rule 37(2) Rules of Court further state that the contracting state in whose territory a witness resides must service any summons. The Court's reach through investigative measures over individuals other than the applicant, such as witnesses or experts, is thus fairly limited. In this constellation, the Court relies on traditional mediation through states.[114]

4.2.3 *Scope of Review*

4.2.3.1 Nature of Review

The primary purpose of the protection system under the Convention is to provide external and complementary judicial review. Insofar as it declares an application admissible, the Court's task is to review whether a state has violated the Convention. Pursuant to Article 19 ECHR the Court ensures the observance of the engagements undertaken by contracting parties in the Convention and the

109 ECtHR, *Gross* v. *Switzerland*, no. 67810/10, Grand Chamber Judgment of September 30, 2014, ECHR 2014-IV, §§ 33 and 36 in particular.

110 Paragraph 1 of Rule A2 Annex Rules of Court reads: The applicant and any Contracting Party concerned shall assist the Court as necessary in implementing any investigative measures.

111 Rule A2 Annex Rules of Court as well as Art. 38 ECHR refer to "necessary facilities".

112 ECtHR, *Shamayev and Others* v. *Georgia and Russia*, no. 36378/02, Judgment of April 12, 2005, ECHR 2005-III, §§ 509 and 511 in particular.

113 ECtHR, *Süheyla Aydin* v. *Turkey*, no. 25660/94, Judgment of May 24, 2005, §§ 137–143.

114 Schabas, *ECHR: A Commentary*, p. 809. In contrast, the supranational authority of international criminal tribunals is much more pronounced in this respect (Marti, "Supranationality Beyond the EU?," pp. 31f.).

protocols thereto. As the Court held in the *Belgian Linguistic case*, it "cannot assume the role of the competent national authorities, for it would thereby lose sight of the subsidiary nature of the international machinery of collective enforcement established by the Convention."[115] The Court's role is limited to reviewing the conformity of state measures with the requirements of the Convention and its Protocols.[116]

At the same time, the judicial review exercised by the ECtHR is sensibly different from adjudicating matters pertaining to interstate relations. Judicial review under the Convention, albeit providing for an external or complementary control, is – in terms of both objects and subjects – similar to domestic (human rights) adjudication.[117] In both instances, the conformity of acts or omissions of domestic authorities is checked against the requirements of fundamental rights. Proportionality analysis by the Court, for instance, prompted analogies to national (constitutional) judicial review.[118] This overlap pertains to the essence of judicial integration. It is why the relationship between domestic courts and Strasbourg is complex and the question of how the two levels relate to each other became a pressing issue.[119] As Cassese noted:

> Whenever different legal systems integrate and lose their exclusivity – no matter what kind of integration occurs –, they assume a set of common general principles and are endowed with a reviewing court; indirect rule is instrumental to avoid collisions (. . .).[120]

As in many other systems,[121] the subsidiarity principle emerged as such indirect rule.[122] Of course, there are competing normative understandings of the principle of subsidiarity, especially among scholars. For instance, a fundamental point of dispute is what, if any, type of control the Court should exercise toward the

115 *Case "Relating to certain aspects of the laws on the use of languages in education in Belgium"* v. *Belgium*, § 10; see also ECtHR, *Schenk* v. *Switzerland*, no. 10862/84, Judgment of July 12, 1988, Series A no. 140, § 45.

116 Ibid.

117 Andreas von Staden, "The Democratic Legitimacy of Judicial Review beyond the State: Normative Subsidiarity and Judicial Standards of Review" (2012) 10 *International Journal of Constitutional Law* 1023–1049 at 1027.

118 Stone Sweet, "Constitutionalization of the Convention," 5f.

119 This has led some to apply the (domestic) notion of separation of powers to the relationship between the Court and the domestic level (Staden, "Democratic Legitimacy").

120 Sabino Cassese, "Ruling Indirectly: Judicial Subsidiarity in the ECtHR" (2015) *Paper prepared for the Seminar to mark the official Opening of the judicial year of the European Court of Human Rights*, www.echr.coe.int/Documents/Speech_20150130_Seminar_Cassese_ENG.pdf (accessed July 23, 2020).

121 The paradigmatic example here is EU law. Instead of many see Gráinne de Búrca, *Reappraising Subsidiarity's Significance After Amsterdam* (Cambridge MA: Harvard Law School 1999).

122 ECtHR, "Subsidiarity: A Two-Sided Coin?" (*Paper prepared for the Seminar to mark the Opening of the Judicial Year of the ECtHR* 2015) 4 www.echr.coe.int/Documents/Seminar_background_paper_2015_ENG.pdf (accessed July 23, 2020).

domestic legislator.[123] In the recent past, the scholarly debate has often focused on concerns of democratic legitimacy. For as the ECtHR exercises broad supranational authority, the need for "a genuine mode of justification that lives up to basic tenets of democratic theory"[124] was felt to be particularly acute. Staden argued, for instance, that the democratic legitimacy of the allocation of competences cannot (anymore) be tied solely to the initial delegation and act of ratification but must be complemented through a democratically informed standard of review in practice.[125]

Subsidiarity, therefore, is not an antitheses to the Court's supranational authority. On the contrary, its emergence is testament to judicial integration as it serves to coordinate and allocate overlapping levels of public authority. Subsidiarity, as put by Carozza in reference to de Búrca, "functions as a conceptual and rhetorical mediator between supranational harmonization and unity, on the one hand, and local pluralism and difference, on the other."[126]

4.2.3.2 Standard of Review: Proportionality, Subsidiarity, and Margin of Appreciation

The Court has always demonstrated awareness about the particular nature of its review and developed different doctrinal tools in its case-law, which specifically aim at negotiating as well as legitimizing its supranational authority. The standard of review applied by the ECtHR in assessing whether a respondent state has lived up to its engagements under the Convention is very much context-specific and depends on a number of factors.

Most ECHR rights are not absolute in that state interference may be justified in certain situations. The classical freedoms enshrined in Articles 8–11 ECHR each contain a limitation clause according to which they can be restricted, if prescribed by law and necessary in order to achieve certain specific and legitimate public interests.[127] In assessing whether a measure is necessary, the Court resorts, *inter*

[123] On whether or to what extent review by the Court is anti-majoritarian and must protect minorities neglected in the domestic political process compare e.g., Besson, "Subsidiarity" and Eyal Benvenisti, "Margin of Appreciation, Consensus and Universal Standards" (1999) 31 *International Law and Politics* 843–854.

[124] Bogdandy and Venzke, *In Whose Name?*, p. 8.

[125] Staden, "Democratic Legitimacy," 1026.

[126] Paolo G. Carozza, "Subsidiarity as a Structural Principle of International Human Rights Law" (2003) 97 *American Journal of International Law* 38–79 at 40.

[127] Art. 8(2) ECHR, for instance, reads: There shall be no interference by a public authority with the exercise of this right except such as is in accordance with the law and is necessary in a democratic society in the interests of national security, public safety or the economic well-being of the country, for the prevention of disorder or crime, for the protection of health or morals, or for the protection of the rights and freedoms of others. For a general account see Steven Greer, *The Exceptions to Articles 8 to 11 of the European Convention on Human Rights* (Strasbourg: Council of Europe Publishing 1997).

alia, to a proportionality analysis, looking at whether there is a "pressing social need" for the interference, whether the interference is proportionate to the legitimate aim pursued and whether the national authorities give justificatory reasons that are "relevant and sufficient."[128] Proportionality analysis also extends beyond the express limitation clauses of Articles 8–11 ECHR. The Court uses it in the context of implicit limitations to procedural guarantees, like for Article 6 ECHR,[129] or to assess whether derogative measures in times of emergency are "strictly required" (Article 15 ECHR).[130] The Court famously held that finding a fair balance "between the general interest of the community and the interests of the individual" is a search for balance which is inherent in the whole of the Convention.[131]

Adopting proportionality analysis was a domestically proven way for the Court to scrutinize state interferences with individual rights, balance competing public interests, and subject state action to its supranational control.[132] However, it also provided a decision-making framework to which the Court has to adhere to. Proportionality analysis has the quality of a meta-principle of judicial governance.[133] It makes sure that the Court provides reasons and renders its deliberative processes transparent.[134] In short, proportionality analysis performs an important dual function: it is "tailor-made for the adjudication of qualified rights in a pluralist setting, and it is the crucial mechanism of coordination (...)."[135]

Under the heading of what was coined substantive or normative subsidiarity,[136] the Court further adopted a pragmatic and flexible approach regarding the intensity of its review, looking to strike a balance between meaningful and independent supranational review on the one hand, and deference to domestic authorities on the other.[137] Depending on the specific circumstances at hand, the Court's intensity

[128] ECtHR, *Sunday Times* v. *the United Kingdom (No. 1)*, no. 6538/74, Plenary Judgment of April 26, 1979, Series A no. 30, § 62; *Handyside* v. *the United Kingdom*, no. 5493/72, Plenary Judgment of December 7, 1976, Series A no. 24, § 58.

[129] E.g., ECtHR, *Ashingdane* v. *the United Kingdom*, no. 8225/78, Judgment of May 28, 1985, Series A no. 93, § 57.

[130] ECtHR, *A. and Others* v. *the United Kingdom*, no. 3455/05, Grand Chamber Judgment of February 19, 2009, § 182.

[131] ECtHR, *Cossey* v. *the United Kingdom*, no. 10843/84, Plenary Judgment of September 27, 1990, Series A no. 184, § 37.

[132] For a critical account see Janneke Gerards, "How to Improve the Necessity Test of the European Court of Human Rights" (2013) 11 *International Journal of Constitutional Law* 466–490 at 467f.

[133] Alec Stone Sweet and Jud Mathews, "Proportionality Balancing and Global Constitutionalism" (2008) 47 *Columbia Journal of Transnational Law* 72–164 at 112.

[134] Stone Sweet and Brunell, "Trustee Courts," 69. Admittedly, different scholars have stressed that in terms of transparency and predictability, there is room for improvement in the way the Court deploys its proportionality analysis (for example Gerards, "Improve the Necessity Test," 466).

[135] Stone Sweet, "Cosmopolitan Legal Order," 74.

[136] ECtHR, "Subsidiarity: A Two-sided Coin?," 6f.

[137] Helfer, "Redesigning the ECtHR," 138. For an early example, *Case "Relating to certain aspects of the laws on the use of languages in education in Belgium"* v. *Belgium*, § 10.

of review operates on a sliding scale from stringent review such as "strict scrutiny," for instance, under rights such as Articles 2 or 3 ECHR,[138] to a more deferential control in respect of rights that require balancing.[139] In particular, the Court developed two doctrines through which it frames deference. The first so-called fourth instance rule applies in the judicial context[140] and provides that it is not the Court's "function to deal with errors of fact or law allegedly committed by a national court."[141] The Court often relies on the fourth instance rule in the context of Article 6 ECHR, restricting itself to challenging factual findings of domestic courts only if they are manifestly arbitrary.[142] Even in the context of Article 3 ECHR, however, the Court has stressed that "in normal circumstances it requires cogent elements to lead it to depart from the findings of fact reached by [domestic] courts."[143] Regarding the application of domestic law, the Court usually only intervenes when domestic courts apply domestic law "manifestly arbitrary or erroneous."[144]

The second tool of deference is the margin of appreciation doctrine, which allows for pluralism in the domestic implementation of Convention rights.[145] In *Handyside* v. *the United Kingdom*, the Court famously recognized that domestic authorities – whether legislative, executive or judicial – may, in principle, "by reason of their direct and continuous contact with the vital forces of their countries (…) be in a better position than the international judge" to interpret and apply the ECHR.[146]

138 For example, ECtHR, *Pretty* v. *the United Kingdom*, no. 2346/02, Judgment of April 29, 2002, ECHR 2002-III, § 37; *Iwanczuk* v. *Poland*, no. 25196/94, Judgment of November 15, 2001, § 53.

139 For instance, ECtHR, *Pla and Puncernau* v. *Andorra*, no. 69498/01, Judgment of July 13, 2004, ECHR 2004-VIII, § 46.

140 Yuval Shany, "Toward a General Margin of Appreciation Doctrine in International Law?" (2005) 16 *European Journal of International Law* 907–940 at 909f.

141 ECtHR, *García Ruiz* v. *Spain*, no. 30544/96, Grand Chamber Judgment of January 21, 1999, ECHR 1999-I, § 28. On the fourth instance rule see CoE/ECtHR, Practical Guide on Admissibility, paras. 381–388.

142 ECtHR, *Sisojeva and Others* v. *Latvia*, no. 60654/00, Judgment of Grand Chamber of January 15, 2007, § 89.

143 ECtHR, *Matko* v. *Slovenia*, no. 43393/98, Judgment of November 2, 2006, § 100.

144 ECtHR, *Pavlović and Others* v. *Croatia*, no. 13274/11, Judgment of April 2, 2015, § 44.

145 Literature on this doctrine is abundant. See, among many others, Eva Brems, "The Margin of Appreciation Doctrine in the Case-Law of the European Court of Human Rights" (1996) 56 *Heidelberg Journal of International Law* 230–314 at 240; Benvenisti, "Margin of Appreciation," 843ff; Steven Greer, *The Margin of Appreciation: Interpretation and Discretion Under the European Convention on Human Rights* (Strasbourg: Council of Europe Publishing 2000); George Letsas, "Two Concepts of the Margin of Appreciation" (2006) 26 *Oxford Journal of Legal Studies* 705–732; Yutaka Arai-Takahashi, *The Margin of Appreciation Doctrine and the Principle of Proportionality in the Jurisprudence of the ECHR* (Cambridge: Intersentia 2002); Janneke Gerards, "Pluralism, Deference and the Margin of Appreciation Doctrine" (2011) 17 *European Law Journal* 80–120; Jan Kratochvil, "The Inflation of the Margin of Appreciation by the European Court of Human Rights" (2011) 29 *Netherlands Quarterly of Human Rights* 324–357; Oddný Mjöll Arnardóttir, "Rethinking the Two Margins of Appreciation" (2016) 12 *European Constitutional Law Review* 27–53.

146 *Handyside* v. *the United Kingdom*, § 48.

As the Court later stressed, part of being "better" positioned also results from the direct democratic legitimation of the domestic level.[147] Determining the precise scope of the margin of appreciation of states has proven difficult, both in abstract as well as in specific cases.[148] There are, however, a number of elements which influence whether states enjoy a wide or narrow margin, or none at all. First, the margin of appreciation doctrine mostly applies in cases of limitations or derogations to human rights that require balancing (Articles 8–11 EHCR, Article 15 ECHR) or where the Convention imposes positive obligations.[149] Regarding absolute rights like Article 3 ECHR or non-discrimination and political rights, the Court only grants a limited if any margin of appreciation.[150] Second, the Court takes into account the quality of the domestic democratic process and the extent to which national authorities applied and considered Convention law.[151] Third, the Court resorts to the comparative law concept of European consensus to ascertain the margin of appreciation: where there is no "European consensus" and reasonable disagreement among contracting states on a specific issue, the margin enjoyed is correspondingly a wide one.[152]

4.2.3.3 Weakening of Review Post-Brighton Declaration?

The operationalization of subsidiarity in the area of review regularly provokes substantial disagreement within the Court, but also among scholars, governments, and politicians.[153] For the Court, applying subsidiarity has therefore, to an extent, always been a question of judicial politics,[154] subjected to general political and

147 ECtHR, *S.A.S.* v. *France*, no. 43835/11, Grand Chamber Judgment of July 1, 2014, ECHR 2014-III, § 129. For a general treatise on this aspect Leach and Donald, Parliaments and the ECHR, pp. 113–154.

148 Kratochvil, "Inflation of the Margin of Appreciation," 325.

149 Greer, *Margin of Appreciation*, pp. 22–33.

150 ECtHR, *Wagner and J.M.W.L.* v. *Luxembourg*, no. 76240/01, Judgment of June 28, 2007, § 96.

151 Matthew Saul, "The European Court of Human Rights' Margin of Appreciation and the Processes of National Parliaments" (2015) 15 *Human Rights Law Review* 745–774; Besson, "Subsidiarity," 81. This has also been refered to as proceduralisation (see fn. 161).

152 Compare e.g., ECtHR, *Leyla Şahin* v. *Turkey*, no. 44774/98, Grand Chamber Judgment of November 10, 2005, ECHR 2005-XI, § 109 with *Bayatyan* v. *Armenia*, no. 23459/03, Grand Chamber Judgment of July 7, 2011, ECHR 2011-IV, § 122f. The literature on the notion of consensus is equally abundant. Instead of many Kanstantsin Dzehtsiarou, *European Consensus and the Legitimacy of the European Court of Human Rights* (Cambridge: Cambridge University Press 2015); Luzius Wildhaber, Arnaldur Hjartarson, and Stephen Donnelly, "No Consensus on Consensus? The Practice of the European Court of Human Rights" (2013) 33 *Human Rights Law Journal* 248–263.

153 Christoffersen therefore rightly noted: "The interaction between the principle of subsidiarity and the standard of protection of the ECHR is perhaps the most important and difficult issue pertaining to contemporary European human rights law, because it touches on the fundamental question of the interaction between national and international authorities" (Christoffersen, *Fair Balance*, pp. 274f).

154 Benvenisti, "Margin of Appreciation," 846.

societal trends as well as constant re-negotiation. There is, however, evidence to suggest that, as of late, increased resistance and criticism have impacted the Court's intensity of review more strongly. In particular, insistence in the Brighton Declaration on subsidiarity – which is now to be codified together with the margin of appreciation in the Preamble of the ECHR[155] – has arguably led the Court to recalibrate its standard and intensity of review.

An early example thereof is *S.A.S.* v. *France*. Relying on a lenient application of the consensus concept and an ambiguous new notion of "living together," the Court afforded France a very wide margin of appreciation in assessing whether a ban to wear face veils in public was proportionate under Articles 8, 9 and 10 ECHR.[156] Empirical studies indeed suggest a trend of increased judicial restraint. Stiansen and Voeten found evidence that member states, in the more recent past, nominated judges adopting a wider interpretation of the margin of appreciation and that consolidated democracies, especially the United Kingdom, increasingly benefit from greater deference.[157] Similarly, Madsen found that the Court's use of the terms "margin of appreciation" and "wide(r) margin of appreciation" increased significantly, in particular in cases under Article 8 ECHR decided at the Chamber level.[158] More generally, commentators stressed that there is, in recent case-law, not only a continuous expansion of the scope of application of the margin of appreciation doctrine[159] but also a trend of focusing on domestic procedural safeguards at the expense of substantive review.[160] This proceduralization, too, arguably creates "a bias that favours Western states, which are assumed to offer more solid legal guarantees."[161] Finally, some went as far as to identify increased deference as a "survival strategy" of human rights institutions at large in face of resurging populism.[162]

While these developments indicate a clear tendency to reduce the intensity of the Court's supranational judicial review, there still remain limits and it is for the Court

155 Art. 1 Protocol 15.

156 S. A. S. v. *France*, § 156f. The Court did so in contradiction to the following statement made earlier in the judgment: "That being said, in view of the flexibility of the notion of 'living together' and the resulting risk of abuse, the Court must engage in a careful examination of the necessity of the impugned limitation" (ibid., § 122). See also the partly dissenting opinion of Judges Nussberger and Jaderblom in the case.

157 Stiansen and Voeten, "Backlash and Judicial Restraint".

158 Madsen, "Rebalancing European Human Rights," 220.

159 Kratochvil, "Inflation of the Margin of Appreciation," 324ff.

160 Patricia Popelier and Catherine J. Van De Heyning, "Subsidiarity Post-Brighton: Procedural Rationality as Answer?" (2017) 30 *Leiden Journal of International Law* 5–23; Robert Spano, "Universality or Diversity of Human Rights?: Strasbourg in the Age of Subsidiarity" (2014) 14 *Human Rights Law Review* 487–502; e.g., ECtHR, *Lalmahomed* v. *the Netherlands*, no. 26036/08, Judgment of February 22, 2011, § 37.

161 Madsen, "Rebalancing European Human Rights," 220.

162 Laurence R. Helfer, "Populism and International Human Rights Institutions" in Gerald L. Neuman (ed.), *Human Rights in a Time of Populism: Challenges and Responses* (Cambridge: Cambridge University Press 2019), pp. 218–249.

to determine those. It gives the final ruling on whether a state has complied with the ECHR and the domestic margin of appreciation always "goes hand in hand with a European supervision" as the Court regularly stresses.[163] Indeed, this aspect is crucial. The Court's supranational authority requires a standard and intensity of review under which the Court retains an inalienable core of autonomy vis-à-vis domestic authorities, for there to be any meaningful external review.

4.3 EXTENDING JUDICIAL INTEGRATION TO THE AREA OF REMEDIES AND ENFORCEMENT

4.3.1 *Declaratory Nature of ECtHR Judgments*

Having discussed the binding force of ECtHR judgments in the preceding part, the focus in the following lies on what exactly Article 46(1) ECHR and undertaking "to abide by the final judgment of the Court" requires. The Court interprets Article 46(1) ECHR in line with the ILC Draft Articles on State Responsibility, the *lex generalis* so to speak.[164] Accordingly, Article 46(1) ECHR imposes a threefold obligation on the state party found in breach of the Convention to (i) cease the breach, (ii) make reparation for it, and (iii) ensure non-repetition of similar violations in future.[165] Making reparation usually requires restitution. Relying on ILC Draft Article 35 and the *Chorzów Factory Case*,[166] the Court held that "if the nature of the breach allows of *restitutio in integrum*, it is for the respondent State to effect it"[167] and that reparation must be made "in such a way as to restore as far as possible the situation existing before the breach."[168] As the Court noted, this reflects the prevailing hierarchy between the different forms of reparation in general international law.[169]

To recall, contracting states rejected the proposal of the European Movement to vest the ECtHR with the power to quash domestic decisions or to directly nullify or invalidate national legislation.[170] As a result, the execution of judgments is both subject

163 *Handyside* v. *the United Kingdom*, § 49; *S.A.S.* v. *France*, § 131.
164 See Arts. 30, 31 and 55 of the ILC Draft Articles on State Responsibility.
165 ECtHR *Papamichalopoulos and Others* v. *Greece (former Article* 50), no. 14556/89, October 31, 1995, Series A no. 330-B, § 34; *Scozzari and Giunta* v. *Italy*, nos. 39221/98 and 41963/98, ECHR 2000-VIII, § 249; Ruedin, *Exécution des arrêts*, p. 123.
166 PCIJ, *Case concerning the Factory at Chorzów (Claim for Indemnity) (Merits)*, Judgment of September 13, 1928, P. C. I. J. (1928) Series A no. 17.
167 *Papamichalopoulos and Others* v. *Greece*, § 34.
168 ECtHR, *Guiso-Gallisay* v. *Italy (Just Satisfaction)*, no. 58858/00, Grand Chamber Judgment of December 22, 2009, § 90. On restitution see Antoine Buyse, "Lost and Regained? Restitution as a Remedy for Human Rights Violations in the Context of International Law" (2008) 68 *Heidelberg Journal of International Law* 129–153.
169 ECtHR, *Verein gegen Tierfabriken Schweiz (VgT)* v. *Switzerland (No. 2)*, no. 32772/02, Grand Chamber Judgment of June 30, 2009, § 86.
170 Chapter 3, Sections 3.2.1–3.2.2.; ECtHR, *Le Compte, Van Leuven and De Meyere (former Article* 50), nos. 6878/75 and 7238/75, Judgment of October 18, 1982, Series A no. 54, § 13.

to and dependent on the adoption of implementing measures by the domestic authorities. In the *Marckx case*, the Court asserted that its judgments are "essentially declaratory,"[171] therefore leaving it to the contracting state, under the supervision of the CoM, to concretize the threefold obligation arising from a violation of the Convention. Following this declaratory approach, the Court usually abstains from determining specific remedies itself. In other words, contracting parties' relative freedom in choosing the means to secure the rights and freedoms guaranteed in the Convention equally applies to the secondary obligations arising from a breach thereof.[172] The Court's declaratory approach is a form of remedial subsidiarity.[173] Similar to the area of judicial review, the Court acknowledged that national authorities are, in principle, better placed than the ECtHR to identify the measures needed to execute a judgment by the Court.[174]

4.3.2 *Beyond Declaratory Relief*

4.3.2.1 Ruling on Compensation

Somewhat at odds with this traditional approach emphasizing implementation freedom is Strasbourg case-law under Article 41 ECHR. The latter stipulates that the Court shall, if necessary, afford just satisfaction to the injured party. The Court developed a long-standing practice under Article 41 ECHR to decide on compensation and award the applicant just satisfaction – a sum of money intended to compensate, *inter alia*, for the pecuniary and non-pecuniary damages suffered – to be paid by the state.[175] Neither the old nor the new Court gave much importance to the negative requirement in the wording of Article 41 ECHR, according to which the Court should afford compensation only in so far as domestic law does not allow complete reparation to be made.[176] On the contrary, the Court often assumes primary and sole authority in deciding on compensation, regardless of whether (partial) restitution could still be granted at the national level.[177] In the context of

171 *Marckx* v. *Belgium*, § 58.

172 *Papamichalopoulos and Others* v. *Greece*, § 34. See Art. 1 ECHR as well as Chapter 6, Section 6.2.2.

173 E.g., Besson, "Subsidiarity," 82f.

174 ECtHR, *Greens and M.T.* v. *the United Kingdom*, nos. 60041/08 and 60054/08, Judgment of November 23, 2010, ECHR 2010-VI (extracts), § 113.

175 On the question whether the Court's case-law could also evolve towards awarding punitive damages see Schabas, *ECHR: A Commentary*, p. 839.

176 The original meaning of this formulation is not entirely clear. Today, it is usually understood as expressing the subsidiary role of the Court as regards damages (Partly Concurring Opinion of Judge Zupančič in ECtHR, *Lucà* v. *Italy*, no. 33354/96, Judgment of February 27, 2001, ECHR 2001-II).

177 Elisabeth Lambert Abdelgawad, "Is There a Need to Advance the Jurisprudence of the European Court of Human Rights with Regard to the Award of Damages?" in Anja Seibert-Fohr and Marc E. Villiger (eds.), *Judgments of the European Court of Human Rights – Effects and Implementation*

reopening of criminal proceedings, for instance, the ECtHR held that the applicant cannot be expected to exhaust domestic remedies several times before being able to obtain compensation.[178] As a result, the Court usually only reserves to rule on the issue of just satisfaction,[179] where corresponding domestic proceedings (e.g. liability proceedings) are already pending.[180]

Despite of its otherwise deferential remedial approach, the Court always considered it part of its supranational authority to rule autonomously and conclusively on compensation. This fact cannot be overestimated from the viewpoint of the individual. That victims can directly obtain damages in Strasbourg represents a tangible consequence of supranational authority, which is arguably perceived as such by the individual concerned.

4.3.2.2 Indication of Individual and General Measures

Around two decades ago, the Court has started to occasionally abandon its deferential remedial practice, also outside the area of compensation, in favor of a more assertive and hybrid approach.[181] Today, the Court may spell out in its judgment what measures it considers necessary on the part of the respondent state in order to repair the violation inflicted.[182] In the words of the Court, it may exceptionally,

(Baden-Baden: Nomos 2014), p. 119. This practice seems to contradict to an extent the view held by the Court that compensation for damages under Art. 41 is, in principle, only a subsidiary form of reparation (Helen Keller and Cedric Marti, "Reconceptualizing Implementation: The Judicialization of the Execution of the European Court of Human Rights' Judgments" (2015) 26 *European Journal of International Law* 829–850 at 844). The Court has, though, refrained from granting just satisfaction, where, as a result of the adverse judgment, domestic proceeding had been re-opened (ECtHR, *Windisch* v. *Austria (former Article 50)*, no. 12489/86, Judgment of June 28, 1993, Series A no. 255-D, §§ 8–15).

178 ECtHR, *Jalloh* v. *Germany*, no. 54810/00, Grand Chamber Judgment of July 11, 2006, ECHR, 2006-IX, § 129.

179 According to Rule 75(1) Rules of Court the Chamber or the Committee can reserve ruling on just satisfaction in whole or in part and fix the further procedure if the question is not ready for decision.

180 E.g., ECtHR, *Kübler* v. *Germany*, no. 32715/06, Judgement of January 13, 2011, § 78.

181 This development has been discussed extensively in scholarship. See, among others, Valerio Colandrea, "On the Power of the European Court of Human Rights to Order Specific Non-Monetary Measures: Some Remarks in Light of the Assanidze, Broniowski and Sejdovic Cases" (2007) 7 *Human Rights Law Review* 396–411; Philip Leach, "No Longer Offering Fine Mantras to a Parched Child? The European Court's Developing Approach to Remedies" in Andreas Føllesdal, Birgit Peters, and Geir Ulfstein (eds.), *Constituting Europe: The European Court of Human Rights in a National, European and Global Context* (Cambridge: Cambridge University Press 2013), pp. 142–180; Jannika Jahn, "Ruling (In)directly through Individual Measures? Effect and Legitimacy of the ECtHR's New Remedial Power" (2014) 74 *Heidelberg Journal of Intenational Law* 1–39; Linos-Alexander Sicilianos, "The Role of the European Court of Human Rights in the Execution of Its Own Judgments: Reflections on Article 46 ECHR" in Anja Seibert-Fohr and Mark E. Villiger (eds.), *Judgments of the European Court of Human Rights – Effects and Implementation* (Baden-Baden: Nomos 2014), pp. 285–316; with further references Keller and Marti, "Reconceptualizing Implementation," 834ff.

182 For an empirical examination see Alice Donald and Anne-Katrin Speck, "The European Court of Human Rights' Remedial Practice and its Impact on the Execution of Judgments," (2019) 19 *Human Rights Law Review* 83–117.

"with a view to helping the respondent State to fulfil its obligations under Article 46 (...) indicate the type of measure that might be taken in order to put an end to a violation it has found to exist."[183] Depending on the situation they address, the remedial measures indicated by the Court may be individual or general in nature; they can be mandatory (so-called consequential orders) or recommendations.

Individual measures address the applicant's particular situation after a breach of his or her Convention right(s). In general international law terms, they aim at cessation and reparation. The award of just satisfaction also falls in this category and it is precisely under Article 41 ECHR that the Court's line of case-law extending the scope of (individual) remedies originated. It was in the case of *Papamichalopoulos and Others* v. *Greece*, in which the Court first abandoned the principle of declaratory relief. The case concerned a de facto expropriation, which the Court found to be incompatible with Article 1 of Protocol 1. In addition to finding a breach of the ECHR, the Court held in the operative part of the judgment that Greece was within six months to return the land in issue to the applicants.[184] The judgment was a silent revolution as the Court not only demanded restitution but actually required specific action from Greece. A few years later, the Court ruled that an unlawfully detained applicant must be released at the earliest possible date.[185] The Court explained that "by its very nature," the violation of Articles 5 and 6 ECHR in the case at hand did not leave any real choice as to the measures required to remedy it.[186] In cases in which an applicant stood an unfair trial, the Court first recommended and later ordered the re-opening of domestic proceedings, if the applicant so wished.[187] It held that re-opening domestic proceedings was the most adequate form of redress for a violation of fair trial rights in criminal proceedings.[188]

A larger line of case-law then emerged through which the Court indicated individual measures also based on Article 46 ECHR.[189] In the context of inhumane

[183] ECtHR, *Oleksandr Volkov* v. *Ukraine*, no. 21722/11, January 9, 2013, ECHR 2013-I, § 195. See also ECtHR, Practice Direction on Just Satisfaction Claims (2007), para. 23.

[184] *Papamichalopoulos* v. *Greece*, point 2 of the operative provisions.

[185] ECtHR, *Assanidze* v. *Georgia*, no. 71503/01, Grand Chamber Judgment of April 8, 2004, ECHR 2004-II, point 14 a) of the operative provisions.

[186] Ibid., § 202.

[187] ECtHR, *Lungoci* v. *Romania*, no. 62710/00, Judgment of January 26, 2006, point 3a) of the operative provisions. The introduction of these re-trial or re-opening clauses was based on the prior practice of the CoM and followed the encouragement of contracting parties "to examine their national legal systems with a view to ensuring that there exist adequate possibilities of re-examination of the case, including reopening of proceedings, in instances where the Court has found a violation of the Convention" (CoM, Recommendation (2000)2, II).

[188] See, for instance, ECtHR, *Gençel* v. *Turkey*, no. 53431/99, Judgment of October 23, 2003, § 27. See, also, CoM, Recommendations (2000)2 and (2004)6.

[189] The change of legal basis can presumably be explained by the introduction of the pilot judgment procedure and the indication of so-called general measures. The Court has yet to find a way to operationalize subsidiarity in this area or render decision-making more transparent at least. Scholars have therefore suggested that the Court is to proceed to a more discernible balancing of those

or unlawful detention, the Court demanded governments, for instance, to replace detention on remand with other less stringent measures[190] or to immediately secure adequate conditions of detention including access to necessary psychiatric treatment and constant medical supervision.[191] In the impactful *Volkov* judgment, the Court even ordered the reinstatement of a judge to the Ukrainian Supreme Court who had been dismissed in disregard of Articles 6 and 8 ECHR.[192] Considering the systemic deficiencies in the Ukrainian judiciary, the Court held that the re-opening of the procedure alone would not have afforded adequate redress.[193] In another case, the Court even ordered the Russian government to bear the costs of the homeless applicants' accommodation pending the enforcement of a domestic judgment that required their resettlement.[194]

Another way by which the Court has taken more influence in the implementation of its judgments is by indicating general measures. When adopting general measures, the Court leaves the realm of individual justice and exercises authority over an indefinite number of persons and situations. General measures aim at protecting persons who are in a situation similar to that of the applicant and ensuring, more generally, that domestic legislation is in conformity with the Convention. The Court introduced general measures as part of the pilot judgment procedure, which originated as a response to systemic human rights problems at the domestic level. Upon request of the Court,[195] the CoM adopted a recommendation suggesting that the Court, in its judgments, identify what it considers the underlying systemic problems, in particular when they are likely to give rise to numerous applications, so as to assist states in finding the appropriate solution and the CoM in supervising the execution of judgments.[196] The pilot judgment procedure and general measures are today codified in Rule 61 Rules of Court.[197]

The Court may adopt general measures whenever a case discloses problems of a systemic nature in a contracting state. General measures are ambitious and wide-reaching in character in that they address a generally defective legal situation. They seek to speedily remedy the systemic or structural problem identified by the Court,

interests that speak in favour or against intervention through the indication of remedies (Keller and Marti, "Reconceptualizing Implementation," 843; Jahn, "Ruling (In)directly," 28).

190 ECtHR, *Aleksanyan* v. *Russia*, no. 46468/06, Judgment of December 22, 2008, § 240.

191 ECtHR, *Sławomir Musiał* v. *Poland*, no. 28300/06, Judgment of January 20, 2009, point 4 a) of the operative provisions.

192 *Volkov* v. *Ukraine*, § 208 and point 9 of the operative provisions.

193 Ibid., § 208.

194 ECtHR, *Pelipenko* v. *Russia*, no. 69037/10, Judgment of January 16, 2014, § 30 and point 1 of the operative provisions.

195 ECtHR, Position Paper, September 12, 2003, CDDH-GDR (2003)024.

196 CoM, Resolution (2004)3.

197 Rule 61(1) Rules of Court reads: The Court may initiate a pilot-judgment procedure and adopt a pilot judgment where the facts of an application reveal in the Contracting Party concerned the existence of a structural or systemic problem or other similar dysfunction which has given rise or may give rise to similar applications.

help bring domestic law and practices in conformity with the Convention and thus prevent future violations.[198] General measures may come in different forms and in varying degrees of specificity.[199] Usually they call for legislative reform, policy changes,[200] large-scale administrative action[201] or changes in judicial practice.[202] If adopted outside the pilot judgment procedure, general measures usually do not figure in the operative part of the judgment,[203] but even in these so-called Article 46 or quasi-pilot judgments, they can be formulated in mandatory terms.[204] Another common type of general measures is the requirement of introducing an effective remedy at the national level. The Court requested states to setup compensatory or preventive mechanisms to remedy rights' violations domestically in cases concerning excessively long proceedings,[205] non-enforcement, and delayed enforcement of domestic judgments[206] or detention conditions violating Article 3 ECHR.[207] The Court may also prescribe transitory measures while domestic (legislative) reform is underway.[208]

4.3.3 *Jurisprudential Developments Conceived as Supranationalization*

The turn in the Court's approach to remedies represented a remarkable and innovative judicial strategy to deal with the high number of repetitive applications and the increasing number of serious Convention violations that the Court faced, in particular after the enlargement of the CoE.[209] At the same time, the practice of indicating individual and general measures enhanced the Court's supranational

198 Hence, they also pertain to states' obligation to prevent future violations and provide assurances of non-repetition. André Nollkaemper, "Constitutionalization and the Unity of the Law of International Responsibility" (2009) 16 *Indiana Journal of Global Legal Studies* 535–563 at fn. 16; Colandrea, "Power of the ECtHR," 409.

199 Leach, "Remedies," p. 163. An example of detailed instructions is ECtHR, *Dimitrov and Hamanov* v. *Bulgaria*, nos. 48059/06 and 2708/09, Judgment of May 10, 2011, § 125; *Ananyev and Others* v. *Russia*, nos. 42525/07 and 60800/08, Judgment of January 10, 2012, §§ 191ff.

200 *Greens and M.T.* v. *the United Kingdom*, point 6 a) of the operative provisions.

201 ECtHR, *Kurić and Others* v. *Slovenia*, no. 26828/06, Grand Chamber Judgment of June 26, 2012, ECHR 2012-IV (extracts), point 9 of the operative provisions.

202 *Broniowski* v. *Poland*, point 4 of the operative provisions.

203 An exception is ECtHR, *Lukenda* v. *Slovenia*, no. 23032/02, Judgment of October 6, 2005, ECHR 2005-X, point 5 of the operative provisions.

204 ECtHR, *Dybeku* v. *Albania*, no. 41153/06, Judgment of December 18, 2007, § 64.

205 ECtHR, *Rumpf* v. *Germany*, no. 46344/06, Judgment of September 2, 2010, point 5 of the operative provisions.

206 ECtHR, *Burdov* v. *Russia (No. 2)*, no. 33509/04, Judgment of January 15, 2009, ECHR 2009-I, point 6 of the operative provisions.

207 ECtHR, *Ananyev and Others* v. *Russia*; *Torreggiani and Others* v. *Italy*, nos. 43517/09, etc., Judgment (Merits and Just Satisfaction) of January 8, 2013, §§ 80–101.

208 *Ananyev and Others* v. *Russia*, § 209.

209 For example, ECtHR, *Broniowski* v. *Poland*, no. 31443/96, Grand Chamber Judgment of June 22, 2004, ECHR 2004-V, §§ 188–194.

authority considerably. Individual and general measures not only extended judicial integration to the area of remedies but also forged new and more direct relationships between the Court, individuals, and domestic authorities, which reinforced, in turn, the latter's integration within the Convention system.

First, the above survey shows how the Court extends judicial integration to the area of remedies. While relief obtained in Strasbourg might still be largely declaratory in nature, the Court can occasionally recommend or even order individual and general remedies and thereby determine directly the legal consequences of an adverse judgment. This is a considerable extension of the Court's autonomous decision-making power in respect to both contracting parties, which are said to enjoy implementation freedom, but also in respect to the intergovernmental CoM, whose responsibility it is to supervise the execution of judgments and whose task the Court may now to an extent legalize and predetermine through indicating remedies.[210] The pilot judgment procedure in particular raised the question whether the Court engaged in procedural lawmaking (*ultra vires*) that would have in fact required formal amendment of the Convention.[211] In general, however, contracting states seem to have accepted that the new remedial dimension is part of judicial integration under the ECHR.[212]

Second, general measures, especially if formulated in mandatory terms and adopted in the context of pilot judgments, have an effect that goes beyond the principle of *res judicata inter partes*.[213] When adopting general measures, the Court leaves the realm of individual justice and exercises authority over an indefinite number of persons and situations. To be sure, in the context of the pilot judgment procedure this may also include other applicants, who already petitioned the Court and whose applications were frozen pending the outcome of Strasbourg proceedings.[214] However, the reach of general measures is much wider, as they also aim to protect potential applicants and persons that are equally affected by the systemic problem at hand.[215] This led some commentators to speak of a "constitutional turn" in ECHR law.[216] The broad and large scale protection through general measures was particularly striking in the Court's first pilot judgment in the case of *Broniowski* v. *Poland*, which revealed the structural problem of Poland

210 Markus Fyrnys, "Expanding Competences by Judicial Lawmaking: The Pilot Judgment Procedure of the European Court of Human Rights" (2010) 12 *German Law Journal* 1231–1260 at 1233.

211 For a detailed analysis see Fyrnys, "Expanding Competences," 1251ff.

212 For general measures see Fyrnys, "Expanding Competences," 1259.

213 Fyrnys, "Expanding Competences," 1246. See, for instance, Brussels Declaration 1.a).

214 Rule 61(6)(a) Rules of Court provides that the Court may adjourn the examination of all similar applications pending the adoption of the remedial measures required by virtue of the operative provisions of the pilot judgment.

215 "Such measures must also be taken *in respect of other persons in the applicant's position*, notably by solving the problems that have led to the Court's findings" (ECtHR, *Olaru and Others* v. *Moldavia*, nos. 476/07 etc., Grand Chamber Judgment of July 28, 2009, § 49 (emphasis added)).

216 Sadurski, "Partnering with Strasbourg," 397ff; Colandrea, "Power of the ECtHR," 406.

in compensating former landowners that had been repatriated from the Bug River area after World War II:

> The Court has already noted that the violation which it has found in the present case has as its cause *a situation concerning large numbers of people*. The failure to implement in a manner compatible with Article 1 of Protocol No. 1 the chosen mechanism for settling the Bug River claims has affected *nearly 80,000 people* (. . .). There are moreover already 167 applications pending before the Court brought by Bug River claimants.[217]

In subsequent pilot judgments, such as *Burdov (No. 2)*, for instance, the Court even went beyond this "class action logic,"[218] in so far as the effective domestic remedy to be adopted should provide redress for a large number of persons that did "not necessarily belong to 'an identifiable class of citizens'."[219]

Third, the Court's hybrid remedial approach contributes to the disaggregation of the state and pierces to a particular degree the state veil.[220] Although performance-specific remedies are formally addressed to the respondent government, by virtue of their content and level of detail, they have a much broader effect on the domestic legal system, responsibilizing, mobilizing, or enabling different domestic actors such as administrative authorities, legislative bodies, or the judiciary. The result is a more direct relationship between the Court and domestic actors. The pilot judgment procedure, for instance, has a strong dialogical element[221] and scholars demonstrated that it resulted in a partnership of Central and Eastern European constitutional courts with the Court against illiberal political action.[222] In the same vein, pilot judgments have been described as decreed lawmaking cooperation between the Court and domestic parliaments to secure compliance with the Convention.[223] The programmative obligations of general measures produced a "catalyzing effect on the domestic democratic legislative process, especially in the ongoing democratic transition in the new state parties of the Central and Eastern Europe."[224] The same effect of government bypassing can also be seen in the context of individual measures. After the regime change in the Ukraine, for instance, the Ukrainian parliament complied with the Court's consequential order and reinstated Mr. Volkov to the supreme court.[225] In fact, the indication of individual measures

217 *Broniowski* v. *Poland*, § 193 (emphasis added).
218 Harmsen, "Reform of the Convention System," p. 139.
219 *Burdov* v. *Russia (No. 2)*, § 129.
220 Sadurski, "Partnering with Strasbourg," 452.
221 Janneke Gerards, "The Pilot Judgment Procedure before the European Court of Human Rights as an Instrument for Dialogue" in Monica Claes, et al.(eds.), *Constitutional Conversations in Europe* (Cambridge: Intersentia 2012), pp. 369ff.
222 Sadurski, "Partnering with Strasbourg," 442ff. On "compliance partners" of ICs more generally see Alter, *New Terrain of International Law*, p. 20.
223 Fyrnys, "Expanding Competences," 1244f.
224 Ibid., 1254.
225 CoM, DH-DD(2015)27.

contributed to ECtHR judgments even having a de facto invalidating effect[226] within certain legal systems. To recall, the ECtHR does not have and never asserted to have the power to annul the domestic decision, legislation or "efface the consequences" of the same.[227] However, by virtue of the Court's jurisprudence on *restitutio in integrum* and the recommendations of the CoM,[228] many states introduced legislation that allows for the re-opening of domestic proceedings, once the applicant has obtained a favorable judgment in Strasbourg.[229] In criminal law matters, the "vast majority of states" allow for re-opening (sometimes even as concerns co-defendants), while in civil law cases states have "broadly accepted the possibility of reopening."[230] In a number of states, judgments by the ECtHR can thus be enforced directly before domestic courts by the individual concerned.

Fourthly, general measures transform the Court's judicial review into a more abstract type of examination of domestic legislation.[231] The Court usually abstains from discussing the compatibility of domestic law with the Convention and focuses, instead, on the concrete implementing measure, usually an administrative or judicial act.[232] This approach is in line with the Court's case-law on victim status under Article 34 ECHR and the fact that the Convention does not enshrine an *actio popularis*.[233] General measures and the pilot judgment procedure, however, though applied in the course of the examination of an individual case, force the Court to take a more generalized and abstract approach to review. Systemic violations are often the result of domestic legislation not living up to Convention standards and as the Court aims at addressing just that, it must necessarily scrutinize domestic legislation. For instance, when the Court requested the United Kingdom to amend its electoral law, it did so on the basis of the general assessment that the blanket ban on voting for prisoners as set forth in section 3 of the Representation of the People Act 1983 was not compatible with the right to free elections (Article 3 Protocol No. 1).[234] Haider therefore rightly

226 Besson, "European Human Rights," p. 112. Chapters 5 and 6 provide a more in-depth examination of the general effect of Convention law (including case-law) in domestic law.

227 Thomas Buergenthal, "The Effect of the European Convention on Human Rights on the Internal Law of Member States" (1965) 11 *International and Comparative Law Quarterly Supplementary Publication* 79–106 at 97.

228 CoM, Recommendations (2000)2 and (2004)6.

229 CDDH, "Overview of the exchange of views held at the 8th meeting of DH-GDR on the provision in the domestic legal order for the re-examination or reopening of cases following judgments of the Court Strasbourg," DH-GDR (2015)008 Rev, February 12, 2016.

230 See the Conclusions of the Round Table on Reopening of Proceedings Following a Judgment of the European Court of Human Rights (2015), available at www.rm.coe.int/CoERMPublicCommonSearchServices/DisplayDCTMContent?documentId=0900001680592 1a0 (accessed July 23, 2020).

231 For a detailed analysis Dominik Haider, *The Pilot-Judgment Procedure of the European Court of Human Rights* (Leiden/Boston: Brill 2013), pp. 129–133.

232 ECtHR, *Sahin* v. *Germany*, no. 30943/96, Grand Chamber Judgment of July 8, 2003, ECHR 2003-VIII, § 87.

233 See earlier Section 4.2.1.1.

234 ECtHR, *Hirst* v. *the United Kingdom (No. 2)*, no. 74025/01, Grand Chamber Judgment of October 6, 2005, ECHR 2005-IX, § 82; *Greens and M. T.* v. *the United Kingdom*, § 77.

submitted that the Court has, through pilot judgments, institutionalized review of domestic legislation to a certain degree.[235] Similar to the Court's practice under Article 41 ECHR, the Court's hybrid remedial approach arguably attracts or mobilizes applicants to petition the Court and simultaneously heightens domestic actors' and the public's perception of the (effectiveness of the) Court's supranational authority.

4.4 EMERGENCE OF COMPLIANCE REVIEW

4.4.1 *Primary Responsibility of the Committee of Ministers*

Closely related to the preceding part is the post-judgment phase. Once the Court delivers its judgment, Article 46(2) ECHR places supervision of the execution process under the intergovernmental oversight of the CoM.[236] At so-called human rights meetings, the respondent state is excepted to inform on the adopted implementing measures, which are then scrutinized by state representatives. It is for the CoM to establish whether all necessary measures have been adopted to comply with the Court's judgment.[237] Admittedly, the CoM is assisted by the Human Rights Directorate, a strong and influential secretariat, and assesses compliance in a fairly technical procedure based on legal criteria.[238] Regardless, supervision remains essentially based on diplomatic dialogue and political peer pressure.[239] In theory, the CoM does have the power to sanction a non-compliant state by suspending its voting rights or, ultima ratio, decide its expulsion from the CoE.[240] Not least because it would be counterproductive, so far, the CoM has not resorted to these possibilities as a response to non-implementation.[241] From a historical and institutional perspective, the political oversight of the execution of judgments is a remain of the originally political and quasi-judicial enforcement structure under the Convention.[242]

235 Haider, *The Pilot-Judgment Procedure*, p. 131.

236 The Brussels Declaration, for instance, reaffirms in section 2.d), "the intergovernmental nature" of the supervisory process of the execution of judgments.

237 If this is the case, it adopts a resolution concluding that its functions have been exercised. On the Committee of Minister's supervisory function see Ruedin, *Exécution des arrêts*, pp. 7–42; Lambert-Abdelgawad, *Execution of Judgments*, pp. 32–43.

238 CoM, Rules for the Supervision of the Execution of Judgments and of the Terms of Friendly Settlements, May 10, 2006; Supervision of the Execution of Judgments and Decisions of the European Court of Human Rights: Implementation of the Interlaken Action Plan – Modalities for a Twin-Track Supervision System, Doc. CM/Inf/DH(2010)37) (2010).

239 For a discussion of the system of peer review see Başak Çali and Anne Koch, "Foxes Guarding the Foxes? The Peer Review of Human Rights Judgments by the Committee of Ministers of the Council of Europe" (2014) 14 *Human Rights Law Review* 301–325.

240 See Art. 8 CoE Statute.

241 On the CoM's new and less drastic means see subsequently Section 4.4.3.

242 Zysset, *ECHR and Human Rights Theory*, p. 115.

In principle, the ECtHR has always been mindful of the separation of competences between itself and the CoM and of the former's primary responsibility in the post-judgment phase. On multiple occasions, the Court stressed that that "it does not have jurisdiction to verify, by reference to Article 46, whether a Contracting Party has complied with the obligations imposed on it by one of the Court's judgments (…)" and that it is for the CoM to evaluate implementing measures.[243] Consequently, applications alleging a state's failure to implement a specific judgment under Article 46 ECHR are usually declared inadmissible.[244]

4.4.2 *Incidental Review of Compliance*

Despite regularly declining jurisdiction to review judgment compliance, the ECtHR has also acknowledged that it may, under very specific circumstances, intervene in the post-judgment phase.[245] In other words, Article 46(2) ECHR does not entail that implementing measures taken by a respondent state would fall completely outside the jurisdiction of the Court.[246] Indeed, three different constellations evidencing a weak form of incidental review of compliance can be distinguished.

First, the Court has asserted jurisdiction to entertain so-called follow-up applications if they raise a new issue, that is, pertain to new information not yet heard by the Court in the context of an earlier judgment.[247] Technically, when examining follow-up applications, the ECtHR only reviews whether there has been a fresh violation of the ECHR in respect of a previous applicant. In reality, however, it is often difficult to distinguish between issues regarding the proper execution of a previous judgment on the one hand and the question of whether the Convention was violated afresh on the other.[248] This has become apparent in the case of *VgT (No. 2)*, for instance, in which the Court held that it must also take "into account the importance in the Convention system of effective execution of the Court's judgments in accordance with Article 46 of the Convention" when examining a follow-up application.[249] In

243 ECtHR, *Kurić and Others* v. *Slovenia (Just Satisfaction)*, no. 26828/06, Judgment of March 12, 2014, § 142.

244 ECommHR, *Times Newspaper Ltd., Giles, Knightley and Potter* v. *the United Kingdom*, no. 10243/83, Decision of March 6, 1985, DR 41, 129; ECtHR, *Haase and Others* v. *Germany*, no. 34499/04, Decision of February 12, 2008.

245 For an in-depth discussion see Lize R. Glas, "The European Court of Human Rights Supervising the Execution of its Judgments" (2019) 37 *Netherlands Quarterly of Human Rights* 228–244.

246 ECtHR, *Lyons and Others* v. *the United Kingdom*, no. 15227/03, Decision of July 8, 2003, ECHR 2003-IX.

247 Art. 35(2)(b) ECHR; ECtHR, *Olsson* v. *Sweden (No. 2)*, no. 13441/87, Judgment of November 27, 1992, Series A no. 250, § 94.

248 ECtHR, *Egmez* v. *Cyprus*, no. 12214/07, Decision of September 18, 2012, § 54. The Court therefore held that only a case by case approach would allow it to establish competence *ratione materiae* without encroaching on the powers of the CoM.

249 ECtHR, *Verein gegen Tierfabriken Schweiz (VgT)* v. *Switzerland (No. 2)*, § 83; see also *Greens and M. T.* v. *the United Kingdom*, point 5 of the operative provisions.

Emre (No. 2), the Court even established a violation of Article 46 ECHR – in conjunction with a fresh violation of Article 8 ECHR – because Switzerland did not comply with *Emre (No. 1)*.[250] In a later judgment, however, the Court regarded it "very doubtful" whether 46(1) ECHR confers an individual right "that can be asserted in proceedings originating in an individual application."[251]

Dissociating the issue of just satisfaction under Article 41 ECHR from the judgment on the merits is another way through which the Court inquired into implementation.[252] Ruling on just satisfaction, the Court may review whether domestic authorities have redressed the violation as found by the Court and "brought about a result as close to *restitutio in integrum* as was possible in the nature of things."[253] In the interstate case of *Cyprus* v. *Turkey*, for instance, the Grand Chamber noted that Turkey had not implemented its judgment on the merits and awarded, as a result, just satisfaction of EUR 90M.[254] Two concurring judges went as far as suggesting that the high sum partly represented a form of punitive damages for Turkey's failure to execute the Court's judgment year after year.[255]

Lastly, the Court also engaged in reviewing implementation in the context of the pilot judgment procedure. On the one hand, the Court must make sure that friendly settlements concluded after the adoption of a pilot judgment are compatible with the "respect for human rights."[256] This may imply a superficial review of compliance. In the case of *Hutten-Czapska* v. *Poland* for instance, the Court approved the settlement reached "having regard to both the general measures for addressing the systemic problem that had been identified and the individual measures afforded to the applicant under the agreement."[257] On the other hand, the re-opening of clone cases, which had been frozen pending the adoption of a pilot judgment, equally necessitates to examine questions of compliance. Rule 61(8) Rules of Court foresees specifically that in the event of the failure of the contracting party concerned to comply with the operative provisions of a pilot judgment, the Court shall resume its examination of the applications which have been adjourned. There are, however,

250 ECtHR, *Emre* v. *Switzerland (No. 2)*, §§ 75 and 77.

251 ECtHR, *United Macedonian Organisation Ilinden – PIRIN and Others* v. *Bulgaria (No. 2)*, nos. 41561/07 and 20972/08, Judgment of October 18, 2011, § 66. The Court confirmed this approach in *Sidabras and Others* v. *Lithuania*, nos. 50421/08 and 56213/08, Judgment of June 23, 2015, §§ 104 and 105. Compare, however, in this case the joint concurring opinion of Judges Spano and Kjølbro with the concurring opinion of Judge Keller.

252 ECtHR, *Barberà, Messegué and Jabardo* v. *Spain (former Art. 50)*, nos. 10588/83, 10589/83 and 10590/83, Judgment of June 13, 1994, Series A no. 285-C; *Pelipenko* v. *Russia*.

253 ECtHR, *De Cubber* v. *Belgium (former Art. 50)*, no. 9186/80, Judgment of September 14, 1987, Series A no. 124-B, § 21.

254 ECtHR, *Cyprus* v. *Turkey*, no. 25781/94, Grand Chamber Judgment of May 12, 2014, ECHR 2014-II, § 63 and operative provisions 4 and 5.

255 *Cyprus* v. *Turkey*, Concurring Opinion of Judge Pinto de Albuquerque joined by Judge Vučinić, §§ 12–19.

256 Art. 37(1) ECHR and Rule 62(3) Rules of Court.

257 *Hutten-Czapska* v. *Poland (Friendly Settlement)*, no. 35014/97, Grand Chamber Judgment of April 28, 2008, § 45.

limits to resuming the examination of adjourned cases as a response to non-compliance. In the *Burmych* case, efficiency concerns and Ukraine's continuous failure to implement the *Ivanov* pilot judgment[258] prompted the Court to strike out all follow-up cases under Article 37(1)(c) ECHR and defer them to the CoM.[259]

The three constellations briefly expounded show the emergence of a weak, fragmented, and incidental review of compliance. Compliance review is thus another, although very limited site of judicial integration. Integration in this area seems less to be the result of the Court's effort to willingly extend its powers into an area, in which it very much respects the primary responsibilities of the CoM. Rather, it appears to be a necessary and incidental consequence of the Court's role in the area of remedies: both awarding just satisfaction and the pilot judgment procedure may require the Court to engage in compliance review.[260] Also, through indicating specific individual and/or general remedies, the Court occasionally transforms the nature of its judgments, which adds to the legal dimension of the otherwise political or diplomatic process of supervising ECtHR judgments.[261]

4.4.3 *Infringement and Interpretation Procedure*

In addition to incidental compliance review, the contracting parties themselves allocated the Court new powers in the post-judgment phase.[262] Protocol 14 introduced a new form of direct review of compliance, the so-called infringement procedure under paras. 4 and 5 of amended Article 46 ECHR.[263]

Modeled after EU law, the infringement procedure adds an important new supranational dimension to the Convention system. Enforcement of the execution of judgments can now be detracted from the intergovernmental and diplomatic sphere, as the CoM may, by a qualified majority vote, take a binding decision to refer a case to the Court.[264] The infringement procedure provides a new means for the CoM to address non-compliance that goes beyond non-binding interim resolutions, but is less drastic or counterproductive than withdrawing voting rights or expulsion from the CoE.[265] The new procedure should allow to overcome potential political disputes in the CoM through a final judicial determination on issues of execution

258 ECtHR, *Yuriy Nikolayevich Ivanov* v. *Ukraine*, no. 40450/04, Judgment of October 15, 2009.
259 ECtHR, *Burmych and Others* v. *Ukraine*, nos. 46852/13 etc., Grand Chamber Judgment of October 12, 2017, §§ 148ff, 167–199.
260 Glas, "Supervising Execution," 243.
261 In neo-functionalist terms, one could argue that judicial integration in the area of remedies provoked spill-over effects extending to the supervision of the execution of ECtHR judgments (compare Lindberg, European Economic Integration, p. 8).
262 Interestingly, the Court itself opposed these changes in the beginning.
263 E.g., Kjetil Mujezinović Larsen, "Compliance with Judgments from the European Court of Human Rights: The Court's Call for Legislative Reforms" (2013) 31 *Nordic Journal of Human Rights* 496–512.
264 Art. 46(4) and (5) ECHR.
265 See earlier Section 4.4.1.

and exert additional pressure on the non-compliant state.[266] A proposal to give the Court the power to impose, on top of that, lump sums – similarly to Article 260(2) TFEU – was discussed at different points in time but ultimately never retained.[267]

Initially, the Court's new power remained rather symbolic.[268] According to the explanatory report to Protocol 14, the CoM should only resort to the infringement proceedings in exceptional circumstances.[269] Considering the hurdle of a two-third majority and reluctance of states to offend their peers, the chances of Article 46(4) ECHR being applied seemed low. The pressure, however, to make use of the new procedure especially in cases of persistent non-compliance gradually increased. Scholars, the PACE, the Court's President, and NGOs alike called upon the CoM to resort to the infringement procedure.[270] For the first and so far only time, the CoM relied on Article 46(4) ECHR in respect of Azerbaijan's failure to provide *restitutio in integrum* to Ilgar Mammadov, a member of the government's opposition who was arbitrarily detained and convicted in violation of the Convention.[271] In its judgment under Article 46(4) ECHR, the Grand Chamber emphasized that while its role was not to displace the CoM supervisory task, it had to make a final determination on the issue of compliance and therefore "take account of all the relevant factors," the moment of the referral by the CoM being "the starting point for its examination."[272] Based on the questions referred by the

266 For a critical appraisal on the usefulness of the procedure see Fiona de Londras and Kanstantsin Dzehtsiarou, "Mission Impossible? Addressing Non-Execution Through Infringement Proceedings in the European Court of Human Rights" (2017) 66 *International and Comparative Law Quarterly* 467ff.

267 As to the context of Protocol 14 see PACE, Opinion on Draft Protocol No. 14 to the Convention for the Protection of Human Rights and Fundamental Freedoms amending the control system of the Convention, no. 251 (2004), April 28, 2004. During the negotiations in the CoM leading up to the Brighton Declaration, the possibility of financial sanctions was considered but quickly discarded given widespread opposition among delegates.

268 Another, arguably secondary reason why the provision has not been invoked so far may be that its wording is fairly ambiguous as to what situations of non-compliance are in fact covered. Paragraph 4 refers to the situation where a state "refuses to abide" (Leach and Donald, *Parliaments and the ECHR*, p. 42).

269 Indeed, it was felt that "[t]he procedure's mere existence, and the threat of using it, should act as an effective new incentive to execute the Court's judgments" (Explanatory Report Protocol No. 14, para. 100).

270 PACE, Recommendation 2079(2015), 1.1; Dean Spielmann, Speech at the Parliamentary Assembly of the Council of Europe, Implementation of judgments of the European Court of Human Rights, September 30, 2015; Ramute Remezaite, "Azerbaijan: Is It Time to Invoke Infringement Proceedings for Failing to Implement Judgments of the Strasbourg Court?" (2017) *EJIL: Talk!* www.ejiltalk.org/azerbaijan-is-it-time-to-invoke-infringement-proceedings-for-failing-to-implement-judgments-of-the-strasbourg-court/ (accessed July 23, 2020).

271 CoM, Interim Resolution (2017)429; Interim Resolution (2017)379. ECtHR, *Ilgar Mammadov* v. *Azerbaijan*, no. 15172/13, Judgment of May 22, 2014; *Ilgar Mammadov* v. *Azerbaijan (No. 2)*, no. 919/15, Judgment of November 16, 2017.

272 ECtHR, *Ilgar Mammadov* v. *Azerbaijan*, no. 15172/13, Grand Chamber Judgment (Art. 46(4) ECHR), of May 29, 2019, §§ 165–171.

CoM, the Court focused on the individual measures and concluded that Azerbaijan was in violation of Article 46(1) ECHR as the limited implementing steps it had taken were insufficient to demonstrate that it acted in good faith and in line with the conclusions and spirit of the first *Mammadov* judgment.[273] It remains to be seen whether a more frequent use of the infringement procedure will ensue in the future.

In addition to the infringement procedure, Protocol 14 also amended Article 46 ECHR to include a new interpretation procedure.[274] Admittedly, the possibility of requesting the Court to clarify a judgment does not give it any power to review compliance.[275] Rather, the aim of the procedure is to enable an interpretative ruling whenever disagreement or uncertainty as to the interpretation of a judgment hinders the CoM's supervision.[276] Nonetheless, Article 46(3) ECHR is equally testament to the fact that the contracting parties bestowed the Court with a (more active) role in the post-judgment phase. Submitting a question of interpretation to the Court also requires a two-third majority and to date, the CoM has not yet made use of it.

4.5 THE COURT'S NEW ADVISORY JURISDICTION

4.5.1 *Existing Advisory Jurisdiction under Article 47 ECHR*

Article 47 ECHR provides for the Court's advisory jurisdiction as introduced by Protocol 2. The Court's jurisdiction under Article 47 ECHR is narrow in scope and was designed to neither interfere with nor prejudice its contentious jurisdiction.[277] Only the CoM may request an advisory opinion and it may do so solely regarding questions that do not pertain to substantive Convention law and cannot otherwise come before the Court.[278] In other words, the ECtHR's advisory jurisdiction under Article 47 ECHR is limited to institutional or procedural questions of legal nature.[279] Whereas advisory opinions are not formally binding, the *travaux*

[273] Ibid., §§ 214–217.

[274] Art. 46(3) ECHR. The parties to a case were already entitled to request within one year after the delivery of a judgment an interpretation thereof (see Rule 79 Rules of Court).

[275] Explanatory Report Protocol 14, para. 97.

[276] Ibid., para. 96.

[277] ECtHR, Decision on the competence of the Court to give an advisory opinion of June 2, 2004, § 33; Kanstantsin Dzehtsiarou and Noreen O'Meara, "Advisory Jurisdiction and the European Court of Human Rights: A Magic Bullet for Dialogue and Docket-Control?" (2014) 34 *Legal Studies* 444–468 at 447.

[278] Art. 47(1) and (2) ECHR. Art. 47(3) ECHR requires a majority vote of the representatives entitled to sit on the Committee.

[279] ECtHR, *Certain legal questions concerning the lists of candidates submitted with a view to the election of judges to the ECtHR*, Advisory Opinion of the Grand Chamber of February 12, 2008, §§ 36f; *Certain legal questions concerning the lists of candidates submitted with a view to the election of judges to the ECtHR (No. 2)*, Advisory Opinion of the Grand Chamber of January 22, 2010, § 29.

préparatoires speak of an "authoritative ruling" by the Court.[280] Given the restrictive terms of Article 47 ECHR, the Court's advisory jurisdiction has remained of limited significance. The Court only rendered two advisory opinions, both relating to questions on the procedure of the election of ECtHR judges.[281]

4.5.2 *Protocol 16*

Paradoxically, it was in times of increased criticism toward the Court and continuous insistence on subsidiarity, that an additional Protocol to the Convention was agreed upon, adding yet another dimension to the Court's jurisdiction. Protocol 16, the so-called dialogue Protocol, was drafted following the Brighton Declaration and extends, or rather transforms, the Court's advisory jurisdiction introducing a new preliminary-type procedure to the Convention system.

The idea of an advisory opinion procedure dates back to the 1960s[282] and was revived by the Group of Wise Persons in its report of 2006 considering the long-term effectiveness of the ECHR control mechanism.[283] A couple of years later, states started considering the idea more seriously. The Brighton Declaration noted "that the interaction between the Court and national authorities could be strengthened by the introduction into the Convention of a further power of the Court (...) to deliver advisory opinions upon request on the interpretation of the Convention (...)" and invited the CoM to draft a Protocol to that effect.[284] The result is Protocol 16, which is open for signature since October 2, 2013, and entered into force on August 1, 2018. So far, sixteen states have ratified, and six additional states have signed the Protocol.[285]

Pursuant to its preamble, the aim of Protocol 16 is to strengthen interaction between the ECtHR and the highest national courts and reinforce the implementation of the Convention in accordance with the principle of subsidiarity.[286] Article 1(1) Protocol 16 foresees that highest courts and tribunals of contracting states may request the Court to give advisory opinions on questions of principle relating to the interpretation or application of the rights and freedoms defined in the Convention

280 Ada Paprocka and Michał Ziółkowski, "Advisory Opinions under Protocol No. 16 to the European Convention on Human Rights" (2015) 11 *European Constitutional Law Review* 274–292 at 290.

281 See earlier fn. 281.

282 See also Andrew Drzemczewski, "The Domestic Status of the European Convention on Human Rights: New Dimensions" (1977) 4 *Legal Issues of Economic Integration* 1–85 at 79ff.

283 Report of the Group of Wise Persons to the Committee of Ministers, CM(2006)203, November 15, 2006, paras. 76–86.

284 Brighton Declaration, 12 d).

285 Status as of March 2021. Art. 8 Protocol 16. For the drafting history see the Explanatory Report Protocol 16, para. 1–6; Dzehtsiarou and O'Meara, "Advisory Jurisdiction," 451–457.

286 Preamble of Protocol 16. For a more detailed discussion of the Protocol's objectives Jannika Jahn, "Normative Guidance from Strasbourg Through Advisory Opinions Deprivation or Relocation of the Convention's Core?" (2014) 74 *Heidelberg Journal of International Law* 821–846.

or the protocols thereto.[287] According to Article 1(2) and (3) Protocol 16, a domestic court or tribunal may only request an advisory opinion in the context of pending proceedings and must give reasons for the request as well as provide the relevant legal and factual background of the case. As to Strasbourg, it is for the Grand Chamber to deliver the advisory opinion and its composition includes, like in contentious cases, the judge elected in respect of the contracting party from which the request originates.[288]

The new advisory procedure is reminiscent of the preliminary reference procedure in the EU,[289] which was a key instrument in securing vertical integration of EU law within domestic legal systems.[290] In April 2019, the ECtHR delivered its first-ever advisory opinion under Protocol 16 upon request of the French Court of Cassation. The opinion concerned the requirements under Article 8 ECHR in respect of the legal recognition of a parent-child relationship between a child born through a gestational surrogacy arrangement abroad and the intended mother.[291] The following provides a tentative outlook on the further operationalization of Protocol 16 and discusses its supranational potential and drawbacks.

4.5.3 *Supranational Potential of the Court's New Advisory Jurisdiction*

On paper, Protocol 16 has considerable supranational potential. First, the advisory procedure pierces the state veil in that it institutionalizes the direct exchange between Strasbourg and the highest domestic courts. It creates a formal channel of communication and interaction between the Court and the domestic judiciary in the context of a particular case. Protocol 16 introduces an interjudicial and multilevel mechanism through which domestic courts will be directly "plugged" into the Convention machinery of protection,[292] reinforcing their position within the interpretative community of the ECHR.[293] It provides an opportunity for the domestic judiciary to enter

[287] For a detailed analysis and interpretation of the different provisions of Protocol 16, see Paprocka and Ziółkowski, "Protocol No. 16," 278ff.

[288] Art. 2(2) and (3) Protocol 16.

[289] Art. 267 TFEU; Report of the Group of Wise Persons, para. 80. For a comparison see Paul Gragl, "(Judicial) Love Is Not a One-Way Street: The EU Preliminary Reference Procedure as a Model for ECtHR Advisory Opinions Under Draft Protocol No. 16" (2013) 38 *European Law Review* 229–247; Janneke Gerards, "Advisory Opinions, Preliminary Rulings and the New Protocol No. 16 to the European Convention of Human Rights: A Comparative and Critical Appraisal" (2014) 21 *Maastricht Journal of European and Comparative Law* 630–651.

[290] Chapter 1, Sections 1.4.2–1.4.3.

[291] ECtHR, *Recognition in domestic law of a legal parent-child relationship between a child born through a gestational surrogacy arrangement abroad and the intended mother*, no. P16-2018-001, Advisory Opinion (Protocol 16) of April 10, 2019.

[292] European Law Institute, Statement on Case-overload at the European Court of Human Rights, July 6, 2012, GT-GDR-C(2012)008, 35; Jahn, "Normative Guidance," 821.

[293] Jahn, "Normative Guidance," 828. On the interpretative community see also Chapter 5, Sections 5.3.2 and 5.4.3.3.

into a (more effective) partnership with the ECtHR,[294] also in respect of other domestic actors.[295] This dialogue is facilitated to the extent that the requesting domestic court can even address the Court in the official national language.[296] From the perspective of the Convention level, the advisory opinion procedure may further promote decentralization of ECHR enforcement for as in addition to individuals (and states), domestic courts may now directly access the Court too and obtain guidance enabling them to ensure respect for Convention rights domestically.[297]

In general, access to the Court under the new advisory jurisdiction is fairly broad. According to the explanatory report it was expected "that the parties to the case in the context of which the advisory opinion had been requested would be invited to take part in the proceedings."[298] Indeed, in the first advisory proceedings, the President of the Grand Chamber invited the parties to the domestic proceedings to submit written observations to the Court, which the concerned family did.[299] As in the context of individual or interstate applications and pursuant to Article 3 Protocol 16, the Commissioner on Human Rights has a right to intervene too. The same provision also foresees that the Court may invite any other high contracting party or person to submit written comments or take part in any hearing, where doing so is in the interest of the proper administration of justice.[300] Again, the broad access rules were relied upon already in the first advisory proceedings: In addition to the French government, the Court received written interventions by three other state parties, different domestic authorities as well as several NGOs.[301]

Secondly, the advisory procedure extends the jurisdiction of the Court by adding a new form of review, which is essentially preventive in nature. Unlike any other judicial function discussed so far, Protocol 16 introduces a mechanism that aims at providing *ex-ante* guidance to domestic courts before they decide a case involving Convention law.[302] They can consult the ECtHR on important aspects of the interpretation and application of Convention law and meanwhile suspend domestic proceedings.[303] As the Court emphasized, the goal of the procedure was "not to transfer the dispute to the European level, but rather to provide guidance to national courts, so that the latter can

294 Gerards, "Advisory Opinions," 638f.
295 Jahn, "Normative Guidance," 825.
296 Explanatory Report Protocol 16, para. 11.
297 ECtHR, *Mennesson* v. *France*, no. 65192/11, Judgment (Merits and Just Satisfaction), June 26, 2014.
298 Explanatory Report Protocol 16, para. 20.
299 *Advisory opinion concerning gestational surrogacy arrangement abroad*, § 4. From a normative perspective of human rights law (Art. 6 ECHR in particular) there is, of course, an important argument to be made that the parties of domestic proceedings should be given access to the Court (Jahn, "Normative Guidance," 843).
300 See also Chapter 5, Section 5.6.
301 *Advisory opinion concerning gestational surrogacy arrangement abroad*, § 6.
302 Explanatory Report Protocol 16, para. 11.
303 Ibid., para. 1.

adjudicate on the matter."[304] This preventive element bolsters the Court's position as final interpreter of Convention law and may thus reinforce integration and convergence.[305] That the Court delivered its first opinion within only six months after the request by the French Court of Cassation indicates that it is willing and capable to provide guidance in a timely and effective manner.[306] In turn, the French Court of Cassation arguably resorted to the advisory opinion procedure precisely to prevent being found in violation of the ECHR a second time.

Potentially, Protocol 16 could further strengthen the limited abstract and general character of the ECtHR's judicial review. Although a request for an advisory opinion must relate to a concrete domestic case and cannot be theoretical in nature,[307] it can also originate in domestic proceedings that pertain to the abstract review of domestic legislation.[308] In fact, this is precisely the type of review that domestic constitutional courts engage in and the latter clearly falls within the ambit of highest domestic courts and tribunals envisaged by Article 1(1) Protocol 16.[309]

4.5.4 *Limits to the New Advisory Jurisdiction*

The Court's advisory jurisdiction also comes with certain limitations, which reduce its supranational potential. First and foremost, the advisory procedure is non-compulsory. Protocol 16 is an additional, not an amending protocol, operating only between those high contracting parties that have chosen to accept it.[310] Furthermore, domestic courts of contracting states that have ratified the Protocol are not obliged to resort to the procedure.[311] It is their discretionary choice to do so, like it is the discretionary choice of the ECtHR to accept or decline delivering an opinion.[312] It was therefore argued that states, which tend to be critical toward the Court or have significant problems in upholding the standard of protection under the Convention, are unlikely to submit to the new procedure; and even if they do, their courts would arguably not make use of the procedure.[313] Whether this holds true or not, the non-compulsory and discretionary nature of the procedure certainly limits the cases, in which it can and will be applied in practice.

304 *Advisory opinion concerning gestational surrogacy arrangement abroad*, § 25.
305 For the same argument in a different context see Lindberg, European Economic Integration, pp. 11f.
306 *Advisory opinion concerning gestational surrogacy arrangement abroad*, § 34.
307 Art. 1(2) Protocol 16; Gerards, "Advisory Opinions," 633.
308 Paprocka and Ziółkowski, "Protocol No. 16," 281.
309 Explanatory Report Protocol 16, para. 8.
310 Art. 6 Protocol 16.
311 Art. 2(1) Protocol 16.
312 The Court may apply similar criteria to those used when deciding on requests for referring cases to the Grand Chamber (Explanatory Report Protocol 16, para. 9).
313 Thomas Voland and Britta Schiebel, "Advisory Opinions of the European Court of Human Rights: Unbalancing the System of Human Rights Protection in Europe?" (2017) 17 *Human Rights Law Review* 1–23 at 14.

Another important limitation is that the Court only renders an advisory "opinion." In a formal sense, the opinion has no binding effect on the domestic court that requested it, the state concerned or any (other) party to the domestic case (Article 5 of Protocol 16). As the Court itself noted, "domestic courts can use (or not use) the advice of the European Court as they see fit."[314] A state which disregards an advisory opinion might arguably frustrate the preventive function of the procedure and a subsequent application under Article 34 ECHR may reveal a violation of the Convention. But there is no formal obligation to abide by the opinion like there is for judgments under Article 46 ECHR.[315] The non-binding outcome of the advisory procedure was a crucial precondition for the adoption of Protocol 16 and said to reflect a more heterarchical and pluralistic ordering of the relationship between the European and domestic level.[316] While legal pluralism and supranationality are not necessarily mutually exclusive, the formally non-binding character does fit squarely with the definition of supranationality adopted. However, when exercising its new advisory function, the Court will also engage in the development of Convention law, which contracting states must generally respect.[317] The explanatory report clearly states that the interpretation of the Convention and its Protocols through advisory opinions has analogous effects to the interpretation in judgments and decisions.[318] Hence, as Gerards noted, the general parts of the advisory opinion benefit from the *res interpretata* effect.[319] Other commentators speculate that the ECtHR's advisory opinion procedure "will display a comparable effect" to the precedential force of CJEU rulings.[320] The Court itself noted that the value of its advisory opinions "also lies in providing the national courts with guidance on questions of principle relating to the Convention applicable in similar cases."[321] The abstract and concise drafting style of the Court's first opinion arguably supports such general guidance, although the Court also framed the issue narrowly limiting the opinion strictly to the question submitted by the requesting court.[322]

Two other qualifications may limit the potential scope of application and impact of Protocol 16. The formalized dialogue is restricted both substantively and procedurally. In terms of substance, the Court will only deliver an opinion on "questions of principle."[323] The drafting history of that wording reveals parallels to Article 43

314 *Advisory opinion concerning gestational surrogacy arrangement abroad*, § 25.

315 Dzehtsiarou and O'Meara, "Advisory Jurisdiction," 465.

316 Jahn, "Normative Guidance," 843.

317 See Chapter 5, Section 5.5.3.

318 Explanatory Report Protocol 16, para. 27.

319 Gerards, "Advisory Opinions," 635f. In comparison to EU law, Gerards even states that "to the extent that the success of the preliminary reference procedure is rooted in the legal or precedential force of the CJEU's rulings, it can be expected that the ECtHR's advisory opinions procedure will display a comparable effect" (644). See also Paprocka and Ziółkowski, "Protocol No. 16," 290f.

320 Voland and Schiebel, "Advisory Opinions," 11.

321 *Advisory opinion concerning gestational surrogacy arrangement abroad*, § 26.

322 Ibid., § 28–34.

323 Art. 1(1) Protocol 16.

ECHR which limits referrals to the Grand Chamber to cases that raise a serious question affecting the interpretation or application of Convention law or a serious issue of general importance.[324] While the Court did not address the question of principle requirement in its first opinion, scholars suggested that the Court may basically deal with three types of issues in an advisory opinion: new and unresolved matters of Convention law, inconsistent case-law, or reversal of existing case-law.[325] On a procedural level, Article 1(1) Protocol 16 only empowers "highest national courts and tribunals" to request an opinion.[326] Lower courts are thus excluded from direct interaction with the ECtHR.[327] Restricting the dialogue with Strasbourg to the highest domestic judiciary reflects the subsidiarity of the Convention system as well as the rule of prior exhaustion of domestic remedies.[328]

4.5.5 *Outlook*

The limitations discussed earlier are primarily regarded such from a comparative perspective, in juxtaposition to the preliminary reference procedure in EU law.[329] In contrast to Protocol 16, Article 267 TFEU sets out an obligatory procedure for both the CJEU and domestic courts, that plays out at an early stage of the domestic proceedings and will lead to a formally binding result for the requesting court and the EU legal order more generally. One should be cautious, however, to draw conclusions from such comparison, as it may fall short of considering the differences between the two legal systems, such as the subsidiary nature of the ECHR or the Court's overlapping jurisdiction alongside that of domestic courts. It might therefore be overly pessimistic to argue that, based on a comparison with EU law, Protocol 16 will necessarily have a modest impact or limited added value.[330]

More generally, scholars have been rather critical toward the new procedure. Some argue that an *ex-ante* control is contrary to the idea of subsidiarity.[331] Others predict that Protocol 16 will likely fail to enhance dialogue or reduce the caseload, or even be counter-productive to the achievement of these objectives.[332] Despite these

324 Explanatory Report Protocol 16, para. 9.

325 For a detailed analysis Paprocka and Ziółkowski, "Protocol No. 16," 284–289.

326 The wording of Art. 1(1) Protocol 16 allows for some flexibility regarding jurisdictions, where there are several highest courts (Explanatory Report Protocol 16, para. 8). Art. 10 Protocol 16 provides that it is for contracting states to indicate the courts or tribunals that qualify for the purposes of Art. 1(1) Protocol 16.

327 Explanatory Report Protocol 16, para. 8.

328 Ibid.

329 Gerards, "Advisory Opinions"; Voland and Schiebel, "Advisory Opinions".

330 Contra Gerards, "Advisory Opinions," 650f.

331 Besson, "Subsidiarity," 105.

332 Dzehtsiarou and O'Meara, "Advisory Jurisdiction," 468; Gerards, "Advisory Opinions," 650f. As to the drawbacks of Protocol 16 on the accession process of the EU to the ECHR see Voland and Schiebel, "Advisory Opinions," 16ff. For a more optimistic assessment Jahn, "Normative Guidance," 821–846, in particular 831.

critical outlooks, the present analysis of Protocol 16 has shown that it transforms the Court's advisory jurisdiction in a significant manner. It represents less an extension of the Court's jurisdiction under Article 47 ECHR than a new form of review altogether, which, from an international law perspective, is quite unique.[333] The fact alone that Protocol 16 was inspired by EU law is testament to the qualitative change of the Court's judicial function. It was, among other things, because of Protocol 16 that the CJEU felt that EU accession to the ECHR would undermine its exclusive jurisdiction over the definitive interpretation of EU law and the autonomy of the EU legal order.[334] While this position was criticized strongly,[335] it, too, shows the far-reaching nature of the new advisory procedure. On a conceptual level, the shift in the Court's role is assessed against the backdrop of the dichotomy of individual *vs.* constitutional justice. In her thorough account, Jahn, for instance, speaks of a paradigm shift and asserts that Protocol 16 has "now openly endorsed the constitutional justice approach" of the ECtHR.[336] In terms of the present conceptualization, Protocol 16 adds another important dimension to judicial integration. In a formal sense, the advisory procedure may fall short of meeting the definition of supranationality, given its voluntary and non-binding character. However, in terms of substance, the transformation of the Court's advisory jurisdiction extends judicial integration both in nature and scope and circumvents, through the institutionalization of the direct interaction between domestic courts and the ECtHR, the national/international divide to a particular degree. Protocol 16 will formally link the domestic and ECHR level of protection and provide for an integrated system of decentralized enforcement. How and to what extent this translates into practice, will largely depend on the willingness of domestic courts to make use of the procedure.[337]

4.6 CONCLUSION

In this chapter, it was argued that supranational adjudication under the ECHR has led to judicial integration in a number of different areas. Discussing and disentangling these different dimensions of judicial integration provided a nuanced and comprehensive picture of the Court's supranational authority, except for the Court's lawmaking function, to which the next chapter is devoted.

333 Tellingly, it has therefore been described as *sui generis* compared to the advisory jurisdictions of other international courts and tribunals (Report of the Group of Wise Persons, para. 81).

334 CJEU, Opinion 2/13 ECLI:EU:C:2014:2454, §§ 196–200; Voland and Schiebel, "Advisory Opinions," 16ff.

335 With further references Voland and Schiebel, "Advisory Opinions," 19.

336 Jahn, "Normative Guidance," 822, 831–843.

337 It was emphasized that Protocol 16 relies, maybe too optimistically, on a presumption of constructive dialogue. Dzehtsiarou and O'Meara, "Advisory Jurisdiction," 454f; Gerards, "Advisory Opinions," 646f.

Notwithstanding certain countertrends, one can witness an incremental supranationalization, a deepening of judicial integration under the ECHR. Today, the supranational authority of the ECtHR goes far beyond its initial function to provide external review and individual redress. The Court has either been given or assumed important new functions in a number of different areas covering the pre-judgment (interim relief, cooperation), the judgment phase (indication of remedies) as well as the post-judgment phase (compliance review). With the operationalization of Protocol 16, this trend still continues, as it links, though on a voluntary basis, the domestic and ECHR level of protection and provides for an integrated system of decentralized enforcement. The result of the deepening of judicial integration under the ECHR is a substantial increase of the ECtHR's autonomy over states, but also a more far-reaching circumvention of the state veil and a more direct interaction of the Court with domestic actors, individuals and courts or state authorities alike, which can leverage the Court. From an interdisciplinary viewpoint, this has opened up new channels of communication and networks, through which Convention law is ultimately constructed, and promoted socialization of domestic actors both civil and public within the Convention framework.[338] On a normative level, it also illustrates how one may find in the particular supranational authority of the ECtHR at the same time part of its legitimacy: the Convention community feeds on numerous individuals daily submitting their arguments to the Court and thus becoming European citizens.[339]

The deepening of judicial integration has led to what could be described as a diversification or complexification of the Court's role and authority, which can no longer be accurately captured within the constitutional *vs.* individual justice dichotomy. Not only has the Court embraced both of these elements, it today exercises comprehensive authority in a wide range of situations and over a continued time span. Acknowledging such complexification may inform the way in which the Court's role and authority are evaluated in the future and allows the adoption of a more context-specific approach in the operationalization of subsidiarity and the wider debate on (democratic) legitimacy and participation.

In many areas including interim relief, cooperation, remedies, or compliance review, the expansion of the Court's judicial function can be traced back, among other reasons, to the enlargement of the CoE in the early nineties.[340] In the new more unstable Europe, the CoE assumed a quite different role than simply safeguarding democratic pluralism: it was more often "concerned with helping its members (...) to become democracies in that full sense of the term."[341] Many of

338 Risse and Sikkink, "Socialization of International Human Rights Norms," p. 5.

339 Lemmens, "Criticising or Misunderstanding?," p. 32.

340 Harmsen, "Reform of the Convention System," p. 121.

341 Catherine Lalumière, "Discussion Paper by the Secretary General on the Development of the Organisation and on the Implications of Continued Enlargement, Particularly of the Russian Federation's Accession" (1994) *The Council of Europe in the New Europe* 1–13 at 3, available at www.cvce.eu/content/publication/2004/4/27/4977d781-d180-4313-b0c7-77f48e3b749e/publishable_en.pdf (accessed July 23, 2020).

the acceding states struggled (or are still struggling) with systemic problems to protect fundamental rights at the domestic level, while, sometimes, displaying a lack of respect for or inability to comply with decisions issued by the Court. Against this background, the Court was in some cases forced to assume a role resembling that of a *first* and *last* instance Court. This in turn, necessarily led to a more direct and perceptible impact of the Court's authority on individuals and victims of human rights violations and a more immediate responsibilization of partnering with state authorities. Once in place, the Court then also began deploying its new powers, such as the pilot judgment procedure, toward other states including Italy, Germany, or the United Kingdom. However, the deepening of judicial integration is not the result of judicial activism alone. In most instances, it was carried by states, be it through resolutions or recommendations in the CoM, formal amendments of the ECHR or additional Protocols.[342] In general, supranational authority remains dependent on contracting states in so far as they can, in theory, withdraw initial grant of jurisdiction to the Court.[343]

342 Keller and Stone Sweet, "Impact of the ECHR," p. 679.
343 Bates, *Evolution of the ECHR*, p. 438.

5

Supranational Lawmaking

5.1 BEYOND THE INDIVIDUAL DISPUTE: THE COURT'S LAWMAKING FUNCTION

Admittedly, any act of (international) judicial interpretation can also be conceived of as lawmaking. Interpretation, especially in the context of international law,[1] concretizes legal rights and obligations and creates normative expectations, which, in turn, may influence the behavior of all those applying and invoking the norms in question.[2] In the words of Hersch Lauterpacht, "judicial lawmaking is a general phenomenon" in every society in which "justice is administered by judicial tribunals."[3] Under the Convention system, however, judicial lawmaking is particularly extensive both in quality and quantity. Today, the text of the ECHR and its Protocols is merely the basis of a much larger notion of Convention law. It is through lawmaking by the ECtHR that the abstract rights guaranteed in the ECHR turned into an ample and autonomous body of law. In fact, normatively speaking, some go as far as arguing that lawmaking, in the sense of setting a general standard of protection, is or ought to be the overriding, "constitutional" mission of the ECtHR.[4] Lawmaking is one important reason that the Convention developed into a "European Bill of Rights,"[5] or to use the Court's own terms, "a constitutional instrument of European public order." In quantitative terms, the Court's extensive lawmaking function can be ascribed to the impressive productivity of the Court. In 2019, the Court disposed of 40,667 applications and delivered 2,187 judgments.[6] If

1 Lacking a central lawmaker, judicial lawmaking is arguably greater in international law compared to the domestic context (Tom Ginsburg, "Bounded Discretion in International Judicial Lawmaking" (2005) 45 *Virginia Journal of International Law* 631–673 at 633).

2 Armin von Bogdandy and Ingo Venzke, "Beyond Dispute: International Judicial Institutions as Lawmakers" (2011) 12 *German Law Journal* 979–1003.

3 Hersch Lauterpacht, *The Function of Law in the International Community (1933)*, reprint (Oxford: Oxford University Press 2011), p. 255.

4 See subsequently the proponents in favor of a system of "constitutional justice" fn. 54.

5 Bates, *Evolution of the ECHR*, pp. 171ff.

6 See the of ECtHR statistics of 2019, available at www.echr.coe.int/Documents/Stats_analysis_2019_ENG.pdf (accessed July 23, 2020).

ECHR lawmaking seems today generally accepted, it does remain a delicate function provoking criticism and the reproach of overreach from both states and commentators. Lawmaking, in particular raising existing protection standards, therefore requires careful justification as well as balancing by the Court: "it is common knowledge that the Court's activity has revolved, revolves and will continue to revolve around issues relating to national sovereignty, interpretation of the more or less strictly worded text, and judicial lawmaking."[7]

The present chapter discusses the qualitative aspect of the Court's extensive lawmaking function in five parts and it is submitted that ECHR lawmaking is uniquely supranational and integrative. Section 5.2 explores the inherently expansive task of interpreting and applying human rights and links this to the special interpretative techniques developed by the Court. Section 5.3 discusses the Court's own appreciation of its lawmaking function as well as the communitarian perspective it has adopted in that regard. Section 5.4 then looks more closely at the judicial methodology that has allowed the Court to develop a common and autonomous European human rights standard, while Section 5.5 analyses how this standard can be re-imposed on states through the *res interpretata* effect of Strasbourg judgments and decisions. Finally, Section 5.6 briefly discusses the importance of third-party interventions in ECtHR proceedings for the Court's role as lawmaker within the Convention community.

At the outset, it is further necessary to clarify the term of lawmaking. Despite the influx of scholarly articles on the subject, there is no authoritative definition of judicial lawmaking by international courts. Some understand the term in a narrow sense, as *extra legem* interpretation of a treaty provision beyond its wording,[8] some focus on gap-filling or norm expansion,[9] and others concentrate on the notion of precedent.[10] Most often perhaps, lawmaking is conceived of in rather a broad fashion and it is this understanding which is adopted here. It is easiest to define lawmaking in this sense in a negative way as the effect of international judicial decisions beyond the settlement of the individual dispute. The premise is that any interpretation and application of international law entails to an extent lawmaking, as it concretizes legal rights and obligations and hence creates normative expectations.[11] As Buergenthal observed, clarifying "existing law (...) of necessity makes new law,

7 Christoffersen, *Fair Balance*, p. 13. Although interpretation is understood here also as a form of lawmaking.

8 Marten Breuer, "Zulässigkeit und Grenzen richterlicher Rechtsfortbildung in der Rechtsprechung des EGMR" (2013) 68 *Zeitschrift für öffentliches Recht* 729–766 at 732.

9 This is often the case in international criminal law and international arbitration. For an example of the former see Mia Swart, "Gap-Filling as Lawmaking: The Examples of the Ad Hoc International Criminal Tribunals" in Hélène Ruiz Fabri, Rüdiger Wolfrum, and Jana Gogolin (eds.), *Select Proceedings of the European Society of International Law*, vol. II (Oxford: Hart 2010), pp. 313–330.

10 Marc Jacob, "Precedents: Lawmaking Through International Adjudication" in Armin von Bogdandy and Ingo Venzke (eds.), *International Judicial Lawmaking: On Public Authority and Democratic Legitimation in Global Governance* (Berlin/Heidelberg: Springer 2012), pp. 35–68.

11 See earlier fn. 2.

not with the broad brush strokes generally employed by legislatures, but by what might be called normative accretion."[12] Lawmaking in this broad sense thus includes a number of processes, not all of which are necessarily perceived as equally intrusive: "developing, adapting, modifying, filling gaps, interpreting, or even branching out in a new direction."[13] Lawmaking can be both procedural or substantive. Examples of procedural lawmaking have already been discussed in the previous chapters (such as establishing the binding character of interim measures or the introduction of the pilot judgment procedure and the category of indirect victims) [14] This chapter, however, is limited to lawmaking under the substantive provisions of the Convention.[15]

5.2 EXPANSIVE NATURE OF ECHR LAWMAKING

5.2.1 *Construction of Human Rights as Perpetual Lawmaking Process*

In 1950, states not only decided against a system of formal adjudication out of concern of an activist Court but also decided to flesh out rights instead of enumerating them to keep the potential loss of sovereignty to a minimum.[16] With the gradual submission and commitment to supranational adjudication, however, contracting states delegated to the ECtHR the authority to "construct" Convention rights.[17] According to Ginsburg's taxonomy on judicial lawmaking states implicitly delegated residual lawmaking powers to the Convention organs and later to the ECtHR.[18] Indeed ECHR rights – or human rights in general for that matter – are open-ended and lawmaking is therefore to a particular degree embedded or inherent in the task of adjudicating ECHR disputes. Even though more or less detailed in their wording, Convention guarantees remain "incomplete" and leave, similar to fundamental rights in the domestic context, considerable room for lawmaking.[19] Legal theorists such as Dworkin and Alexy have regarded fundamental rights as principles that need concretization as opposed to rules that furnish definitive

12 Thomas Buergenthal, "Lawmaking by the ICJ and Other International Courts" (2009) 103 *Proceedings of the Annual Meeting (American Society of International Law)* 403–406 at 403.
13 Robert Y. Jennings, "The Judicial Function and the Rule of Law", *International Law at the Time of its Codification: Essays in Honour of Roberto Ago*, vol. III (Milan: Giuffrè 1988), p. 145. See also Mohamed Shahabuddeen, *Precedent in the World Court* (Cambridge: Cambridge University Press 1996), p. 91.
14 Chapter 4, Sections 4.2.1.1, 4.2.2.2 and 4.3.2.2.
15 Procedural rights such as Art. 6 ECHR are, of course, equally covered.
16 Chapter 3, Section 3.2.3.
17 Stone Sweet, "Constitutionalization of the Convention," 4.
18 Ginsburg, "Bounded Discretion," 643f. Although Ginsburg's taxonomy does not seem to fit entirely the context of human rights adjudication.
19 Stone Sweet, "Constitutionalization of the Convention," 3.

reasons.[20] The stability of human rights norms is therefore a necessary illusion:[21] while human rights are abstract, "conduct is relentlessly particular," which "constantly triggers disputes, and disputes end up modifying the rules."[22] In other words, interpretation and application of human rights norms to specific circumstances, whether domestic or international, leads to almost perpetual lawmaking.

Moreover, societal conditions evolve beyond what was or could have been anticipated by the drafters of the Convention. The ECtHR must therefore decide in how far the content of Convention guarantees should evolve to reflect these changes. It may resort to the living instrument doctrine (evolutive interpretation) in order to update under certain conditions the ECHR by interpreting it as "a living instrument" and "in the light of present-day conditions."[23] Responsiveness to changing societal circumstances is central to the construction of human rights and also an important bedrock principle for the Court's lawmaking function. As Wildhaber stated:

> Our Court is to a certain extent a lawmaking body. How could it be otherwise? How is it possible to give shape to Convention guarantees such as the prohibition of torture, equality of arms, freedom of expression or private and family life, if – like Montesquieu – you see in the judge only the mouthpiece of the law? Such guarantees are programmatic formulations, open to the future, to be unfolded and developed in the light of changing conditions.[24]

In short, human rights as principles as well as applying them in the case at hand, especially to changing societal conditions, entail that adjudication under the ECHR results in lawmaking.

5.2.2 *Objective Obligations and Interpretative Autonomy*

An objective or lawmaking treaty such as the ECHR must not necessarily imply lawmaking through adjudication.[25] If vested with interpreting institutions, however, lawmaking treaties, because of their content and nature, lend themselves to special interpretative techniques. To recall, the Court emphasized already in *Wemhoff* the link between the Convention's character as a lawmaking treaty and interpretation:

[20] Robert Alexy, *A Theory of Constitutional Rights* (Oxford: Oxford University Press 2009). Ronald Dworkin, *Taking Rights Seriously* (Cambridge MA: Harvard University Press 1978).

[21] Wayne Sandholtz, "Expanding Rights: Norm Innovation in the European and Inter-American Courts" in Alison Brysk and Michael Stoh (eds.), *Expanding Human Rights* (Cheltenham: Edward Elgar 2017), p. 156.

[22] Sandholtz, "Expanding Rights," p. 156.

[23] *Tyrer* v. *the U.K*, § 31.

[24] Luzius Wildhaber, "The European Court of Human Rights: The Past, the Present, the Future" (2007) 22 *American University International Law Review* 521–538 at 525.

[25] Chapter 3, Section 3.3.1.2.

> Given that it is a lawmaking treaty, it is also necessary to seek the interpretation that is most appropriate in order to realise the aim and achieve the object of the treaty, not that which would restrict to the greatest possible degree the obligations undertaken by the Parties.[26]

Indeed, the objective nature of the ECHR was one of the grounds on which the Court justified recurring to doctrines such as autonomous interpretation, the principle of effectiveness, and evolutive interpretation.[27] Those techniques, in turn, allowed the Court to gain considerable autonomy in interpreting the Convention and provided the basis for the Court's extensive norm-generating function. The Court's "interpretative ethic," which rejects textualism and intentionalism,[28] paved the way for assuming a more pronounced and autonomous lawmaking function. It enabled the Court, as Letsas pointed out, to recognize rights (i) which do not expressly figure in the Convention (such as the right to court access[29] or the right to be free from environmental nuisance[30]) (ii) which contracting states could not have intended to protect (such as the freedom from human trafficking)[31] or (iii) which contracting states even explicitly rejected to protect (such as the freedom of deciding not to belong to a trade union)[32].[33] The last constellation, however, remains rare. The ECtHR will be reluctant to "create" rights that would clearly contradict either the wording or a systemic interpretation of the ECHR and its Protocols.[34] The Court has itself always asserted that there are limits to judicial lawmaking through evolutive interpretation and usually abstains from establishing specific guarantees, where this would clearly sidestep formal amendment of the Convention or the adoption of an additional Protocol.[35] Of course, whether one conceives of a specific evolutive interpretation as a creation of a new right, an *ultra vires* act, or as extending the scope of protection of an existing right, is in itself a question open to diverging interpretations, also among judges.[36]

26 *Wemhoff* v. *Germany*, § 8.
27 Chapter 3, Section 3.3.2.
28 George Letsas, "Strasbourg's Interpretive Ethic: Lessons for the International Lawyer" (2010) 21 *European Journal of International Law* 509–541 at 523ff.
29 ECtHR, *Golder* v. *the United Kingdom*.
30 For example, ECtHR, *López Ostra* v. *Spain*, no. 16798/90, Judgment of December 9, 1994, Series A no. 303-C.
31 ECtHR, *Rantsev* v. *Cyprus and Russia*, no. 25965/04, Judgment of January 7, 2010, ECHR 2010-I (extracts).
32 *Young, James and Webster* v. *the United Kingdom*.
33 Letsas, "ECHR as a Living Instrument," pp. 122f.
34 *Öcalan* v. *Turkey*, § 162. Although Breuer submits that the Court's judgment in *Schalk and Kopf v. Austria* is precisely an example of interpretation *contra legem* (see subsequently fn. 97).
35 See, also, for an early example ECtHR, *Johnston and Others* v. *Ireland*, no. 9697/82, Plenary Judgment of December 18, 1986, Series A no. 12, § 53.
36 In defense of the latter view Laurens Lavrysen, "The Scope of Rights and the Scope of Obligations: Positive Obligations" in Eva Brems and Janneke Gerards (eds.), *Shaping Rights in the ECHR* (Cambridge: Cambridge University Press 2013), pp. 173f. See, for instance, ECtHR, *Di Trizio* v. *Switzerland*, no. 7186/09, Judgment of February 2, 2016, Joint Dissenting Opinion of Judges Keller, Spano, and Kjølbro.

Evolutive interpretation also calls for a flexible doctrine of precedent.[37] As the Court stated in *Pretty* v. *the United Kingdom*, "judgments issued in individual cases establish precedents albeit to a greater or lesser extent."[38] It has regularly reiterated that although it "is not formally bound to follow its previous judgments, it is in the interests of legal certainty, foreseeability, and equality before the law that it should not depart, without good reason, from precedents laid down in previous cases."[39] With this approach the Court secures a certain level of normative stability as regards lawmaking, while remaining open to adjust the ECHR's interpretation, if societal and legal changes so require.[40] In this sense and as Feldman put it, precedents of the Court are no more or no less than "authoritative interpretations of the ECHR under social and moral conditions and the state of scientific knowledge *current at the time of the decision*."[41]

In short, autonomy through special interpretative techniques is crucial for the Court in discharging its supranational role as European standard setter and translates also into an autonomous European human rights law as such.[42]

5.3 THE ECTHR AS A COMMUNITY COURT

5.3.1 *Lawmaking as a Secondary but Standalone Function*

The integrative dimension of ECHR lawmaking is also owed to the ECtHR's understanding of its role and mandate.[43] Lawmaking by international courts

37 Luzius Wildhaber, "Precedent in the European Court of Human Rights" in Paul Mahoney et al. (eds.), *Protection des droits de l'homme: la perspective européenne /Protecting Human Rights: The European Perspective: Mélanges à la mémoire de /Studies in memory of Rolv Ryssdal* (Cologne: Heymanns 2000), pp. 1530ff.

38 *Pretty* v. *the United Kingdom*, § 75. On the doctrine of precedent in the ECHR system, see, among others, Katia Lucas-Alberni, *Le revirement de jurisprudence de la Cour européenne des droits de l'homme* (Brussels: Bruylant 2008); Alastair Mowbray, "An Examination of the European Court of Human Rights' Approach to Overruling Its Previous Case Law" (2009) 9 *Human Rights Law Review* 179–201; Yonatan Lupu and Erik Voeten, "Precedent in International Courts: A Network Analysis of Case Citations by the European Court of Human Rights" (2012) 42 *British Journal of Political Science* 413–439; Wildhaber, "Precedent in the ECtHR."

39 For example, *Goodwin v. the United Kingdom*, § 74.

40 Ibid.

41 David Feldman, "Precedent and the European Court of Human Rights," *Appendix C to Law Commission Consultation Paper No. 157, Criminal Law Bail and the Human Rights Act 1998: A Consultation Paper* (London: The Stationery Office 1999), pp. 114f. It is usually up to the Grand Chamber to overturn precedents, which secures a certain internal cohere of the Court's case-law. The Chamber has for instance the possibility to relinquish a case to the Grand Chamber, where its outcome would result in inconsistencies with previous judgments delivered by the Court (Art. 30 ECHR).

42 Madsen called this the boomerang effect of Strasbourg institutions (Mikael Rask Madsen, "France, the UK and the 'Boomerang' of the Internationalisation of Human Rights (1945–2000)" in Simon Halliday and Patrick Schmidt (eds.), *Human Rights Brought Home – Socio-Legal Perspectives of Human Rights in the National Context* [Oxford: Hart 2004]), pp. 57–86.

43 As submitted for European economic integration by Lindberg, European Economic Integration, pp. 8 and 10.

has been captured by referring to the adjudicator's role "beyond individual dispute settlement."[44] While this holds true for the ECHR context too, lawmaking under the Convention has always been more than a simple by-product of adjudication. To an extent, lawmaking developed into a standalone function of the Court. Early on, the Court distinguished lawmaking from the settlement of disputes and from providing redress to individuals on a case by case basis. In fact, the Court was, since *Ireland* v. *the United Kingdom*, surprisingly open as to its norm generating function. To recall, the Court held therein that, although the UK admitted to having breached the Convention, it must hear the case because its "judgments in fact serve not only to decide those cases brought before" it but, "more generally, to *elucidate, safeguard and develop the rules instituted by the Convention*, thereby contributing to the observance by the States of the engagements undertaken by them as Contracting Parties (Article 19) (art. 19)."[45] In the following, the Court elucidated its lawmaking function further. In *Karner* v. *Austria*, which concerned the discrimination of homosexuals under Austrian succession law, the Court refused to strike out the case, although the applicant had died and no heirs wished to pursue the application.[46] The Court stressed that "human rights cases before the Court generally also have a moral dimension, which must be taken into account when considering whether the examination of an application after the applicant's death should be continued," which was "all the more so if the main issue raised by the case transcends the person and the interests of the applicant."[47] It is against this background that the Court not only referred to its famous statement in *Ireland* v. *the United Kingdom* but further elaborated:

> Although the primary purpose of the Convention system is to provide individual relief, its mission is also to determine issues on public-policy grounds in the common interest, thereby raising the general standards of protection of human rights and extending human rights jurisprudence throughout the community of the Convention States (. . .).[48]

The Court concluded that the issue at hand, i.e., the difference in treatment of homosexuals as regards succession to tenancy, indeed concerned an "important question of general interest not only for Austria but also for other states parties to the Convention."[49] The Court followed the same approach in *Markin* v. *Russia*.[50] In its

[44] See earlier fn. 2.
[45] *Ireland* v. *the United Kingdom*, § 154.
[46] ECtHR, *Karner* v. *Austria*, §§ 20–28.
[47] Ibid., § 25.
[48] Ibid., § 26.
[49] Ibid., § 27.
[50] *Markin* v. *Russia*, § 89.

judgment, in this case, the Court established a violation of Article 8 in conjunction with Article 14 ECHR (discrimination based on gender) because domestic authorities refused to grant a male intelligence operator parental leave from the military (servicewomen being entitled to such leave).[51] The Russian government argued that the matter had been resolved given that the applicant had ultimately been granted parental leave, including financial aid. Nonetheless, the Court refused to strike out the case as it considered that the difference in treatment between male and female military personnel as regards entitlement to parental leave is an issue of "general interest" not only for Russia but also for other CoE states.[52]

Both the *Karner* and *Markin* case confirmed that, as *Ireland* v. *the United Kingdom* suggested, lawmaking under the Convention is to an extent freestanding. The Court literally conceives of lawmaking as a function that it performs for the entire community of Convention states and in certain situations, this is by itself sufficient to maintain the Court's jurisdiction. There are thus instances, in which the Court acts "more as a general and prospective lawmaker than as a judge whose reach is primarily particular and retrospective."[53] Advocates of a system of constitutional justice under the ECHR wish to see the self-sufficiency of lawmaking further strengthened. Ultimately, they assert that lawmaking in the sense of setting a general standard of protection is the only function which the Court can reasonably be excepted to perform given the great number of applications.[54] As *Karner* v. *Austria* shows, however, the Court today still maintains a certain hierarchy among its different functions. Lawmaking, even though free-standing in certain circumstances, remains "secondary" compared to the "primary purpose" of the Convention system, which is delivering individual justice.[55]

Similar to the area of judicial review, there is some evidence to suggest that resistance against the ECtHR, in particular following the Brighton Declaration, has prompted it to use its lawmaking powers more cautiously.[56] Stiansen and Voeten, for instance, have found that the proportion of judgments going beyond simply applying existing case-law has dropped.[57] Further, granting states a broader margin of appreciation is usually the result of the Court not finding a sufficient European consensus on an issue, which also prevents evolutive lawmaking.[58] It is, however, important to recognize that the Court has (so far) not retracted from the

51 Ibid.

52 *Markin* v. *Russia*, § 90.

53 Keller and Stone Sweet, "Impact of the ECHR," p. 703.

54 With further references Steven Greer, *The European Convention on Human Rights – Achievements, Problems and Prospects* (Cambridge: Cambridge University Press 2006), pp. 169ff.

55 Greer, for instance, has called this hierarchy into question and submitted that it lacks justification and reflection (Greer, *ECHR*, pp. 169ff).

56 Chapter 4, Section 4.2.3.3.

57 Stiansen and Voeten, "Backlash and Judicial Restraint," 13.

58 See subsequently Sections 5.4.2–5.4.3.

understanding of its mandate as articulated in *Ireland* v. *the United Kingdom* or *Karner v. Austria*.

5.3.2 *Progressive Realization of Human Rights*

In 1950, there was considerable disagreement on whether the ECHR should represent a common minimum denominator of fundamental rights or provide the basis for lifting the fundamental rights protection standard across CoE states.[59] Looking at the drafting history discussed in Chapter 3, it is safe to say that if a view prevailed, it was that of the ECHR securing "rights minimalism."[60] Nonetheless, the Preamble of the ECHR always included a dynamic element with its reference to the "achievement of greater unity between its members" and "the maintenance and further realization of Human Rights and Fundamental Freedoms" as a method to reach this aim. And as the Court later held, "any interpretation of the rights and freedoms guaranteed has to be consistent with 'the general spirit of the Convention, an instrument designed to maintain and promote the ideals and values of a democratic society'."[61]

In *Ireland* v. *the United Kingdom*, the Court already referred to its task "to develop the rules instituted by the Convention,"[62] and since *Karner*, it explicitly asserts that "raising the general standards of protection of human rights and extending human rights jurisprudence throughout the community of the Convention States" is part of its duty as adjudicator.[63] Moreover, the Court also emphasized "the increasingly high standard being required in the area of the protection of human rights" which necessitates "greater firmness in assessing breaches of the fundamental values of democratic societies."[64] In other terms, the Court acknowledged that lawmaking may serve the specific purpose of realizing a progressive human rights standard across CoE states. Progressive realization includes the creation of new guarantees or the expansion of existing ones, either by extending the scope of persons protected or the scope of situations covered by that right. It also entails that once a certain level of protection is established, it will generally function as a minimum baseline which, in principle, cannot be undercut anymore, neither by domestic authorities, nor by the Court itself.[65] Generally speaking, the Court thus overturns its precedents to the

59 Nicol Danny, "Original Intent and the European Convention on Human Rights Public Law" (2005) *Public Law* 152–172.

60 Chapter 3, Section 3.2.3; Danny, "Original Intent"; Stone Sweet, "Cosmopolitan Legal Order," 73.

61 ECtHR, *Soering* v. *the United Kingdom*, no. 14038/88, Plenary Judgment of July 7, 1989, Series A no. 161, § 87.

62 *Ireland* v. *the United Kingdom*, § 154.

63 *Karner* v. *Austria*, § 26.

64 *Demir and Baykara* v. *Turkey*, § 146.

65 Arts. 19 and 53 ECHR. Although the notion of non-regression is largely absent in the Court's case-law (for an exception see the Partly Dissenting Opinion of Judge Casadevall in ECtHR, *Gorou* v. *Greece (No. 2)*, no. 12686/03, Grand Chamber Judgment of March 20, 2009, § 8).

benefit of those protected, not in order to reduce protection.[66] In sum and to use the words of Keller and Stowe Sweet:

> (...) "going to Strasbourg" will be attractive to those who wish to see new rights recognized, or to raise standards of protection for established rights. It is an important function of the Court to respond to these demands and to participate fully in the progressive development of rights in Europe (...).[67]

This statement also illustrates that in the end progressive lawmaking goes back to and is initiated by the ultimate legal subjects of the Convention system. Indeed, citizens by petitioning the Court and less so its judges insist on expanding Convention rights. The many applications received by the Court can therefore be regarded as its "daily plebiscite."[68] That the ECtHR explicitly invoked the community notion when discussing its lawmaking function can further be seen as a recognition that the interpretation of the Convention constitutes an important way of protecting as well as supplementing community interests norms.[69]

The ECtHR never understood its (lawmaking) function as one of ensuring uniform application of Convention law. The particular nature of human rights as both complementary and evolutive rights encourages, if not demands, a certain level of rights diversity across regional contexts.[70] Convention law represents a standard, which, on the one hand, and as long as it is met, allows for different forms and ways of protection granting states a certain margin of appreciation.[71] On the other hand, states are encouraged to exceed Convention protection and develop their own, more protective interpretation of Convention or domestic human rights (Article 53 ECHR). Diversity across the CoE is an important source of interpretation for the Court and, therefore, precondition for the progressive realization of human rights.[72] Variation in the interpretation and application of Convention law, within the boundaries established by the Court, is thus an inherent feature of the ECHR system. Rather than being contrasted to progressive lawmaking, it has to be viewed as the latter's foundation.[73]

66 Mowbray, "Overruling of Previous Case Law," 200.

67 Keller and Stone Sweet, "Impact of the ECHR," p. 707.

68 Lemmens, "Criticising or Misunderstanding?," p. 39.

69 Besson, "Community Interests in International Law," p. 42.

70 See also Chapter 6, Sections 6.2.2.3 and 6.3.4.

71 The institutional requirements derived from Art. 6(1) ECHR, for instance, allow states a leeway in the setting up and organization of their judiciaries. For example, ECtHR, *Kleyn and Others* v. *the Netherlands*, nos. 39343/98, 39651/98 and 43147/98, Grand Chamber Judgment of May 6, 2003, ECHR 2003-VI, § 193.

72 Samantha Besson, "The 'Erga Omnes' Effect of Judgments of the European Court of Human Rights – 'What's in a Name?'" in Samantha Besson (ed.), *La Cour europeéenne des droits de l'homme après le Protocole 14 – premier bilan et perspectives* (Zurich: Schulthess 2011), pp. 165–168.

73 Bjorge, *Domestic Application of ECHR*, p. 23.

5.4 ESTABLISHING A PAN-EUROPEAN HUMAN RIGHTS STANDARD

5.4.1 *Sources of Lawmaking*

The methodology through which the Court has engaged in progressive lawmaking is discussed in more detail in the following sections. It will become clear that lawmaking cannot be disconnected from the wider legal and societal developments. As the Court stressed, the ECHR does not operate in a vacuum.[74] While the Court often resorts to the concept of consensus, it is sometimes difficult to pinpoint relevant sources, determine their respective weight and ascertain the level of convergence needed for there to actually be "consensus."[75] Through a comparative lens, the Court may consider a broad variety of (legal) sources such as domestic legislation, case-law or public opinion (including civil society concerns as represented by NGOs), EU law but also international law including treaties, international case-law or soft law (both within or outside the European context). Access to and knowledge about pertinent sources therefore becomes an important element of lawmaking under the Convention.[76]

To recall, any international judge engages in autonomous decision-making in that he or she must by definition decide in an independent and binding fashion. However, the judicial methodology adopted by the ECtHR renders lawmaking particularly autonomous and therefore also supranational (if one ignores for a moment the other constitutive aspect of supranational decision-making, which is the involvement of individuals).[77] The following survey groups the Court's methodology into two categories in ascending order of autonomy at play: the majoritarian method and relying on international trends and common values. These two categories, which remain a scholarly approximation, are sometimes presented as subsequent developments,[78] though recent practice rather points to their parallel existence.[79] However, increased criticism towards the ECtHR has arguably resulted in the ECtHR being reluctant to rely on trends and emerging consensus as opposed to the majoritarian method.[80]

74 ECtHR, *Loizidou* v. *Turkey (Merits)*, no. 15318/89, Grand Chamber Judgment of December 18, 1996, Reports 1996-VI, § 43.

75 For an analysis on the different types of consensus and their interaction see Dzehtsiarou, *European Consensus*, pp. 38–71.

76 On the importance of custom, usage but also knowledge in international regimes see Krasner, "Structural Causes and Regime Consequences," pp. 202–204.

77 On this aspect see subsequently Sections 5.4.2.3 and 5.4.3.3; Chapter 2, Section 2.3.2.

78 For example, Letsas, "ECHR as a Living Instrument," pp. 115ff.

79 Dzehtsiarou, *European Consensus*, pp. 38–71.

80 See earlier Section 5.3.1.

5.4.2 *Majoritarian Method*

5.4.2.1 Comparative Approach

The Court usually grounds its evolutive interpretation on a majoritarian approach. As soon as a sufficient number of contracting states have recognized a certain right or regard a restriction thereof as impermissible, the Court will raise the Convention standard to that level and impose it on states, which lag behind.[81] This method requires a detailed comparative analysis of how contracting states regulate a given issue. The Court compiles comparative data on relevant domestic legislation and practice. Initially, the comparative analysis was limited in scope and depth. In *Tyrer*, for instance, in which the Court applied evolutive interpretation to establish that corporal punishment is contrary to Article 3 ECHR, the Court held – almost in passing and without citing any sources – that in "the great majority of the member States of the Council of Europe, judicial corporal punishment is not, it appears, used and, indeed, in some of them, has never existed in modern times (. . .)."[82] Over the years, however, the comparative method has become more sophisticated and mathematical. Today, the Court is assisted by a special research division composed of lawyers with expertise in the various domestic legal systems and it can rely on a statistical reading of a lot of comparative data.[83] In a way, the Court's comparative approach constitutes a practical necessity to understand a specific legal issue, map the possible range of solutions, and get inspiration. It, however, also reflects the Court's subsidiary position and renders its jurisgenerative function (more) legitimate.[84]

As early as *Golder*, the Court established that the Convention must be interpreted in the light of the rules on treaty interpretation codified in the VCLT[85] and its comparative method does find support in Article 31(3) VCLT, which provides for the possibility to take into account subsequent developments, namely any subsequent agreement between the parties regarding the interpretation of the treaty or the application of its provisions[86] (a) as well as any subsequent practice in the application of the treaty which establishes the agreement of the parties regarding its interpretation (b).[87] As to

[81] *A, B and C* v. *Ireland*, § 234.
[82] *Tyrer* v. *the United Kingdom*, § 38.
[83] Dzehtsiarou, *European Consensus*, pp. 40ff.
[84] Bjorge, *Domestic Application of ECHR*, p. 65.
[85] Arts. 31–33 VCLT.
[86] The question of whether a certain practice or conduct reflects a position "in the application of" the treaty or "regarding its interpretation" raises thorny issues of delimitation (ILC, Second Report on Subsequent Agreements and Subsequent Practice in Relation to the Interpretation of Treaties by Georg Nolte, A/CN.4/671, para. 10).
[87] The Court usually does not distinguish whether a specific practice falls under Art. 31(3)(b) VCLT or amounts to "an agreement between" the parties in the sense of Art. 31(3)(a) VCLT. Also, as to Art. 31(3)(b), it simply presumes that states "act in a way which reflects their *bona fide* understanding of their obligations" under the Convention (Georg Nolte, "Second Report on Subsequent Agreements and

the latter, common ground among the parties is sufficient and the ICJ does not require a qualified form of collective and uniform practice.[88]

5.4.2.2 Illustrating Consensus

Two examples should illustrate how the Court uses a majoritarian approach to determine the protection standard under the ECHR. The case of *Vinter and Others* v. *the United Kingdom* serves as an example in which the Court confirmed the existence of a European consensus in order to interpret the Convention dynamically.[89] As *Tyrer*, the case concerned Article 3 ECHR, more precisely the question of whether a life sentence without the possibility of parole is permissible under the Convention. A detailed comparative analysis revealed that in only six countries, not including the respondent state, domestic law precluded parole for life prisoners. Whereas nine countries didn't provide for life imprisonment in the first place, thirty-two countries allowed for life sentences to be reviewed in one form or another after a certain period of time.[90] Referring, *inter alia*, to this "large majority" of contracting states,[91] the Court raised the protection standard and found that Article 3 ECHR must henceforth be read as requiring the possibility of reviewing life sentences:

> (...) Article 3 must be interpreted as requiring reducibility of the sentence, in the sense of a review which allows the domestic authorities to consider whether any changes in the life prisoner are so significant, and such progress towards rehabilitation has been made in the course of the sentence, as to mean that continued detention can no longer be justified on legitimate penological grounds. (...)
>
> It follows from this conclusion that, where domestic law does not provide for the possibility of such a review, a whole life sentence will not measure up to the standards of Article 3 of the Convention.[92]

Inversely, the Court's methodology consists of not raising protection when a European consensus is lacking. The case of *Schalk and Kopf*, a same-sex couple denied marriage in Austria, is a telling example.[93] The couple invoked in Strasbourg a violation of the right to marry as guaranteed in Article 12 ECHR. Following

Subsequent Practice in Relation to the Interpretation of Treaties," vol A/CN.4/671 paras. 14 and 46). Exceptionally, however, the Court has referred to the interpretation of the Convention (e.g., ECtHR, *Banković and Others* v. *Belgium and Others*, no. 52207/99, Grand Chamber Decision of December 12, 2001, ECHR 2001-XII, § 62).

88 ICJ, *Kasikili/Sedudu Island (Botswana* v. *Namibia)*, Judgment of December 13, 1999, I. C. J. Reports 1999 1045, paras. 47–50 and 63.

89 ECtHR, *Vinter and Others* v. *the United Kingdom*, nos. 6069/09 and 130/10 3896/10, Grand Chamber Judgment of July 9, 2013, ECHR 2013-III (extracts).

90 Ibid., § 68.

91 Ibid., § 117.

92 Ibid., §§ 119 and 121.

93 ECtHR, *Schalk and Kopf* v. *Austria*, no. 30141/04, Judgment of July 24, 2010, ECHR 2010-IV.

a "traditional" conception of marriage, the ECtHR opined that the Convention's drafters must have had the union among people of different sex in mind when wording Article 12 ECHR.[94] The question then was whether Article 12 ECHR should be interpreted dynamically, as obliging contracting states to grant same-sex couples access to marriage. At the time of the judgment, six states allowed same-sex marriage, thirteen states some form of registered partnership, and nineteen states neither possibility.[95] Against this background, the Court held:

> Although, (...) the institution of marriage has undergone major social changes since the adoption of the Convention, the Court notes that there is no European consensus regarding same-sex marriage. At present no more than six out of forty-seven Convention States allow same-sex marriage (...).[96]

The Court abandoned its previous position that Article 12 ECHR necessarily pertains to marriage between two persons of the opposite sex,[97] but stated that, as matters stand, it remains up to contracting states to decide whether or not to allow same-sex marriage.[98]

A key question is what level of convergence is needed for the Court to proceed to evolutive interpretation. The Court's case-law is not entirely clear on this point. While consensus as a mode of (intergovernmental) decision-making is commonly understood as denoting a situation of absence of objection,[99] the Court's use of the notion points to a form of qualified majority: it usually uses adjectives such as "large,"[100] "clear"[101] or "overwhelming"[102] to describe the majorities that amount to consensus. Naturally, any finding regarding the (non-)existence of consensus will partly be predetermined by how narrowly or broadly the comparative issue in question is framed.[103]

94 Ibid., §§ 54 and 55. Art. 12 ECHR speaks of "men and women of marriageable age." The French version reads: *"l'homme et la femme ont le droit de se marier."*

95 Ibid., §§ 27–34.

96 Ibid., § 58.

97 This not only leaves the door open for future development but also is, in itself, an example of lawmaking *contra legem* in reference to standards outside the CoE framework (see subsequently Section 5.4.3.3). The Court did defend this reversal relying on Art. 9 EU Fundamental Rights Charter (Breuer, "Rechtsprechung des EGMR," 739f).

98 *Schalk and Kopf* v. *Austria*, § 61.

99 Rüdiger Wolfrum and Jakob Pichon, "Consensus" in Rüdiger Wolfrum (ed.), *Max Planck Encyclopedia of Public International Law*, online ed. (Oxford: Oxford University Press 2006), n. 1.

100 *Vinter and Others* v. *the United Kingdom*, § 117.

101 *A contrario*, ECtHR, *T.* v. *the United Kingdom*, no. 24724/94, Grand Chamber Judgment of December 16, 1999, §§ 71f.

102 *Bayatyan* v. *Armenia*, §§ 103, 108 and 124.

103 In S.A.S v. *France*, for instance, the Court defended that a general ban to wear full-face veil in public was compatible with the ECHR, although similar legislation was absent in forty-five out of forty-seven member states of the CoE (S.A.S v. *France*, Joint Partly Dissenting Opinion of Judges Nussberger and Jäderblom, § 19).

5.4.2.3 Conceptual Analysis

The mathematical approach of counting and comparing the position of CoE member states on a certain issue has prompted analogies to the situation of majority decision-making in an intergovernmental context, which is a hallmark of supranationality.[104] Stone Sweet and Brunell, for instance, make the argument that the ECtHR engages in majoritarian activism:

> (…) judges have developed techniques of assessing aggregate state practice in order to arrive at some measure of the extent of regime consensus on a relevant policy issue; the degree of policy consensus is then treated as an important fact bearing on the case at hand. This practice enables judges to pursue a strategy of majoritarian activism (…). Majoritarian activism refers to the disposition of judges to produce rulings that reflect outcomes that states might adopt under majoritarian, but not unanimity, decision rules.[105]

Of course, the Court's comparative approach does not hinge upon the position of governments as representatives of their citizens. Instead, the Court looks behind the state veil at the general legal situation in CoE member states.[106] It is with this caveat in mind, that the Court's method in applying evolutive interpretation could be regarded supranational in so far as it allows to impose a general standard of protection "against the will" of certain contracting states. A commonly accepted, European-wide position trumps the particular national approach in question.

Majoritarianism was identified as a judicial strategy which combines relative autonomy over states, while at the same time mitigating risks of a generalized backlash against the ECtHR. It "helps (…) manage judicialization, mitigate the legitimacy problems associated with judicial lawmaking under supremacy, and render efforts at curbing the growth of (…) authority improbable or ineffective."[107] Certain scholars, however, criticize the method for not being autonomous or supranational enough. Benvenisti's point of critique, for instance, is that the notion of consensus and the margin of appreciation doctrine still remain rooted in the concept of state sovereignty and state consent. By relying primarily on state practice, the Court would eschew its responsibility and fail to perform its task of providing external control.[108] Benvenisti therefore explicitly criticizes the limited supranational dimension of majoritarian lawmaking: "the court (…) relinquishes its

104 Chapter 2, Section 2.3.2.

105 Stone Sweet and Brunell, "Trustee Courts," 63.

106 Although states' governments are likely to defend in an intergovernmental context their domestic legal policies, this remains an assumption that must not necessarily hold true.

107 Stone Sweet and Brunell, "Trustee Courts," 64.

108 Benvenisti, "Margin of Appreciation," 850ff; see also Susanna Mancini, "The Crucifix Rage: Supranational Constitutionalism Bumps Against the Counter-Majoritarian Difficulty" (2010) 6 *European Constitutional Law Review* 66–27 at 25f.

duty to set universal standards from its unique position as a *collective supranational voice* of reason and morality."[109] Letsas, too, demands a judicial methodology, which is effectively more supranational. Within his framework of a moral reading of the Convention, he challenges the Court's reliance on majoritarianism: "if human rights are distinctively counter-majoritarian then it makes no sense conditioning their scope and meaning on what the majority itself believes."[110] Doing so would be to deny protection to minorities altogether, because majoritarian preferences are typically biased against them.[111]

5.4.3 *International Trends and Common Ground*

5.4.3.1 Beyond Consensus

Instead, or sometimes complementary to the majoritarian method, the Court may rely on international trends or common grounds as a source of lawmaking. Sometimes, the Court also refers to the notion of emerging consensus,[112] although consensus in this context must not necessarily be European but can also be of an international character.[113] The approach of relying on international trends or common grounds is less principled and structured than the majoritarian method and it might be exaggerated to speak of a particular judicial methodology at all. It was traced back to the *Marckx* case, in which the Court only invoked an abstract "common ground (...) amongst modern societies" to proceed to evolutive interpretation.[114] Compared to the majoritarian approach, relying on international trends usually enhances the Court's autonomy in lawmaking vis-à-vis contracting states. The threshold to be met in terms of empirical sources is much lower and evolutive interpretation does not depend on prior recognition of the new protection standard by a majority of CoE states. International trends may comprise legal developments at the international but also at the domestic level outside CoE member states. The former may include international treaties, EU law, non-binding international instruments (soft law) as well as decisions of other international courts and quasi-judicial bodies. In general international law terms, the Court leaves the realm of Article 31(3)(a) and (b) VCLT and enters the sphere of Article 31(3)(c) VCLT instead, according to which "any relevant rules of international law applicable in the relations between the parties" should be taken into account.[115] In *Loizidou*, for instance, the Court held that "the principles underlying

109 Benvenisti, "Margin of Appreciation," 852 (emphasis added).
110 Letsas, "ECHR as a Living Instrument," p. 123.
111 Ibid., p. 123.
112 *Demir and Baykara* v. *Turkey*, § 85.
113 Dzehtsiarou, *European Consensus*, p. 39.
114 *Marckx* v. *Belgium*, § 41; Letsas, "ECHR as a Living Instrument," p. 115.
115 The Court stressed the importance of this provision (*Golder* v. *the United Kingdom*, § 29: for a study on the reception of international law in the ECtHR see Forowicz, *Reception of International Law*).

the Convention cannot be interpreted and applied in a vacuum" and due regard must be paid to "any relevant rules of international law."[116] Accordingly, the Court strives, in so far as possible, to interpret the ECHR in harmony with other rules of international law (of which it forms part).[117]

5.4.3.2 Illustrating International Trends and Common Grounds

The following discussion should illustrate how the Court relies on international trends or common grounds as conclusive element to advance ECHR protection. A prominent example is the case of *Goodwin* v. *the United Kingdom*.[118] Christine Goodwin unsuccessfully sought to have her operative gender re-assignment legally recognized before domestic authorities. The Court's Grand Chamber had to address the question of what, if any, positive obligations Article 8 ECHR imposes on states in this area. At the outset of its reasoning, the Court recalled its so far rather conservative case-law on transsexualism, while stressing that it must maintain a dynamic and evolutive stance on the issue.[119] It prefaced its analysis by proposing "to look at the situation within and *outside* the Contracting State to assess in the light of 'present-day conditions' what is now the appropriate interpretation and application of the Convention (…)."[120] As in earlier cases,[121] the Grand Chamber reiterated that there was still no "common European approach as to how to address the repercussions which the legal recognition of a change of sex may entail for other areas of law such as marriage, filiation, privacy or data protection."[122] This time, however, the lack of a European consensus did not prevent the Court from engaging in evolutive interpretation. On the contrary, the Grand Chamber held, that it

> (…) attaches less importance to the lack of evidence of a common European approach to the resolution of the legal and practical problems posed, than to the clear and uncontested evidence of a *continuing international trend* in favour not only of increased social acceptance of transsexuals but of legal recognition of the new sexual identity of post-operative transsexuals.[123]

116 *Loizidou* v. *Turkey (Merits)*, § 43.

117 ECtHR, *Al-Adsani* v. *the United Kingdom*, no. 35763/97, Grand Chamber Judgment of November 21, 2001, ECHR 2001-XI, § 55; *Hassan* v. *the United Kingdom*, Grand Chamber Judgment of September 16, 2014, no. 29750/09, ECHR 2014-VI, § 77.

118 ECtHR, *Christine Goodwin* v. *the United Kingdom*, no. 28957/95, Grand Chamber Judgment of July 11, 2002, ECHR 2002-VI.

119 Ibid., §§ 71–75.

120 Ibid., § 75.

121 ECtHR, *Sheffield and Horsham* v. *the United Kingdom*, nos. 22985/93 and 23390/94, Judgment of July 30, 1998, ECHR 1998-V, § 35. Although the Grand Chamber already observed an emerging consensus domestic law of CoE states being in a state of flux.

122 *Goodwin* v. *the United Kingdom*, § 85.

123 Ibid.

The Court ascertained a continuing international trend based on a comparative report submitted by Liberty, an NGO and third-party intervener in the case. The NGO's report concluded that while there was no statistical increase of relevant data in Europe, an increasing number of states outside Europe gave full legal recognition of gender re-assignment including countries such as Singapore, Canada, South Africa, Israel, Australia, New Zealand, and the United States.[124] Against this background, the Court concluded that Article 8 ECHR imposes a duty to legally recognize the applicant's new gender.[125]

Goodwin is an example in which the Court abandoned its usual method in proceeding to evolutive lawmaking. First, the Court's comparative reasoning was global instead of European, including countries as far away – both geographically and culturally – as Singapore. Secondly, rather than proceeding to statistical and numerical preponderance, the Court was satisfied (or had to be)[126] with general trends. And third, international trends outweighed the lack of a European consensus rather than confirming an emerging one. In sum, in terms of sources, *Goodwin* represents an important shift away from the state-centric and majoritarian approach, which primarily looks at ECHR parties and their position on a specific legal question.

The case of *Rantsev* v. *Cyprus and Russia* provides another example of the Court deviating from its usual majoritarian method. The case concerned a young Russian woman who came to Cyprus on an artist visa and tragically died trying to escape from her employer's apartment.[127] Taking into account different international legal instruments,[128] the ECtHR interpreted Article 4 ECHR and the prohibition of slavery and forced labor contained therein dynamically. It considered human trafficking within the meaning of Article 3(a) of the Palermo Protocol and Article 4(a) of the CoE Anti-Trafficking Convention to be a modern form of slavery[129] falling within the scope of Article 4 ECHR.[130] On that basis, the Court developed far-reaching positive obligations regarding human trafficking: Article 4 ECHR requires states to put in place a framework to prohibit and punish trafficking[131],

124 Ibid., § 56.

125 Ibid., § 93.

126 Admittedly, a majority requirement would become difficult to ascertain, let alone meet, once the borders of the CoE as a geographical area of reference are crossed.

127 *Rantsev* v. *Cyprus and Russia*, § 41.

128 Ibid., § 274. The ECtHR cited various instruments related to trafficking such as the Palermo Protocol, the CoE Convention on Action against Trafficking in Human Beings, different CoM and PACE recommendations, EU legislation, and relevant ICTY case-law on contemporary forms of slavery.

129 Though the Court refrained to specify whether it falls under the category of slavery, servitude, or forced labor. This was regarded as a failure to provide a more precise engagement with the constituent elements of trafficking as human exploitation (Jean Allain, "Rantsev v Cyprus and Russia: The European Court of Human Rights and Trafficking as Slavery" (2010) 10 *Human Rights Law Review* 546–557).

130 *Rantsev* v. *Cyprus and Russia*, § 282.

131 *Rantsev* v. *Cyprus and Russia*, § 285.

regulate businesses or immigration,[132] take operational steps to protect victims and potential victims of trafficking[133] or cooperate in cases of cross-border trafficking.[134] The Court grounded its evolutive interpretation conclusively on regional and universal international law standards, incorporating them into Article 4 ECHR. The Court was little concerned about whether the relevant international instruments were binding in respect of the two respondent states or CoE states more generally.[135] In *Demir and Baykara* v. *Turkey*, the Court acknowledged the same in a surprisingly open manner:

> In this context, it is not necessary for the respondent State to have ratified the entire collection of instruments that are applicable in respect of the precise subject matter of the case concerned. It will be sufficient for the Court that the relevant international instruments denote *a continuous evolution in the norms and principles applied in international law* or in the domestic law of the majority of member States of the Council of Europe and show, in a precise area, that there is *common ground* in modern societies (. . .).[136]

International or European law trends also served the Court as a basis for dynamic interpretation in the *Scoppola (No. 2)* judgment.[137] In this case, the Grand Chamber reversed previous Strasbourg case-law according to which Article 7(1) ECHR only included a prohibition of imposing more stringent criminal laws retrospectively, not, however, an obligation to vest more lenient criminal law with retroactive effect. The Court, again, relied on a number of different international documents such as Article 6 ACHR, Article 49(1) Charter of Fundamental Rights of the European Union as well the ICC Statute and ICTY case-law,[138] which did not necessarily pertain to the respondent state or CoE states more generally for that matter.[139]

5.4.3.3 Conceptual Analysis

What transpires from the Court's case-law is a very broad understanding of systemic integration as provided for by Article 31(3)(c) VCLT.[140] As Tzevelekos found, the ECtHR uses Article 31(3)(c) VCLT in a way "that provides greater human rights

[132] Ibid.
[133] Ibid., §§ 284, 286f.
[134] Ibid., § 289.
[135] Breuer, "Rechtsprechung des EGMR," 737. The cited CoE Anti Trafficking Convention, for instance, was only ratified by Cyprus, whereas the European Convention on Mutual Assistance in Criminal Matters was only ratified by Russia. For a similar approach see ECtHR, *Scoppola* v. *Italy (No. 2)*, no. 10249/03, Grand Chamber Judgment of September 17, 2009.
[136] *Demir and Baykara* v. *Turkey*, §§ 85 and 86.
[137] *Scoppola* v. *Italy (No. 2)*.
[138] Ibid., § 105.
[139] Critical thereof Breuer, "Rechtsprechung des EGMR," 746.
[140] To be sure, the Court does not always invoke this provision explicitly and there are different ways, in which the Court has applied it, including more restrictive ones. For a detailed analysis of ECtHR case-law and systemic integration see Forowicz, *Reception of International Law*, pp. 47ff; Vassilis

protection but that can also easily *extend further than or against state will.*"[141] Admittedly, the restriction in the wording of Article 31(3)(c) to "any relevant rules of international law applicable *in the relations between the parties*" has provoked controversy in international law scholarship.[142] For some, systemic integration presupposes identity of parties between both the treaty to be interpreted and the treaty to be taken into account.[143] Others require that all parties to the dispute also be parties to the treaty to be taken into account.[144] A third position consists of allowing systemic integration also in the absence of (complete) identity of membership in so far as international norms are at play, which reflect, even though not necessarily customary law, some (implicitly) accepted "common understanding" or "state of the art."[145] As *Rantsev* and *Scoppola (No. 2)* show, the ECtHR doesn't attach much importance to the principle of state consent, which is at play in the limitation phrase of Article 31(3)(c) VCLT and it sometimes may go beyond even the third and most inclusive position found among scholars.[146] Furthermore, relying on Article 31(3)(c) VCLT might be questionable in the first place, if the goal is "to update" ECHR guarantees in order for them to match up with more protective international standards rather than to harmonize conflicting international obligations.[147] For these reasons, the Court's reliance on international trends alone was criticized as unlawful judicial lawmaking and as being contrary to the VCLT framework.[148]

Both *Goodwin* and *Rantsev* exemplify a category of cases, in which the Court departed from the majoritarian and comparative law technique in favor of a more autonomous lawmaking method, in the context of which the position of ECHR states and their consent becomes less important, if not irrelevant altogether. In *Goodwin*, the Court's conclusive argumentation was based on global developments

P. Tzevelekos, "The Use of Article 31(3)(c) of the VCLT in the Case Law of the ECtHR: An Effective Anti-Fragmentation Tool or a Selective Loophole for the Reinforcement of Human Rights Teleology" (2010) 31 *Michigan Journal of International Law* 621–690; Breuer, "Rechtsprechung des EGMR," 756ff.

141 Tzevelekos, "Use of Article 31(3)(c)," 685f (emphasis added).

142 For a detailed analysis and with further references see ILC, Fragmentation of International Law, 206–243; Panos Merkouris, *Article 31(3)(c) VCLT and the Principle of Systemic Integration: Normative Shadows in Plato's Cave* (Leiden/Boston: Brill Nijhoff 2015).

143 For instance, Ulf Linderfalk, "Who Are 'The Parties'? Article 31, Paragraph 3(c) of the 1969 Vienna Convention and the 'Principle of Systemic Integration' Revisited" (2008) 55 *Netherlands International Law Review* 343–364.

144 Duncan French, "Treaty Interpretation and the Incorporation of Extraneous Legal Rules" (2006) 55 *International and Comparative Law Quarterly* 281–314 at 306f.

145 ILC, Fragmentation of International Law, 239. This, or a similar position is defended by Joost Pauwelyn, *Conflict of Norms in Public International Law* (Cambridge: Cambridge University Press 2003), pp. 257ff; Campbell McLachlan, "The Principle of Systemic Integration and Article 31(3)(c) of the Vienna Convention" (2005) 54 *International and Comparative Law Quarterly* 279–320 at 314f.

146 Tzevelekos, therefore, speaks of a less voluntarist interpretation of the Convention through reliance on systemic integration (Tzevelekos, "Use of Article 31(3)(c)," 688).

147 Breuer, "Rechtsprechung des EGMR," 761.

148 Ibid.

in states around the world, whereas in *Rantsev*, the Court relied on systemic integration to incorporate standards from international instruments, which were not necessarily applicable in respect of the respondent states or all CoE states. As Letsas observed, the Court moved "away from placing decisive weight on the absence of consensus amongst contracting states and from treating it as the ultimate limit on how far it can evolve the meaning and scope of Convention rights" and instead "treats the ECHR as a living instrument by looking for common values and emerging consensus in international law."[149] It is this increase in autonomy that renders the Court's approach of relying on international trends more supranational than the majoritarian method. Letsas' analysis also reveals the particular communitarian dimension of operating with international trends as opposed to consensus. That the Court is looking for "common values"[150] echoes the Court's function as standard setter for the Convention community[151] and his role in identifying the (inter-)subjective and cohesive element making up the community.[152]

5.5 (RE-)IMPOSING THE EUROPEAN PROTECTION STANDARD

5.5.1 *Beyond the* Res Judicata *Effect*

In addition to autonomy in decision-making, the supranational aspect of ECHR lawmaking lies in the fact that its product is binding: the protection standard developed by the ECtHR is applicable throughout the Convention system and can be (re-)imposed on all contracting states. This aspect pertains to the general effect of ECtHR case-law, not by virtue of the principle of *res judicata* (Article 46 ECHR)[153] but based on the principle of *res interpretata*.

To recall, under Article 46(1) ECHR contracting states only undertake to abide by judgments of the Court delivered in cases to which they are a party. Helfer described this limited binding effect of international adjudication as "an artifact of sovereignty."[154] In the present-day Convention system, however, the argument can be made that this artifact has, at least in part, been overcome. Indeed, it would seem contradictory for the Court to assume the function of a lawmaker, whose task it is to raise the standard of human rights protection, while denying the latter a wider significance beyond the individual case. The same goes for the commitment to a system of precedents. It would make little sense for the Court to adhere to its precedents, while not expecting contracting states to live up to the standards developed

149 Letsas, "ECHR as a Living Instrument," pp. 121f.
150 Ibid.
151 See earlier Section 5.3.
152 Ibid.
153 Compare Chapter 4, Section 4.2.2.1.
154 Laurence R. Helfer, "The Effectiveness of International Adjudicators" in Cesare P. R. Romano, Karen J. Alter, and Chrisanthi Avgerou (eds.), *The Oxford Handbook of International Adjudication* (Oxford: Oxford University Press 2013), p. 471.

therein.[155] In fact, the structure of ECtHR judgments and decisions reflects the latter's *res interpretata* effect. In each case, the Court lays out the general principles flowing from established case-law before applying them to the case at hand.[156] Moreover, several Convention provisions underline the importance of the Court's case-law and the precedent-based system (e.g., Articles 28(1)b), 30 and 43 ECHR). While the *res judicata* flows from the decisional authority of the Court, the *res interpretata* is the result of the Court's jurisprudential or interpretative authority and describes the effect of the generalizable parts of a judgment (or a decision).[157] The notion of *erga omnes* effect can be used synonymously, bearing in mind, however, that the *erga omnes* effect in the ECHR context is always limited to the contracting parties (*erga omnes inter partes*) and to the interpretative value of a judgment (i.e., can never pertain to the operative provisions and the Court's decisional authority).[158]

5.5.2 *Legal Basis of the* Res Interpretata *Effect*

It seems fair to say that the Court's jurisprudential authority stands on somewhat shaky ground. Article 46 ECHR only incorporates the principle of *res judicata* and the Convention is silent on the general effects of Strasbourg case-law. There is an argument to be made that the Court has acknowledged the *res interpretata* principle through its case-law, but if it did, then only indirectly, and without much vigor. In *Opuz* v. *Turkey*, a case concerning domestic violence, the Court held that

> [i]n carrying out this scrutiny, and bearing in mind that the Court provides final authoritative interpretation of the rights and freedoms defined in Section I of the Convention, the Court will consider whether the national authorities have sufficiently taken into account the principles flowing from its judgments on similar issues, even when they concern other States.[159]

This statement presupposes that states are required to conform to the Court's case-law in order to live up to their obligations under the Convention and prevent being found in violation thereof (should a similar case concerning their legal system be brought to Strasbourg). Put differently, if the Court may find a violation of the Convention because a state does not respect Strasbourg case-law, there appears to be a corresponding legal duty to observe this very case-law in the first place. More generally, the statement in *Opuz* v. *Turkey* suggests that Strasbourg case-law becomes an integral part of the corresponding ECHR rights and of the broader notion of Convention law (*corpus juris conventionis*).[160] Yet, the Court has barely

155 Besson, "Erga Omnes Effect," p. 135.
156 Gerards, "Shared Responsibility," p. 23.
157 Besson, "Erga Omnes Effect," pp. 129f, 132.
158 Ibid.
159 ECtHR, *Opuz* v. *Turkey*, no. 33401/02, Judgment of June 9, 2009, ECHR 2009-III, § 163.
160 Besson, "Erga Omnes Effect," pp. 129f, 138.

reiterated the position it voiced in *Opuz* v. *Turkey* in subsequent judgments and the author is not aware of any other cases, which address the *res interpretata* issue more upfront.[161] The Court did emphasize that its judgments all have "the same legal value" and "interpretative authority."[162] However, one can observe a certain discrepancy, between the Court's clear position on its extensive lawmaking and its relative silence on the general effects of its case-law.

At the intergovernmental level, contracting states also demonstrated reluctance to recognize a full and formal *erga omnes* effect of ECtHR judgments. The Interlaken Declaration does call upon state parties "to commit themselves to taking into account the Court's developing case-law, also with a view to considering the conclusions to be drawn from a judgment finding a violation of the Convention by another State, where the same problem of principle exists within their own legal system,"[163] whereas the Brighton Declaration states that "courts and tribunals should take into account the Convention and the case law of the Court."[164] The wording of these formulations is rather soft, however, and points to a desirability rather than a conventional duty or obligation. This seems to be the prevailing view at the intergovernmental level still today,[165] although some commentators also interpreted the Interlaken or Brighton Declaration to the contrary, as embracing the *erga omnes* effect of the Court's judgments by and large.[166]

In general, there remain controversies and a certain confusion regarding the subject, including whether there is a duty of states – legal or otherwise – to follow the Court's case-law.[167] The Parliamentary Assembly, for instance, held early on and

161 For the sake of completeness, it is worth mentioning that it has been addressed more directly in separate opinions. Judge Pinto de Albuquerque, for instance, held that the "erga omnes res interpretata effect" of Strasbourg case-law goes "far beyond its inter partes res judicata effect" and derives from the "nature of the Court as the European Constitutional Court" (ECtHR, *Al-Dulimi and Montana Management Inc.* v. *Switzerland*, no. 5809/08, Grand Chamber Judgment of June 21, 2016, ECHR 2016-III, Concurring Opinion of Judge Pinto de Albuquerque joined by Judges Hajiyev, Pejchal and Dedoval, § 60; see also *G.I.E.M. S.r.l. and Others* v. *Italy*, nos. 1828/06, 34163/07 and 19029/11, Grand Chamber Judgment of June 28, 2018, Partly Concurring, Partly Dissenting Opinion of Judge Pinto de Albuquerque, §§ 72ff).

162 *G.I.E.M. S.r.l. and Others* v. *Italy*, § 252.

163 Interlaken Declaration, Action Plan, B.4)c).

164 Brighton Declaration, A.7) and 9)c)iv).

165 CDDH, Report on the Longer-term Future of the System of the European Convention on Human Rights, CDDH(2015)R84 Addendum I, December 11, 2015, para. 37 (emphasis added).

166 Mirjana Lazarova Trajkovska, "Ways and Means to Recognise the Interpretative Authority of Judgments against Other States," Conference on Subsidiarity, Skopje, October 1–2, 2010, AS/Jur/Inf (2010)04, 12.

167 It was with the drastic influx of applications to the Court that the topic gained traction and became a recurring theme in the debate on the reform of the Convention system. Strengthening the general effects of ECtHR case-law (and the principles derived therefrom) was identified as a preventive tool that could relieve the overburdened Court and increase primary protection at the domestic level instead. For an overview of relevant CoE soft law instruments see Adam Bodnar, "Res Interpretata: Legal Effect of the European Court of Human Rights' Judgments for Other States Than Those Which Were Party to the Proceedings" in Eva Brems and Yves Haeck (eds.), *Human Rights and Civil*

in clear terms that "[t]he principle of solidarity implies that the case-law of the Court forms part of the Convention, thus extending the legally binding force of the Convention erga omnes (to all the other parties)."[168] According to the PACE, "this means that the states parties (...) have to take into consideration the possible implications which judgments pronounced in other cases may have for their own legal system and legal practice."[169] In contrast, the Group of Wise Persons[170] found that "under the present system, judgments are given in a particular case and do not apply to other States, even if they are judgments establishing a general principle,"[171] while, submitting that "the dissemination of the Court's case-law and recognition of its authority above and beyond the judgment's binding effect on the parties would no doubt be important elements in ensuring the effectiveness of the Convention."[172] In a similar vein, former and present judges have underlined the absence of a formal *erga omnes* effect or a system of de jure precedence, albeit stressing the interpretative authority of the Court or referring to a de facto *erga omnes* effect.[173] As a result, the picture conveyed is that the *erga omnes* effect of ECtHR judgments is not established *qua* Convention law but something granted de facto, either by Convention states themselves or indirectly through enforcement via Article 34 ECHR, or simply a desirability *de Coventione feranda*.

Some of the ambiguities may be due to a lack of terminological clarity, especially as concerns the notion of *erga omnes*. If the notion of *erga omnes* effect is understood, as it should not be, as the generalization of the *res judicata*, then ECtHR judgments or decisions indeed lack such effect (more precisely, they could never have such effect to begin with).[174] Also, the de facto qualification often leads to a conflation of

Liberties in the 21st Century (Berlin/Heidelberg: Springer 2014), pp. 229ff. PACE, Committee on Legal Affairs and Human Rights, "The Future of the Strasbourg Court and Enforcement of ECHR Standards: Reflections on the Interlaken Process," Conclusions of the Chairperson (Herta Däubler-Gmelin), Paris, December 16, 2009, AS/Jur (2010)06, 3ff.

168 PACE, Resolution 1226(2000), 3. The Resolution does however neither specify the legal basis of the principle of solidarity nor of the *erga omnes* effect. Point 2 simply reads: "The system of the Convention is based in particular on two principles: subsidiarity and solidarity."

169 Ibid.

170 To recall, this group was tasked by the CoM in 2005 to develop ideas to secure the long-term effectiveness of the ECHR system.

171 Interim Report of the Group of Wise Persons to the Committee of Ministers, CM(2006)88, May 10, 2006, para. 50.

172 Report of the Group of Wise Persons, para. 66 (emphasis added).

173 Jean Paul Costa, "The Authority of the Case-law of the ECtHR," Proceedings of the Regional Conference on the Role of Supreme Courts in the Domestic Implementation of the ECHR, September 20–21, 2007 (Council of Europe 2008) 17; Julia Laffranque, "Can't Get Just Satisfaction" in Anja Seibert-Fohr and Mark E. Villiger (eds.), *Judgments of the European Court of Human Rights – Effects and Implementation* (Farnham: Ashgate 2014), p. 71; contra Dean Spielmann, "Keynote Address" in Anja Seibert-Fohr and Mark E. Villiger (eds.), *Judgments of the European Court of Human Rights – Effects and Implementation* (Farnham: Ashgate 2014), p. 28.

174 For a similar view see Oddný Mjöll Arnardóttir, "Res Interpretata, Erga Omnes Effect and the Role of the Margin of Appreciation in Giving Domestic Effect to the Judgments of the European Court of Human Rights" (2017) 28 *European Journal of International Law* 819–843 at 826. She, therefore,

the factual and normative level. Indeed, CoE documentation as well as scholarly studies show that the interpretative authority of ECtHR judgments has found wide acceptance on the national plane.[175] Yet, the position that the interpretative authority of the ECtHR solely exists because national judges allow and observe it,[176] seems difficult to reconcile with states' primary duty to live up to the Convention standards, including principles flowing from its case-law.[177] A similar reservation applies to conditioning the interpretative effect of case-law on enforcement in a future case before the Court.[178] Given the level of abstraction of Convention rights, this view equally questions states' primary obligation to secure Convention rights and prevent violations thereof under Article 1 ECHR.[179]

Unsurprisingly, legal scholars, too, have recognized the *res interpretata* or *erga omnes* effect to varying degrees. Some deny the existence of an *erga omnes* effect in the formal or legal sense but assert that judgments are vested with something comparable, equally resorting to some sort of "de facto" or "quasi-" qualification.[180] Other scholars, however, have argued that an obligation to respect the Court's *res interpretata* may be inferred from the Convention itself, namely from Article 1 ECHR in conjunction with Articles 19 and 32 ECHR.[181] The argument is that by ratifying the Convention (and its Protocols), states have accepted to respect and secure Convention rights (Article 1 ECHR) as well as tasked the Court with the final interpretation thereof (Article 19 ECHR). Accordingly, the principles of ECHR case-law are just as important for contracting states as the Convention provision they pertain to.[182] In other words, the interpretation of the ECHR becomes an integral part of the corresponding Convention guarantees.[183] This view, although never confirmed

objects at least to an unqualified use of the *erga omnes* notion in the ECHR context and appears preferring to speak of *res interpretata* or de facto *erga omnes effect*.

175 PACE, Committee on Legal Affairs and Human Rights, Contribution to the Conference on the Principle of Subsidiarity, Skopje, October 1–2, 2010, "Strengthening Subsidiarity: Integrating the Strasbourg Court's Case Law into National Law and Judicial Practice," AS/Jur/Inf (2010)04, November 25, 2010.

176 ECtHR, Interlaken Follow-up, Principle of Subsidiarity, Note by the Jurisconsult, July 8, 2010.

177 *Opuz* v. *Turkey*, § 163.

178 It is unclear to the author how the Court can find a violation of the Convention, because a specific state measure is in contradiction to Strasbourg jurisprudence, if there is no corresponding duty to duly consider the Court's interpretation of Convention rights in the first place.

179 See also Chapter 6, Section 6.2.2.1.

180 Ress, "Decisions and Judgments of the ECtHR," 374. Ress, "Supranationaler Menschenrechtsschutz," 630; Luzius Wildhaber, "A Constitutional Future for the European Court of Human Rights" (2002) 23 *Human Rights Law Journal* 161–165 at 163. Breuer, "Principled Resistance," pp. 333ff, in particular 336.

181 See, for instance, Gerards, "Shared Responsibility," pp. 21–23; Bodnar, "Res Interpretata," pp. 223–262.

182 Bodnar, "Res Interpretata," pp. 226f.

183 ECtHR, *Scordino and Others* v. *Italy (No. 1)*, no. 36813/97, Decision of March 27, 2003, ECHR 2003-IV.

by the ECtHR, appears most in line with both the Court's extensive lawmaking function and its statement in *Opuz* v. *Turkey* on the effect of ECtHR judgments vis-à-vis other state parties.[184]

5.5.3 *Scope and Content of the* Res Interpretata

Not least because of the lack of guidance by the ECtHR, it is difficult to ascertain what precisely the *res interpretata* effect amounts to.[185] The following analysis is therefore in large parts based on legal scholarship. Similar to the *res judicata*, the *res interpretata* effect has a personal, material, and temporal scope.[186] *Ratione personae*, the Court's jurisprudential authority extends to all forty-seven contracting states and all individuals therein, as protected under the ECHR.[187] *Ratione temporis*, an interpretative principle or precedent is valid from the moment the respective judgment or decision has become final and so long as it is not overturned by the ECtHR. Given the dynamic nature of human rights in general and the evolutive dimension of lawmaking under the Convention in particular, the *res interpretata* effect generally lacks retroactivity.[188] Lastly, in terms of *ratione materiae*, the *res interpretata* can only pertain to the generalizable parts of judgments and decisions,[189] which establish interpretative principles.[190] While this excludes the facts of a specific case as well as the operative provisions, there are virtually no substantive restrictions, meaning that the *res interpretata* extends to all Convention rights, all notions interpreted by the Court but also to tests applied such as the proportionality analysis.[191]

The content of the obligation to respect the *res interpretata* is somewhat harder to pin down. Respect for the Court's interpretative authority cannot be viewed in isolation from the broader context of states' obligation to apply the ECHR in good faith and secure Convention rights domestically.[192] Looking at the Court's limited case-law, soft law instruments as well as legal scholarship, one may observe the crystallization of a three-pronged duty incumbent on states. Firstly, it appears logical that respecting the *res interpretata* effect requires some measure of awareness and

184 *Opuz* v. *Turkey*, § 163.

185 Exceptions are Besson, "Erga Omnes Effect"; Bodnar, "Res Interpretata"; Arnardóttir, "Erga Omnes Effect."

186 Following Besson, "Erga Omnes Effect," pp. 159ff.

187 Ibid.

188 Besson, "Erga Omnes Effect," p. 160.

189 Decisions may include important developments regarding admissibility criteria but can also shape the content of substantive guarantees when they address, for instance, whether an application is manifestly ill-founded. For example, ECtHR, *Rappaz* v. *Switzerland*, no. 73175/10, Decision of March 26, 2013. On the importance of decisions for the *res interpretata* see Bodnar, "Res Interpretata," p. 224, fn 1.

190 The same arguably applies to advisory opinions (Chapter 4, Section 4.5.3).

191 Besson, "Erga Omnes Effect," p. 161.

192 Chapter 6, Sections 6.2.2.1 and 6.2.3-6.2.5.

knowledge about Strasbourg case-law. Only when state authorities keep track of and understand the judicial output by the ECtHR, are they able to consider it. The Court held that states must facilitate domestic courts' knowledge of ECtHR case-law[193] and the CoM, PACE as well as contracting states stressed in various instruments the importance of activities such as dissemination, translation, or teaching for the interpretative authority of the Court.[194]

Second, state authorities must identify which interpretative principles are actually relevant or applicable to their domestic legal system and/or the proceedings in question. This is to an extent a discretionary assessment, although the focus should lie on the underlying principles of Strasbourg case-law instead of overconcentration on specific and individual cases.[195] As to judicial proceedings, the *res interpretata* will follow the applicable ECHR right(s),[196] while for the legislative, the CoM stressed the importance of having due regard to the entirety of the Court's case-law,[197] which contracting states also reiterated in the Brussels Declaration.[198]

Third and lastly, the principles identified as relevant and applicable must be "taken into account."[199] Respect for the Court's jurisprudential authority, especially by the domestic judiciary, does not require blind obedience. On the contrary, as Convention standards are to evolve constantly and provide minimum guarantees (Article 53 ECHR), it is for the domestic judge to keep sight of changing realities or more protective domestic guarantees, and to, if called for, develop or maybe even second guess the state of Convention law as it stands.[200] By so doing, the domestic judiciary enters into a dialogue with Strasbourg over the interpretation of ECHR rights.[201] Save for exceptions, however, there is an argument to be made in favor of a general duty to follow in good faith the principles established in case-law.[202] Such duty would also include the obligation of domestic courts to render their engagement with ECtHR

193 ECtHR, *Scordino* v. *Italy (No. 1)*, no. 36813/97, Grand Chamber Judgment of March 29, 2006, ECHR 2006-V, § 82.

194 For example, PACE, Resolution 1856(2012), 3; PACE, Recommendation (2002)13; Interlaken Declaration, Action Plan, Section B; Izmir Declaration, Action Plan, Section B; Brussels Declaration, Action Plan, Section B1; CoM, Recommendation (2002)13; CoM, Appendix to Recommendation (2004)5, 25f.

195 With references to domestic case-law Bjorge, *Domestic Application of ECHR*, p. 45.

196 Besson, "Erga Omnes Effect," p. 165.

197 CoM, Recommendation (2004)5, in particular paras. 25 and 26 of the Appendix.

198 Brussels Declaration, Action Plan, B.1.d).

199 Interlaken Declaration, Action Plan, B.4)c); Brighton Declaration, A.7) and 9)c)iv). As regards judicial proceedings, the ECtHR made the remarkable statement that national courts "must be in a position, under domestic law, to directly apply Strasbourg case-law" (*Scordino* v. *Italy (No. 1)*, § 82). The context of the statement, however, has remained unclear and the Court's dictum does not seem to have gained any wider significance.

200 See on relative supremacy Chapter 6, Section 6.3.4.

201 Besson, "Erga Omnes Effect," pp. 164–168.

202 See earlier fn. 179 and 185; Breuer, "Principled Resistance," p. 340. Raffaela Kunz, "Judging International Judgments Anew? The Human Rights Courts before Domestic Courts" (2019) 30 *European Journal of International Law* 1129–1163.

case-law transparent.[203] Indeed, this seems a precondition for any real and constructive dialogue[204] and was confirmed by the Court to the extent that it is regularly affording diligent courts and legislatures, which take due account of Convention law, a broader margin of appreciation when it comes to applying the relevant principles to the case or circumstances at hand.[205] Different scholars moreover agreed that there is a graduation in the interpretative value of Strasbourg case-law depending on a number of different factors such as the deciding composition of the Court,[206] agreement/disagreement among judges or whether or not a given interpretative principle forms part of a well-established case-law.[207] However, the Court recently clarified that "its judgments all have the same legal value" and that "interpretative authority cannot therefore depend on the formation by which they were rendered."[208] If, formally speaking, the legal value might therefore be the same for all judgments, the room for argumentation in the sense of differentiation or reversal might arguably still be greater or smaller depending on whether or not, for instance, a specific issue has been decided by the Grand Chamber or is subject of well-established case-law.

5.6 THIRD-PARTY INTERVENTIONS

Article 36(2) ECHR grants the possibility to seek leave to intervene as a third party. It allows the President of the Court to invite any contracting state which is not a party to the proceedings or any person concerned who is not the applicant to submit written comments or take part in hearings, if this is in the interest of the proper administration of justice.[209] Third-party interventions in the sense of Article 36(2) ECHR include *amicus curiae*, contracting state as well as actual third-party interventions.[210] In the course of the development towards a system of supranational adjudication, third-party access was progressively broadened in Strasbourg proceedings. This was interpreted in Chapter 3 as a general recognition by the Court that it is part of and impacts a broader legal community.[211] The present context allows to

203 Helen Keller and Cedric Marti, "Berücksichtigung der EGMR-Praxis durch innerstaatliche Gerichte – Eine rechtsmethodische Anleitung für den richterlichen Dialog mit Strassburg" (2015) 1 *Justice – Justiz – Giustizia*.
204 Lambrecht, "Assessing Criticism," p. 547.
205 Arnardóttir, "Erga Omnes Effect," 830–841.
206 Art. 43(2) ECHR.
207 For a comprehensive account see Bodnar, "Res Interpretata," p. 237. Although he rather discusses the factors from the perspective of legitimacy. See also Besson, "Erga Omnes Effect," p. 168f.
208 *G.I.E.M. S.r.l. and Others* v. *Italy*, § 252.
209 Given the sweeping impact of ECtHR case-law, one may even raise the question whether the discretionary wording of Art. 36(2) ECHR should not be replaced by an actual legal right to intervene.
210 Nicole Bürli, *Third-Party Interventions before the European Court of Human Rights* (Cambridge: Intersentia 2017), p. 183.
211 Chapter 3, Section 3.3.4.

concretize this communitarian interpretation: Article 36(2) ECHR can be conceived of as an expression and justification of the general lawmaking power of the Court as well as its interpretative authority throughout the Convention system.[212]

States ought to respect the general interpretative authority of the Court and the Convention standard introduced through lawmaking can be held against them.[213] For individuals, the interpretation of "their" rights under the ECHR is concerned, which, through the *res interpretata* effect, may also affect their domestic legal position more or less directly.[214] In short, the Court's lawmaking function impacts European society at large. Third-party interventions, therefore, provide an opportunity for governments, individuals but also for civil society to take part actively in the lawmaking process and exert influence over the general interpretation of Convention rights (by submitting legal arguments, relevant information or provide evidence on the existence or absence of consensus or international trends for instance).[215] The potential of taking influence becomes particularly evident following both a constructivist and communitarian premise.[216] Third-party interventions are a formalized element of the intersubjective dialogue through which norms but also interests and collective expectations are constituted.[217] While it is difficult to measure the result of this process, empirical research suggests that interventions, especially *amici curiae*, do in fact have a bearing on the Court's decision-making.[218]

Participation based on Article 36(2) ECHR not only enhances process legitimacy but also contributes to the general legitimacy of ECHR lawmaking.[219] *Amici curiae*, for instance, strengthen argumentative representation, principled decision-making, and the acceptance of the Court's authority. This becomes of particular significance in cases in which the Court decides politically sensitive issues or scrutinizes the domestic legislator.[220]

212 Bürli, *Third-Party Interventions*, pp. 183ff.

213 For example, the intervention of the Italian government in ECtHR, *Tarakhel* v. *Switzerland*, no. 29217/12, Grand Chamber Judgment of November 4, 2014, ECHR 2014-VI (extracts), § 76; the intervention of the government of Belgium in *S.A.S* v. *France* or the different interventions in *Lautsi* v. *Italy*, no. 30814/06, Grand Chamber Judgment of March 18, 2011, ECHR 2011-III (extracts), in *M.S.S.* v. *Belgium and* Greece, no. 30696/09, Grand Chamber Judgment of January 21, 2011, ECHR 2011-I or in *Al-Dulimi and Montana Management Inc.* v. *Switzerland*.

214 Many states in fact allow for Strasbourg case-law to be applied directly (Chapter 6, Section 6.3.3).

215 See earlier Section 5.4.

216 Chapter 2, Section 2.4.2.

217 Advocacy groups may even use Art. 36(2) ECHR to leverage the Court to indirectly exert influence over domestic processes.

218 Bürli, *Third-Party Interventions*, pp. 188–193.

219 Besson, "Erga Omnes Effect," p. 173.

220 Bürli, *Third-Party Interventions*, pp. 183–185.

5.7 CONCLUSION

This chapter discussed lawmaking understood as the general effect of Strasbourg case-law beyond the individual case. The topic was addressed from a Convention perspective, while leaving the domestic status and treatment of Strasbourg case-law to the subsequent chapter. It was argued that the expansive task of interpreting human rights as well as the Court's particular understanding of its mandate lie at the basis of the integrative dimension of ECHR lawmaking: human rights are transverse, open-ended, and dynamic principles that need constant (re-)interpretation by way of judicial practice. At the same time, the ECtHR has conceived of itself as a Community court, whose task it is to set and progressively raise a common protection standard. While evolutive lawmaking can and has therefore been viewed as a particular form of judicial activism, it is still the citizen, which, by petitioning the Court, ultimately insists on expanding Convention rights. When acting as lawmaker, the ECtHR does not seek to impose uniformity in the application of the ECHR, but pluralism and diversity remain the very foundation of ECHR lawmaking.

In the remainder of the chapter, it was argued that evolutive lawmaking by the ECtHR can be viewed as a form of supranational decision-making for two reasons. First, the Court applies an interpretative methodology that disregards state consent to a greater or lesser extent. Whereas the majoritarian approach allows the Court to impose a pan-European standard against the will of a minority of contracting parties, state consent becomes irrelevant altogether where the Court is relying on international trends and uses harmonious interpretation beyond the confines of the VCLT. In both instances, the standard set is supranational in that it embodies norms for a regional community transcending domestic human rights. Admittedly, the precise contours of the scope and breadth of the protection standard – or inversely the remaining margin of appreciation of states – will always be subject to disagreement among different actors and determined as a result of an ongoing debate or dialogue. At the moment, the trend in Strasbourg may well be to resort less often to evolutive lawmaking and grant states more leeway. Even in times of backlash and increased criticism, however, Convention law will likely conserve a supranational core or minimum. If human rights protection under the Convention were to become the mere reflection of domestic human rights and could only develop in complete lockstep with the latter, then, after all, the ECHR would be obsolete. Secondly, the product of the Court's lawmaking may be (re-)imposed on states by virtue of the Court's interpretative authority, states' primary duty to secure Convention rights as well as Article 34 ECHR. Whatever the term used – *res interpretata* or (de facto/quasi-) *erga omnes* effect – the Court's interpretative authority extends beyond the parties to the dispute, to use its own words: "throughout the community of Convention States." States ought to follow Strasbourg case-law in good faith, unless there are cogent reasons not to. In sum, lawmaking is supranational in so far as the Court determines a generalizable and autonomous protection standard which then must be observed throughout the community of Convention states and can be directly enforced by individuals relying on Article 34 ECHR. This suggests that the Convention system has dispelled another myth of state sovereignty. It is testament to the maturity of the Convention as a legal community.

Lastly, the possibility of third-party interventions pursuant to Article 36(2) ECHR was identified as corollary of the Court's lawmaking power and interpretative authority. Drawing on constructivist regime theory discloses how through Article 36(2) ECHR any contracting state or non-state actor may effectively intervene in a case with a view to taking part in the construction of ECHR rights.

6

From Supranational Adjudication to Supranational Law?

6.1 SUPRANATIONALIZATION OF CONVENTION LAW

For the most part, Chapters 4 and 5 dealt with the international level, investigating horizontal integration and the multifaceted supranational authority exercised by the ECtHR. It is indispensable, however, to also analyze the interface between domestic law and the Convention. This last chapter, therefore, looks in more detail at the high degree of penetration or vertical integration of Convention law into domestic legal orders of contracting states – an aspect which, so far, has been discussed in reference to terms such as domestification or embeddedness of the ECHR.[1] In this chapter, the assumption is tested that by virtue of the strong supranational adjudication and lawmaking by the Court, the ECHR (or Convention law more broadly) has itself become supranationalized and could, for that matter, be considered supranational law in terms of its effect in domestic legal systems. To be sure, this chapter does not aim at demonstrating a particular structuring effect on domestic law. It investigates whether Convention law has been integrated within the domestic legal orders to the extent that it can be directly invoked and applied, sometimes even notwithstanding conflicting domestic law. The methodology adopted here differs from most accounts on the domestic reception of the ECHR. The hypothesis of vertical integration is verified by adopting a twofold approach analyzing both the perspective of the Court and the point of view of national legal orders.

Section 6.2 analyses the issue from a top-down perspective. It looks at what the ECHR and the Court say about the domestic authority of Convention law. In this context, it is argued that it is necessary to revisit the standard account that, based on a traditional international law approach, emphasizes implementation freedom.[2] Taking a closer look at the Convention level, it is argued, reveals how the Court has in fact ruled on and strengthened domestic implementation of the ECHR

[1] Keller and Stone Sweet, "Impact of the ECHR"; Helfer, "Redesigning the ECtHR."

[2] To be sure, there are exceptions to the standard account, which acknowledge and look at the international factors of implementation. See, for example, Polakiewicz, "Status of the Convention."

through a subtle but sophisticated framework of obligations, which could be termed supranationality lite. Section 6.3 then tests the hypothesis of supranationalization of Convention law from the perspective of national legal orders. This perspective is important as supranational law was defined as the result of the interaction of both the domestic and international legal order. To recall, it must be stressed that this section does not and cannot aim at providing an in-depth comparative study. The focus lies on providing a synthesis of existing research, discussing some examples, and addressing recent developments.

Further terminological and methodological considerations ought to be addressed at the outset. In contrast to previous chapters, the term implementation as used in this chapter refers to the primary duty of states to secure and observe Convention rights domestically (Article 1 ECHR), not to the execution of judgments (Article 46 ECHR). While implementation in this sense may refer to various forms of domestic processes (legislative, administrative, judicial, societal, etc.), the focus lies on the domestic application of the ECHR by state authorities, the judiciary in particular, because it is in this area that vertical integration becomes most visible.[3]

6.2 BEYOND IMPLEMENTATION FREEDOM: SUPRANATIONALITY LITE

6.2.1 *Revisiting the Standard Account on Implementation (Freedom)*

International obligations are usually formulated as obligations of result not of conduct: States remain free to choose the means through which they conform to their international obligations and an issue of state responsibility only arises when they fail, *in concreto*, to meet the prescribed result.[4] This seems to be no different for the ECHR, as an analysis of Article 1 ECHR and the Court's case-law under this article will show. Indeed, the Court has always emphasized implementation freedom and never entertained minority views by scholars or judges that the Convention itself, similarly to EU law, would establish its direct effect or supremacy in domestic legal orders (Section 6.2.2).

At the same time, it would be flawed to assert that the Court turns a blind eye to the domestic status of the Convention. The Court has ruled on and strengthened domestic implementation of the ECHR in subtle ways. For one, it has developed a detailed framework for implementation through crossover doctrines such as positive duties, proceduralization, and proportionality analysis (Section 6.2.3). For another, under Article 13 ECHR the Court requires states to grant the ECHR

[3] This is not to say, of course, that taking Convention law into account in the legislative, political, or administrative processes is not of importance for the respect of states' primary duties.

[4] ILC, Report of the Commission to the General Assembly on the Work of its Twenty-ninth Session, *Yearbook of the ILC* (vol. II) (1977), 19ff paras. 1–2, 26.

indirect effect domestically in that Convention rights must in substance be enforceable within the domestic legal order (Section 6.2.4). A facet of this indirect effect is the development of an obligation of consistent interpretation (Section 6.2.5). The result of this practice, it is submitted, could be termed "supranationality lite." The overall claim submitted is that the discretion enjoyed by states in implementing the ECHR has shrunk considerably. Through different crossover doctrines and meta-principles as well as requiring indirect effect, Convention law imposes implementation-specific duties.

6.2.2 *Implementation Freedom*

6.2.2.1 General Duty to Secure Human Rights: Article 1 ECHR

Implementation freedom is undoubtedly a key paradigm under the ECHR.[5] The ILC cites the ECHR as a typical example of an international instrument whose provisions only specify the results to be achieved, while leaving the choice of means up to state parties.[6] As the ILC put it, it is implicit in the Convention guarantees "that the State is free to choose whatever means it considers best calculated to ensure that no one can be held in slavery, that everyone's security is assured, etc."[7] In short, the general view is that the ECHR falls short of imposing any uniform standard as regards its internal effect.

The central provision of the Convention regarding its internal effect is Article 1 ECHR containing the obligation to respect human rights. It requires contracting states to secure to everyone within their jurisdiction the rights and freedoms guaranteed in the ECHR. Article 1 ECHR reflects the customary principle of *pacta sunt servanda* according to which contracting states have a duty to perform their treaty obligations in good faith.[8] The Court has construed Article 1 ECHR in line with the law of state responsibility, which treats states, internationally, as monolithic entities.[9] Responsibility for a breach of the Convention may thus "arise for the acts of all State organs, whether they belong to the legislature, the executive or the judiciary"[10] and irrespective of the level of political organization (federal, local, communal, etc.).[11] A state may also be held liable for the conduct of

5 Polakiewicz, "Status of the Convention," p. 33.

6 ILC, Report of the Commission to the General Assembly on the Work of its Twenty-Ninth Session, *Yearbook of the ILC* (vol. II) (1977), 27 para. 7.

7 Ibid., fn. 66.

8 *Ireland* v. *the United Kingdom*, § 238; Art. 26 VCLT; Schabas, *ECHR: A Commentary*, p. 90.

9 See, in particular, Art. 2 of the ILC Draft Articles on State Responsibility.

10 ECtHR, *Andrejeva* v. *Latvia*, no. 55707/00, Grand Chamber Judgment of February 18, 2009, ECHR 2009-II, § 56; *Sejdić and Finci* v. *Bosnia and Herzegovina*, nos. 27996/06 and 34836/06, Grand Chamber Judgment of December 22, 2009, ECHR 2009-VI, § 56.

11 *Ireland* v. *the United Kingdom*, § 159. Also, this results, *a contrario*, from the Court's jurisprudence under Art. 34 ECHR denying "governmental organizations" *locus standi*. For example, ECtHR, *Danderyds Kommun* v. *Sweden*, no. 525591/99, Decision of June 7, 2001. *Assanidze* v. *Georgia*, § 146.

private persons or entities,[12] although the Court did not "consider it desirable, let alone necessary, to elaborate a general theory concerning the extent to which the Convention guarantees should be extended to relations between private individuals *inter se*."[13]

The *travaux* indicate that the scope of the obligation to respect human rights under Article 1 ECHR was understood to include the duty "to give full effect to the provisions of the Convention from the moment the State has given its adherence."[14] Giving full effect entails to ensure that domestic law, including constitutional provisions, are compatible with Convention requirements.[15] As the Court explicitly stated, contracting states have undertaken "to ensure that their domestic legislation is compatible with it."[16]

Interestingly, the Teitgen Report adopted in the Consultative Assembly in 1949 included an article entitled "implementation freedom." It foresaw that "every Member State, signatory to the Convention, shall be entitled to establish the rules by which the guaranteed rights and freedoms shall be organized within its territory."[17] The provision did not make it into the 1950 Convention and the guarantees in the Convention ultimately gained more concrete shape as opposed to the mere catalogue of rights suggested by the Teitgen Report.[18] Its absence in the Convention text, however, did not prevent implementation freedom from becoming an important paradigm of Convention law. The Court regularly reiterates that the ECHR does not "lay down for the Contracting States any given manner for ensuring within their internal law the effective implementation of any of the provisions of the Convention."[19] As a result, contracting parties are said to enjoy inherent and wide discretion as regards the choice of means through which they want to afford the protection required by the Convention.[20]

6.2.2.2 Rejection of an Obligation of Incorporation

Implementation freedom also meant that the Court always rejected to derive from the Convention an obligation to incorporate the latter into domestic law.[21] There is

12 Andrew Clapham, "The 'Drittwirkung' of the Convention" in Ronald Macdonald, Franz Matscher, and Herbert Petzold (eds.), *The European System for the Protection of Human Rights* (Leiden: Martinus Nijhoff 1993), pp. 163ff.

13 ECtHR, *Verein gegen Tierfabriken Schweiz (VgT)* v. *Switzerland*, no. 24699/94, Judgment of June 28, 2001, ECHR 2001-VI, § 46.

14 Travaux Préparatoires ECHR, vol. IV, 216.

15 *Sejdić and Finci* v. *Bosnia and Herzegovina*, § 56.

16 ECtHR, *Maestri* v. *Italy*, no. 39748/98, Grand Chamber Judgment of February 17, 2004, ECHR 2004-I, § 47.

17 Travaux Préparatoires ECHR, vol. I, 105.

18 Chapter 3, Section 3.2.2.

19 ECtHR, *Swedish Engine Drivers' Union* v. *Sweden*, no. 5614/72, Judgment of February 6, 1976, Series A no. 20, § 50.

20 Christoffersen, *Fair Balance*, pp. 296–298. The margin of appreciation doctrine is sometimes used synonymously in this respect.

21 For example, ECtHR, *James and Others* v. *the United Kingdom*, no. 8793/79, Plenary Judgment of February 21, 1986, Series A no. 98, § 84.

no obligation to grant the ECHR direct effect or make it directly applicable before domestic authorities either.[22] This is not to say that the ECtHR could not have taken a different stance on these issues. In the 1960s, coincidentally with the CJEU handing down its landmark decisions,[23] different scholars actually defended the view that Article 1 ECHR in conjunction with Article 13 ECHR must be read as entailing a duty of contracting states to incorporate the ECHR and make it part of the internal legal order.[24] Buergenthal was one of the proponents of this view:

> Accordingly, it is vital that the rights guaranteed by the Convention have the status of directly enforceable domestic law. If these rights can only be vindicated through the cumbersome process of an appeal to an international institution like the Commission, they lose that immediacy and reality which is associated with domestic law and with it the preventive function such law performs.
>
> (...) self executing nature means enforceable: thus, if a treaty was designed to give individuals certain rights directly enforceable in the domestic tribunals, it follows that the State parties to it have, by ratifying it, assumed the obligation to remove all domestic obstacles standing in the way of such a result.
>
> Read in the context of Article 1, and keeping in mind the precise and individual-oriented language of the remaining provisions of the Convention, I cannot but share the conclusion reached by Dr. Golsong and Professor Silsterhenn that Article 13 creates an obligation on the part of each adhering State to transform the Convention into directly applicable domestic law.[25]

The view that Articles 1 and 13 ECHR give rise to an obligation of incorporation and direct applicability is sometimes still defended today.[26] It has, however, moved to the background as the Court itself never endorsed it. Yet, it is noteworthy that ECtHR judges were divided on the subject too. Judge Martens, for instance, argued in a partly dissenting opinion in the case of *Ahmet Sadik* v. *Greece* in favor of moving beyond treating direct effect as a mere desirability from the Convention's perspective.[27] In reference to the Court's, at that point, quasi-compulsory jurisdiction and the *Loizidou* dictum on the special character of the ECHR as a constitutional instrument of the European public order,[28] Martens submitted

22 Polakiewicz, "Status of the Convention," pp. 31–33.

23 Chapter 1, Section 1.4.2.

24 Buergenthal, "Effect of the ECHR," 82. See also Ralph Beddard, "The Status of the European Convention of Human Rights in Domestic Law" (1967) 16 *International and Comparative Law Quarterly* 206–217. For a detailed discussion and references to proponents and critics of this view Drzemczewski, "Domestic Status of the ECHR," pp. 12–20.

25 Buergenthal, "Effect of the ECHR," 80f.

26 Polakiewicz, "Status of the Convention," p. 35f.

27 ECtHR, *Ahmet Sadik* v. *Greece*, no. 18877/91, Judgment of November 15, 1996, Reports 1996-V, Partly Dissenting Opinion of Judge Martens joined by Judge Foighel.

28 Ibid., §§ 4 and 11.

that under the Convention the same rule applies as has been accepted by the Court of Justice of the European Communities with respect to Community law: *in those cases where domestic courts, under their national law, are in a position to apply the Convention ex officio, those courts must do so under the Convention*. That is an obvious demand of the effectiveness both of the Convention as a constitutional instrument of European public order (ordre public) and of the "national human right systems."[29]

Martens' view follows the "in for a penny, in for a pound" logic and can be compared to the obligation established by the Court to grant the re-opening of domestic proceedings, in so far as such a possibility exists domestically.[30] If the Court has never adopted the proposition that direct effect becomes a Convention based requirement so long as domestic law allows for it, this view would in fact find some support in the *travaux* of the Convention.[31] As stated in a report by the Venice Commission, "from the legal history of the European Convention on Human Rights it appears that its drafters intended its substantive provisions to be self-executing in those Contracting States where they form part of the domestic legal order."[32]

6.2.2.3 Silence on Supremacy

So far, the Court has renounced any explicit claims of supremacy regarding the Convention. While from the Court's perspective, the ECHR prevails over domestic law of any kind,[33] it usually avoids discussing the Convention's internal rank vis-à-vis conflicting domestic law, which is precisely reflecting the general indifference of international law as to its internal effect.[34]

Here too, however, the Court's case-law could look different today. There is the argument that, at the end of the day, EU law supremacy is nothing less than a teleological reading of international law supremacy,[35] which could equally be applied to the ECHR.[36] As explained earlier, the Court, following Article 27 VCLT, always rejected the argument that a violation of the ECHR can be justified by

[29] Ibid., § 11 (emphasis added).

[30] *Verein gegen Tierfabriken Schweiz (VgT)* v. *Switzerland (No. 2)*.

[31] Travaux Préparatoires ECHR (vol. V), 26–27, 34–35, 66–67, 74–75.

[32] Venice Commission, Report on the Implementation of International Human Rights Treaties in Domestic Law and the Role of Courts 31.

[33] ECtHR, *United Communist Party of Turkey* v. *Turkey*, no. 19392/92, Grand Chamber Judgment of January 30, 1998, Reports 1998-I, § 30.

[34] The limits of indirect effect under Art. 13 ECHR also show that the Court has thus far refrained from requiring supremacy. As explained below, the Court does not require *contra legem* interpretation in this context (see subsequently Section 6.2.5).

[35] Ole Spiermann, "The Other Side of the Story: An Unpopular Essay on the Making of the European Legal Order" (1999) 10 *European Journal of International Law* 763–789.

[36] See, for example, Polakiewicz, "Status of the Convention," pp. 31f. On the supremacy of international law see Chapter 2, Section 2.3.3.3.

invoking conflicting domestic law, including domestic constitutional law.[37] Some have therefore suggested that the international supremacy of the ECHR also translates into domestic supremacy. For example, Jean-Paul Costa, former President of the Court, went so far as to make an analogy to top-down imposed EU law supremacy: "this reasoning is important because it suggests that the Convention *prevails over national constitutions*, even if it does not state it as directly as the Luxembourg Court has done in relation to the primacy of Community law."[38] In the same vein, Judge de Albuquerque (joined by three other judges) argued in a concurring opinion in the *Al-Dulimi* case that "the principles of primacy and direct effect developed by the CJEU are to be found in the Court's case-law as well."[39]

Scholars have also grounded supremacy of the ECHR in the effective enforcement structure set up through Article 34 ECHR,[40] or in its particular substance and normative force. The latter is often tied to viewing ECHR rights as (international) constitutional or suprapositive rights:[41] the special substance of human rights would translate into supremacy over other international norms, but also over conflicting law in the domestic realm. Admittedly, the Court has held in *Loizidou* that the ECHR, because of its particular content, is a document of constitutional nature and formal definitions of constitutionalism usually posit higher status of constitutional norms.[42] Hence, in the precited concurring opinion in the *Al-Dulimi* case, Judge Pinto de Albuquerque also asserted the supremacy of the ECHR over both domestic and international law because of the ECHR's constitutional character. He argued that the Convention's

> transformational role emphatically proclaimed in the preamble as an instrument for building a closer union of European States and developing human rights on a pan-European basis, the Convention is subordinated neither to domestic constitutional rules, nor to allegedly higher rules of international law, *since it is the supreme law of the European continent*. In the Council of Europe's own internal hierarchy of norms, United Nations law is equal to any other international

37 *United Communist Party of Turkey* v. *Turkey*, § 30; *Sejdić and Finci* v. *Bosnia and Herzegovina*, § 56.

38 Jean-Paul Costa, Inaugural Speech during the Visit of the ECtHR Judges to the Russian Constitutional Court, May 10–11, 2007 (referenced by Martinico and Pollicino, *Interaction between Europe's Legal Systems*, p. 178).

39 *Al-Dulimi and Montana Management Inc.* v. *Switzerland*, Concurring Opinion of Judge Pinto De Albuquerque joined by Judges Hajiyev, Pejchal, and Dedov, fn. 112.

40 As individuals may enforce their rights in Strasbourg (Art. 34 ECHR) and states are under an obligation to execute an eventual judgment and bring domestic law in conformity with the ECHR (Art. 46 ECHR), the latter would enjoy supremacy (Ress, "Supranationaler Menschenrechtsschutz"; Gardbaum, "Human Rights as International Constitutional Rights," 247).

41 Gardbaum, "Human Rights as International Constitutional Rights," 243; Gerald L. Neuman, "Human Rights and Constitutional Rights: Harmony and Dissonance" (2003) 55 *Stanford Law Review* 1863–1900 at 1868f.

42 *Loizidou* v. *Turkey (Preliminary Objections)*, § 75; Chapter 2, Sections 2.4.1.1–2.4.1.2 .

agreement and subordinated to the primacy of the Convention as a constitutional instrument of European public order.[43]

The ECtHR may, however, have had good reasons not to develop any strong supremacy claims. Although the Court must ensure respect for its supranational standard, a strict supremacy rule could endanger rights diversity and the complementarity of the ECHR as set forth in Article 53 ECHR.[44] The same goes for the dynamic nature of Convention law. ECHR rights feed on bottom-up developments regarding both changing societal conditions as well as progressing legal protection standards.[45] A strict supremacy rule could be difficult to reconcile with the demand for such openness. The inherent tension between safeguarding the effectiveness of ECHR protection and the requirement of openness may explain why the Court seeks to avoid, as far as possible, open clashes and renounces any hierarchical conceptualization.[46] At the same time and as will be demonstrated in the following, the Court has found other, more subtle ways to secure domestic effectiveness and integration of Convention law.

6.2.3 *Concretizing the Duty to Respect Human Rights through Cross-Over Doctrines*

6.2.3.1 Positive Obligations and Proceduralization

The widespread application of the doctrine of positive obligations has constrained implementation freedom under Article 1 ECHR.[47] Positive obligations are usually contrasted to negative obligations as they require a state to take action and perform

[43] *Al-Dulimi and Montana Management Inc.* v. *Switzerland*, Concurring Opinion of Judge Pinto De Albuquerque joined by Judges Hajiyev, Pejchal, and Dedoval, § 59 (emphasis added).

[44] The Court held that domestic authorities are particularly well placed to concretize and develop human rights (e.g., ECtHR, *Animal Defenders International* v. *the United Kingdom*, no. 48876/08, Grand Chamber Judgment of April 22, 2013, 2013-II (extracts), § 111).

[45] Chapter 5, Sections 5.2.1 and 5.3.2.

[46] Venice Commission, Report on the Implementation of International Human Rights Treaties in Domestic Law and the Role of Courts 114. Krisch, *Beyond Constitutionalism*, pp. 109ff.

[47] On positive obligations under the ECtHR see, among others, Alastair Mowbray, *The Development of Positive Obligations under the European Convention on Human Rights by the European Court of Human Rights* (Oxford: Hart 2004); Matthias Klatt, "Positive Obligations under the European Convention on Human Rights" (2011) 71 *Zeitschrift für ausländisches öffentliches Recht und Völkerrecht* 691–718; Heike Krieger, "Positive Verpflichtungen unter der EMRK: Unentbehrliches Element einer gemeineuropäischen Grundrechtsdogmatik, leeres Versprechen oder Grenze der Justiziabilität?" (2014) 74 *Zeitschrift für ausländisches öffentliches Recht und Völkerrechtt* 187–213; Lavrysen, "Positive Obligations"; Dimitris Xenos, *The Positive Obligations of the State under the European Convention of Human Rights* (London: Routledge 2012). On positive obligations in human rights law in general see Sandra Fredman, *Human Rights Transformed: Positive Rights and Positive Duties* (Oxford: Oxford University Press 2008).

specific tasks.[48] According to Shue's classical tripartite typology of duties, positive obligations impose a duty to protect or fulfil instead of a mere obligation to respect.[49] The state bears positive obligations in those situations, in which the ability to exercise a right or a freedom requires to create the conditions allowing one to do so in the first place. Therefore, positive obligations have been justified in reference to the principle that protection under the Convention must be practical and effective.[50] The Court's stance on positive obligations is marked by pragmatism. It did not consider it necessary "to develop a general theory of the positive obligations which may flow from the Convention," adopting, instead, a case by case approach.[51] Furthermore, the Court has maintained that the distinction between positive and negative duties is not always clear-cut[52] and in some instances even irrelevant given that "the applicable principles are broadly similar."[53]

Some ECHR rights already refer explicitly to positive duties, like the right to a fair trial, for example, and its guarantee under the criminal limb to be informed promptly of the nature and cause of an accusation (Article 6(3)a) ECHR). Most Convention rights, however, are framed as negative duties obliging states not to unduly interfere within their scope of protection.[54] In conjunction with Article 1 ECHR, these rights may contain implicit positive duties.[55] Implicit positive duties go back to the *Belgian Linguistic case*, in which the Court noted that, although the negative formulation of the right to education (Article 2 Protocol 2) indicated that states are not required "to establish at their own expense, or to subsidize, education of any particular type or at any particular level," it didn't mean "that the State has no positive obligation to ensure respect for such a right."[56] In *Marckx*, the Court went

48 David Harris, Michael O'Boyle, and Colin Warbrick, *Law of the European Convention on Human Rights*, 3rd ed. (Oxford: Oxford University Press 2014), p. 22.

49 Henry Shue, *Basic Rights: Subsistence, Affluence, and U.S. Foreign Policy*, 2nd ed. (Princeton: Princeton University Press 1996).

50 Mowbray, *Positive Obligations under the ECHR*, p. 221.

51 ECtHR, *Plattform 'Ärzte für das Leben'* v. *Austria*, no. 10126/82, Judgment of June 21, 1988, Series A no. 139, § 31.

52 It holds regularly "that the boundaries between the State's positive and negative obligations (...) do not lend themselves to precise definition" (e.g., ECtHR, *Keegan* v. *Ireland*, no. 28867/03, Judgment of July 18, 2006, 2006-X, § 49).

53 ECtHR, *Hatton and Others* v. *the United Kingdom*, no. 36022/97, Grand Chamber Judgment of July 8, 2003, 2003-VII, §§ 98 and 119. The Court's approach in dealing with positive obligations, especially as regards the determination of the precise scope and content of positive obligation in a specific case, has led to criticism in scholarship. See e.g., Lavrysen, "Positive Obligations," pp. 165ff. She argues in favor of a symmetrical approach that, like for negative obligations, requires a twofold approach distinguishing the question of whether a right was infringed from the question of whether the infringement was justified (the latter calling for a legality, legitimacy, and proportionality test).

54 Lavrysen, "Positive Obligations," p. 163.

55 E.g., ECtHR, A. v. *the United Kingdom*, no. 25599/94, Judgment of September 23, 1998, Reports 1998-VI, § 22.

56 *Case "Relating to certain aspects of the laws on the use of languages in education in Belgium"* v. *Belgium*, §§ 27 and 3.

a step further and held that Article 8 ECHR "does not merely compel the State to abstain from (…) interference: in addition to this primarily negative undertaking, there may be positive obligations inherent in an effective 'respect' for family life."[57] Ever since, the Court has gradually developed and extended the concept of positive obligations, applying it, today across virtually all Convention rights,[58] including Articles 2,[59] 3,[60] 4,[61] 6[62] ECHR or Article 1 Protocol 1,[63] requiring a diverse range of measures such as (criminal) investigations, criminalization, victim protection or the adoption of appropriate legal and administrative frameworks.

A particular category of positive duties emerged from what can be termed the proceduralization of substantive rights. Again in the context of Article 8 ECHR, the Court found that it may scrutinize the process leading up to a limitation of Article 8 "to determine whether it has been conducted in a manner that, in all the circumstances, is fair and affords due respect to the interests protected by Article 8."[64] Proceduralization, especially as regards Articles 2, 3, 4, and 5 ECHR, provides for a catching function in cases, in which a violation of substantive obligations presents itself difficult to prove.[65] In general, the Court's approach to positive duties has become more and more innovative. The Court held, for instance, that peaceful religious pluralism (Article 10 ECHR) may require "to place restrictions on the freedom to manifest one's religion or belief,"[66] or established a right of access to information in environmental law and pollution cases stressing that contracting states must, under Article 8 ECHR, produce information enabling those affected to assess the environmental risks and those for their health.[67] In addition, the emergence of positive obligations was paralleled by the extension of the horizontal effect of the Convention – that is, its effect on the relationships

57 *Marckx* v. *Belgium*, § 31. In *Marckx*, the positive duty derived by the Court consisted of providing for legal safeguards in domestic law, which ensure that an unmarried mother and her child may live a normal life and the child is integrated within the family.

58 For a comprehensive overview see Mowbray, *Positive Obligations under the ECHR*.

59 ECtHR, *Nachova and Others* v. *Bulgaria*, nos. 43577/98 and 43579/98, Grand Chamber Judgment of July 6, 2005, ECHR 2005-VII, § 96; *Osman* v. *the United Kingdom*, no. 23452/94, Grand Chamber Judgment of October 28, 1998, Reports 1998-VIII, § 115.

60 E.g., *Nachova and Others* v. *Bulgaria*.

61 *Rantsev* v. *Cyprus and Russia*.

62 ECtHR, *Zimmermann and Steiner* v. *Switzerland*, no. 8737/79, Judgment of July 13, 1983, Series A no. 66, § 29; *Airey* v. *Ireland*, § 25.

63 ECtHR, *Campbell and Cosans* v. *the United Kingdom*, nos. 7511/76 and 7743/76, Judgment of February 25, 1982, Series A no. 48, § 37.

64 ECtHR, *B* v. *the United Kingdom*, no. 9840/82, Judgment of July 8, 1987, Series A no. 121-B, §§ 63–64. As a result, parents must, for instance, be granted participatory rights in childcare cases (*Olsson* v. *Sweden (No. 1)*, no. 10465/83, Judgment of March 24, 1988, Series A no. 130, §§ 81–83).

65 Krieger, "Positive Verpflichtungen unter der EMRK," 191.

66 ECtHR, *H.C.W. Schilder* v. *the Netherlands*, no. 2158/12, Decision of October 16, 2012, § 21.

67 ECtHR, *Guerra and Others* v. *Italy*, no. 14967/89, Grand Chamber Judgment of February 19, 1998, Reports 1998-I, § 60.

between individuals – into areas such as labor or tenancy law.[68] As regards Article 3 ECHR, the Court explicitly held that states must take measures "designed to ensure that individuals within their jurisdiction are not subjected to torture or inhuman or degrading treatment or punishment, including such ill treatment administered by private individuals."[69]

Through positive obligations the Court achieves a considerable concretization of the obligation to secure the implementation of Convention rights. Applicable to virtually all ECHR rights, positive obligations provide guidelines that states have to take into account when implementing the Convention domestically. Granted, they usually come themselves with a certain margin of appreciation for states, especially when pertaining to the legislative realm.[70] Nonetheless, positive obligations structure and therefore limit the general freedom of implementation to an important degree. In fact, in some instances, the margin of appreciation may even be reduced to a minimum, which has provoked criticism of overdetermination.[71] In addition to their concretization, positive duties have also transformed the nature of primary obligations under the ECHR. In contrast to negative duties and non-interference, positive duties often require legislative reforms and, henceforth, more fundamental change and adaption at the domestic level.[72] As a result, implementation is not a question of (in)direct effect or enforceability alone.[73] In short, positive duties have added to the obligation of result a sometimes thick layer of obligations of specific conduct.[74]

6.2.3.2 Proportionality Framework

Another way through which the Court has concretized the general obligation to respect Convention rights was by developing and imposing proportionality analysis.[75] Proportionality analysis operates as a key principle or doctrine guiding the Court when exercising its complementary review function over state action.[76] Inversely, however, the Court also expects domestic authorities, courts, in particular,

[68] E.g., ECtHR, *Immobiliare Saffi* v. *Italy*, no. 22774/93, Grand Chamber Judgment of July 28, 1999, ECHR 1999-V. Early on the topic of Drittwirkung and domestic effect of the ECHR see Drzemczewski, "Domestic Status of the ECHR," pp. 66ff.

[69] ECtHR, *A.* v. *the United Kingdom*, § 22.

[70] ECtHR, *Women on Waves and Others* v. *Portugal*, no. 31276/05, Judgment of February 3, 2009, § 40; *Hatton and Others* v. *the United Kingdom*, § 100. Klatt, therefore, speaks of the disjunctive structure of positive obligations (Klatt, "Positive Obligations," 694).

[71] For an account on this critique Klatt, "Positive Obligations," 712.

[72] Krieger, "Positive Verpflichtungen unter der EMRK," 197. This is not to say that negative obligations do not affect the legislator's work.

[73] Therefore, the costs of discharging positive obligations are usually perceived as higher than those arising in the context of negative obligations. Lavrysen, "Positive Obligations," p. 172.

[74] The implications are reminiscent of the developments analyzed in Chapter 4 pertaining to the secondary obligations arising from a violation of the Convention (Chapter 4, Sections 4.3-4.4).

[75] Stone Sweet, "Cosmopolitan Legal Order," 74.

[76] Chapter 4, Section 4.2.3.2.

to use proportionality analysis in dealing with and adjudicating fundamental rights issues.

The Court has long held that the right to an effective remedy at the domestic level (Article 13 ECHR)[77] requires alleged violations of Convention rights to be reviewed with a certain intensity. As regards restrictions of qualified rights, this means that the competent domestic authority must be able to perform a proportionality review. The case of *Smith and Grady* is a famous example, concerning two applicants that were discharged from the Royal Navy because of their homosexuality.[78] In its judgment, the Court reprimanded the British "Wednesbury (un)reasonableness" test because it limited judicial review of governmental policies to grounds of irrationality and thereby excluded the examination of whether the applicants' dismissal answered a pressing social need and was proportionate to the national security and public order aims pursued.[79] As a result, the Court found a violation of Article 8 in conjunction with Article 13 ECHR.[80]

In addition to Article 13 ECHR, the more specific guarantees of judicial review contained in Article 5(4) ECHR and Article 6(1) ECHR also require proportionality analysis. Article 6(1) ECHR requires access to a tribunal, which by definition must exercise "full jurisdiction" and examine all relevant factual and legal questions relevant to the dispute before it.[81] In the case of *Diennet* v. *France*, for instance, the Court held that full jurisdiction also entails a domestic tribunal's power to assess whether a disciplinary penalty was proportionate to the misconduct in question.[82] Similarly, in the context of Article 5(4) ECHR, the domestic court reviewing the lawfulness of a person's detention must be able to strike a balance between the right to liberty and opposing public interests.[83] Finally, an implicit obligation to apply proportionality analysis also derives from the various substantive and qualified rights of the Convention. As reiterated earlier, the Court itself applies proportionality analysis and it expects domestic authorities to do so too.[84]

Surely, proportionality is a crucial principle of substantive human rights law in general, allowing to weigh and to balance individual rights against each other or against public interests: "to speak of human rights in the twenty-first century is to speak of proportionality."[85] Because of its overriding importance, however, the Court imposed proportionality as a general mode of argumentation under the

77 More on Art. 13 ECHR subsequently Section 6.2.4.

78 ECtHR, *Smith and Grady* v. *the United Kingdom*, nos. 33985/96 and 33986/96, Judgment of September 27, 1999, ECHR 1999-VI.

79 Ibid., § 138.

80 Ibid.

81 ECtHR, *Beaumartin* v. *France*, no. 15287/89, Judgment of November 24, 1994, Series A no. 296-B, § 38.

82 ECtHR, *Diennet* v. *France*, no. 18160/91, Judgment of September 26, 1995, Series A no. 325-A, § 34.

83 ECtHR, *Suso Musa* v. *Malta*, no. 42337/12, Judgment of July 23, 2013, § 50; *Nowicka* v. *Poland*, no. 30218/96, Judgment of December 3, 2002, § 61.

84 Chapter 4, Section 4.2.3.2.

85 Grant Huscroft, Bradley W. Miller, and Grégoire Webber (eds.), "Introduction," *Proportionality and the Rule of Law* (Cambridge: Cambridge University Press 2014), pp. 1–20, p. 1. See also, among many,

Convention's procedural as well as substantive guarantees. As Stone Sweet noted, it is less "a list of norms defined in a lowest-common denominator manner" which is characteristic for the Convention system, "but a mode of argumentation, and justification: the proportionality framework."[86] The Court complemented the result-oriented dimension of the duty to secure Convention rights domestically by developing a process-based principle, which national authorities must adopt as a mode of reasoning when evaluating whether rights' interferences are justified. It is a principle, which itself does not comprise any substantive obligations,[87] but should guarantee, if applied correctly, an outcome which is defensible from the Convention's perspective:

> This means that on application this principle (. . .) requires saturation by arguments that are context sensitive and most likely subject to normative and empirical challenges. Its usefulness does not lie in providing a definitive answer in any specific context. But it structures inquiries in a way that is likely to be sensitive to the relevant empirical and normative concerns.[88]

Also, proportionality analysis directly responsibilizes domestic authorities, especially ordinary judges, as protectors of Convention rights and entrusts or empowers them with some sort of de facto constitutional role.[89] Proportionality analysis is further a tool to concretize rights as principles.[90] In Christoffersen's words, the "principle of proportionality entails a measure of concretization and provides a means to move from the level of principles to the level of rules."[91] In short, proportionality analysis is central to the concretization and hence implementation of states' primary obligations under the Convention.

6.2.4 *Requiring Indirect Effect: Enforcement "in Substance"*

Another crucial provision regarding domestic implementation is Article 13 ECHR. As touched upon earlier, Article 13 ECHR provides that everyone whose rights and freedoms as set forth in the Convention are violated shall have an effective remedy before a national authority, through which he or she can obtain appropriate relief. The right to an effective remedy is an accessory procedural guarantee, which only comes into play, where there is an arguable claim of a violation of another

Yutaka Arai-Takahashi, "Proportionality" in Dinah Shelton (ed.), *The Oxford Handbook of International Human Rights Law* (Oxford: Oxford University Press 2013), pp. 446–468.

86 Stone Sweet, "Cosmopolitan Legal Order," 74. See also Stone Sweet and Keller, "Reception of the ECHR," pp. 10f.

87 Christoffersen, *Fair Balance*, p. 224.

88 Mattias Kumm, "The Legitimacy of International Law: A Constitutionalist Framework of Analysis" (2004) 15 *European Journal of International Law* 907–931 at 921.

89 Keller and Stone Sweet, "Impact of the ECHR," p. 699.

90 Robert Alexy, A *Theory of Constitutional Rights*, pp. 66ff.

91 Christoffersen, *Fair Balance*, p. 224.

Convention right.[92] Article 13 ECHR operates at the interface between the substantive Convention guarantees and the enforcement structure at the supranational level.[93] The requirement of an effective domestic remedy aims at establishing the pre-condition for the subsidiary or complementary nature of the ECHR and Strasbourg proceedings. In the Court's words, "it is fundamental to the machinery of protection established by the Convention that the national systems themselves provide redress for breaches of its provisions, the Court exerting its supervisory role subject to the principle of subsidiarity."[94] Because individuals enjoy a remedy to complain about Convention violations domestically, they are required to exhaust domestic remedies before coming to Strasbourg.[95] A remedy, however, is only considered effective, if national authorities are in a position to render a binding decision and, if indicated, acknowledge, either expressly or in substance, a breach of the Convention as well as afford redress for it.[96]

As mentioned, the Court never understood Article 13 ECHR to require states to incorporate the Convention into domestic law or grant the latter direct effect therein.[97] It did however hold that Article 13 ECHR "guarantees the availability of a remedy at national level *to enforce* – and hence *to allege non-compliance* with – the *substance of the Convention rights and freedoms* (. . .)."[98] The Court thus presupposes not only the enforcement but also the invocability by individuals of at least the substance of Convention rights before domestic authorities. Tulkens, former Judge at the ECtHR, expressed this in similar terms by stressing that "the object of the Convention is to be directly applicable in the domestic law of the member States."[99] Drawing on the foundations of vertical integration developed in Chapter 2, Article 13 ECHR requires states to grant the ECHR at least indirect effect in the sense that the substance of the Convention guarantees must be enforced through a domestic provision either incorporating, implementing, or overlapping with the former.[100] Individuals may have to rely on parallel domestic fundamental rights, but the latter

92 *Klass and Others* v. *Germany*, § 64.

93 Marten Breuer, "Artikel 13. Recht auf wirksame Beschwerde" in Ulrich Karpenstein and Franz C. Mayer (eds.), *EMRK Konvention zum Schutz der Menschenrechte und Grundfreiheiten Kommentar*, 2nd ed. (Munich: C. H. Beck 2015), n. 1.

94 ECtHR, Z v. *the United Kingdom*, no. 29392/95, Grand Chamber Judgment of May 10, 2001, § 103.

95 *Selmouni* v. *France*, § 74.

96 The latter follows from the Court's case-law concerning the victim requirement under Art. 34 ECHR. E.g., ECtHR, *Amuur* v. *France*, no. 19776/92, Judgment of June 25, 1996, Reports, 1996-III, § 36.

97 For a convincing critique of this restrictive position see Christoffersen, *Fair Balance*, pp. 384ff.

98 ECtHR, *Boyle and Rice* v. *the United Kingdom*, nos. 9659/82 and 9658/82, Plenary Judgment of April 27, 1988, Series A no. 131, § 52 (emphasis added).

99 Françoise Tulkens, "The European Convention on Human Rights between International Law and Constitutional Law," *Dialogue between Judges* (Strasbourg: European Court of Human Rights, Council of Europe 2007) www.echr.coe.int/Documents/Dialogue_2007_ENG.pdf (accessed July 23, 2020).

100 The same obligation of indirect effect may also arise in the context of other, more stringent procedural Convention guarantees such as Art. 6(1) or 5(4) ECHR, which, if applicable, usually supersede Art. 13 ECHR as *lex specialis* (in more detail see Christoffersen, *Fair Balance*, pp.

have, in substance, to be congruent with Convention rights in order to stand up to scrutiny under Article 13 ECHR. The Court demands that the ECHR's object or substance is integrated into the domestic legal order, even in (or despite of) the absence of incorporation (or direct effect). Considering that Article 13 ECHR contains a guarantee of general character, applicable across all Convention rights, this is both far-reaching and remarkable.

Two elements, however, qualify the requirement of indirect effect under Article 13 ECHR to a certain extent. First, the Court has always affirmed that Article 13 ECHR does not guarantee a remedy capable of challenging domestic legislation as such.[101] Accordingly, Article 13 ECHR does not require states to provide for (judicial) review of formal legislation[102] and if a Convention violation is directly attributable to the legislature, the right to an effective remedy usually doesn't apply.[103] This also limits the requirement of indirect effect in the context of conflicting domestic laws.[104] Second, unlike Article 6(1) ECHR, Article 13 ECHR normally only requires a remedy before an independent domestic authority, not a court or tribunal.[105] Hence, enforcement of the substance of the Convention as required by Article 13 ECHR doesn't necessarily need to take place within or through the judiciary (although this will usually be the case). It is with these two caveats in mind that one can speak of a general obligation derived from Article 13 ECHR to render the ECHR indirectly effective within domestic legal systems.

That the Court did not go as far as requiring direct effect of the Convention could partly be due to the abstract and broad nature of ECHR rights, which usually find in most states some correspondence in domestic (constitutional) law.[106] Many states already possessed some form of fundamental rights catalogue and the ECtHR could settle for a requirement of indirect enforceability without fearing (too much) for the effectiveness of Convention protection.

367–374). The Court has held that domestic courts must closely examine alleged Convention violations, where Art. 6 ECHR establishes a right to court access (*Fabris* v. *France*, § 73) and that in the context of the right of everyone deprived of his liberty to challenge the lawfulness of his detention (Art. 5(4) ECHR), the notion of lawfulness not only includes relevant domestic law but also the conditions under which detention is lawful under the ECHR in the first place (see Art. 5(1) ECHR; ECtHR, *Van Droogenbroeck* v. *Belgium*, no. 7906/77, Plenary Judgment of June 24, 1982, Series A no. 50, § 48).

101 *James and Others* v. *the United Kingdom*, § 85.

102 Laws adopted by the executive branch, however, do fall within the scope of Art. 13 ECHR (ECtHR, *Silver and Others* v. *the United Kingdom*, nos. 5947/72 etc., Judgment of March 25, 1983, Series A no. 61, § 118).

103 See, however, ECtHR, *Riener* v. *Bulgaria*, no. 46343/99, Judgment of May 23, 2006, §§ 141–143. This practice raises delicate questions of delimitation.

104 More on that subsequently Sections 6.2.4–6.2.5.

105 ECtHR, *Golder* v. *the United Kingdom*, § 33; *Klass* v. *Germany*, § 67; *Silver* v. *the United Kingdom*, §§ 114f; ECtHR, *De Souza Ribeiro* v. *France*, no. 22689/07, Grand Chamber Judgment of December 13, 2012, ECHR 2012-VI, § 79.

106 A notable exception was the United Kingdom.

6.2.5 *Obligation of Consistent Interpretation*

The requirement to give the ECHR at least indirect effect is also expressed by the fact that the Court has stressed the importance of interpreting domestic law in accordance with the Convention. Consistent interpretation is a way to give (indirect) effect to international law domestically, especially in the absence of transposition of international norms into the domestic legal order.[107] In accordance with the standard view, consistent interpretation of the ECHR is usually treated from a domestic perspective.[108] While this is not flawed in general,[109] the ECtHR has in fact on several occasions explicitly touched upon the issue of consistent interpretation.

The Court addressed the issue of consistent interpretation on several occasions and under the heading of different provisions including substantive provisions such as Article 8 ECHR,[110] but also under Article 46 ECHR in respect of a state's secondary obligations following the delivery of a judgment.[111] The most assertive stance it has arguably taken in the context of the rule on the exhaustion of domestic remedies (Article 35 ECHR) and Article 13 ECHR. In its decision in the case of *Scordino and Others* v. *Italy (No. 1)*, it held that "it follows from the principle of subsidiarity outlined above that the national courts *must*, where possible, interpret and apply domestic law in accordance with the Convention."[112] The Court further linked consistent interpretation to Article 1 ECHR by holding that the responsibility of the respondent state for a breach of the Convention may be engaged because of the manner in which a domestic court interprets domestic law.[113] The Court stated that

> (. . .) in exercising the European supervision incumbent on it, it cannot remain passive where a national court's interpretation of a legal act, be it a testamentary disposition, a private contract, a public document, a statutory provision or an administrative practice appears unreasonable, arbitrary, discriminatory or, more broadly, inconsistent with the principles underlying the Convention (. . .).[114]

107 Chapter 2, Section 2.3.3.2.

108 Martinico and Pollicino, *Interaction between Europe's Legal Systems*, pp. 129ff; Martinico, "ECHR and EU Law before National Courts," 407ff. For an exception see Gerards, "Shared Responsibility," p. 127; Christoffersen, *Fair Balance*, pp. 367ff.

109 Even for general international law, one may today argue that state practice has led to the emergence of an international duty of consistent interpretation (Betlem and Nollkaemper, "Giving Effect to Public International Law," 574. More critical Davíd Thór Björgvinsson, *The Intersection of International Law and Domestic Law* (Cheltenham: Edward Elgar Publishing 2015), p. 106.

110 *Pla and Puncernau* v. *Andorra*, § 62; ECtHR, *Paulic* v. *Croatia*, no. 3572/06, Judgment of October 22, 2009, § 42.

111 *Fabris* v. *France*, § 75.

112 *Scordino and Others* v. *Italy (No. 1)* (emphasis added).

113 ECtHR, *Khurshid Mustafa and Tarzibachi* v. *Sweden*, no. 23883/06, Judgment of December 16, 2008, § 34; *Storck* v. *Germany*, no. 61603/00, Judgment of June 16, 2005, ECHR 2005-V, § 148.

114 *Khurshid Mustafa and Tarzibachi* v. *Sweden*, § 33.

Generally, Convention states' autonomy in determining the conditions and consequences of consistent interpretation is limited.[115] As regards the scope of the obligation of consistent interpretation, the ECtHR has held that the obligation of consistent interpretation pertains to any provision of domestic law and is thus not limited to domestic human rights, for instance.[116] Also, in referring generally to "principles underlying the Convention,"[117] the Court arguably suggests that the duty of consistent interpretation equally pertains to Strasbourg case-law. Finally, the Court also expressed itself on the limits of consistent interpretation. As stated in the *Scordino (No. 1)* decision, consistent interpretation must only be carried out "where possible":[118] in particular the scope and wording of the domestic provision concerned must actually allow for consistent interpretation.[119] For another, the Court mentioned in *Fabris* v. *France* that regard must be paid to the principle of legal certainty.[120] Similar to EU law,[121] consistent interpretation may thus hinge upon whether or not the retroactive limitation of acquired rights was foreseeable for the individual concerned.[122] In short, there are several indications that the Court may infer an obligation of consistent interpretation from the ECHR and that the latter prescribes the scope and limits of consistent interpretation to an extent.

6.2.6 *Encouraging Incorporation and Direct Effect*

Indirect effect represents the minimum requirement under Article 13 ECHR, beyond which the Court has long voiced its preference for granting the ECHR direct effect. In the context of substantive provisions, the Court confirmed that Convention rights lend themselves to direct application. In *Vermeire* v. *Belgium*, the Court rejected the claim of the Belgian government that the Convention guarantees were not "sufficiently precise and comprehensive" and "thus not suitable for direct application by the domestic courts." As regards Article 8 ECHR, it found that there was "nothing imprecise or incomplete about the rule which prohibited

115 On this autonomy (especially compared to EU law) see Betlem and Nollkaemper, "Giving Effect to Public International Law," 575.
116 ECtHR, *Stankova* v. *Slovakia*, no. 7205/02, Judgment of October 9, 2007, § 24 (emphasis added).
117 *Khurshid Mustafa and Tarzibachi* v. *Sweden*, § 33.
118 See earlier fn. 112.
119 Betlem and Nollkaemper, "Giving Effect to Public International Law," 576. With this *contra legem* reservation, the ECtHR has adopted a well-known principle of consistent interpretation under EU law (e.g., CJEU, Case 14/83, *Sabine von Colson and Elisabeth Kamann* v. *Land Nordrhein-Westfalen* [1984] ECR 1891; Christoffersen, *Fair Balance*, p. 375).
120 *Fabris* v. *France*, §§ 40–42.
121 Betlem and Nollkaemper, "Giving Effect to Public International Law," 580.
122 *Fabris* v. *France*, §§ 40–42 and 67–72.

discrimination between children born in and out of wedlock."[123] Moreover, in the context of Articles 5 and 6 ECHR the Court stressed "the importance and the consequences of incorporating the Convention into domestic law (...) and of the direct applicability of the Convention (...)"[124] and held that its supervisory role will be easier "in respect of States that have effectively incorporated the Convention into their legal system and consider the rules to be directly applicable, since the highest courts of these States will normally assume responsibility for enforcing the principles determined by the Court."[125] In short, while indirect effect is a strict necessity, the Court strongly encourages direct effect.

6.2.7 *Preliminary Conclusion: Supranationality Lite*

The first part of the present chapter questioned the standard account on the domestic effect of Convention law, which treats implementation as a matter governed exclusively by domestic law. Case-law under different ECHR provisions points to a growing legal framework, through which Convention law partly claims to govern the domestic effect and implementation of Convention rights.[126] First, positive obligations, proceduralization, and proportionality analysis have entailed a structural transformation of the nature of the duty to secure human rights enshrined in Article 1 ECHR. Although they did not lead to an erosion of implementation freedom, they clearly introduced new obligations of means, both at the general/abstract level (e.g., adoption of legislative measures) as well as on an individual level as regards decision-making by domestic authorities (e.g., participation and proportionality test). As these doctrines remain largely processed-based, they don't impose a specific outcome and states retain discretion. Still, the Court prescribes the tools to be used in order to discharge the duty to secure Convention rights and therefore adds an important measure of concretization but also responsibilization. Second, Article 13 ECHR requires indirect effect of the ECHR whenever there is an arguable claim of a violation of the Convention. This means that at least the substance of Convention rights has to be both invocable and enforceable before domestic authorities. The Court also insinuated that an obligation of consistent interpretation flows from different ECHR provisions and that Convention law may not only govern the sources but also the scope and limits of consistent interpretation. In short, the Court imposed the permeability or integration of the object of Convention law into domestic law.

123 ECtHR, *Vermeire* v. *Belgium*, no. 12849/87, Judgment of November 29, 1991, Series A no. 214-C, §§ 23–24.
124 *Van Droogenbroeck* v. *Belgium*, § 55.
125 *Scordino* v. *Italy (No. 1)*, § 191.
126 The result is a certain discrepancy in Strasbourg practice: The Court "introduced – in substantive contexts – an implementation obligation, which it has been unwilling to establish in a formal context" (Christoffersen, *Fair Balance*, p. 378).

This preliminary conclusion shows that the ECtHR has fallen short of establishing defining elements of supranational law like direct invocability or supremacy.[127] Yet, the Court moved far away from being satisfied with individual reparation or prospective modification of domestic legislation.[128] The implementation framework developed by the Court aims at directly securing the domestic effectiveness of Convention law by requiring integration and enforceability in substance. It guarantees that individuals can rely on Convention protection domestically and conceptualizes domestic authorities as institutions of the Convention community.[129] Proportionality analysis, indirect effect, and consistent interpretation are tools that enable and responsibilize domestic judges to enforce ECHR rights, scrutinize domestic law and practices with regard to Convention law, and produce outcomes, which are Convention compatible. As these are largely process-based tools and the Court renounced to formulate any stare and formal supremacy claims, the implementation framework remains flexible and thus in line with the special and complementary nature of ECHR rights. Maybe more so than requiring the integration of specific substantive rules, the Court introduced meta-principles and modes of legal reasoning into domestic law. Given this subtle approach taken by the Court to secure and bolster the domestic effect and effectiveness of the ECHR, one may speak of supranationality lite.

6.3 VERTICAL INTEGRATION *QUA* DOMESTIC LAW

6.3.1 *Convention Law as Received by Domestic Legal Orders*

The argument expounded in this second part of the chapter is that of the domestic integration of Convention law *qua* domestic law.[130] This claim will largely be based on a survey of existing comparative studies researching the domestic reception,[131] implementation,[132] or effect[133] of Convention law. Inquiries into the domestic effect of Convention law usually follow the classical approach of studying the domestic effect of international law, distinguishing between monist and dualist traditions and

127 Chapter 2, Section 2.3.3.

128 Compare Janneke Gerards and Joseph Fleuren, "Comparative Analysis" in Janneke Gerards and Joseph Fleuren (eds.), *Implementation of the European Convention on Human Rights and of the Judgments of the ECtHR in National Case-law* (Cambridge: Intersentia 2014), p. 351.

129 See Conclusion, Members.

130 For earlier studies see, for example, Buergenthal, "Effect of the ECHR," 84ff; Drzemczewski, "Domestic Status of the ECHR" in Robert Blackburn and Jörg Polakiewicz (eds.), *Fundamental Rights in Europe: The European Convention on Human Rights and Its Member States, 1950–2000* (Oxford: Oxford University Press 2001).

131 Stone Sweet and Keller, "Reception of the ECHR," pp. 23ff.

132 Gerards and Fleuren, "Comparative Analysis."

133 Ress, "Decisions and Judgments of the ECtHR."

looking at validity, direct effect, and the rank of Convention law domestically.[134] Accordingly, the focus lies on domestic constitutional conditions, including the competence of domestic courts and authorities to give effect to the Convention.[135] Some studies have focused on Western,[136] some on Eastern European states,[137] and still others have worked with a representative selection covering both.[138] One of the leading treatise on the subject by Keller and Stone Sweet provides a comprehensive account covering the social, legal, political and scholarly processes and adaptions, which took place in response to the exposure of domestic systems to Convention law.[139] While their in-depth study of 2008 focused on sixteen countries, Stone Sweet later extended this research on domestic reception to cover all forty-seven state parties to the ECHR.[140] A synthesis of this body of research will reveal the domestification (Section 6.3.2), the direct invocability as well as the relative supremacy of Convention law (Sections 6.3.3–6.3.4). Domestic systems have by and large integrated the ECHR over time, which has justifiably prompted claims of a de facto supranationalization (Section 6.3.5). The last section is devoted to the question of whether increased criticism toward the ECtHR challenges domestic integration of the ECHR (Section 6.3.6).

6.3.2 *Domestification*

A key observation confirmed by many comparative studies is that the ECHR has become an integral part of domestic law, either automatically or by way of incorporation or transformation (through a constitutional provision, legislation, or the judiciary).[141] Incorporation in this wide sense can be understood as an incremental[142] process of domestification.[143] One could argue that given the need for a transformative act in dualist states, the ECHR loses its international character and simply becomes domestic

134 Gerards and Fleuren, "Comparative Analysis," pp. 335ff, 338f.

135 Keller and Stone Sweet, "Impact of the ECHR," p. 687; Bjorge, *Domestic Application of ECHR*, p. 4.

136 Gerards and Fleuren, "Comparative Analysis."

137 Iulia Motoc and Ineta Ziemele (eds.), *The Impact of the ECHR on Democratic Change in Central and Eastern Europe: Judicial Perspectives* (Cambridge: Cambridge University Press 2016).

138 Keller and Stone Sweet, "Impact of the ECHR."

139 Ibid., pp. 677ff.

140 Stone Sweet, "Cosmopolitan Legal Order," 85. As he stressed himself, his findings, which he presented in a tabular summary, must be read with caution as they do not capture the complexity and nuances of the domestic effect of Convention law.

141 Stone Sweet, "Cosmopolitan Legal Order," 84f; Besson, "European Human Rights," p. 505.

142 Compare Drzemczewski, "Domestic Status of the ECHR". For the United Kingdom, for example, domestification did not become reality until 2000 and the entry into force of the Human Rights Act 1998.

143 Keller and Stone Sweet, "Impact of the ECHR," pp. 682f.

law.[144] This argument applies in particular to states, in which the ECHR is only partially incorporated or in adapted form like in the United Kingdom.[145] Research, however, shows that the monism/dualism paradigm and the mode of incorporation are of limited importance in practice.[146] Also, as will be shown subsequently, while the formal legal source of "transformed" Convention rights may possibly be regarded domestic in nature, the same would be more difficult to defend for Strasbourg case-law.[147]

6.3.3 *Direct Invocability of Convention Rights*

Stone Sweet demonstrated that the ECHR is endowed with direct effect in all contracting states.[148] He defines direct effect as the Convention's direct applicability: the fact that ECHR rights "can be pleaded by individuals at bar, and judges can enforce them (applying them to resolve the case)."[149] For monist states, direct effect may hinge upon the self-executing nature of ECHR provisions, whereas for dualist states one might, again, object that it is not the ECHR which is directly applied, but rather the domestic provisions transforming Convention rights.[150] Yet, decisive is that the subjective rights as guaranteed in the Convention can be invoked by individuals across the CoE,[151] in many instances also in disputes among private parties.[152]

Direct effect, as defined by Stone Sweet, refers to Convention rights, including the Court's case-law.[153] From the perspective of domestic legal orders, Strasbourg case-law, generally speaking, forms part of the Convention and is therefore equally covered by the latter's internal validity and direct

144 E.g., UK House of Lords, *Re P and Others (Ap) (Appellants) (Northern Ireland)* [2008] UKHL 38; [2009] 1 AC 173; [2008] 3 WLR 76. Bjorge, *Domestic Application of ECHR*, pp. 108ff. Contra Andrew Le Sueur, Maurice Sunkin, and Jo Eric Khushal Murkens, *Public Law: Text, Cases, and Materials*, 3rd ed. (Oxford: Oxford University Press 2016), p. 749.

145 On full and partial incorporation see David Sloss (ed.), "Treaty Enforcement in Domestic Courts: A Comparative Analysis," *The Role of Domestic Courts in Treaty Enforcement* (Cambridge: Cambridge University Press 2009), pp. 18f and 22f. For a similar but slightly different terminology see Venice Commission, Report on the Implementation of International Human Rights Treaties in Domestic Law and the Role of Courts 9f.

146 Polakiewicz, "Status of the Convention," p. 43.

147 ECtHR case-law usually also benefits from direct invocability (see subsequently Section 6.3.3).

148 Stone Sweet, "Cosmopolitan Legal Order," 84f.

149 Ibid., 85.

150 Support for such an argument can be found in the fact that the HRA does not make reference to Art. 13 ECHR, for instance, which, therefore, cannot be directly invoked by individuals in the UK.

151 For a similar assessment see Gerards and Fleuren, "Comparative Analysis," p. 343; Besson, "European Human Rights," p. 106.

152 For an early analysis see Drzemczewski, "Domestic Status of the ECHR," pp. 70ff.

153 Stone Sweet, "Cosmopolitan Legal Order," 85 (emphasis added).

effect.[154] While in some countries such as the Ukraine, the United Kingdom, or Ireland, domestic law explicitly obliges courts to observe Strasbourg case-law,[155] national courts usually take the Court's interpretation into account when applying the Convention or domestic fundamental rights, either implicitly or through more or less systematic references. They thereby recognize both the *res interpretata* effect and the direct applicability of ECtHR case-law.[156] In some jurisdictions, domestic practice expressly reflects that direct applicability of ECtHR case-law also entails direct invocability. In *Gorgülü*, for example, the German Constitutional Court expanded the constitutional complaint procedure to include challenges alleging failure to take into account Strasbourg case-law.[157] Similarly, the Swiss Federal Supreme Court has found that ECtHR case-law can be invoked directly by individuals.[158] It is in this sense that if today the Court renders a new judgment, it can be considered immediately valid and effective within the legal orders of Convention states.[159] There remain, of course, still important differences, especially as regards respect for Strasbourg case-law.[160] In certain states such as Turkey, Russia, Poland, or Hungary, general awareness and visibility of Convention law remain lower and direct effect as observed by Stone Sweet does not necessarily or always translate into a high(er) domestic impact or observance of Convention law.[161]

6.3.4 *Relative Supremacy*

Another element to be considered is the rank of the ECHR within the domestic hierarchy of sources. Stone Sweet has grouped contracting states into the following

[154] This includes, for instance, Austria, Belgium, Croatia, Cyprus, Estonia, France, Ireland, Germany, Greece, Latvia, Lithuania, Macedonia, Poland, the Netherlands, Turkey, Russia, Spain, Slovakia, Slovenia, Sweden, Switzerland, United Kingdom, and Ukraine. With references to domestic practice PACE, The Interpretative Authority (*Res Interpretata*) of the Strasbourg Court's Judgments: Compilation of Background Material, AS/Jur/Inf (2010)04, 17ff; Gerards and Fleuren, "Comparative Analysis," p. 357; Besson, "Erga Omnes Effect," p. 141f; Martinico, "ECHR and EU Law before National Courts," 407ff; Polakiewicz, "Status of the Convention," p. 51; Lambrecht, "Assessing Critisicm," p. 536f.

[155] Art. 2(1) HRA 1998 (UK); Art. 4 ECHR Act 2003 (Ireland); Section 4 Law No. 3477–IV 2006 (Ukraine). UK Supreme Court, *Brigid McCaughey and another for Judicial Review (Northern Ireland)* [2011] UKSC 20; [2012] 1 AC 725; [2011] 2 WLR 1279. Bjorge, *Domestic Application of ECHR*, p. 21. In the UK, the so-called mirror principle requires courts to keep pace with Strasbourg jurisprudence.

[156] To be sure, the *res interpretata* effect may also call for the adoption of legislative measures or changes in administrative practices. As Polakiewicz held, "incorporation should not be a pretext for passivity by the legislature (...)" (Polakiewicz, "Status of the Convention," p. 50). Explicit references to ECtHR case-law have increased steadily among highest supreme courts (Lambrecht, "Assessing Criticism," 537f).

[157] Federal Constitutional Court of Germany, *Gorgülü*, BVerfGE 111, 307 paras. 60–63.

[158] Federal Supreme Court of Switzerland, 130 II 113, consideration 6.4.

[159] This applies to the interpretative effect of the judgment and not to the *res iudicata* effect in the individual case.

[160] Besson, "Erga Omnes Effect," p. 142.

[161] Lambrecht, "Assessing Criticism," pp. 507 and 536f.

four different categories depending on the Convention's internal status: supra-constitutional, constitutional, supra-legislative, and infra-legislative.[162] Striking is that with the exception of the UK and Ireland, ECHR rights are in virtually all states effectively enforceable in respect to conflicting domestic legislation, even if the latter was enacted after the ECHR entered into force.[163] In fact, this holds true even for states following a dualist tradition such as Belgium, Sweden, Norway, Germany, or Italy, in which the status of international law is usually determined by the rank of the incorporating act (i.e., ordinary law).[164] Instead of the *lex posterior* rule, which would frustrate ECHR enforcement vis-à-vis subsequent conflicting statutes, the *lex specialis* rule and consistent interpretation dictate practice.[165] In Germany, for instance, where the ECHR formally only has the rank of its incorporating statute,[166] the *lex posterior* rule was qualified and conflicts are generally resolved in favor of the Convention.[167] On the one hand, the Federal Constitutional Court has held that domestic legislation, regardless of its date of issuance, must be interpreted in conformity with the Convention.[168] On the other hand, because of the "openness to international law" (*Völkerrechtsfreundlichkeit*) of the German Basic Law as well as the paramount importance of human rights, the Convention and its case-law serve as interpretation aids (*Auslegungshilfe*) for the fundamental rights of the German Basic Law.[169] Similarly, the Italian Constitutional Court has held that Convention rights, although formally incorporated at the level of ordinary legislation, are inviolable in the sense of Article 2 of the Italian Constitution, which means that they cannot be abrogated through subsequent legislation. As a result, the Convention ranks in Italy, too, half-way between statutory law and constitutional norms.[170] Consistent

[162] Stone Sweet, "Cosmopolitan Legal Order," 85.

[163] Ibid., 71f. See also Besson, "European Human Rights," p. 106; Lambrecht, "Assessing Criticism," pp. 506ff.

[164] Keller and Stone Sweet, "Impact of the ECHR," p. 685.

[165] Polakiewicz, "Status of the Convention," p. 43.

[166] So-called *Zustimmungsgesetz* according to Art. 59(2) of the German Basic Law. For a detailed account see Thomas Giegerich, "Wirkung und Rang der EMRK in den Rechtsordnungen der Mitgliedstaaten" in Oliver Dörr, Rainer Grote, and Thilo Marauhn (eds.), *EMRK/GG: Konkordanzkommentar zum europäischen und deutschen Grundrechtsschutz*, vol. I, 2nd ed. (Tübingen: Mohr Siebeck 2013), pp. 57–98.

[167] Bjorge, *Domestic Application of ECHR*, p. 91. Hence, the Federal Constitutional Court has so far never had to apply the *lex posterior* rule in disregard of the Convention to give way to a conflicting statute. However, and in contrast to the earlier discussed case-law, the German Federal Administrative Tribunal appears to have gone as far as giving the ECHR supra-constitutional status (Marten Breuer, "Streikverbot vor dem Bundesverwaltungsgericht: Auf dem Weg zur supranationalen EMRK?" (2014) *Verfassungsblog* www.verfassungsblog.de/streikverbot-bundesverwaltungsgericht-auf-weg-zur-supranationalen-emrk/ (accessed July 23, 2020)).

[168] German Federal Constitutional Court, *Unschuldsvermutung I*, BVerfGE 74, 358 para. 39; *Gorgülü*, BVerfGE 111, 307 paras. 29ff; *Sicherungsverwahrung I*, BVerfGE 128, 326 paras. 88ff; *Sicherungsverwahrung II*, BVerfGE 131, 286.

[169] German Federal Constitutional Court, *Sicherungsverwahrung I*, BVerfGE 128, 326 para. 86. Article 1(1)(2) of the German Basic Law.

[170] Constitutional Court of Italy, Judgments nos. 348-349/2007 of October 22 and 24, 2007.

interpretation further allowed some states to grant ECHR rights primacy over ordinary domestic legislation even in the absence of formal incorporation.[171] In short, national courts are by and large in a position to grant the ECHR interpretative priority,[172] set aside, disapply, or even declare void conflicting domestic law.[173] Even the United Kingdom and Ireland, the only exceptions to the rule, grant the ECHR privileged status.[174] While British courts may only issue a declaration of incompatibility in case of conflict and are barred from setting aside domestic legislation that is contrary to Convention law,[175] judges often resort to harmonious interpretation to avoid open conflicts. Section 3(1) of the HRA 1998 explicitly foresees that "so far as it is possible to do so, primary legislation and subordinate legislation must be read and given effect in a way which is compatible with the Convention rights." In fact, Section 3(1) is understood to allow courts a very wide interpretative margin when construing statutes so as to reach at most an outcome which complies with Convention law standards.[176] As Bjorge recently argued, domestic courts go a long way in respecting the ECHR and act as faithful trustees of Convention law: they regard their task as being first-line defenders of Convention rights that take part in the development of Convention law, even in areas where clear guidance from Strasbourg is lacking.[177]

ECHR supremacy in the above sense does not mean that the ECHR would also take precedence over domestic constitutions. In only few states does the ECHR rank equal to or above domestic constitutions.[178] Indeed, the constitutional courts of Germany,[179] Italy,[180] Austria,[181] and Russia,[182] but also the UK Supreme Court[183] explicitly asserted that Convention law must respect the constitution.[184] Spanish, French, and Belgian

171 This was the case in Iceland. Björgvinsson, *Intersection of International Law*, pp. 107 and 119.

172 Martinico, "ECHR and EU Law before National Courts," 412, citing the example of Nordic countries or Germany.

173 This is the case in Italy, France, Portugal, Spain, or Romania, for example. Martinico, "ECHR and EU Law before National Courts," 412ff. Lambrecht, "Assessing Criticism," pp. 534f.

174 Lambrecht, "Assessing Criticism," p. 509.

175 Section 4 Human Rights Act 1998.

176 UK House of Lords, *Ghaidan* v. *Godin-Mendoza* [2004] UKHL 30; [2004] 2 AC 557; [2004] 3 WLR 113. On this Bjorge, *Domestic Application of ECHR*, p. 288.

177 Bjorge, *Domestic Application of ECHR*, p. 248.

178 According to Stone Sweet, supra-constitutional status of the ECHR is only to be found in the Netherlands, Belgium, Slovakia, Macedonia, and Albania (Stone Sweet, "Cosmopolitan Legal Order," 74f).

179 Federal Constitutional Court of Germany, *Gorgülü*, BVerfGE 111, 307. See also Art. 79(3) of the German Basic Law.

180 Constitutional Court of Italy, Judgment no. 311/2009 of November 16, 2009; Judgment no. 264/2012 of November 19, 2012.

181 Austrian Constitutional Court, *Miltner*, Judgment of October 14, 1987, VfSlg 11500/1987.

182 Russian Constitutional Court, Judgment no. 21-P/2015 of July 14, 2015.

183 UK Supreme Court, *R* v. *Horncastle and Others* [2009] UKSC 14; [2010] 2 AC 373; [2009] WLR (D) 358.

184 In the case of the United Kingdom, the fundamental parts of domestic law must be respected (ibid.).

case-law can be interpreted in a similar fashion.[185] Considering that even for EU law absolute and unconditional supremacy over domestic constitutions was rejected,[186] this case-law is not surprising. It corroborates Martinico's point that states – their constitutional courts in particular – may qualify the general acceptance of ECHR supremacy by some sort of constitutional counter-limit doctrine of the *Solange* type.[187] Preserving constitutional primacy may itself be a sign of the pervasive effect of the ECHR. In Italy, for instance, "the progressive importance acquired by the Convention in the case-law of the Italian Corte Costituzionale" was regarded "a success which has sometimes converted a valuable ally into a thorny interlocutor."[188]

To be sure, constitutional reservations, if applied towards the ECtHR, are particularly powerful and may challenge the ECHR's domestic effectiveness.[189] Unlike the *Solange* constellation, (irresolvable) conflicts between constitutional law and the ECHR usually result precisely from concurring interpretations of one and the same right, particularly as regards so-called multipolar rights situations,[190] the principle of separation of powers, or the rule of law.[191] Yet, conflicts between constitutional principles of contracting states and the ECHR have remained rather singular so far. Even the UK Supreme Court, for instance, which is more assertive than most domestic courts in this regard, held that only "rare occasions" would justify not to follow Strasbourg case-law.[192] And in Germany, for example, an irresolvable conflict between the ECHR and German Basic Law did so far not arise.[193]

185 For France and Spain see Krisch, *Beyond Constitutionalism*, pp. 114ff. For Belgium see Gerards and Fleuren, "Comparative Analysis," p. 363.

186 Chapter 2, Section 2.3.3.3.

187 Martinico, "ECHR and EU Law before National Courts," 419ff; see also Gerards and Fleuren, "Comparative Analysis," pp. 364 and 359. Bjorge has approached this issue partly under the heading of respect for domestic separation of powers and judicial dialogue. Bjorge, *Domestic Application of ECHR*, pp. 36ff, 49ff.

188 Leandro Mancano, and Giuseppe Martinico, "An Italian Tale of Two Courts. Judgment no. 49/2015 of the Italian Constitutional Court and its Relationship with Strasbourg" (2016) 58 *Revista española de derecho europeo* 199–214 at 212.

189 Breuer, "Principled Resistance," pp. 4f. Therefore Breuer speaks of "principled resistance" regarding situations, in which ECtHR judgments cannot be implemented on grounds of domestic constitutional law.

190 E.g., Federal Constitutional Court of Germany, *Gorgülü*, BVerfGE 111, 307 para. 50.

191 As to the latter see Bjorge, *Domestic Application of ECHR*, pp. 49ff.

192 UK Supreme Court, *R* v. *Horncastle & Others* [2009] UKSC 14, para. 11. In France, too, only exceptional reasons may justify deviating from ECtHR case-law (French State Council, *Bitouzet*, July 3, 1998, no. 1585929, Conclusions of the Government Commissioner M. Abraham).

193 Sauer submits that the role of the constitutional limits doctrine developed in the *Görgülü* judgment (see earlier fn. 179) is overrated in practice (Heiko Sauer, "Principled Resistance against ECtHR Judgments in Germany" in Marten Breuer (ed.), *Principled Resistance against ECtHR Judgments – A New Paradigm?* [Berlin/Heidelberg: Springer 2019], pp. 55–87).

6.3.5 *De facto Supranationalization*

The preceding sections shows that there exists a very strong measure of convergence regarding key issues such as domestification, invocability, and relative supremacy of Convention law despite the variety of domestic constitutional arrangements.[194] Contracting states allow for a high degree of penetration and effectiveness of the Convention, which, from an international law perspective, was described as strongly monist.[195] While states usually uphold the primacy of their constitution also vis-à-vis Convention law, this practice seems so far to confirm rather than question the high degree of vertical integration.

The domestic treatment of Convention law points to a process of de facto supranationalization. By granting direct effect and relative supremacy to the ECHR, contracting states went beyond what the ECHR formally requires and elevated Convention law de facto to supranational law.[196] As Keller and Stone Sweet stressed, "national officials are being steadily socialized into a Europe whose Convention not only binds the state, as a matter of international law, but also binds domestic officials, *as a matter of enforceable national law*."[197] The idea of a de facto supranationalization is also reflected in Martinico and Pollicino's finding that the domestic application of EU and ECHR law converges to a large degree. In the context of both EU law and the ECHR, consistent interpretation, disapplication of domestic law, and domestic counter-limit doctrines operate as important instruments.[198] Since the structural principles of EU law such as direct effect and supremacy were extended to the ECHR, Martinico speaks of "supranational laws" in respect of both systems.[199] Indeed, other scholars investigating the Europeanization of domestic law have used "supranational law" as an umbrella term for both EU and Convention law.[200] To be sure, sometimes the convergence of EU and ECHR law as regards domestic effect is simply the result of domestic legal systems not making any distinction. Also, in some countries, there remain important differences between EU law and the ECHR. In the pre-Brexit United Kingdom, for instance, EU law, unlike the ECHR, enjoyed formal supremacy over domestic legislation.[201] And the Italian Constitutional Court explicitly upheld a distinction between the Convention

194 See also Martinico, "ECHR and EU Law before National Courts," 404; Keller and Stone Sweet, "Impact of the ECHR," pp. 685f, 693.

195 Keller and Stone Sweet, "Impact of the ECHR," p. 683.

196 Besson, "European Human Rights," p. 106. This is the opposite of what is observed in the context of regional economic integration outside the EU, where the challenge seems to lie in transposing de jure into de facto supranationality (Caserta, "Regional Integration," 592ff, 600).

197 Keller and Stone Sweet, "Impact of the ECHR," p. 694 (emphasis added).

198 Martinico, "ECHR and EU Law before National Courts," 423. See also Giuseppe Martinico and Oreste Pollicino, *The National Judicial Treatment of the ECHR and EU Laws* (Groningen: Europa Law Publishing 2010).

199 Martinico and Pollicino, *Interaction between Europe's Legal Systems.*

200 Lebeck, "European Law in Scandinavia."

201 UK House of Lords, *Regina* v. *Secretary of State for Transport Ex Parte Factortame Ltd (No. 2)* [1990] UKHL 13; [1991] 1 AC 603; [1990] 3 WLR 818; see also the European Communities Act of 1972.

and EU law, asserting that the former was "only" an international treaty that did not entail a limitation of sovereignty in terms of Article 11 of the Italian Constitution with the result that the ECHR must respect the entire Italian Constitution, not just some constitutional core principles as is the case for EU law.[202] These caveats, however, do not question the general finding that Convention law's domestic integration has become comparable to that of EU law.

Even the constitutional counter-doctrines may reflect a trend of de facto supranationalization.[203] The development of more sophisticated approaches regarding the limits of the internal effect of the ECHR can be framed as a response to the ever-growing domestic impact of the Convention and its particular internal effectiveness. Disregard for Convention law based on domestic constitutional law is thus the rare exception confirming the general rule of relative ECHR supremacy.[204] This also transpires from Bjorge's narrative and his response to, inter alia, Krisch's account on the pluralist and frictious relationship between domestic legal systems and the ECHR. Discussing the *Preventive Detention II case* by the German Constitutional Court he noted:

> The German Constitutional Court's statement in Preventive Detention II to the effect that all organs of the state are under a duty "not only to take into account" the European Convention but also "to avoid conflict" between it and national law, seems to go against the grain of Krisch's account of the approach taken in German law. So does the exhortation, in the same ruling, that the openness of the Basic Law *expresses an understanding of sovereignty which not only does not oppose international and supranational integration but presupposes and expects it.*[205]

Not all states have embraced and observe Convention law to the same degree in domestic practice.[206] Given the overlap in comparative findings on the domestic status of the ECHR, however, it seems nonetheless possible to argue that generally speaking, contracting parties have endowed Conventional law with the characteristics of supranational law and that this is also reflected in the legal practice in a majority of countries

The reasons why states allow for such a high level of domestic integration of the ECHR are manifold and difficult to trace. The Court's subtle approach of fostering implementation may be one but is certainly not the only reason.[207] In addition, scholars identified several important factors. EU law,

202 Italian Constitutional Court, Judgments nos. 348-349/2007 of October 22 and 24, 2007. For a detailed analysis see Oreste Pollicino, "Italy: Constitutional Court at the Crossroads between Constitutional Parochialism and Co-Operative Constitutionalism. Judgments No. 348 and 349 of 22 and 24 October 2007" (2008) 4 *European Constitutional Law Review* 363–382.

203 Martinico, "ECHR and EU Law before National Courts," 423.

204 Bjorge, *Domestic Application of ECHR*, p. 61.

205 Ibid., pp. 62f (emphasis added).

206 Lambrecht, "Assessing Criticism," pp. 507 and 536f.

207 See Conclusion, Driving Factors.

for instance, forced especially dualist states to accept fundamental changes in order to accommodate direct effect, supremacy, and proportionality analysis, which in sorts paved the way for the Convention's integration into domestic law.[208] The Convention's domestic function further plays a significant role. The fact that the ECHR operates in some states as a surrogate for non-existent or ineffective domestic fundamental rights clearly favors supranationalization.[209] The same holds true for states, in which the ECHR served as an external pillar supporting transition processes towards democracy and as a model for the development of newly introduced human rights catalogues.[210] Besides ratifying the Convention, ensuring the latter's domestic effectiveness is a tool to "lock-in" – to use Moravcsik's terms – newly established democracies against future backlash.[211] The special normative force of human rights reflecting their constitutional status or nature may also have been an important factor.[212] The assumption is that protection of the individual and human dignity is paramount and, therefore, to an extent supreme.[213] A last and somewhat neglected aspect is that vertical integration can also be a means for states to actually (re-)gain control over and/or participate in the development of Convention law. Indeed, granting Convention law direct effect, for instance, appears to be a pre-condition for any systematic engagement by domestic courts with Strasbourg case-law and, therefore, their faculty to take influence on the latter. In a sense, therefore, supranationalization provides a basis for meaningful judicial dialogue.

6.3.6 *Signs of Disintegration?*

The question arises whether recent assessments within the backlash or resistance discourse challenge previous findings of domestic loyalty to and effectiveness of the ECHR. As already mentioned, the application of constitutional reservations toward the ECHR is particularly powerful and may challenge the authority of the

208 Keller and Stone Sweet, "Impact of the ECHR," p. 681. Moreover, by construing Convention law as part of EU law, the CJEU has helped in bolstering the normative impact of the ECHR in EU member states at least within the realm and scope of application of EU law (Art. 6 TEU; Polakiewicz, "Status of the Convention," p. 37). If the EU's accession to the ECHR should become reality after all, this impact could receive a more formal legal basis.

209 On the ECHR as a shadow constitution Keller and Stone Sweet, "Impact of the ECHR," p. 686.

210 This is arguably the case for some Eastern European states formally part of the Soviet Republic, which have incorporated the ECHR in a particularly faithful manner. Polakiewicz, "Status of the Convention," pp. 40ff.

211 Andrew Moravcsik, "The Origins of Human Rights Regimes: Democratic Delegation in Postwar Europe" (2000) 54 *International Organization* 217–252 at 220.

212 Along these lines, for example, Federal Supreme Court of Switzerland, 125 II 417 *(PKK)*, consideration 4c/d; see Erika Wet and Jure Vidmar, *Hierarchy in International Law* (Oxford: Oxford University Press 2012).

213 Bjorge, *Domestic Application of ECHR*, pp. 58ff.

ECtHR and the ECHR more or less directly.[214] But are states actually invoking their constitution or national identity more frequently to shield themselves from Convention law and, if yes, to an extent that calls the general picture of vertical integration into question?

The most prominent examples of recent clashes between domestic (constitutional) law and the ECHR concern the United Kingdom and Russia. Both countries have recently refused to execute specific ECtHR judgments because of (an alleged) conflict with domestic (constitutional) law.[215] As to the United Kingdom, the ECtHR kept reiterating for more than a decade that the blanket disenfranchisement of British prisoners was in violation of Article 3 Protocol 1.[216] UK parliament openly refused to follow the Court's judgments and the government could not bring forward legislative proposals to bring domestic law in line with Convention standards.[217] In 2017, a compromise was found, which was accepted by the CoM and consists of an administrative measure allowing about 100 prisoners to vote.[218] However, the enfranchisement remains minimal and the United Kingdom did not amend the impugned Representation of the People Act 1983.[219] This *Hirst* saga has been understood as an assertion of national and particularly parliamentary supremacy over the ECHR including the Court's interpretation thereof.[220]

In Russia, the Duma amended the law on the Russian Constitutional Court enabling the latter to declare decisions of international courts impossible to implement if they contradict the Russian Constitution and non-execution is the only way to avoid such conflict.[221] The law followed increased political and public pressure on Strasbourg and basically codified a previous dictum by the Russian Constitutional Court according to which the execution of an ECtHR judgment could eventually be blocked if it contradicted the constitution.[222] The Constitutional Court first applied the new provision with respect to the ECtHR's

214 Breuer, "Principled Resistance," pp. 18f.

215 This is basically what Breuer coined principled resistance (Breuer, "Principled Resistance," pp. 20f.) Ed Bates, "Analysing the Prisoner Voting Saga and the British Challenge to Strasbourg" (2014) 14 *Human Rights Law Review* 503–540; Ed Bates, "Principled Criticism and a Warning from the 'UK' to the ECtHR?" in Marten Breuer (ed.), *Principled Resistance to ECtHR Judgments – A New Paradigm?* (Berlin/Heidelberg: Springer 2019), pp. 219ff; Stiansen and Voeten, "Backlash and Judicial Restraint," 7f.

216 See, among others, *Hirst* v. *the United Kingdom (No. 2)*; *Firth and Others* v. *the United Kingdom*, nos. 47784/09, 47806/09 and 47812/09, Judgment of August 12, 2014.

217 *Greens and M.T.* v. *the United Kingdom*.

218 CoM, Resolution CM/ResDH(2018)467.

219 Bates, "Principled Criticism," p. 221.

220 Ibid., pp. 193–244, 219.

221 Federal Constitutional Law of December 14, 2015, N 7-FKZ; Vladislav Starzhenetskiy, "The Execution of ECtHR Judgements and the 'Right to Object'" in Marten Breuer (ed.), *Principled Resistance to ECtHR Judgments – A New Paradigm?* (Berlin/Heidelberg: Springer 2019), pp. 255f and 259f.

222 Russian Constitutional Court, Judgment no. 21-P/2015 of July 14, 2015; Judgment no. 27-P/2013 of December 6, 2013.

judgment in *Anchugov and Gladkov*, which reproved, as the British cases, the disenfranchisement of prisoners.[223] Later, the Constitutional Court also denied execution of the 2014 *Yukos* judgment, in which Russia was ordered to pay close to EUR 1.9B in just satisfaction to former Yukos shareholders.[224] The Constitutional Court's response to the *Yukos* judgment even raised the question of whether the execution of ECtHR judgments may be blocked in cases of conflicts below the constitutional threshold.[225]

Resistance in this form from Russia and the United Kingdom both concern the specific issue of disenfranchisement and primarily challeng the binding effect of judgments under Article 46 ECHR.[226] It is difficult to ascertain how much it also impacts the general domestic status of the Convention in these countries or beyond.[227] Lambrecht, for instance, found that "deliberate refusal to implement an ECtHR judgment is highly exceptional," while general compliance problems usually do not coincide with increased criticism.[228] There certainly is the danger that deliberate non-execution could become a more widespread phenomenon.[229] Also, the example of the United Kingdom and the Brighton Declaration show that non-execution can spark off wider political resistance, which may translate into (attempts) of institutional backlash.[230]

The judgment no. 49/2015 by the Italian Constitutional Court has also been treated as an example of resistance.[231] Unlike the Russian and British examples, it deals more directly with the domestic status of ECHR law. The Italian Constitutional Court held that Italian courts should only be obliged to follow a rule derived from Strasbourg case-law, if it forms part of established practice.[232] While this certainly introduces a limitation to the domestic effectiveness of

223 Russian Constitutional Court, Judgment No. 12-P/2016 of April 19, 2016; ECtHR, *Anchugov and Gladkov* v. *Russia*, nos. 11157/04 and 15162/05, Judgment of July 4, 2013. Natalia Chaeva, "The Russian Constitutional Court and Its Actual Control over the ECtHR Judgement in Anchugov and Gladkov" (2016) *EJIL: Talk!* www.ejiltalk.org/the-russian-constitutional-court-and-its-actual-control-over-the-ecthr-judgement-in-anchugov-and-gladko/ (accessed July 23, 2020).

224 Russian Constitutional Court, Judgment no. 1-P/2017 of January 19, 2017; ECtHR, *Oao Neftyanaya Kompaniya Yukos* v. *Russia*, no. 14902/04, Judgment of July 31, 2014.

225 Breuer, "Principled Resistance," pp. 331f.

226 In respect of the United Kingdom, this danger was somewhat alleviated. Although it is questionable, whether the compromise reached in the CoM (fully) implements the Court's judgments, it did help Strasbourg to save face, which is, interestingly, a solution also known from the context of challenges to EU law supremacy (Breuer, "Principled Resistance," p. 332). In contrast, the use of its new veto powers by the Constitutional Court regarding execution is unprecedented.

227 Although in the case of Russia, the argument could indeed be made that the mere possibility of declaring a potential judgment from the ECtHR finding a violation of the ECHR non-enforceable, could prompt domestic courts to also more readily disregard Convention law in the first place.

228 Lambrecht, "Assessing Criticism," p. 531.

229 Philip Leach and Alice Donald, "Russia Defies Strasbourg: Is Contagion Spreading?" (2015) *EJIL: Talk!* www.ejiltalk.org/russia-defies-strasbourg-is-contagion-spreading/ (accessed July 23, 2020).

230 Stiansen and Voeten, "Backlash and Judicial Restraint," 7ff; Chapter 4, Section 4.2.1.3.

231 Giuseppe Martinico, "Judicial Disobedience and the ECtHR: The Italian Case" in Marten Breuer (ed.), *Principled Resistance to ECtHR Judgments – A New Paradigm?* (Berlin/Heidelberg: Springer 2019), pp. 153ff.

232 Italian Constitutional Court, Judgment no. 49/2015 of March 26, 2015, para. 7.

Convention law, the judgment must be read in the specific context in which it was rendered. Essentially, the Italian Constitutional Court's point was that the ECtHR's *Varvara* judgment could be interpreted in a manner consistent with Italian law, not least because it did not (yet) represent established case-law.[233] The judgment no. 49/2015 is thus not a case of simply disregarding Strasbourg practice but reflects a specific understanding of the *res interpretata* and the authority flowing Strasbourg case-law. Although the Court later clarified that, from its perspective, all judgments enjoy the same legal value, support for a graduation in the Court's interpretative authority can in fact be found in scholarship.[234] Also, the Constitutional Court explicitly framed its findings in reference to the notion of judicial dialogue stating that domestic courts are not simply passive receptors of Convention law, but take on an active role in its development.[235] Furthermore, judgment no. 49/2015 is still an expression of the classical reservation of many states that Convention law must not violate their constitution. The Italian Constitutional Court did in fact recall and adhere to the supra-legislative status of the Convention.[236] Arguably, judgment no. 49/2015 might therefore rather be a sign of constitutional maturity and a case of application of judicial dialogue than an actual backlash.[237]

Another example of resistance concerning the domestic effect of the ECHR has come out of Switzerland. In 2016, the Swiss National Popular Party (SVP) launched a popular initiative that sought to establish primacy of the Swiss Constitution over international law and limit the applicability of those international agreements on which no popular referendum was held.[238] In reality, the initiative mainly targeted the ECtHR, at the risk of having to withdraw from the ECHR.[239] The promise of the initiative was to protect Switzerland from illegitimate interferences of "foreign judges," especially those at the ECHR.[240] The initiative also took issue with the judiciary in general, including the Swiss Federal Supreme Court. Swiss resistance remained populistic rather than legalistic or principled,[241] and it did not yield the desired results. The Swiss government

[233] Ibid.

[234] See Chapter 5, Section 5.5.3.

[235] Mancano and Martinico, "Italian Tale of Two Courts," 208.

[236] Italian Constitutional Court, Judgment no. 49/2015 of March 26, 2015.

[237] Mancano and Martinico, "Italian Tale of Two Courts," 212.

[238] So-called Self-determination Initiative of the Swiss Popular Party. The text of the initiative is reproduced in the Message of the Federal Council of July 5, 2017 published in the Federal Gazette 2017 5355, 5360f; Tilmann Altwicker, "Switzerland: The Substitute Constitution in Times of Popular Dissent" in Patricia Popelier, Sarah Lambrecht, and Koen Lemmens (eds.), *Criticism of the European Court of Human Rights. Shifting the Dynamics of the Convention System: Counter-Dynamics at the National and EU level* (Cambridge: Intersentia 2016), pp. 385–412.

[239] Message of the Federal Council, Federal Gazette 2017 5355, 5384 fn. 96.

[240] Freely translated, the SVP's popular initiative was subtitled "Swiss law instead of foreign judges" (see earlier fn. 238).

[241] Helen Keller and Reto Walther, "Resistance in Switzerland: Populist rather than Principled" in Marten Breuer (ed.), *Principled Resistance against ECtHR Judgments – A New Paradigm?* (Berlin/Heidelberg: Springer 2019), pp. 161–191.

recommended voting against the initiative and the Swiss people clearly rejected it by popular vote in 2018.[242] As the initiative targeted the ECtHR in particular, its rejection at the ballot can be understood as a commitment by the Swiss people to the ECHR.

The above examples show that constitutional primacy has gained in importance both in practice and scholarship. It serves to justify resistance or disobedience when there is strong disagreement over the interpretation of Convention rights. Nonetheless, it seems difficult to infer a larger trend of increased readiness to invoke constitutional conflict to deny the ECHR domestic effectiveness. So far, "the Russian Court is (...) the only court having clearly enunciated the incompatibility of ECtHR standards with the national constitution."[243] We also lack empirical evidence that the domestic status of the ECHR has significantly changed as a result of occasional disobedience.[244] In the context of a comprehensive study on criticism towards the ECtHR, Lambrecht reaches the conclusion that disobedience based on substantive issues still remains very rare and "in the majority of countries, no clear increase of criticism is visible and criticism is generally not widespread, temporary in nature and case-specific."[245] Similarly, Breuer didn't answer in the positive the question posed in the title of his volume on resistance towards the ECtHR: whether there has been a change of paradigm.[246] Ultimately, resistance in its current form must not necessarily be understood as an antithesis to supranationalization or integration, but can equally be regarded epiphenomenal. For instance, the parallel one finds in ECHR scholarship on resistance to the national (constitutional) identity discourse under EU law points to the assumption that legal integration under the ECHR deepened to an extent that affects national identities.[247]

242 Federal Gazette 2019 5931, 5932f.

243 Breuer, "Principled Resistance," p. 333.

244 As concerns Russia see Madsen, Cebulak and Wiebusch, "Backlash against International Courts," 211.

245 Lambrecht, "Assessing Criticism," pp. 551, 512–514 and 541.

246 Instead, he concludes that principled resistance comes down to the question of proper allocation of powers: "Who is the final arbiter and therefore has the last word – the national legislator, the national constitutional court, or the Court in Strasbourg" (Breuer, "Principled Resistance," p. 349). This quandary has already been at the heart of the *Von Hannover* cases (e.g., ECtHR, *Von Hannover v. Germany (No. 2)*, nos. 40660/08 and 60641/08, Grand Chamber Judgment of February 7, 2012, ECHR 2012-I).

247 Schmahl described the concept of constitutional identity as a constitutional self-image that is rather an expression of the concern over Europeanization than of normative prerequisites. Stefanie Schmahl, "The National Identity Criterion in the Crossfire between European Integration and the Preservation of National Sovereignty" in Marten Breuer (ed.), *Principled Resistance against ECtHR Judgments – A New Paradigm?* (Berlin/Heidelberg: Springer 2019), p. 320f.

6.4 CONCLUSION

This chapter has analyzed the interface between Convention law and the domestic legal orders of contracting states. The assumption was tested whether Convention law can be considered supranational law in terms of its effect in domestic legal systems. An attempt was made to answer this question in two steps. The first part of the chapter took issue with the traditional, yet still widely accepted view that neither the Convention nor the ECtHR have much to say about the domestic status and effect of Convention law. It was asserted that this view should be abandoned, given that the Court developed a subtle framework to secure and bolster the domestic effect and effectiveness of the ECHR. This implementation framework, it was submitted, could be termed supranationality lite as it requires vertical integration of the Convention's substance and responsibilizes domestic courts as defenders of ECHR rights through the imposition of different mostly processed based cross-over doctrines. The second part of the chapter analyzed the domestic effect of the ECHR from the perspective of national legal orders. It has shown that virtually all CoE states have incorporated the ECHR and endowed it – including Strasbourg case-law – with direct effect and supremacy (at least) over ordinary legislation. For these reasons, scholars rightly ascertained that domestic legal systems treat Convention law de facto as supranational law.

Although not formally conceptualizing the ECHR as supranational law, the Court has provided strong incentives and impetus for contracting parties and courts to do exactly that. To simply conclude that bottom-up or de facto supranationalization is self-imposed and CoE states have voluntarily gone beyond what is formally required under the Convention, would be to underestimate both the requirements and the influence of the supranationality lite framework. Generally speaking, endowing the ECHR with supranational effect may simply be regarded as the most effective way of implementing the Convention.[248] At least indirectly, this point has also been stressed by the Court when it ruled incorporation and direct effect to be a desirability from the Convention's perspective. In fact, given the Court's extensive lawmaking function, massive judicial output as well as the ever-evolving and dynamic body of case-law, respecting the jurisprudentially developed Convention standards is difficult, unless domestic authorities can take them directly into account. On the one hand, to just afford compensation on an individual basis would be to deny the ECtHR its lawmaking function and expose states to a series of adverse judgments from Strasbourg.[249] On the other hand, from a practical perspective, a continuous transformation into domestic law of Strasbourg case-law through legislative or administrative adaptations does not

[248] It may also reflect respect for the principle of *pacta sunt servanda* (Bjorge, *Domestic Application of ECHR*, pp. 42ff, 65).

[249] Keller and Stone Sweet, "Impact of the ECHR," p. 703; Bjorge, *Domestic Application of ECHR*, p. 22.

appear feasible.[250] Moreover, the Court's requirement of indirect effect works on the assumption that contracting states (at least) have a parallel set of fundamental rights, which correspond in substance to the ECHR and can be invoked domestically. However, even where there is an entrenched domestic catalogue of fundamental rights, the congruence can never be perfect and, as a result, there remain instances, where domestic law does not provide a remedy, although Convention law requires one. In other words, not making Convention rights directly enforceable bears a special risk in these situations of being found in breach of Article 13 ECHR.[251] The procedural guarantees of the Convention (Articles 13, 6(1), and 5(4) ECHR) required domestic legal systems to intensify and extend judicial review and strengthen the competences of judges to grant appropriate relief in order to live up to Convention standards.[252] This in turn, equally removed (constitutional) obstacles and paved the way for the domestic judiciary to apply and effectively enforce ECHR rights.[253] What is more, Article 13 ECHR in particular, obliges domestic authorities to engage with alleged human rights violations and form their own opinion as to whether Convention law was breached. Subsidiarity is an important reason for domestic courts to display such a high degree of readiness to act as first-line defenders of Convention rights and to faithfully apply as well as give full effect to Convention law.[254]

The consecutively discussed international and domestic perspectives can be brought together as follows. If one can speak today of Convention law as (de facto) supranational law, it is because it is, by and large, directly invocable by individuals vis-à-vis domestic authorities and effectively enforceable within national legal systems, following a moderated principle of supremacy that allows accommodating the complementary and evolving nature of human rights as well as the inviolability of states' constitutions. On the one hand, this is owed to a subtle yet consistent pressure from the Court to integrate at least the object of Convention law into domestic legal systems, make it enforceable, and adopt tools that lead to Convention compatible outcomes; and on the other hand, to the general readiness of domestic legal systems to recognize that not only forms the Convention integral part of domestic law but also represents a general protection standard, which domestic courts must uphold directly, if need be notwithstanding contrary domestic legislation. The result is a vertical integration of Convention law into domestic legal systems, without that the

250 This is not to say that far-reaching changes of domestic law would not be necessary at times in addition to the direct application of ECtHR case-law.

251 Polakiewicz, "Status of the Convention," pp. 33 and 35f.

252 For a detailed analysis and further references to relevant country reports see Helen Keller and Cedric Marti, "Der EGMR als Schöpfer von Verwaltungsprozessrecht" in A. von Bogdandy, P. M. Huber, and Paužaitė-Kulvinskienė J. (eds.), *Ius Publicum Europaeum*, vol. IX (forthcoming).

253 Holding a similar view Gerards and Fleuren, "Comparative Analysis," p. 352.

254 Bjorge, Domestic Application of ECHR, p. 12.

former would (fully) lose its European origin or source.[255] One may hypothesize that this integration is also reflected in that, today, individual and legal persons arguably perceive Convention law as an important body of law that regulates their daily life directly and can be relied upon before domestic authorities in all kinds of disputes and areas of law.

255 Melissa A. Waters, "Creeping Monism: The Judicial Trend Toward Interpretive Incorporation of Human Rights Treaties" (2007) 107 *Columbia Law Review* 628–705.

Conclusion

Framing a Convention Community

SUPRANATIONAL ASPECTS OF THE CONVENTION

The Convention system combines two seemingly antagonistic aspects. On the one hand, the ECtHR remains an international court based on an international treaty, governed by international law and, at least theoretically, open to withdrawal on the part of contracting states. It is not an appeals court formally embedded in domestic judicial systems. What is more, the ECtHR is not part of some larger constitutional or political setting, which could justify qualifying the ECtHR as a federal or constitutional court in a narrow or formal sense. While it was established and operates under the auspices of the CoE, the ECtHR remains a treaty organ of the Convention. In any case, the CoE itself is a classical intergovernmental IO, which was explicitly denied playing any meaningful role regarding political integration in Europe. Rather, the CoE is characterized by a strong position of governments and a low level of binding obligations.[1] On the other hand, however, there is a particularly high degree of overlap both in terms of substance and functions between the Convention system and domestic legal orders. Moreover, the Court exercises public authority over individuals and domestic authorities in a number of ways, which goes far beyond its function of reviewing individual cases of alleged human rights violations.[2] Convention law has become an integral part of domestic legal orders, not least because the Court requires at least the Convention's substance to be permeable into and effective in domestic systems. Individuals can rely on Convention law domestically.[3]

Unlike previous approaches, this dual disposition of the ECHR has not been analyzed by recurring to concepts such as special, self-contained, or *sui generis* regimes, nor by drawing domestic analogies and resorting to constitutionalist theories. Instead, it was submitted that the ECHR system's autonomy, integrative force, and penetrating powers make it display supranational aspects. This study has defined supranationality as a relational concept to refer to law beyond the state that seeks to

[1] Introduction, Aim of the Study: The Convention through the Prism of Supranationality; Chapter 3, Section 3.2.2; Chapter 4, Section 4.1.
[2] Chapter 4, Section 4.1; Chapter 5, Section 5.3.
[3] Chapter 6, in particular Sections 6.2.4 and 6.3.3.

achieve a form of legal integration, either horizontally, through international institutions which can bypass states in their ability to determine the legal position of individuals, or vertically, in that law beyond the state is entrenched in the domestic legal order in a way that allows individuals to rely on it directly. In so far, the notion denotes those international regimes, in which, (i) decision-making power has shifted from states to independent institutions, (ii) the structure of international rules is inward targeted, overlapping with domestic law in that individuals are the addresses and beneficiaries of international norms, (iii) certain rules enjoy a particular degree of normativity or authority, and (iv) permeate the domestic legal order.[4] All of these aspects were found to be present under the Convention system, which combines both sites of vertical and horizontal integration. The study has analyzed in more detail the establishment of a permanent Court with compulsory jurisdiction to deal with complaints from individuals (Chapter 3), the expansion of the Court's judicial function and competences (Chapter 4), lawmaking under the ECHR (Chapter 5), as well as the domestic effect and status of Convention law (Chapter 6). For each of these areas, the concept of supranationality has particular analytical force to capture and expose the competences and authority of the ECtHR as well as the effect of Convention law both over and in contracting states.

In addition, the study revealed a dynamic aspect. The findings made in the context of the area-specific inquiries reflect a wider trend and fit within an overall narrative of supranationalization of the ECHR. A general and incremental deepening of legal integration is ascertainable. In the following, an attempt is made to offer some general observations on this process, which naturally is multifaceted, complex, and dependent on a variety of factors. These factors have not been researched systematically in this study, but the analysis undertaken has nevertheless brought to light some of them. They are, among other aspects, addressed in the following.

A NARRATIVE OF SUPRANATIONALIZATION

Incrementalism and Legitimacy

Supranationality under the ECHR has proven to be the result of a process, which unfolds over the entire lifespan of the ECHR system and continues up to date. While it took almost half a century for the Court to become a supranational Court, its forays into the field of the execution of judgments is a more recent development. The same goes for vertical integration. That the supranationalization of Convention law was a gradual process becomes apparent when comparing more recent studies on the domestic status of the ECHR with those that were conducted in the 1980s, for

[4] Chapter 2, Section 2.5.

instance, or in the early 2000s.[5] We thus deal with grown structures, rather than supranationality by design. Incrementalism has certainly played an important role for the legitimacy of the process of supranationalization from the perspective of the contracting parties. The long and gradual path toward supranational adjudication is a telling example.[6] As is the fact that the idea of an advisory opinion procedure, proposed as early as in the 1960s, is being operationalized only now.[7]

The present study has also shown that supranationalization cannot be reduced to judicial activism. Through formal amendments of the ECHR, decisions in the CoM or political declarations states have in many ways been complicit in expanding the roles of the Court.[8] The same holds true for vertical integration. The special status granted to the ECHR by domestic legal orders is a crucial part of domestic integration and effectiveness of Convention law.[9]

Driving Factors

Throughout the study, the special nature of human rights revealed to be an important factor of supranationalization. It was a pivotal argument for the Court (and Commission) in distinguishing enforcement of the Convention from ordinary international dispute settlement, establishing interpretative autonomy, and developing its lawmaking function.[10] The special nature of human rights is equally invoked in support of the direct effect and supremacy of the ECHR over ordinary legislation.[11] By the special nature of human rights is meant that human rights (i) are inward targeted, governing the relationship between individuals and the state, (ii) are opened-end and need constant concretization in the light of changing social conditions, and (iii) embody rights derived from human dignity itself and therefore enjoy special moral force and normativity. In short, the structure and subject matter of the norms at play appear to be a significant factor for the supranationalization of the ECHR regime.

The enlargement of the CoE in the early 1990s also had a considerable impact on supranationalization. After Protocol 11 took effect and supranational adjudication had been formally established, the number of CoE states increased rapidly. The profound challenges faced by the entire system as a result of the enlargement are well known. Against the background of systemic problems and more frequent disrespect for its judgments and orders, the Court saw itself forced to adapt and

[5] Chapter 6, Section 6.3.2.
[6] Chapter 3.
[7] Chapter 4, Section 4.5.2.
[8] Ibid., Section 4.6.
[9] Chapter 6, Section 6.4.
[10] Chapter 3, Section 3.3; Chapter 5, Section 5.2.
[11] Chapter 6, Sections 6.3.3–6.3.4.

assume, in some cases, a role resembling that of a first and last instance Court. Chapter 4 has shown that in areas such as interim relief, cooperation, remedies, or compliance review, the expansion of the Court's judicial function and its more assertive stance can be traced back to this new *post*-enlargement role.[12] A similar correlation is visible with respect to vertical integration. Chapter 6 has shown that young democracies, which joined the CoE in the context of its enlargement, granted the ECHR supranational effect as a measure of self-protection.[13] In that sense, this study confirms the observation that the enlargement of the CoE represented a break in the development of the Convention system with fundamental impact.[14]

At the same time, supranationalization should not too easily be dismissed as a phenomenon exclusive in respect of states which show a comparatively weak level of domestic human rights protection. Admittedly, the Court may be more reluctant to deploy its supranational authority towards liberal states, especially in times of increased criticism, and in the area of judicial review, the Court may adjust its intensity of review depending on the quality of domestic processes.[15] Also, structural deficiencies and a low level of compliance may have been impetus for supranationalization in certain areas. Yet, once in place and generally accepted, the Court did not shy away from using its new powers toward established democracies. Interim measures, for instance, are binding for any contracting party to which they are addressed; as are orders to cooperate.[16] The Court engaged in compliance review in regards to states such as Switzerland and it has made use of the pilot judgment procedure against Italy, Germany, and the United Kingdom.[17] Furthermore, other sites of supranationalization do not appear to stand in any direct or causal relationship to the domestic level of protection. The Court's sweeping lawmaking function and the *res interpretata* effect of its judgments, for instance, are of a general nature and, therefore, cannot by definition discriminate between different states. The same goes for the supranationality lite framework, which forced states like France, for instance, to embrace proportionality analysis.[18] And even though constitutional courts of established democracies have shown some reluctance in applying Convention law and embracing the Court's jurisprudential authority, it appears that today this finding has at least to be relativized.[19]

12 Chapter 4, Section 4.6.
13 Chapter 6, Section 6.3.5.
14 Harmsen, "Reform of the Convention System," p. 121.
15 Chapter 4, Section 4.2.3.3 and Chapter 5, Section 5.3.1.
16 Chapter 4, Sections 4.2.2.2–4.2.2.3.
17 Ibid., Section 4.6. This confirms the following, more general observation of Stone Sweet and Brunell: "From the perspective of Western states, Protocol no. 11 remade the regime into an efficient mechanism for monitoring domestic politics in regions that could pose serious threats to peace and stability on the continent. The cost to Western states was stronger supervision of their own systems of rights protection" (Stone Sweet and Brunell, "Trustee Courts," 77f).
18 Chapter 6, Section 6.2.3.2.
19 Chapter 5, Section 5.5; Chapter 6, Section 6.3.3.

Finally, it can be hypothesized that the interplay between different supranational aspects of the ECHR has also been a driving factor for supranationalization.[20] Support for this hypothesis can be found in integration studies, which have highlighted the feedback and spillover effects of supranational mandates.[21] The establishment of supranational adjudication with Protocol 11 provided the basis for both horizontal and vertical legal integration under the Convention.[22] It rendered the Court's review function compulsory and laid the foundation for the diversification of its judicial function in areas such as the execution of judgments, compliance review, and preventive review (advisory opinion procedure), whereas the right to individual application (Article 34 ECHR) was central to the expansion of the Court's decision-making powers in areas such as interim relief and cooperation. At the same time, the high number of applications reaching the Court through Article 34 ECHR allowed it to fully activate its lawmaking function.[23] In turn, the scope and depth of the Court's case-law coupled with the *res interpretata* effect exposed states to constant pressure of adaption and made vertical integration of Convention law into domestic legal orders almost an inevitability, at least from a practical perspective.[24] Also, it seems that vertical integration is a precondition for the Court's new advisory jurisdiction for instance. Only if domestic courts are in a position to apply Convention rights, does it make sense for them to ask the Court for its interpretation.[25] There appears, however, to be a negative correlation between the supranational powers of the Court and integration of Convention law in domestic legal orders: if ECHR rights can be relied upon effectively at the domestic level, the Court is more likely to exercise restraint or it does not need to intervene at all. This negative correlation corresponds, in fact, to those conceptions of subsidiarity, which stress the primary obligations of states to secure ECHR rights domestically.[26]

Counter Dynamics and Resistance

Supranationalization is neither irreversible nor devoid of counter dynamics. Chapters 3–6 have all revealed that there are certain countertrends to both horizontal and vertical integration. The deepening and diversification of the Court's judicial function is accompanied by the curtailing of the Court's classic role. Accessing the Court is ever more difficult for individuals and in substantive terms there is evidence for a trend, post-Brighton, toward relaxing the standard of review through the margin

20 On this self-propelling element, see Chapter 1, Section 1.4.1.
21 Lindberg, *European Economic Integration*, p. 10.
22 Chapter 3, Section 3.4; Chapter 4, Section 4.1.
23 Chapter 5, Section 5.3.2.
24 Ibid., Sections 5.1, 5.2.1 and 5.5; Chapter 6, Section 6.4.
25 This might explain why (some) contracting parties agreed upon the Court's optional advisory jurisdiction only recently and after all states had incorporated Convention guarantees in one way or another (Drzemczewski, "Domestic Status of the ECHR," p. 78).
26 For example, Christoffersen, *Fair Balance*, pp. 359ff.

of appreciation doctrine and proceduralization. In the same vein, the Court might today be more cautious to engage in evolutive lawmaking and progressively raise protection standard under the ECHR. At the domestic level, one occasionally witnesses more principled resistance to follow Strasbourg judgments. The *Hirst* saga or the new veto powers of the Russian Constitutional Court are singular yet telling examples,[27] which may suggest that domestic courts could, today, be less reluctant to invoke their constitution to deny the ECHR domestic effectiveness. The worrying democratic retrenchment in several CoE countries such as Hungary, Poland, or Turkey may further exacerbate domestic resistance.[28]

However, it appears that these counter dynamics do not (yet) fundamentally question the general observation of integration under the ECHR. Criticism vis-à-vis Strasbourg and challenges to the ECtHR's practice are an inherent part of the system. The ECtHR deals by nature with politically sensitive issues and interpreting Convention rights is the result of a sometimes frictious interaction with domestic law.[29] Backlash in the sense of extraordinary resistance, in turn, still remains the exception. It is mostly limited to a few member states and non-compliance with specific, unwarranted judgments. The Brighton Declaration showed how resistance can prompt institutional or judicial changes. But the basis of the Court's supranational authority established with Protocol 11 is relatively robust and would need collective action by all member states to dismantle.[30] What is more, contracting states continue to further expand the Court's mandate and even created a new mechanism with Protocol 16 to integrate the highest domestic courts more directly into the Convention system. Moreover, it seems difficult to conceptualize resistance as a clear and linear trend.[31] Attempts at backlash are not always successful. They may be blocked and deflected by counter-mobilizations[32] or even have the adverse effect of bolstering the system. The British proposal, for instance, to seriously curtail the right to access the Court was rejected and states reiterated in the Brighton Declaration their unfettered commitment to the right to individual application.[33] Similarly, by rejecting the popular initiative against interference from "foreign judges" at the ballot, the Swiss public essentially voted in favor of (remaining party to) the ECHR.[34] After all, perpetuating the idea of backlash against the ECtHR may also reflect a normative agenda rather than actual (judicial) practices.

All this points to resistance, at least partly, still being epiphenomenal. Indeed, criticism or resistance may confirm rather than question the supranational authority of the Court and the Convention. More pronounced criticism may be explained by the

[27] Chapter 6, Section 6.3.6.
[28] Helfer, "Populism."
[29] Chapter 5, Section 5.5.3; Chapter 6, Sections 6.2.2.3 and 6.3.4.
[30] Madsen, Cebulak, and Wiebusch, "Backlash against International Courts," 198.
[31] See, in particular, Chapter 6, Section 6.3.6; Lambrecht, "Assessing Criticism," p. 551 and 512–514.
[32] Madsen, Cebulak, and Wiebusch, "Backlash against International Courts," 217.
[33] Chapter 4, Section 4.2.1.3.
[34] Chapter 6, Section 6.3.6.

privileged status of the Convention and the uncomfortable realization that "the citizen is the instigator of a process that could lead to a decision of a supranational court that limits the ability for politicians to set out a policy."[35] Resistance, from both states and civil society, reflects the far-reaching (domestic) impact of the ECHR. The observation that backlash or pushback is "evidence of the importance of ICs in contemporary globalizing society" thus holds particularly true for the ECtHR.[36] Unsurprisingly, proposals to confront increased resistance – such as mobilizing domestic actors or increase involvement of the ECtHR within the public debate – speak to the ECHR's supranational character too.[37] In other words, recent tensions may partly be the result of increased openness and integration and could lead to a constructive dialogue as well as reconsideration and refinement of Convention law.[38]

THE CONVENTION COMMUNITY

Giving Shape to the Notion

Considering the high degree of integration on both a horizontal and vertical plane, one may ask whether the general notion of regime or system is still specific enough to describe the Convention in its widest sense. As Keller and Stone Sweet observed, "in post-Protocol no. 11 Europe, it makes little sense to conceptualize the ECHR as an international regime, external to the Contracting States."[39] Indeed, even following a hybrid definition, the notion of regime usually puts emphasis on relative autonomy toward general international law or other international regimes and is thus often limited to the international sphere, thereby neglecting the interplay between domestic and the international level. Similar reservations apply to the popular term of Convention system. While it promulgates a more comprehensive approach to the ECHR including actors other than the Court or contracting states, it is a rather broad and technical term that fails to capture legal integration. At the other end of the spectrum, Stone Sweet went as far as placing the ECHR within a cosmopolitan legal order, in which each public official bears a duty to protect human rights.[40] However, this could be read as claim that the ECHR itself has become a (separate) legal order in respect to both international and domestic law, which would arguably be difficult to reconcile with the Court's understanding of the Convention.[41] Instead, it is

35 Lambrecht, "Assessing Criticism," pp. 509 and 514; Lemmens, "Criticising or Misunderstanding?," pp. 38f.
36 Madsen, Cebulak, and Wiebusch, "Backlash against International Courts," 217.
37 Helfer, "Populism"; Chapter 5, Section 5.6. The merits of a communitarian perspective on resistance and potential responses will be discussed in more detail subsequently.
38 Martinico, "Judicial Disobedience," p. 156; see also Lemmens, "Criticising or Misunderstanding?," pp. 38ff; Lambrecht, "Assessing Criticism," p. 547ff.
39 Keller and Stone Sweet, "Impact of the ECHR," p. 710.
40 Stone Sweet, "Cosmopolitan Legal Order," 53.
41 Chapter 5, Section 5.4.2.1; Chapter 6, Section 6.2.2.

suggested to revive the notion of Convention community. Both ECHR scholars[42] and the Court[43] have in fact used this term before, mostly without further explanation, however.[44] Hence, general criticism that the notion of community is ambiguous and vague thus proves to be true in the ECHR context so far.[45]

Whereas supranationality refers to the legal-institutional aspects of integration, community, especially when drawing on constructivist insights, can be viewed as both a precondition and product of legal integration. Indeed, the term community points to greater normative integration.[46] It was shown throughout the book that many of the ECHR's supranational aspects also lend themselves to a communitarian perspective. In addition, the term community captures the strong dialogical character of the construction of Convention rights, which was described as an "open-ended product of interactive social processes."[47] In short, it is submitted that the findings of the present study enable us to give shape to the notion of Convention community. In a sense, this book was an exercise in deconstruction, the results of which should now serve to frame a Convention community. It is argued that the Convention community is characterized by (i) human rights as community interest norms, for the protection of which the Courts enjoys an inalienable core of autonomy, (ii) direct membership of domestic authorities and natural and legal persons, as well as (iii) subsidiarity and (iv) moderated supremacy of Convention law as ordering principles.

Community Interests, Collective Identity, and the Inalienable Core of Autonomy

To recall, a community is characterized by a minimum of cohesion between its members expressed through shared or common values.[48] Signs of such collective identity can be found in the ECHR's preamble, which mentions the common heritage of political traditions, ideals, freedom, and the rule of law among European countries and echoes the CoE's aim to achieve greater unity through maintaining and further realizing human rights. CoE membership evolved significantly since the adoption of the Convention and there are good reasons to challenge the idea of an intersubjective or collective identity across the diverse CoE. However, as a human rights instrument, the ECHR serves to protect fundamental values, which are also community interest norms.[49] When enforcing and interpreting the

42 Mahoney, "New Challenges for the ECtHR," 104; Wildhaber, "Place of the ECtHR," p. 4.
43 *Markin* v. *Russia*, § 89.
44 See, however, for an insightful approach regarding the global constitutional community Peters, "Global Constitutional Community."
45 Chapter 2, Section 2.4.2.
46 Tams, "International Community."
47 Keller and Stone Sweet, "Impact of the ECHR," p. 678.
48 Chapter 2, Section 2.4.2.
49 Besson, "Community Interests in International Law," p. 39.

Convention, the ECtHR thus takes on an important role in protecting and identifying community interests. This prompted the ECtHR to speak of a Community of Convention states[50] and may in fact contribute to the constitution of a community in the first place.[51] Lawmaking especially entails a harmonization among CoE states within the scope of Convention law. Europeanization of domestic law has long been identified as a factor of convergence, leveling domestic legal systems, different legal traditions, and cultures as well as various forms of judicial organization.[52] Underlying the Convention community is "the common belief in fundamental freedoms"[53] and in protecting and developing them collectively as demonstrated by the term collective enforcement[54] and more recently the notion of shared responsibility.[55]

To protect community interests, the ECtHR enjoys an inalienable core of autonomy over states in interpreting and enforcing ECHR rights. To be sure, any international court must enjoy some degree of autonomy in order to settle disputes independently. However, the scope of the Court's autonomy is particular. The far-reaching breakthrough of the consensual and voluntarist paradigm of international law has run like a common thread through Chapters 3–5. Regarding enforcement, Chapter 3 has shown how the Court and the Commission early on differentiated the collective protection system under the Convention from interstate and state-controlled adjudication. They rejected the idea that they primarily serve governments or only settle disputes *strictu sensu* and conceptualized their task as one of being adjudicators of a community instead, upholding the common values of the European public order. As to supervision, it was discussed in Chapter 4 that any margin of appreciation of states must go hand in hand with European control. For its external review function to be meaningful, there must be areas, in which the ECtHR exercises (full) scrutiny in reviewing state action. In the words of Letsas: "contracting states cannot have their cake and eat it: set up a *supranational* institution to protect people's real human rights but expect the institution to condone violations when it is convenient for them."[56] Lastly, in terms of lawmaking and general determination of the content of ECHR rights, Chapter 5 revealed that the Court uses a methodology that may go well beyond the consensual confines of the VCLT, in order to impose a common and binding pan-European protection standard that is more than a mere mirror image of domestic human rights standards. In all these areas, a central aspect

50 *Markin* v. *Russia*, § 89.

51 Besson, "Community Interests in International Law," p. 39.

52 With further references and for an in-depth analysis regarding judicial review in administrative law, see Keller and Marti, "EGMR als Schöpfer von Verwaltungsprozessrecht."

53 See Preamble to the ECHR.

54 Chapter 3, Sections 3.3.1 and 3.3.4.

55 Gerards, "Shared Responsibility," pp. 13ff.

56 Letsas, "ECHR as a Living Instrument," p. 124.

of the Court's supranational authority is an inalienable core of autonomy. The precise scope of this core is context-dependent and thus impossible to pin down in a general sense. It evolves constantly and is subject to and the product of continuous re-negotiating among different interest groups and actors within the Community.

Members

A communitarian perspective looks beyond states and their governments.[57] Indeed, the disaggregation of Convention states and the bypassing of their governments is another common theme of the present book. In addition to Convention states, natural and legal persons but also domestic authorities are to be understood as direct members of the Convention community.

Within the unique ECHR framework, the individual can enforce its international rights and, therefore, becomes an active international legal subject,[58] over which the ECtHR exercises direct public authority.[59] This is first and foremost the case for the victim who comes to Strasbourg and utilizes the review function of the Court discussed in Chapter 4. Pending the outcome of a case, applicants may be put under interim protection, and judgments, today, may include the determination of specific remedies to the benefit of the victim. However, the ECtHR's judgments and decisions have much broader implications for individuals living in the Convention community. With general measures, for instance, the Court leaves the realm of individual justice and exercises authority over an indefinite number of individuals, seeking to protect them from systemic deficiencies at the domestic level. Also, Convention law today has by and large direct effect.[60] The community notion puts emphasis on the direct invocability of Convention law and the individual as the ultimate legal subject in the Convention community.[61]

It can be hypothesized that the exercise of authority over individuals coupled with the de facto supranational status of Convention law domestically has led individuals to be increasingly aware of Strasbourg's significance in governing their everyday life. The growing interest in the Court over the last couple of years by the media and domestic actors, such as political parties, interest groups, or NGOs, may be reflective of that.[62] Indeed, it seems that Strasbourg's impact has become more perceptible to the public and politically sensitive issues, in particular, may engender opposition

57 Chapter 2, Section 2.4.2.

58 Peters, "Global Constitutional Community," pp. 160f.

59 Chapter 4, Section 4.1.

60 Chapter 6, Section 6.3.3.

61 Hersch Lauterpacht, *International Law and Human Rights* (London: Stevens & Sons 1950), pp. 60–79. For the international community Peters, "Global Constitutional Community," p. 155.

62 As to NGOs see Chapter 5, Section 5.6.

beyond elite circles such as lawyers, public officials, or politicians.[63] As a result, and rightly so, the Court is no longer scrutinized by governments or domestic courts alone but also European citizens themselves.[64] This might explain why criticism has sometimes become less legal or diplomatic and more direct and political in nature.[65] At the same time, the ECtHR itself appears to have adopted a more active role in shaping its perception within the European public space. Through the compilation of fact sheets, for instance, it provides enhanced access to information about the work and functioning of the Court. In the same vein, the Court seeks to establish more direct relations with its constituencies, inviting, for instance, the press or different domestic actors to seminars and visits in Strasbourg. Paradoxically, the backlash discourse could further this communitarian aspect of the Convention. Or put differently, a communitarian perspective can help in overcoming state-centrism in the backlash debate. Fostering outreach and advocacy by the ECtHR, for example, was identified as a strategy to mobilize domestic actors in confronting (populistic) resistance against Strasbourg.[66] In so doing, the Court may, for instance, intervene to correct misguided public perception regarding its work, provide justifications for its judgments or publicize human rights violations. Some measure of resistance may thus have the positive effect of broader accountability and increased participation in public discourse. So far, the ECtHR has been predominately scrutinized by insiders or elites and it could in the long run benefit from broader critical input.[67]

The communitarian perspective also speaks to domestic authorities, in addition to individuals, being conceptualized as direct members of the Convention community. The ECtHR regards domestic authorities as "Convention organs" as has become apparent in the area of remedies[68] but also within the framework regarding the implementation of primary obligations.[69] By imposing specific or general remedies as well as Convention-specific tools such as proportionality analysis, the ECtHR directly responsibilizes, mobilizes, or enables different domestic actors, including the legislature and courts, to uphold Convention standards. Especially from a viewpoint of Article 13 ECHR, domestic courts play a crucial role as first-line defenders of Convention guarantees.[70] While the direct responsibilization of domestic authorities comes with specific obligations, it also represents an opportunity to

63 Madsen, Cebulak, and Wiebusch, "Backlash against International Courts," 205; Ran Hirschl, "The Judicialization of Mega-Politics and the Rise of Political Courts" (2008) 11 *Annual Review of Political Science* 93–118 at 94.

64 Discussing this aspect in the context of Italian crucifix cases Mancini, "Crucifix Rage," 26f.

65 Madsen, Cebulak, and Wiebusch, "Backlash against International Courts," 207.

66 Helfer, "Populism."

67 Madsen, Cebulak, and Wiebusch, "Backlash against International Courts," 205, 217; Başak Çali, Anne Koch, and Nicola Bruch, "The Legitimacy of Human Rights Courts: A Grounded Interpretivist Analysis of the European Court of Human Rights" (2013) 35 *Human Rights Quarterly* 955–984 at 957.

68 Chapter 4, Section 4.3.3.

69 Chapter 6, Section 6.2.7.

70 Bjorge, *Domestic Application of ECHR*, p. 248; Chapter 6, Section 6.2.4.

take influence over both the outcome of a potential application to the Court and the general lawmaking process in Strasbourg.[71] Chapter 6 has further revealed that domestic authorities actually embrace their role as community members, though to varying degrees.[72] It was observed that domestic courts (still) show increasing loyalty to both the ECtHR and the overall community interest of securing the protection of fundamental rights.[73] The participation of domestic judges in the broader development of Convention law discussed under the heading of judicial dialogue is only one example. The advisory opinion procedure marks a new step in the interaction between the ECtHR and domestic courts and the latter's integration and socialization within the Convention community.[74] It is not argued, that states or governments have been superseded as primary and democratic representatives of their citizens. After all, states remain internationally responsible to uphold Convention standards. Rather their presence has been complemented to a particular extent by the inclusion, responsibilization, and empowerment of other domestic actors, which take on an active role in the inter-subjective construction of community interests and their protection.

Subsidiarity as the Structuring Principle

Subsidiarity has become the structuring principle of the Convention community. As Keller and Stone Sweet observed: "the ECHR does not provide a blueprint for an integrated system of human rights protection for Europe, nor does it establish how the Court should interact with its national counterparts."[75] With the exception of Protocol 16, which institutionalized direct interaction between the domestic judiciary and Strasbourg,[76] this observation remains certainly true. Yet, because of the high degree of legal integration and the overlapping exercise of authority, the question of how the European and national level interact has taken center stage. Subsidiarity emerged as the principle used to coordinate the ECtHR's functions with those of domestic authorities.[77] Stressing this point might seem obvious, but it is nonetheless important because it is precisely legal integration that triggered the need for a structuring principle in the first place. One may argue that IHRL has always been subsidiary in nature, and procedural subsidiarity, for instance, existed all along as reflected by the rule of exhaustion of domestic remedies. However, subsidiarity only gradually emerged from a peripheral to a central notion of Convention law. The Court began endorsing a broader understanding of subsidiarity, including

71 Chapter 5, Section 5.4.1; Chapter 6, Section 6.3.5.
72 Chapter 6, Section 6.3.5.
73 Bjorge, *Domestic Application of ECHR*, pp. 245f; Lambrecht, "Assessing Criticism," p. 552.
74 On socialization see Keller and Stone Sweet, "Impact of the ECHR," p. 710.
75 Keller and Stone Sweet, "Impact of the ECHR," p. 705.
76 Chapter 4, Sections 4.5.3 and 4.5.5.
77 For example, Chapter 4, Section 4.1.

normative subsidiarity, and the operationalization of the principle remains an ongoing process, which is not (yet) developed equally across the different sites of judicial integration analyzed.[78] If recently the "age of subsidiarity" has been proclaimed in Strasbourg,[79] a (positive) way to interpret this would be to regard it as testament to the maturity of the Convention.

The principle of subsidiarity has come with an important rhetorical shift. In Chapter 3, some early cases were analyzed in which states attempted to rely on the notion of sovereignty in their defense.[80] Not only were these attempts vain, the notion of sovereignty appears to play only a marginal role within the Convention community. Arguably, subsidiarity and the notion of the margin of appreciation have replaced sovereignty in general legal and political discourse. States rarely invoke sovereignty (anymore), they rely on subsidiarity and the margin of appreciation doctrine to defend a certain domestic measure or interpretation of the ECHR.[81] This shift is not just semantics. It goes, in fact, a long way to show that governments are aware and accept that they belong to a community – or at least a multilevel system of public authority.[82] At the same time, supranationalization also exacerbated legitimacy concerns. The more supranational the ECtHR and the ECHR become, the more there is a need for accountability.[83] Although states certainly retain a key role as regards legitimacy,[84] supranationalization has provoked a shift in the legitimacy and accountability debate. In the Convention community, state-centered approaches have been complemented by cosmopolitan avenues of strengthening legitimacy such as process legitimacy, judicial dialogue, and the participation of civil society.[85]

Moderated Supremacy of Convention Law

The Convention community is characterized by a certain measure of flexibility. The Court retains the last word in matters regarding the interpretation and application of

78 Chapter 4, Section 4.6. It appears that the principle of proportionality has the potential of becoming a key principle in terms of legitimacy and as regards the operationalization of subsidiarity. Accordingly, the Court would be compelled to engage in a balancing exercise that precedes its intervention, that is, to reason why it is better placed and needs to intervene in respect to a certain issue.

79 Spano, "Universality or Diversity?," 487.

80 Chapter 3, Section 3.3.1.1.

81 See, for instance, Chapter 4, Section 4.2.3.2.

82 See earlier Community Interests, Collective Identity, and the Inalienable Core of Autonomy and Members.

83 In respect of autonomy for IOs, see Peters, "Global Constitutional Community." The same has held true for the EU. On the latter and democratic supranationalism, see Chapter 1, Section 1.4.3.

84 See earlier Incrementalism and Legitimacy.

85 See earlier Members; Chapter 5, Section 5.6.

the Convention, its orders are binding on states and its case-law benefits from the *res interpretata* effect.[86] Moreover, Convention law imposes the requirement that it be effectively enforced in domestic legal systems.[87] In return, almost all contracting states allow for Convention law to take precedence over conflicting domestic legislation.[88] Yet, the Court has renounced to develop a stare rule of internal supremacy regarding the effect of both its case-law and the ECHR, and many states have reserved the right to exceptionally deviate from Convention law, in particular, where it conflicts with their constitutions.[89] In other words, the Convention community operates based on a moderated or flexible rule of supremacy. Moderated supremacy allows to reconcile the antagonistic principles of effectiveness and openness within the Convention community. It secures that the protection of ECHR rights is not being subverted, while accommodating, simultaneously, the complementary and evolutive nature of human rights, which is based on rights diversity and pluralism and requires the Court to constantly reconsider its own case-law.[90] This is also why the *res interpretata* effect of ECtHR case-law mostly imposes process-based obligations.[91] Conflicts over the interpretation of Convention rights are an inherent feature of the Convention community and an expression of the dialogical character of the interpretative process.[92] To be sure, disobeying the ECtHR must remain – and mostly has remained so far – a bona fide exception that places domestic authorities under a particular duty of justification.[93] If such contestation is received in Strasbourg, it may ultimately even lead to a stronger level of convergence.[94]

Although increased resistance toward the ECtHR has not (yet) caused any fundamental changes, it revealed that the Convention community may be more fragile than believed so far. The Brighton Declaration in particular demonstrated that the ECtHR is not insulated from politics.[95] The Court had to adjust to a more hostile (political) climate. Trends such as relaxing the standard of review, proceduralization, or reluctance to engage in evolutive lawmaking challenge the inalienable core of the Court's autonomy as well as (perceived) equality within the Convention community, if, as some empirical studies suggest,[96] certain states "benefit" from

86 Chapter 4, Section 4.2.2; Chapter 5, Sections 5.5.2–5.5.3.
87 Chapter 6, Sections 6.2.4 and 6.2.7.
88 Ibid., Section 6.3.4.
89 Ibid., Sections 6.2.2.3 and 6.3.4.
90 Chapter 5, Section 5.3.2; Chapter 6, Sections 6.2.7 and 6.3.4.
91 Chapter 5, Section 5.5.3.
92 Martinico, "Judicial Disobedience," p. 156; see also Monica Hakimi, "Constructing an International Community" (2017) 111 *American Journal of International Law* 317–356.
93 Breuer, "Principled Resistance," pp. 339f.
94 For the same argument in a different context, see Lindberg, *European Economic Integration*, pp. 6f and 10f.
95 Madsen, "Rebalancing European Human Rights," 221.
96 Chapter 4, Section 4.2.3.3; Chapter 5, Section 5.3.1.

them more than others. Additionally, the ECHR faces other, partly related challenges such as the rise of populism, increasing societal cleavages, or more frequent invocation of state of emergencies. Fundamentally, the commitment to the common goal of human rights protection and thus whether European states and their citizens continue to "belong" to the Convention community is put to the test more frequently and directly at present.

Bibliography

Abbott K. W. and Snidal D., "Why States Act through Formal International Organizations" (1998) 42 *The Journal of Conflict Resolution* 3–32
Alexy R., *A Theory of Constitutional Rights* (Oxford: Oxford University Press 2009)
Allain J., "Rantsev v Cyprus and Russia: The European Court of Human Rights and Trafficking as Slavery" (2010) 10 *Human Rights Law Review* 546–557
Alter K. J., *Establishing the Supremacy of European Law* (Oxford: Oxford University Press 2003)
The New Terrain of International Law: Courts, Politics, Rights (Princeton: Princeton University Press 2014)
Alter K. J. and Helfer L. R., "Transplanting the European Court of Justice: The Experience of the Andean Tribunal of Justice" (2012) 60 *American Journal of Comparative Law* 629–664
Transplanting International Courts, vol. I (Oxford: Oxford University Press 2017)
Altwicker T., "Switzerland: The Substitute Constitution in Times of Popular Dissent" in P. Popelier, S. Lambrecht, and K. Lemmens (eds.), *Criticism of the European Court of Human Rights. Shifting the Dynamics of the Convention System: Counter-Dynamics at the National and EU Level* (Cambridge: Intersentia 2016), pp. 385–412
Amerasinghe C. F., *Principles of the Institutional Law of International Organizations*, 2nd ed. (Cambridge: Cambridge University Press 2005)
Arai-Takahashi Y., *The Margin of Appreciation Doctrine and the Principle of Proportionality in the Jurisprudence of the ECHR* (Cambridge: Intersentia 2002)
"Proportionality" in D. Shelton (ed.), *The Oxford Handbook of International Human Rights Law* (Oxford: Oxford University Press 2013), pp. 446–468
Arnardóttir O. M., "Rethinking the Two Margins of Appreciation" (2016) 12 *European Constitutional Law Review* 27–53
"Res Interpretata, Erga Omnes Effect and the Role of the Margin of Appreciation in Giving Domestic Effect to the Judgments of the European Court of Human Rights" (2017) 28 *European Journal of International Law* 819–843
Barents R., *The Autonomy of Community Law* (Alphen aan den Rijn: Kluwer Law International 2004)
Bates E., *The Evolution of the European Convention on Human Rights* (Oxford: Oxford University Press 2010)
"Analysing the Prisoner Voting Saga and the British Challenge to Strasbourg" (2014) 14 *Human Rights Law Review* 503–540

"Principled Criticism and a Warning from the 'UK' to the ECtHR?" in M. Breuer (ed.), *Principled Resistance to ECtHR Judgments – A New Paradigm?* (Berlin/Heidelberg: Springer 2019), pp. 193–244

Bebr G., "Directly Applicable Provisions of Community Law: The Development of a Community Concept" (1970) 19 *International and Comparative Law Quarterly* 257–298

Beddard R., "The Status of the European Convention of Human Rights in Domestic Law" (1967) 16 *International and Comparative Law Quarterly* 206–217

Benvenisti E., "Margin of Appreciation, Consensus and Universal Standards" (1999) 31 *International Law and Politics* 843–854

Bernier I., *International Legal Aspects of Federalism* (London: Longman 1973)

Besson S., "How International Is the European Legal Order? Retracing Tuori's Steps in the Exploration of European Legal Pluralism" (2008) 5 *NoFo* 50–70

"The Authority of International Law – Lifting the State Veil" (2008) 31 *Sydney Law Review* 343–380

"European Human Rights, Supranational Judicial Review and Democracy – Thinking Outside the Judicial Box" in P. Popelier, C. J. Van de Heyning, and P. Van Nuffel (eds.), *Human Rights Protection in the European Legal Order: The Interaction between the European and the National Courts* (Cambridge: Intersentia 2011), pp. 97–145

"The 'Erga Omnes' Effect of Judgments of the European Court of Human Rights – 'What's in a Name?'" in S. Besson (ed.), *La Cour europeéenne des droits de l'homme après le Protocole 14 – premier bilan et perspectives* (Zurich: Schulthess 2011), pp. 125–175

"Sovereignty" in R. Wolfrum (ed.), *Max Planck Encyclopedia of Public International Law*, online ed. (Oxford: Oxford University Press 2012)

"The Truth about Legal Pluralism" (2012) 8 *European Constitutional Law Review* 354–361

"Subsidiarity in International Human Rights Law – What Is Subsidiary about Human Rights?" (2016) 61 *American Journal of Jurisprudence* 69–107

"Community Interests in International Law: Whose Interests Are They and How Should We Best Identify Them?" in G. Nolte and E. Benvenisti (eds.), *Community Interests Across International Law* (Oxford: Oxford University Press 2018), pp. 36–49

Besson S. and Cebulak P., "Introduction" in S. Besson and N. Levrat (eds.), *L'Union européenne et le droit international – The European Union and International Law* (Zurich/Paris: Schulthess/LDGJ 2015), pp. 5–14

Betlem G. and Nollkaemper A., "Giving Effect to Public International Law and European Community Law before Domestic Courts" (2003) 14 *European Journal of International Law* 569–589

Bickerton C. J., Hodson D., and Puetter U., "The New Intergovernmentalism and the Study of European Integration" in C. J. Bickerton, D. Hodson, and U. Puetter (eds.), *The New Intergovernmentalism* (Oxford: Oxford University Press 2015), pp. 1–50

Binder C., "The Prohibition of Amnesties by the Inter-American Court of Human Rights" in A. von Bogdandy and I. Venzke (eds.), *International Judicial Lawmaking* (Berlin/Heidelberg: Springer 2012), pp. 295–328

Bindschedler R. L., "Internationale Organisation (Grundfragen)" in H.-J. Schlochauer and K. Strupp (eds.), *Wörterbuch des Völkerrechts* (Berlin: De Gruyter 1961), pp. 70–89

Bjorge E., *Domestic Application of the ECHR – Courts as Faithful Trustees* (Oxford: Oxford University Press 2015)

Björgvinsson D. T., *The Intersection of International Law and Domestic Law* (Cheltenham: Edward Elgar Publishing 2015)

Blackburn R. and Polakiewicz J. (eds.), *Fundamental Rights in Europe: The European Convention on Human Rights and Its Member States, 1950–2000* (Oxford: Oxford University Press 2001)

Bodansky D., "The Legitimacy of International Governance: A Coming Challenge for International Environmental Law" (1999) 93 *American Journal of International Law* 596–624

Bodansky D. and Crook J. R., "Symposium on the ILC's State Responsibility Articles: Introduction and Overview" (2002) 96 *American Journal of International Law* 773–791

Bodnar A., "Res Interpretata: Legal Effect of the European Court of Human Rights' Judgments for Other States Than Those Which Were Party to the Proceedings" in E. Brems and Y. Haeck (eds.), *Human Rights and Civil Liberties in the 21st Century* (Berlin/Heidelberg: Springer 2014), pp. 223–262

Bogdandy A. von, *Supranationaler Föderalismus als Wirklichkeit und Idee einer neuen Herrschaftsform* (Baden-Baden: Nomos 1999)

"Pluralism, Direct Effect, and the Ultimate Say: On the Relationship between International and Domestic Constitutional Law" (2008) 6 *International Journal of Constitutional Law* 397–413

Bogdandy A. von, Dann P., and Goldmann M., "Developing the Publicness of Public International Law: Towards a Legal Framework for Global Governance Activities" in A. von Bogdandy et al. (eds.), *The Exercise of Public Authority by International Institutions* (Berlin/Heidelberg: Springer 2010), pp. 3–32

Bogdandy A. von and Venzke I., "Beyond Dispute: International Judicial Institutions as Lawmakers" (2011) 12 *German Law Journal* 979–1003

"Beyond Dispute: International Judicial Institutions as Lawmakers" in A. von Bogdandy and I. Venzke (eds.), *International Judicial Lawmaking* (Berlin/Heidelberg: Springer 2012), pp. 3–33

In Whose Name?: A Public Law Theory of International Adjudication (Oxford: Oxford University Press 2014)

Boisson de Chazournes L. , "Functionalism! Functionalism! Do I Look like Functionalism?" (2015) 26 *European Journal of International Law* 951–956

Bonner D., "Ireland v. United Kingdom" (1978) 27 *International and Comparative Law Quarterly* 897–907

Brems E., "The Margin of Appreciation Doctrine in the Case-Law of the European Court of Human Rights" (1996) 56 *Heidelberg Journal of International Law* 230–314

Human Rights: Universality and Diversity (Leiden/Boston: Martinus Nijhoff 2001)

Breuer M., "Zulässigkeit und Grenzen richterlicher Rechtsfortbildung in der Rechtsprechung des EGMR" (2013) 68 *Zeitschrift für öffentliches Recht* 729–766

"Streikverbot vor dem Bundesverwaltungsgericht: Auf dem Weg zur supranationalen EMRK?" (2014) *Verfassungsblog* https://verfassungsblog.de/streikverbot-bundesverwaltungsgericht-auf-weg-zur-supranationalen-emrk/ [accessed July 23, 2020]

"Artikel 13. Recht auf wirksame Beschwerde" in U. Karpenstein and F. C. Mayer (eds.), *EMRK Konvention zum Schutz der Menschenrechte und Grundfreiheiten Kommentar*, 2nd ed. (Munich: C. H. Beck 2015), pp. 366–385

"Artikel 46. Verbindlichkeit und Vollzug der Urteile" in U. Karpenstein and F. C. Mayer (eds.), *EMRK Konvention zum Schutz der Menschenrechte und Grundfreiheiten Kommentar*, 2nd ed. (Munich: C. H. Beck 2015), pp. 663–691

"'Principled Resistance' to ECtHR Judgments: Dogmatic Framework and Conceptual Meaning" in M. Breuer (ed.), *Principled Resistance against ECtHR Judgments – A New Paradigm?* (Berlin/Heidelberg: Springer 2019), pp. 3–34

"'Principled Resistance' to ECtHR Judgments: An Appraisal" in M. Breuer (ed.), *Principled Resistance to ECtHR Judgments – A New Paradigm?* (Berlin/Heidelberg: Springer, 2019), pp. 323–350

Brilmayer L., "From 'Contract' to 'Pledge': The Structure of International Human Rights Agreements" (2007) 77 *British Yearbook of International Law* 163–202

Brölmann C., "Law-Making Treaties: Form and Function in International Law" (2005) 74 *Nordic Journal of International Law* 383–403

The Institutional Veil in Public International Law (Oxford: Hart 2007)

"Typologies and the 'Essential Juridical Character' of Treaties" in M. J. Bowman and D. Kritsiotis (eds.), *Conceptual and Contextual Perspectives on the Modern Law of Treaties* (Cambridge: Cambridge University Press 2018), pp. 79–102

Brown H. B., "The Proposed International Prize Court" (1908) 2 *American Journal of International Law* 476–489

Brunnée J. and Toope S. J., "Constructivism and International Law" in J. L. Dunoff and M. A. Pollack (eds.), *Interdisciplinary Perspectives on International Law and International Relations: The State of the Art* (Cambridge: Cambridge University Press 2012), pp. 119–145

Buergenthal T., "The Effect of the European Convention on Human Rights on the Internal Law of Member States" (1965) 11 *International and Comparative Law Quarterly Supplementary Publication* 79–106

"Self-Executing and Non-Self-Executing Treaties in National and International Law," *Collected Courses of the Hague Academy of International Law*, vol. 235 (Leiden/Boston: Brill Nijhoff 1992), pp. 303–400

"Lawmaking by the ICJ and Other International Courts" (2009) 103 *Proceedings of the Annual Meeting (American Society of International Law)* 403–406

Bürli N., *Third-Party Interventions before the European Court of Human Rights* (Cambridge: Intersentia 2017)

Buyse A., "Lost and Regained? Restitution as a Remedy for Human Rights Violations in the Context of International Law" (2008) 68 *Heidelberg Journal of International Law* 129–153

Çali B., "The Logics of Supranational Human Rights Litigation, Official Acknowledgment, and Human Rights Reform: The Southeast Turkey Cases before the European Court of Human Rights, 1996–2006" (2010) 35 *Law and Social Inquiry* 311–337

The Authority of International Law (Oxford: Oxford University Press 2015)

Çali B. and Koch A., "Foxes Guarding the Foxes? The Peer Review of Human Rights Judgments by the Committee of Ministers of the Council of Europe" (2014) 14 *Human Rights Law Review* 301–325

Çali B., Koch A., and Bruch N., "The Legitimacy of Human Rights Courts: A Grounded Interpretivist Analysis of the European Court of Human Rights" (2013) 35 *Human Rights Quarterly* 955–984

Cançado Trindade A. A., *The Access of Individuals to International Justice* (Oxford: Oxford University Press 2011)

Capotorti F., "Supranational Organizations" in R. Bernhardt (ed.), *Encyclopedia of Public International Law*, vol. IV (Amsterdam: Elsevier 2000)

Carozza P. G., "Subsidiarity as a Structural Principle of International Human Rights Law" (2003) 97 *American Journal of International Law* 38–79

Caserta S., "Regional Integration through Law and International Courts – the Interplay between De Jure and De Facto Supranationality in Central America and the Caribbean" (2017) 30 *Leiden Journal of International Law* 579–601

Cassese A., "Remarks on Scelle's Theory of 'Role Splitting' (dédoublement fonctionnel) in International Law" (1990) 1 *European Journal of International Law* 210–231

Five Masters of International Law: Conversations with R-J Dupuy, E Jimenez de Arechaga, R Jennings, L Henkin and O Schachter (Oxford: Hart 2011)

Cassese S., "Is There a Global Administrative Law?" in A. von Bogdandy et al. (eds.), *The Exercise of Public Authority by International Institutions* (Berlin/Heidelberg: Springer 2010), pp. 761–776

"Ruling Indirectly: Judicial Subsidiarity in the ECtHR" (2015) *Paper prepared for the Seminar to mark the official Opening of the judicial year of the European Court of Human Rights* www.echr.coe.int/Documents/Speech_20150130_Seminar_Cassese_ENG.pdf (accessed July 23, 2020)

Chaeva N., "The Russian Constitutional Court and Its Actual Control over the ECtHR Judgement in Anchugov and Gladkov" (2016) *EJIL: Talk!* www.ejiltalk.org/the-russian-constitutional-court-and-its-actual-control-over-the-ecthr-judgement-in-anchugov-and-gladko/ (accessed July 23, 2020)

Chapuis C., *Die Übertragung von Hoheitsrechten auf supranationale Organisationen* (Basel: Helbing & Lichtenhahn 1993)

Charney J. I., "Is International Law Threatened by Multiple International Tribunals?," *Collected Courses of the Hague Academy of International Law*, vol. 271 (Leiden/Boston: Brill Nijhoff 1998), pp. 101–188

Chernishova O. and Vajic N., "The Court's Evolving Response to the States' Failure to Cooperate" in D. Spielmann (ed.), *The European Convention on Human Rights: A Living and Dynamic Instrument – Liber Amicorum in Honour of Judge Rozakis* (Brussels: Bruylant 2011), pp. 47–79

Christoffersen J., *Fair Balance: Proportionality, Subsidiarity and Primarity in the European Convention on Human Rights* (Leiden/Boston: Martinus Nijhoff 2009)

Christoffersen J. and Madsen M. R., "Introduction: The European Court of Human Rights between Law and Politics" in J. Christoffersen and M. R. Madsen (eds.), *The European Court of Human Rights between Law and Politics* (Oxford: Oxford University Press 2011), pp. 1–13

Churchill R. R. and Ulfstein G., "Autonomous Institutional Arrangements in Multilateral Environmental Agreements: A Little-Noticed Phenomenon in International Law" (2000) 94 *American Journal of International Law* 623–659

Clapham A., "The 'Drittwirkung' of the Convention" in R. Macdonald, F. Matscher, and H. Petzold (eds.), *The European System for the Protection of Human Rights* (Leiden: Martinus Nijhoff 1993), pp. 163–206

Cohen J. L., *Globalization and Sovereignty* (Cambridge: Cambridge University Press 2012)

Colandrea V., "On the Power of the European Court of Human Rights to Order Specific Non-Monetary Measures: Some Remarks in Light of the Assanidze, Broniowski and Sejdovic Cases" (2007) 7 *Human Rights Law Review* 396–411

Collins R. and White N. D. (eds.), *International Organizations and the Idea of Autonomy: Institutional Independence in the International Legal Order* (London: Routledge 2011)

Conway G., *EU Law* (London: Routledge 2015)

Cotterrell R., "What Is Transnational Law?" (2012) 37 *Law & Social Inquiry* 500–524

Craven M., "Legal Differentiation and the Concept of the Human Rights Treaty in International Law" (2000) 11 *European Journal of International Law* 489–519

Danny N., "Original Intent and the European Convention on Human Rights" (2005) *Public Law* 152–172

De Baere G., Chané A.-L., and Wouters J., "The Contribution of International and Supranational Courts to the Rule of Law: A Framework for Analysis" in G. De Baere and J. Wouters (eds.), *The Contribution of International and Supranational Courts to the Rule of Law* (Cheltenham: Edward Elgar 2015), pp. 19–81

De Brabandere E., "The Impact of Supranationalism on State Sovereignty from the Perspective of the Legitimacy of International Organisations" in D. French (ed.), *Statehood and Self-Determination* (Cambridge: Cambridge University Press 2013), pp. 450–470

De Búrca G., *Reappraising Subsidiarity's Significance After Amsterdam* (Cambridge MA: Harvard Law School 1999)

De Schutter O., "Sur l'émergence de la société civile en droit international: le rôle des associations devant la Cour européenne des droits de l'homme" (1996) 7 *European Journal of International Law* 372–410

De Vylder H. and Haeck Y., "The Duty of Cooperation of the Respondent State During the Proceedings before the European Court of Human Rights" in E. Brems and Y. Haeck (eds.), *Human Rights and Civil Liberties in the 21st Century* (Berlin/Heidelberg: Springer 2014), pp. 37–68

De Witte B., "The European Union as an International Legal Experiment" in G. de Búrca and J. H. H. Weiler (eds.), *The Worlds of European Constitutionalism* (Cambridge: Cambridge University Press 2012), pp. 19–56

Delbrück J., "Transnational Federalism: Problems and Prospects of Allocating Public Authority Beyond the State" (2004) 11 *Indiana Journal of Global Legal Studies* 31–55

Delvaux L., "La notion de supranationalité dans le traité du 18 avril 1951, créant la Communauté européenne du chabron et de l'acier," *Actes officiels du Congrès international d'études sur la Communauté européenne du charbon et de l'acier (Milan and Stresa, 31 May – 9 June 1957)*, vol. II (Milan: Giuffrè 1957)

Diggelmann O., "Supranationalität in geschichtlicher Perspektive: Die 'Articles of Confederation' (1781–1789)" in T. Bruha (ed.), *Europäischer Föderalismus im Licht der Verfassungsgeschichte* (Schaan: Verlag der Liechtensteinischen Akademischen Gesellschaft 2011), pp. 117–147

"Georges Scelle (1878–1961)" in B. Fassbender and A. Peters (eds.), *The Oxford Handbook of the History of International Law* (Oxford: Oxford University Press 2012), pp. 1162–1166

Donald A. and Speck A.-K., "The European Court of Human Rights' Remedial Practice and its Impact on the Execution of Judgments" (2019) 19 *Human Rights Law Review* 83–117

Doyle M. W., "The UN Charter – A Global Constitution?" in J. L. Dunoff and J. P. Trachtman (eds.), *Ruling the World?* (Cambridge: Cambridge University Press 2012), pp. 113–132

Drzemczewski A., "The Domestic Status of the European Convention on Human Rights: New Dimensions" (1977) 4 *Legal Issues of Economic Integration* 1–85

"The Sui Generis Nature of the European Convention on Human Rights" (1980) 29 *International and Comparative Law Quarterly* 54–63

"A Major Overhaul of the European Human Rights Convention Control Mechanism: Protocol No. 11" (1995) IV/2 *Collected Courses of the Academy of European Law* 121–244

Dulitzky A. E., "An Inter-American Constitutional Court? The Invention of the Conventionality Control by the Inter-American Court of Human Rights" (2015) 50 *Texas International Law Journal* 45–93

Dupuy R.-J., "Images de Georges Scelle" (1990) 1 *European Journal of International Law* 235–239

Dworkin R., *Taking Rights Seriously* (Cambridge MA: Harvard University Press 1978)

Dzehtsiarou K., *European Consensus and the Legitimacy of the European Court of Human Rights* (Cambridge: Cambridge University Press 2015)
Dzehtsiarou K. and O'Meara N., "Advisory Jurisdiction and the European Court of Human Rights: A Magic Bullet for Dialogue and Docket-Control?" (2014) 34 *Legal Studies* 444–468
Edward D. and Bengoetxea J., "The Status and Rights of Sub-State Entities in the Constitutional Order of the European Union" in A. Arnull et al. (eds.), *A Constitutional Order of States? Essays in EU Law in Honour of Alan Dashwood* (Oxford: Hart 2011), pp. 25–38
Elazar D. J., *Exploring Federalism* (Tuscaloosa/London: University of Alabama Press 1987)
Constitutionalizing Globalization: The Postmodern Revival of Confederal Arrangements (Lanham: Rowman & Littlefield 1998)
Ellis D. C., "On the Possibility of 'International Community'" (2009) 11 *International Studies Review* 1–26
El Zeidy M. M., *The Principle of Complementarity in International Criminal Law* (Leiden/Boston: Brill 2008)
Eysinga W. J. M. van, "Supranational" in W. Schätzel and H. J. Schlochauer (eds.), *Rechtsfragen der internationalen Organisation: Festschrift für Hans Wehberg zu seinem 70. Geburtstag* (Frankfurt/Main: Klostermann 1956), pp. 130–132
Fabbrini F., "The Constitutionalization of International Law: A Comparative Federal Perspective" (2013) 6 *European Journal of Legal Studies* 7–26
Feldman D., "Precedent and the European Court of Human Rights," *Appendix C to Law Commission Consultation Paper No. 157, Criminal Law Bail and the Human Rights Act 1998: A Consultation Paper* (London: The Stationery Office 1999), pp. 112–124
Føllesdal A., "Subsidiarity and International Human-Rights Courts: Respecting Self-Governance and Protecting Human Rights – or Neither?" (2016) 79 *Law and Contemporary Problems* 147–163
Forowicz M., *The Reception of International Law in the European Court of Human Rights* (Oxford: Oxford University Press 2010)
Forteau M., "The Role of the International Rules of Interpretation for the Determination of Direct Effect of International Agreements" in H. P. Aust and G. Nolte (eds.), *The Interpretation of International Law by Domestic Courts* (Oxford: Oxford University Press 2016), pp. 96–112
Franck M., *Fairness in International Law and Institutions* (Oxford: Oxford University Press 1998)
Fredman S., *Human Rights Transformed: Positive Rights and Positive Duties* (Oxford: Oxford University Press 2008)
French D., "Treaty Interpretation and the Incorporation of Extraneous Legal Rules" (2006) 55 *International and Comparative Law Quarterly* 281–314
Fyrnys M., "Expanding Competences by Judicial Lawmaking: The Pilot Judgment Procedure of the European Court of Human Rights" (2010) 12 *German Law Journal* 1231–1260
Gardbaum S., "Human Rights as International Constitutional Rights" (2008) 19 *European Journal of International Law* 749–768
"Human Rights and International Constitutionalism" in J. L. Dunoff and J. P. Trachtman (eds.), *Ruling the World?: Constitutionalism, International Law, and Global Governance* (Cambridge: Cambridge University Press 2009), pp. 233–257
Gerards R., *Die Europäische Menschenrechtskonvention im Konstitutionalisierungsprozess einer gemeineuropäischen Grundrechtsordnung* (Frankfurt/Main: Peter Lang 2007)

Gerards J., "Judicial Deliberations in the European Court of Human Rights" in N. Huls, J. Bomhoff, and M. Adams (eds.), *The Legitimacy of Highest Courts' Rulings – Judicial Deliberations and Beyond* (The Hague: T.M.C. Asser Press 2009), pp. 407–436

"Pluralism, Deference and the Margin of Appreciation Doctrine" (2011) 17 *European Law Journal* 80–120

"The Pilot Judgment Procedure before the European Court of Human Rights as an Instrument for Dialogue" in M. Claes et al. (eds.), *Constitutional Conversations in Europe* (Cambridge: Intersentia 2012), pp. 237–276

"How to Improve the Necessity Test of the European Court of Human Rights" (2013) 11 *International Journal of Constitutional Law* 466–490

"Advisory Opinions, Preliminary Rulings and the New Protocol No. 16 to the European Convention of Human Rights: A Comparative and Critical Appraisal" (2014) 21 *Maastricht Journal of European and Comparative Law* 630–651

"The European Court of Human Rights and the National Courts: Giving Shape to the Notion of 'Shared Responsibility'" in J. Fleuren and J. Gerards (eds.), *Implementation of the European Convention on Human Rights and of the Judgments of the ECtHR in National Case-law* (Cambridge: Intersentia 2014), pp. 13–94

Gerards J. and Fleuren J., "Comparative Analysis" in J. Fleuren and J. Gerards (eds.), *Implementation of the European Convention on Human Rights and of the Judgments of the ECtHR in National Case-law* (Cambridge: Intersentia 2014), pp. 333–374

Ghandhi S., "The Human Rights Committee and Interim Measures of Relief" (2007) 13 *Canterbury Law Review* 203–226

Giegerich T., "Wirkung und Rang der EMRK in den Rechtsordnungen der Mitgliedstaaten" in O. Dörr, R. Grote, and T. Marauhn (eds.), *EMRK/GG: Konkordanzkommentar zum europäischen und deutschen Grundrechtsschutz*, vol. I, 2nd ed. (Tübingen: Mohr Siebeck 2013), pp. 57–98

Ginsburg T., "Bounded Discretion in International Judicial Lawmaking" (2005) 45 *Virginia Journal of International Law* 631–673

Glas L. R., "The European Court of Human Rights Supervising the Execution of its Judgments" (2019) 37 *Netherlands Quarterly of Human Rights* 228–244

Gormley W. P., *The Procedural Status of the Individual before International and Supranational Tribunals* (Leiden: Martinus Nijhoff 1966)

Gragl P., "(Judicial) Love Is Not a One-Way Street: The EU Preliminary Reference Procedure as a Model for ECtHR Advisory Opinions Under Draft Protocol No. 16" (2013) 38 *European Law Review* 229–247

Greer S., *The Exceptions to Articles 8 to 11 of the European Convention on Human Rights* (Strasbourg: Council of Europe Publishing 1997)

The Margin of Appreciation: Interpretation and Discretion Under the European Convention on Human Rights (Strasbourg: Council of Europe Publishing 2000)

The European Convention on Human Rights – Achievements, Problems and Prospects (Cambridge: Cambridge University Press 2006)

Greer S. and Wildhaber L., "Revisiting the Debate about 'Constitutionalising' the European Court of Human Rights" (2012) 12 *Human Rights Law Review* 655–687

Guieu J.-M., "Introduction. Le Congrès de La Haye (7–10 Mai 1948), 'Porte-parole de l'Europe'?" in J.-M. Guieu and C. Le Dréau (eds.), *Le Congrès de l'Europe à La Haye (1948–2008)* (Bruxelles: Peter Lang 2009), pp. 15–44

Haas E. B., *Beyond the Nation-State: Functionalism and International Organization* (Stanford: Stanford University Press 1964)

Hahn H. J., "International and Supranational Public Authorities" (1961) 26 *Law and Contemporary Problems* 638–665

Haider D., *The Pilot-Judgment Procedure of the European Court of Human Rights* (Leiden/ Boston: Brill Nijhoff 2013)

Hakimi M., "Constructing an International Community" (2017) 111 *American Journal of International Law* 317–356

Halberstam D., "Federalism: Theory, Policy, Law" in M. Rosenfeld and A. Sajó (eds.), The *Oxford Handbook of Comparative Constitutional Law* (Oxford: Oxford University Press 2012)

Hallstein W., *Der unvollendete Bundesstaat: Europäische Erfahrungen und Erkenntnisse* (Wien: Econ 1969)

Harmsen R., "The Reform of the Convention System: Institutional Restructuring and the (Geo-)Politics of Human Rights" in J. Christoffersen and M. R. Madsen (eds.), *The European Court of Human Rights between Law and Politics* (Oxford: Oxford University Press 2011), pp. 119–143

Harris D., O'Boyle M., and Warbrick C., *Law of the European Convention on Human Rights*, 3rd ed. (Oxford: Oxford University Press 2014)

Hay P., "International and Supranational Organizations: Some Problems of Conceptualization" (1965) *University of Illinois Law Forum* 733–770

Federalism and Supranational Organizations: Patterns for New Legal Structures (Urbana/ London: University of Illinois Press 1966)

Helfer L. R., "Redesigning the European Court of Human Rights: Embeddedness as a Deep Structural Principle of the European Human Rights Regime" (2008) 19 *European Journal of International Law* 125–159

"The Effectiveness of International Adjudicators" in C. P. R. Romano, K. J. Alter, and C. Avgerou (eds.), *The Oxford Handbook of International Adjudication* (Oxford: Oxford University Press 2013), pp. 464–482

"Populism and International Human Rights Institutions" in G. L. Neuman (ed.), *Human Rights in a Time of Populism: Challenges and Responses* (Cambridge: Cambridge University Press 2019), pp. 218–249

Helfer L. R. and Slaughter A.-M., "Toward a Theory of Effective Supranational Adjudication" (1997) 107 *The Yale Law Journal* 273–391

Hirschl R., "The Judicialization of Mega-Politics and the Rise of Political Courts" (2008) 11 *Annual Review of Political Science* 93–118

Howse R. and Nicolaidis K. (eds.), "Introduction," *The Federal Vision* (Oxford: Oxford University Press 2001), pp. 1–28

Hull W. I., "The Primary Sources of International Obligations" (1911) 5 *American Society of International Law Proceedings* 257–288

Huscroft G., Miller B. W., and Webber G. (eds.), "Introduction," *Proportionality and the Rule of Law* (Cambridge: Cambridge University Press 2014), pp. 1–20

Ipsen H. P., "Über Supranationalität" in H. Ehmke (ed.), *Festschrift für Ulrich Scheuner zum 70. Geburtstag* (Berlin: Duncker & Humblot 1973), pp. 211–226

Iwasawa Y., "The Doctrine of Self-Executing Treaties in the United States: A Critical Analysis" (1985) 26 *Virginia Journal of International Law* 627–650

Jackson J. L., "Broniowski v. Poland: A Recipe for Increased Legitimacy of the European Court of Human Rights as a Supranational Constitutional Court" (2006) 39 *Connecticut Law Review* 759–806

Jacob M., "Precedents: Lawmaking Through International Adjudication" in A. von Bogdandy and I. Venzke (eds.), *International Judicial Lawmaking: On Public*

Authority and Democratic Legitimation in Global Governance (Berlin/Heidelberg: Springer 2012), pp. 35–68

Jaenicke G., "Die Sicherung des übernationalen Charakters der Organe internationaler Organisationen" (1951) 14 *Zeitschrift für ausländisches öffentliches Recht und Völkerrecht* 46–117

"Der übernationale Charakter der Europäischen Wirtschaftsgemeinschaft" (1958) 19 *Zeitschrift für ausländisches öffentliches Recht und Völkerrecht* 153–196

Jahn J., "Normative Guidance from Strasbourg Through Advisory Opinions Deprivation or Relocation of the Convention's Core?" (2014) 74 *Heidelberg Journal of International Law* 821–846

"Ruling (In)directly through Individual Measures? Effect and Legitimacy of the ECtHR's New Remedial Power" (2014) 74 *Heidelberg Journal of International Law* 1–39

Jennings R. Y., "The Judicial Function and the Rule of Law," *International Law at the Time of its Codification: Essays in Honour of Roberto Ago*, vol. III (Milan: Giuffrè 1988), pp. 139–151

Jessup P. C., *Transnational Law* (New Haven: Yale University Press 1956)

Karp B., "The Draft Constitution for a European Political Community" (1954) 8 *International Organization* 181–202

Kaufmann W., *Die Rechtskraft des internationalen Rechtes und das Verhältniss der Staatsgesetzgebungen und der Staatsorgane zu demselben* (Stuttgart: F Enke 1899)

Keck M. E. and Sikkink K., *Activists beyond Borders: Advocacy Networks in International Politics* (Ithaca/London: Cornell University Press 1998)

Keller H. and Garin A., "Câmpeanu: quo vadis? – Le recours individuel en péril" (2017) 111 *Revue trimestrielle des droits de l'homme* 485–510

Keller H. and Marti C., "Der EGMR als Schöpfer von Verwaltungsprozessrecht" in A. von Bogdandy, P. M. Huber, and J. Paužaitė-Kulvinskienė (eds.), *Ius Publicum Europaeum*, vol. IX (forthcoming)

"Interim Relief Compared: Use of Interim Measures by the UN Human Rights Committee and the European Court of Human Rights" (2013) 73 *Heidelberg Journal of International Law* 325–372

"Berücksichtigung der EGMR-Praxis durch innerstaatliche Gerichte – Eine rechtsmethodische Anleitung für den richterlichen Dialog mit Strassburg" (2015) 1 *Justice – Justiz – Giustizia*

"Reconceptualizing Implementation: The Judicialization of the Execution of the European Court of Human Rights' Judgments" (2015) 26 *European Journal of International Law* 829–850

Keller H. and Stone Sweet A. (eds.), "Assessing the Impact of the ECHR on National Legal Systems," *A Europe of Rights: The Impact of the ECHR on National Legal Systems* (Oxford: Oxford University Press 2008), pp. 677–712

Keller H. and Walther R., "Resistance in Switzerland: Populist rather than Principled" in M. Breuer (ed.), *Principled Resistance against ECtHR Judgments – A New Paradigm?* (Berlin/Heidelberg: Springer 2019), pp. 161–191

Kennedy D., "International Law and the Nineteenth Century: History of an Illusion" (1996) 65 *Nordic Journal of International Law* 385–420

Klabbers J., "The Paradox of International Institutional Law" (2008) 5 *International Organizations Law Review* 151–173

"Setting the Scene" in J. Klabbers, A. Peters, and G. Ulfstein (eds.), *The Constitutionalization of International Law* (Oxford: Oxford University Press 2009), pp. 1–44

An Introduction to International Institutional Law, 1st ed. (Cambridge: Cambridge University Press 2009)

An Introduction to International Organizations Law, 3rd ed. (Cambridge: Cambridge University Press 2015)

Klatt M., "Positive Obligations under the European Convention on Human Rights" (2011) 71 *Zeitschrift für ausländisches öffentliches Recht und Völkerrecht* 691–718

Kohler J., "Völkerrechtliche Studien" (1912) 6 *Zeitschrift für Völkerrecht und Bundesstaatsrecht* 89–124

Koskenniemi M., *The Gentle Civilizer of Nations* (Cambridge: Cambridge University Press 2001)

"The Subjective Dangers of Projects of World Community" in A. Cassese (ed.), *Realizing Utopia: The Future of International Law* (Oxford: Oxford University Press 2012), pp. 3–13

Krabbe H., *Die moderne Staatsidee*, 2nd ed. (Leiden: Martinus Nijhoff 1919)

Krasner S. D., "Structural Causes and Regime Consequences: Regimes as Intervening Variables" (1982) 36 *International Organization* 185–205

Kratochvil J., "The Inflation of the Margin of Appreciation by the European Court of Human Rights" (2011) 29 *Netherlands Quarterly of Human Rights* 324–357

Krieger H., "Positive Verpflichtungen unter der EMRK: Unentbehrliches Element einer gemeineuropäischen Grundrechtsdogmatik, leeres Versprechen oder Grenze der Justiziabilität?" (2014) 74 *Zeitschrift für ausländisches öffentliches Recht und Völkerrechtt* 187–213

Krisch N., *Beyond Constitutionalism – The Pluralist Structure of Postnational Law* (Oxford: Oxford University Press 2010)

Krisch N. and Kingsbury B., "Introduction: Global Governance and Global Administrative Law in the International Legal Order" (2006) 17 *European Journal of International Law* 1–13

Kritsiotis D., "Imagining the International Community" (2002) 13 *European Journal of International Law* 961–992

"The Legitimacy of International Law: A Constitutionalist Framework of Analysis" (2004) 15 *European Journal of International Law* 907–931

Kunz J. L., "Supra-National Organs" (1952) 46 *American Journal of International Law* 690–698

"Treaty Establishing the European Defense Community" (1953) 47 *American Journal of International Law* 275–281

Kunz R., "Judging International Judgments Anew? The Human Rights Courts before Domestic Courts" (2019) 30 *European Journal of International Law* 1129–1163

Laffranque J., "Can't Get Just Satisfaction" in A. Seibert-Fohr and M. E. Villiger (eds.), *Judgments of the European Court of Human Rights – Effects and Implementation* (Farnham: Ashgate 2014), pp. 75–114

Lalumière C., "Discussion Paper by the Secretary General on the Development of the Organisation and on the Implications of Continued Enlargement, Particularly of the Russian Federation's Accession" (1994) *The Council of Europe in the New Europe* 1–13, www.cvce.eu/content/publication/2004/4/27/4977d781-d180-4313-b0c7-77f48e3b749e/publishable_en.pdf (accessed July 23, 2020)

Lambert-Abdelgawad E., *The Execution of Judgments of the European Court of Human Rights*, 2nd ed. (Strasbourg: Council of Europe Publishing 2008)

"Is There a Need to Advance the Jurisprudence of the European Court of Human Rights with Regard to the Award of Damages?" in A. Seibert-Fohr and M. E. Villiger (eds.),

Judgments of the European Court of Human Rights – Effects and Implementation (Baden-Baden: Nomos 2014), pp. 115–136
Lambrecht S., "Assessing the Existence of Criticism of the European Court of Human Rights" in P. Popelier, S. Lambrecht, and K. Lemmens (eds.), *Criticism of the European Court of Human Rights: Shifting the Convention System: Counter-dynamics at the National and EU Level* (Cambridge: Intersentia 2016), pp. 505–554
Larsen K. M., "Compliance with Judgments from the European Court of Human Rights: The Court's Call for Legislative Reforms" (2013) 31 *Nordic Journal of Human Rights* 496–512
Lauterpacht H., *International Law and Human Rights* (London: Stevens 1950)
The Function of Law in the International Community (1933), reprint (Oxford: Oxford University Press 2011)
Lavrysen L., "The Scope of Rights and the Scope of Obligations: Positive Obligations" in E. Brems and J. Gerards (eds.), *Shaping Rights in the ECHR* (Cambridge: Cambridge University Press 2013), pp. 162–182
Leach P., "No Longer Offering Fine Mantras to a Parched Child? The European Court's Developing Approach to Remedies" in A. Føllesdal, B. Peters, and G. Ulfstein (eds.), *Constituting Europe: The European Court of Human Rights in a National, European and Global Context* (Cambridge: Cambridge University Press 2013), pp. 162–182
Leach P. and Donald A., "Russia Defies Strasbourg: Is Contagion Spreading?" (2015) *EJIL: Talk!* www.ejiltalk.org/russia-defies-strasbourg-is-contagion-spreading/ (accessed July 23, 2020)
Parliaments and the European Court of Human Rights (Oxford: Oxford University Press 2016)
Le Sueur A., Sunkin M., and Murkens J. E. K., *Public Law: Text, Cases, and Materials*, 3rd ed. (Oxford: Oxford University Press 2016)
Lebeck C., "Sliding Towards Supranationalism? The Constitutional Status of EU Framework Decisions after Pupino" (2007) 8 *German Law Journal* 501–531
"Supranational Law in a Cold Climate: European Law in Scandinavia" (2010) 4 *Stals Research Paper* www.stals.sssup.it/files/stals_Lebeck_042010.pdf (accessed July 23, 2020)
Lemmens K., "Criticising the European Court of Human Rights or Misunderstanding the Dynamics of Human Rights Protection?" in P. Popelier, S. Lambrecht, and K. Lemmens (eds.), *Criticism of the European Court of Human Rights: Shifting the Convention System: Counter-dynamics at the National and EU Level* (Cambridge: Intersentia 2016), pp. 23–40.
Lenaerts K., "Constitutionalism and the Many Faces of Federalism" (1990) 38 *American Journal of Comparative Law* 205–263
"Federalism and the Rule of Law: Perspectives from the European Court of Justice" (2011) 33 *Fordham International Law Journal* 1338–1387
"Direct Applicability and Direct Effect of International Law in the EU Legal Order" in I. Govaere et al. (eds.), *The European Union in the World* (Leiden/Boston: Brill Nijhoff 2013), pp. 45–64
Lenaerts K. et al., *European Union Law*, 3rd ed. (London: Sweet & Maxwell 2011)
Lester A., "The European Court of Human Rights after 50 Years" in J. Christoffersen and M. R. Madsen (eds.), *The European Court of Human Rights between Law and Politics* (Oxford: Oxford University Press 2011), pp. 98–118
Letsas G., "The Truth in Autonomous Concepts: How to Interpret the ECHR" (2004) 15 *European Journal of International Law* 279–305
"Two Concepts of the Margin of Appreciation" (2006) 26 *Oxford Journal of Legal Studies* 705–732

A *Theory of Interpretation of the European Convention on Human Rights* (Oxford: Oxford University Press 2007)

"Strasbourg's Interpretive Ethic: Lessons for the International Lawyer" (2010) 21 *European Journal of International Law* 509–541

"The ECHR as a Living Instrument: Its Meaning and Legitimacy" in A. Føllesdal, B. Peters, and G. Ulfstein (eds.), *Constituting Europe* (Cambridge: Cambridge University Press 2013), pp. 106–141

Lindberg L. N., *The Political Dynamics of European Economic Integration* (Stanford: Stanford University Press 1963)

Lindeiner-Wildau K. von, *La supranationalité en tant que principe de droit* (Leiden: A. W. Sijthoff 1970)

Linderfalk U., "Who Are 'The Parties'? Article 31, Paragraph 3(c) of the 1969 Vienna Convention and the 'Principle of Systemic Integration' Revisited" (2008) 55 *Netherlands International Law Review* 343–364

Lindseth P. L., "Supranational Organizations" in I. Hurd, I. Johnstone, and J. Katz Cogan (eds.), *Oxford Handbook of International Organizations* (Oxford: Oxford University Press 2016), pp. 152–170

Liszt F. von, "Das Wesen des völkerrechtlichen Staatenverbandes und der Internationale Prisenhof," *Festgabe der Berliner juristischen Fakultät für Otto Gierke zum Doktorjubiläum 21. August 1910*, vol. III (Breslau: M & H Marcus 1910), pp. 19–44

Londras F. de and Dzehtsiarou K., "Mission Impossible? Addressing Non-Execution Through Infringement Proceedings in the European Court of Human Rights" (2017) 66 *International and Comparative Law Quarterly* 467–490

Loth W., *Building Europe: A History of European Unification* (Berlin: De Gruyter Oldenbourg 2015)

Lucas-Alberni K., *Le revirement de jurisprudence de la Cour européenne des droits de l'homme* (Brussels: Bruylant 2008)

Lüder S. R., "The Legal Nature of the International Criminal Court and the Emergence of Supranational Elements in International Criminal Justice" (2002) 84 *International Review of the Red Cross* 79–92

Lupu Y. and Voeten E., "Precedent in International Courts: A Network Analysis of Case Citations by the European Court of Human Rights" (2012) 42 *British Journal of Political Science* 413–439

Madsen M. R., "France, the UK and the 'Boomerang' of the Internationalisation of Human Rights (1945–2000)" in S. Halliday and P. Schmidt (eds.), *Human Rights Brought Home – Socio-Legal Perspectives of Human Rights in the National Context* (Oxford: Hart 2004), pp. 57–86

"From Cold War Instrument to Supreme European Court: The European Court of Human Rights at the Crossroads of International and National Law and Politics" (2007) 32 *Law & Social Inquiry* 137–159

"The Protracted Institutionalization of the Strasbourg Court: From Legal Diplomacy to Integrationist Jurisprudence" in J. Christoffersen and M. R. Madsen (eds.), *The European Court of Human Rights between Law and Politics* (Oxford: Oxford University Press 2011), pp. 43–60

"Rebalancing European Human Rights: Has the Brighton Declaration Engendered a New Deal on Human Rights in Europe?" (2018) 9 *Journal of International Dispute Settlement* 199–222

Madsen M. R., Cebulak P., and Wiebusch M., "Backlash against International Courts: Explaining the Forms and Patterns of Resistance to International Courts" (2018) 14 *International Journal of Law in Context* 197–220

Maduro M. P., "Three Claims of Constitutional Pluralism" in M. Avbelj and J. Komárek (eds.), *Constitutional Pluralism in the European Union and Beyond* (Oxford: Hart 2012), pp. 67–84

Mahoney P., "Developments in the Procedure of the European Court of Human Rights: The Revised Rules of Court" (1983) 3 *Yearbook of European Law* 127–167

"New Challenges for the European Court of Human Rights Resulting from the Expanding Case Load and Membership" (2002) 21 *Penn State International Law Review* 101–114

Malanczuk P., *Akehurst's Modern Introduction to International Law*, 7th ed. (London: Routledge 1997)

Mancano L. and Martinico G., "An Italian Tale of Two Courts. Judgment no. 49/2015 of the Italian Constitutional Court and its Relationship with Strasbourg" (2016) 58 *Revista española de derecho europeo* 199–214

Mancini F., "The Making of a Constitution for Europe" (1989) 26 *Common Market Law Review* 595–614

Mancini S., "The Crucifix Rage: Supranational Constitutionalism Bumps Against the Counter-Majoritarian Difficulty" (2010) 6 *European Constitutional Law Review* 6–27

Marquis J., *La qualité pour agir devant la Cour européenne des droits de l'homme* (Zurich: Schulthess 2017)

Marsh N. S., "Supranational Planning Authorities and Private Law: An English Approach to a New Aspect of Comparative Law" (1955) 4 *American Journal of Comparative Law* 189–207

Marti C., "Supranationality Beyond the EU?" in S. Besson and N. Levrat (eds.), *L'Union européenne et le droit international – The European Union and International Law* (Zurich/Paris: Schulthess/LDGJ 2015), pp. 18–38

Martinico G., "Is the European Convention Going to Be 'Supreme'? A Comparative-Constitutional Overview of ECHR and EU Law before National Courts" (2012) 23 *European Journal of International Law* 401–424

"Judicial Disobedience and the ECtHR: The Italian Case" in M. Breuer (ed.), *Principled Resistance to ECtHR Judgments – A New Paradigm?* (Berlin/Heidelberg: Springer 2019), pp. 137–160

Martinico G. and Pollicino O., *The National Judicial Treatment of the ECHR and EU Laws* (Groningen: Europa Law Publishing 2010)

The Interaction between Europe's Legal Systems: Judicial Dialogue and the Creation of Supranational Laws (Cheltenham: Edward Elgar 2012)

Mason H. L., *The European Coal and Steel Community: Experiment in Supranationalism* (Leiden: Martinus Nijhoff 1955)

Mattli W., *The Logic of Regional Integration: Europe and Beyond* (Cambridge: Cambridge University Press 1999)

McLachlan C., "The Principle of Systemic Integration and Article 31(3)(c) of the Vienna Convention" (2005) 54 *International and Comparative Law Quarterly* 279–320

Mégret F., "Private Actor Litigation and the Evolving Legitimacy of Supranational Adjudication" (2012) *RSCAS Policy Papers – Courts, Social Change and Judicial Independence* 3–10

Mendez M., *The Legal Effects of EU Agreements* (Oxford: Oxford University Press 2013)

Menkel-Meadow C., "Why and How to Study 'Transnational Law'" (2010) 1 *UC Irvine Law Review* 97–129

Merkouris P., *Article 31(3)(c)VCLT and the Principle of Systemic Integration: Normative Shadows in Plato's Cave* (Leiden/Boston: Brill Nijhoff 2015)

Milward A. S., *The Reconstruction of Western Europe, 1945–51* (Berkeley/Los Angeles: University of California Press 1984)
Mitrany D., *A Working Peace System* (Chicago: Quadrangle Books 1966)
Monaco R., "La Communità sopranazionale nell'ordinamento internazionale" (1953) 8 *La Comunità Internazionale* 441–458
Moravcsik A., "The Origins of Human Rights Regimes: Democratic Delegation in Postwar Europe" (2000) 54 *International Organization* 217–252
Mosler H., "Supra-National Judicial Decisions" (1981) 4 *Hastings International and Comparative Law Review* 425–472
Motoc I. and Ziemele I. (eds.), *The Impact of the ECHR on Democratic Change in Central and Eastern Europe: Judicial Perspectives* (Cambridge: Cambridge University Press 2016)
Mowbray A., *The Development of Positive Obligations under the European Convention on Human Rights by the European Court of Human Rights* (Oxford: Hart 2004)
"A New Strasbourg Approach to the Legal Consequences of Interim Measures" (2005) 5 *Human Rights Law Review* 377–386
"The Creativity of the European Court of Human Rights" (2005) 5 *Human Rights Law Review* 57–79
"An Examination of the European Court of Human Rights' Approach to Overruling Its Previous Case Law" (2009) 9 *Human Rights Law Review* 179–201
"Between the Will of the Contracting Parties and the Needs of Today: Extending the Scope of Convention Rights and Freedoms beyond What Could Have Been Foreseen by the Drafters of the ECHR" in E. Brems and J. Gerards (eds.), *Shaping Rights in the ECHR* (Cambridge: Cambridge University Press 2013), pp. 17–37
Münch F., "Délimitation du domaine du droit des Communautés supranationales par rapport au droit étatique," *Actes officiels du Congrès international d'études sur la Communauté européenne du charbon et de l'acier (Milan and Stresa, 31 May – 9 June 1957)*, vol. II (Milan: Giuffrè 1957), pp. 271–298
"Die Abgrenzung des Rechtsbereiches der supranationalen Gemeinschaft gegenüber dem innerstaatlichen Recht" (1958) 2 *Verhandlungen der Tagung der Deutschen Gesellschaft für Völkerrecht* 73–93
Murphy S. D., "Does International Law Obligate States to Open Their National Courts to Persons for the Invocation of Treaty Norms That Protect or Benefit Persons?" in D. Sloss (ed.), *The Role of Domestic Courts in Treaty Enforcement* (Cambridge: Cambridge University Press 2009), pp. 61–119
Neuman G. L., "Human Rights and Constitutional Rights: Harmony and Dissonance" (2003) 55 *Stanford Law Review* 1863–1900
Nigoul C., "René-Jean Dupuy et le fédéralisme: de Georges Scelle à Alexandre Marc," *Humanité et droit international: Mélanges René-Jean Dupuy* (Paris: A. Pédone 1991), pp. 233–240
Nijman J. and Nollkaemper A. (eds.), "Beyond the Divide," *New Perspectives on the Divide between National and International Law* (Oxford: Oxford University Press 2007), pp. 341–360
Nijman J., *The Concept of International Legal Personality – An Inquiry into the History and Theory of International Law* (The Hague: T.M.C. Asser Press 2004)
Nollkaemper A., "Constitutionalization and the Unity of the Law of International Responsibility" (2009) 16 *Indiana Journal of Global Legal Studies* 535–563
"Rethinking the Supremacy of International Law" (2010) 65 *Zeitschrift für öffentliches Recht* 65–85

National Courts and the International Rule of Law (Oxford: Oxford University Press 2011)
"The Duality of Direct Effect of International Law" (2014) 25 *European Journal of International Law* 105–125
Ophüls C. F., "Europas partieller Bundesstaat" (1951) 6 *Die Gegenwart* 25–29
Oppong R. F., *Legal Aspects of Economic Integration in Africa* (Cambridge: Cambridge University Press 2011)
Orakhelashvili A., "Restrictive Interpretation of Human Rights Treaties in the Recent Jurisprudence of the European Court of Human Rights" (2003) 14 *European Journal of International Law* 529–568
Paprocka A. and Ziółkowski M., "Advisory Opinions under Protocol No. 16 to the European Convention on Human Rights" (2015) 11 *European Constitutional Law Review* 274–292
Paulus A., "International Community" in R. Wolfrum (ed.), *Max Planck Encyclopedia of International Law*, online ed. (Oxford: Oxford University Press 2013)
Pauwelyn J., *Conflict of Norms in Public International Law* (Cambridge: Cambridge University Press 2003)
Peters A., "Global Constitutionalism Revisited" (2005) 39 *International Legal Theory* 39–67
"Supremacy Lost: International Law Meets Domestic Constitutional Law" (2009) 3 *Vienna Journal on International Constitutional Law* 170–198
"Membership in the Global Constitutional Community" in J. Klabbers, A. Peters, and G. Ulfstein (eds.), *The Constitutionalization of International Law* (Oxford: Oxford University Press 2009), pp. 153–262
"Rechtsordnungen und Konstitutionalisierung: Zur Neubestimmung der Verhältnisse" (2010) 65 *Zeitschrift für öffentliches Recht* 3–63
Beyond Human Rights (Cambridge: Cambridge University Press 2016)
Polakiewicz J., "The Status of the Convention in National Law" in R. Blackburn and J. Polakiewicz (eds.), *Fundamental Rights in Europe: The European Convention on Human Rights and Its Member States, 1950–2000* (Oxford: Oxford University Press 2001), pp. 31–54
Politis N. E., *Les nouvelles tendances du droit international* (Paris: Hachette 1927)
Pollicino O., "Italy: Constitutional Court at the Crossroads between Constitutional Parochialism and Co-Operative Constitutionalism. Judgments No. 348 and 349 of 22 and 24 October 2007" (2008) 4 *European Constitutional Law Review* 363–382
"The New Relationship between National and the European Courts after the Enlargement of Europe: Towards a Unitary Theory of Jurisprudential Supranational Law?" (2010) 29 *Yearbook of European Law* 65–111
Popelier P. and Van De Heyning C. J., "Subsidiarity Post-Brighton: Procedural Rationality as Answer?" (2017) 30 *Leiden Journal of International Law* 5–23
Portmann R., *Legal Personality in International Law* (Cambridge: Cambridge University Press 2010)
Rasmussen M., "Revolutionizing European Law: A History of the Van Gend En Loos Judgment" (2014) 12 *International Journal of Constitutional Law* 136–163
Remezaite R, "Azerbaijan: Is It Time to Invoke Infringement Proceedings for Failing to Implement Judgments of the Strasbourg Court?" (2017) *EJIL: Talk!* www.ejiltalk.org/azerbaijan-is-it-time-to-invoke-infringement-proceedings-for-failing-to-implement-judgments-of-the-strasbourg-court/ (accessed July 23, 2020)
Ress G., "Supranationaler Menschenrechtsschutz und der Wandel der Staatlichkeit" (2004) 64 *Zeitschrift für ausländisches öffentliches Recht und Völkerrecht* 621–639
"The Effect of Decisions and Judgments of the European Court of Human Rights in the Domestic Legal Order" (2005) 40 *Texas International Law Journal* 359–382

Reuter P., "Le plan Schuman – La Communauté européenne du charbon et de l'acier," *Collected Courses of the Hague Academy of International Law*, vol. 81 (Leiden/Boston: Brill Nijhoff 1952), pp. 532–572

Rietiker D., "The Principle of 'Effectiveness' in the Recent Jurisprudence of the European Court of Human Rights: Its Different Dimensions and Its Consistency with Public International Law – No Need for the Concept of Treaty Sui Generis" (2010) 79 *Nordic Journal of International Law* 245–277

Risse T. and Sikkink K., "The Socialization of International Human Rights Norms into Domestic Practices: Introduction" in T. Risse, S. C. Ropp, and K. Sikkink (eds.), *The Power of Human Rights: International Norms and Domestic Change* (Cambridge: Cambridge University Press 1999), pp. 1–38

Rittberger V., Zangl B., and Kruck A., *Internationale Organisationen* (Berlin/Heidelberg: Springer 2013)

Robertson A. H., "Legal Problems of European Integration," *Collected Courses of the Hague Academy of International Law*, vol. 91 (Leiden: Brill Nijhoff 1957), pp. 105–211

Rosenstiel F., *Le principe de supranationalité: essai sur les rapports de la politique et du droit* (Paris: A. Pédone 1962)

Ruedin X.-B., *Exécution des arrêts de la Cour européenne des droits de l'homme: procédure, obligations des Etats, pratique et réforme* (Basel: Helbing Lichtenhahn 2009)

Ruffert M. and Walter C., *Institutionalisiertes Völkerrecht*, 2nd ed. (Munich: C. H. Beck 2015)

Ruggie J. G., *Constructing the World Polity: Essays on International Institutionalization* (London: Routledge 2000)

Sadurski W., "Partnering with Strasbourg: Constitutionalisation of the European Court of Human Rights, the Accession of Central and East European States to the Council of Europe, and the Idea of Pilot Judgments" (2009) 9 *Human Rights Law Review* 397–453

Salerno F., "Treaties Establishing Objective Regimes" in E. Cannizzaro (ed.), *The Law of Treaties Beyond the Vienna Convention* (Oxford: Oxford University Press 2011), pp. 225–243

Sandholtz W., "Expanding Rights: Norm Innovation in the European and Inter-American Courts" in A. Brysk and M. Stoh (eds.), *Expanding Human Rights* (Cheltenham: Edward Elgar 2017), pp. 156–176

Sandholtz W. and Stone Sweet A., "Neo-Functionalism and Supranational Governance" in E. Jones, A. Menon, and S. Weatherill (eds.), *The Oxford Handbook of the European Union* (Oxford: Oxford University Press 2012), pp. 18–33

Sands P. and Klein P., *Bowett's Law of International Institutions*, 6th ed. (London: Sweet & Maxwell 2009)

Sauer H., "Principled Resistance against ECtHR Judgments in Germany" in M. Breuer (ed.), *Principled Resistance against ECtHR Judgments – A New Paradigm?* (Berlin/Heidelberg: Springer 2019), pp. 55–87

Saul M., "The European Court of Human Rights' Margin of Appreciation and the Processes of National Parliaments" (2015) 15 *Human Rights Law Review* 745–774

Scelle G., *Précis de droit des gens. Principes et systématique* (Paris: Recueil Sirey 1932)

Manuel élémentaire de droit international public (Paris: Domat-Montchrestien 1943)

"Quelques réflexions sur l'abolition de la competence de guerre" (1954) 58 *Revue générale de droit international public* 5–22

Schabas W. A., *The European Convention on Human Rights: A Commentary* (Oxford: Oxford University Press 2015)

Schermers H. G. and Blokker N. M., *International Institutional Law*, 5th ed. (Leiden/Boston: Brill Nijhoff 2011)

Schmahl S., "The National Identity Criterion in the Crossfire between European Integration and the Preservation of National Sovereignty" in M. Breuer (ed.), *Principled Resistance against ECtHR Judgments – A New Paradigm?* (Berlin/Heidelberg: Springer 2019), pp. 299–322
Schmalenbach K., "International Organizations or Institutions, General Aspects" in R. Wolfrum (ed.), *Max Planck Encyclopedia of Public International Law*, online ed. (Oxford: Oxford University Press 2014)
Schmitz K., *Durchgriffswirkung von Massnahmen der UN und ihrer Sonderorganisationen unter besonderer Berücksichtigung von Resolutionen des UN-Sicherheitsrates: Die Entwicklung supranationaler Strukturen* (Frankfurt/Main: Peter Lang 2003)
Schout A. and Wolff S., "The 'Paradox of Lisbon': Supranationalism-Intergovernmentalism as an Administrative Concept" in F. Laursen (ed.), *The EU's Lisbon Treaty: Institutional Choices and Implementation* (Farnham: Ashgate 2012), pp. 21–39
Schroeder W. and Müller A. T., "Elements of Supranationality in the Law of International Organizations" in U. Fastenrath et al. (eds.), *From Bilateralism to Community Interest: Essays in Honour of Judge Bruno Simma* (Oxford: Oxford University Press 2011), pp. 358–378
Schütze R., *From Dual to Cooperative Federalism* (Oxford: Oxford University Press 2009)
European Constitutional Law (Cambridge: Cambridge University Press 2012)
Schwantes K. D., *Die Supranationalität: Eine Untersuchung internationaler wirtschaftlicher Organisationen Europas im 19. und 20. Jahrhundert* (Cologne: University of Cologne 1962)
Seidl-Hohenveldern I. and Loibl G., *Das Recht der internationalen Organisationen einschliesslich der supranationalen Gemeinschaften*, 6th ed. (Cologne/Berlin: Heymanns Verlag 2000)
Shaffer G. C. (ed.), "Transnational Legal Ordering and State Change," *Transnational Legal Ordering and State Change* (Cambridge: Cambridge University Press 2012), pp. 1–22
Shahabuddeen M., *Precedent in the World Court* (Cambridge: Cambridge University Press 1996)
Shany Y., "Toward a General Margin of Appreciation Doctrine in International Law?" (2005) 16 *European Journal of International Law* 907–940
Shelton D., "The Participation of Nongovernmental Organizations in International Judicial Proceedings" (1994) 88 *American Journal of International Law* 611–642
"Introduction" in D. Shelton (ed.), *International Law and Domestic Legal Systems – Incorporation, Transformation, and Persuasion* (Oxford: Oxford University Press 2011), pp. 1–22
"Significantly Disadvantaged? Shrinking Access to the European Court of Human Rights" (2016) 16 *Human Rights Law Review* 303–322
Shue H., *Basic Rights: Subsistence, Affluence, and U.S. Foreign Policy*, 2nd ed. (Princeton: Princeton University Press 1996)
Sicilianos L.-A., "The Role of the European Court of Human Rights in the Execution of Its Own Judgments: Reflections on Article 46 ECHR" in A. Seibert-Fohr and M. E. Villiger (eds.), *Judgments of the European Court of Human Rights – Effects and Implementation* (Baden-Baden: Nomos 2014), pp. 285–316
Sidjanski D., *Le principe supranational et le processus d'intégration dans les Communautés européennes* (Paris: Association des études internationales 1962)
The Federal Future of Europe: From the European Community to the European Union (Ann Arbor: University of Michigan Press 2000)

Simma B., "Reservations to Human Rights Treaties – Some Recent Developments" in G. Hafner et al. (eds.), *Liber Amicorum Professor Ignaz Seidl-Hohenveldern: In Honour of His 80th Birthday* (The Hague: Kluwer Law International 1998), pp. 659–682

Simma B. and Pulkowski D., "Of Planets and the Universe" (2006) 17 *European Journal of International Law* 483–530

Skordas A., "Supranational Law" in R. Wolfrum (ed.), *Max Planck Encyclopedia of Public International Law*, online ed. (Oxford: Oxford University Press 2012)

Sloss D. (ed.), "Treaty Enforcement in Domestic Courts: A Comparative Analysis," *The Role of Domestic Courts in Treaty Enforcement* (Cambridge: Cambridge University Press 2009), pp. 1–60

Snow A. H., "The Law of Nations" (1912) 6 *American Journal of International Law* 890–900

Spano R., "Universality or Diversity of Human Rights?: Strasbourg in the Age of Subsidiarity" (2014) 14 *Human Rights Law Review* 487–502

Spaventa E., "Opening Pandora's Box: Some Reflections on the Constitutional Effects of the Decision in Pupino" (2007) 3 *European Constitutional Law Review* 5–24

Spielmann D., "Keynote Address" in A. Seibert-Fohr and M. E. Villiger (eds.), *Judgments of the European Court of Human Rights – Effects and Implementation* (Farnham: Ashgate 2014), pp. 25–32

Spiermann O., "The Other Side of the Story: An Unpopular Essay on the Making of the European Legal Order" (1999) 10 *European Journal of International Law* 763–789

Staden A. von, "The Democratic Legitimacy of Judicial Review beyond the State: Normative Subsidiarity and Judicial Standards of Review" (2012) 10 *International Journal of Constitutional Law* 1023–1049

Stein E., "Lawyers, Judges, and the Making of a Transnational Constitution" (1981) 75 *American Journal of International Law* 1–27

Stiansen Ø. and Voeten E., "Backlash and Judicial Restraint: Evidence from the European Court of Human Rights" (2020) 64 *International Studies Quarterly* 770–784

Stone Sweet A., "On the Constitutionalization of the Convention: The European Court of Human Rights as a Constitutional Court" (2009) 80 *Revue trimestrielle des droits de l'homme* 1–14

"A Cosmopolitan Legal Order: Constitutional Pluralism and Rights Adjudication in Europe" (2012) 1 *Global Constitutionalism* 53–90

Stone Sweet A. and Brunell T. L., "Trustee Courts and the Judicialization of International Regimes" (2013) 1 *Journal of Law and Courts* 61–88

Stone Sweet A. and Keller H. (eds.), "Introduction: The Reception of the ECHR in National Legal Orders," *A Europe of Rights: The Impact of the ECHR on National Legal Systems* (Oxford: Oxford University Press 2008), pp. 11–36

Stone Sweet A. and Mathews J., "Proportionality Balancing and Global Constitutionalism" (2008) 47 *Columbia Journal of Transnational Law* 72–164

Stone Sweet A. and Sandholtz W., "European Integration and Supranational Governance" (1997) 4 *Journal of European Public Policy* 297–317

Swart M., "Gap-Filling as Lawmaking: The Examples of the Ad Hoc International Criminal Tribunals" in H. R. Fabri, R. Wolfrum, and J. Gogolin (eds.), *Select Proceedings of the European Society of International Law*, vol. II (Oxford: Hart 2010), pp. 313–330

Swedberg R. and Agevall O., *The Max Weber Dictionary: Key Words and Central Concepts*, 2nd ed. (Stanford: Stanford University Press 2016)

Szasz P. C., "The Complexification of the United Nations System" (1999) 3 *Max Planck Yearbook of United Nations Law* 1–57

Tams C. J., "The 'International Community' as a Legal Concept" in J. d'Aspremont and S. Singh (eds.), *Concepts for International Law: Contributions to Disciplinary Thought* (Cheltenham: Edward Elgar 2019), pp. 505–523

Thierry H., "The European Tradition in International Law: Georges Scelle" (1990) 1 *European Journal of International Law* 193–209

Tomuschat C., *Human Rights: Between Idealism and Realism* (Oxford: Oxford Uiversity Press 2014)

Tsebelis G. and Garrett G., "The Institutional Foundations of Intergovernmentalism and Supranationalism in the European Union" (2001) 55 *International Organization* 357–390

Tulkens F., "The European Convention on Human Rights between International Law and Constitutional Law," *Dialogue between Judges* (Strasbourg: European Court of Human Rights, Council of Europe 2007) www.echr.coe.int/Documents/Dialogue_2007_ENG.pdf (accessed July 23, 2020)

Tuori K., "Transnational Law" in M. Maduro, K. Tuori, and S. Sankari (eds.), *Transnational Law: Rethinking European Law and Legal Thinking* (Cambridge: Cambridge University Press 2014), pp. 11–58

Tzevelekos V. P., "The Use of Article 31(3)(c) of the VCLT in the Case Law of the ECtHR: An Effective Anti-Fragmentation Tool or a Selective Loophole for the Reinforcement of Human Rights Teleology" (2010) 31 *Michigan Journal of International Law* 621–690

Ulfstein G., "Institutions and Competences" in J. Klabbers, A. Peters, and G. Ulfstein (eds.), *The Constitutionalization of International Law* (Oxford: Oxford University Press 2009), pp. 45–80

"Treaty Bodies and Regimes" in D. B. Hollis (ed.), *The Oxford Guide to Treaties* (Oxford: Oxford University Press 2012), pp. 428–447

Van de Heyning C. J., "The Natural 'Home' of Fundamental Rights Adjudication: Constitutional Challenges to the European Court of Human Rights" (2012) 31 *Yearbook of European Law* 128–161

Vazquez C. M., "The Four Doctrines of Self-Executing Treaties" (1995) 89 *American Journal of International Law* 695–723

Venzke I. and Thio L., *The Internal Effects of ASEAN External Relations* (Cambridge: Cambridge University Press 2016)

Verdross A. von, "On the Concept of International Law" (1949) 43 *American Journal of International Law* 435–440

Vetsika S.-E. and Tzevelekos V. P., "In Integration We Trust? The Reception of Supranational Law in the Greek Legal Order: 'A Tale of Love and Darkness'" (2010) 5 *Stals Research Paper* www.stals.sssup.it/files/stals_Vassilis_052010.pdf (accessed July 23, 2020)

Vila M. I., "Subsidiarity, Margin of Appreciation and International Adjudication within a Cooperative Conception of Human Rights" (2017) 15 *International Journal of Constitutional Law* 393–413

Villalpando S. "Definition and Classification of International Organizations: A Legal Approach" in G. Abi-Saab (ed.), *The Concept of International Organization* (Paris: UNESCO 1981), pp. 50–66

"The Legal Dimension of the International Community: How Community Interests Are Protected in International Law" (2010) 21 *European Journal of International* 387–419

Voland T. and Schiebel B., "Advisory Opinions of the European Court of Human Rights: Unbalancing the System of Human Rights Protection in Europe?" (2017) 17 *Human Rights Law Review* 1–23

Wassenberg B., *History of the Council of Europe* (Strasbourg: Council of Europe 2013)
Waters M. A., "Creeping Monism: The Judicial Trend Toward Interpretive Incorporation of Human Rights Treaties" (2007) 107 *Columbia Law Review* 628–705
Weber M., "Die 'Objektivität' sozialwissenschaftlicher und sozialpolitischer Erkenntnis" (1904) 19 *Archiv für Sozialwissenschaft und Sozialpolitik* 22–87
Weil P., "Towards Relative Normativity in International Law?" (1983) 77 *The American Journal of International Law* 413–442
Weiler J. H. H., "The Community System: The Dual Character of Supranationalism" (1981) 1 *Yearbook of European Law* 267–306
"The Transformation of Europe" (1991) 100 *Yale Law Journal* 2403–2483
Westbrook J. L., "Legal Integration of NAFTA Through Supranational Adjudication" (2008) 43 *Texas International Law Journal* 349–358
Wet E. and Vidmar J., *Hierarchy in International Law* (Oxford: Oxford University Press 2012)
Wheare K. C., *Federal Government* (Oxford: Oxford University Press 1946)
Wildhaber L., "Precedent in the European Court of Human Rights" in P. Mahoney et al. (eds.), *Protection des droits de l'homme: la perspective européenne /Protecting Human Rights: The European Perspective: Mélanges à la mémoire de /Studies in memory of Rolv Ryssdal* (Cologne: Heymanns 2000), pp. 1529–1546
"A Constitutional Future for the European Court of Human Rights" (2002) 23 *Human Rights Law Journal* 161–165
"The Place of the European Court of Human Rights in the European Constitutional Landscape," *Conference of European Constitutional Courts XIIth Congress* (2002) www.confeuconstco.org/reports/rep-xii/Report%20ECHR-EN.pdf
"The European Court of Human Rights: The Past, the Present, the Future" (2007) 22 *American University International Law Review* 521–538
"The European Convention on Human Rights and International Law" (2007) 56 *International and Comparative Law Quarterly* 217–232
"Rethinking the European Court of Human Rights" in J. Christoffersen and M. R. Madsen (eds.), *The European Court of Human Rights between Law and Politics* (Oxford: Oxford University Press 2011), pp. 204–230
Wildhaber L., Hjartarson A., and Donnelly S., "No Consensus on Consensus? The Practice of the European Court of Human Rights" (2013) 33 *Human Rights Law Journal* 248–263
Wolfrum R. and Pichon J., "Consensus," *Max Planck Encyclopedia of Public International Law*, online ed. (Oxford: Oxford University Press 2006)
Xenos D., *The Positive Obligations of the State under the European Convention of Human Rights* (London: Routledge 2012)
Zysset A., *The ECHR and Human Rights Theory: Reconciling the Moral and the Political Conceptions* (London: Routledge 2017)

Index

access to ECtHR, 88–94, 125
admissibility, of applications to ECtHR, 92–94, 95, 157
advisory jurisdiction of ECtHR, 122–129
  compared to EU law, 128–129
  limits to, 126–129
  non-binding outcome of, 126
  preventive nature of, 125–126
  supranational potential of, 124–126
  under Art.47, 122–123
  under Protocol No.16, 123–124
advisory opinion procedures, 122–124
Ahmet Sadik v. Greece case, 167–168
Albuquerque, Judge Pinto de, 169–170
Al-Dulimi case, 169–170
Alexy, Robert, 134, 175
Anchugov and Gladkov vs. Russia case, 191–192
Andean Community, 47, 48
Annex Rules of Court (of ECtHR), 101
anthropocentrism, 15
applicants to ECtHR
  representatives of, 78
  rights of, 78–79
  victim requirement and, 89–91
applications to ECtHR, admissibility of, 92–94, 95, 157
Articles of ECHR
  1, 164, 165–168
  3, 105
  6, 76, 105, 171
  8–11, 103–104
  13, 164–165, 166–168, 175–177, 196
  19, 101–102
  34, 88–91, 92–94, 97, 99–100, 202
  35, 92
  36(2), 159–160
  38, 98–99, 101
  41, 109–110, 111
  46, 97, 111–112, 120–122
  46(1), 94–95, 108, 152
  47, 122–123
assistance to ECtHR, 101
ATJ (Court of Justice of the Andean Community), 47
Austria v. Italy case, 67, 70
autonomy. *see also* supranational authority
  in general, 30, 40–41
  of ECtHR
    in general, 83, 206–207
    in interpretation, 75–77, 135–137

Bates, Ed, 62, 81
Belgian Linguistic cases, 68–69, 89, 102, 171
Benvenisti, Eyal, 146–147
Besson, Samantha, 43, 57, 60, 86
binding force. *see also* non-binding force
  in general, 30, 40–41, 152
  of ECtHR judgments and decisions, 83, 94–101
Bjorge, Eirik, 186, 189
Blokker, Niels M., 30, 32, 41
Bogdandy, Armin von, 56, 74
Breuer, Marten, 194
Brighton Declaration, 93–94, 123, 154, 192, 203
British law, 186, 191
Brölmann, Catherine, 74
Broniowski v. Poland case, 114–115
Brunell, Thomas L., 146
Brussels Declaration, 117, 158
Buergenthal, Thomas, 133–134, 167
Burdov case, 115
Burmych case, 120

CACJ (Central American Court of Justice), 47
Çali, Başak, 4, 49
Câmpeanu case, 90–91
Cassese, Sabino, 41, 102

Central American Community, 47, 48
Central American Court of Justice (CACJ), 47
Chané, Anna-Luise, 43
Charter of Human Rights, 61
children
  illegitimacy of, 77, 179–180
  language education of, 68–69
Chorzów Factory case, 108
Christoffersen, Jonas, 175
Churchill, Winston, 16
CJEU (Court of Justice of the European Union), 47
Cohen, Jean, 55, 56
Committee of Ministers (CoM, of CoE), 37, 111, 117–118, 120–121, *see also* Table of International Instruments
communities
  interests of, 57–58
  intersubjective nature of, 58–59
  notion of, 56–59
compensation/reparations, 108, 109–110
complementary reviews. *see* subsidiarity
compliance reviews, 117–120
Congress of Europe (1948), 16, 61–63
consensus, 144–145, 147–148
consistent interpretations, 45, 178–179
constitutionalism, 6, 51–53
constructivism, 58–59
contextualization of supranationality, 51–59
  constitutionalism and, 52–53
  federalism and, 53–56
  monism and, 51–52
  notion of community and, 56–59
  pluralism and, 52
Convention community. *see also* communities; domestic courts
  in general, 3, 7–8
  collective identity of, 205
  Convention states within, 209, 210
  direct members of, 207–209
  domestic authorities within, 208–209
  ECHR and, enforcement, 206
  ECtHR and
    as community court, 137–141
    external review of, 206
    lawmaking of, 137–140, 206–207
  individuals within, 207–208
  interests of, 205–206
  sovereignty, role within, 210
  subsidiarity and, 209–210
  use of term, 204–205
Convention regime, use of term, 204
Convention states. *see also* domestic courts
  within Convention community, 209, 210
  ECHR, freedom of implementation of, 164–170
    in general, 164–165
    general duty to secure human rights and, 165–166
    obligation of incorporation and, 166–168
    positive obligations and, 170–173
    proportionality analysis and, 173–175
  sovereignty of, 210
Convention system, use of term, 204
cooperation, ECtHR and, 98–101
Costa E.N.E.L case, 25, 27
Council of Europe (CoE). *see also* Table of International Instruments
  Committee of Ministers of, 37, 111, 117–118, 120–121
  ECHR and, 2, 63–64
  ECtHR and, 87
  enlargement of, 130, 200–201
  as IO, 37, 63, 198
  post-judgement phase of ECtHR and, 117–118, 120–121
  rejection of an early supranational court and, 63–64
Court of Justice of the Andean Community (ATJ), 47
Court of Justice of the European Union (CJEU), 47, *see also* Table of Cases
Cyprus v. Turkey case, 119

De Baere, Geert, 43
dédoublement fonctionnel, 14
Delbrück, Jost, 44
dialogues, formalized, 127–128
Diennet v. France case, 174
direct effect. *see also* indirect effect; invocability
  in general, 42, 45–48
  of ECHR, 179–180, 183–184
  of European treaties, 23–24
  supranationality and, 25, 30
disenfranchisements, 191–192
dissemination, of ECtHR's case-law, 155, 157–158
domaine réservé (reserved domain), 68–69
domestic authorities, within Convention community, 208–209
domestic courts
  ECtHR and, 123–124, 128, 157–159, 208–209
  proportionality analysis and, 173–174
domestic fundamental rights, 85–86
domestic law
  and ECHR
    supremacy of ECHR over, 210–212
  ECHR and, 175–177, 181–194
    in general, 2, 6–8, 181–182
    consistent interpretation and, 178–179

domestic law (cont.)
constitutional reservations towards, 186–187, 190–194, 203
direct applicability of, 183–184
domestification of, 182–183
implementation freedom and, 166–168
supranationalization of, 188–190, 195–197
supremacy of ECHR over, 168–170, 184–187
ECtHR and, 7, 91–92, 108–109
international law and, 14–15, 48–50
vs. supranational law, 51
supranationality in
invocability and, 45–48
penetration of, 44–45
domestic violence, 153–154
Draft Articles on State Responsibility (of ILC), 108
Draft European Convention on Human Rights (1949), 61–62, 64
'Dual Character of Supranationalism' (Weiler), 25
Dworkin, Ronald, 134, 177
dynamic interpretation. *see* evolutive/dynamic interpretation

ECHR. *see* European Convention on Human Rights (ECHR)
ECJ (European Court of Justice), 24–25
EComHR (European Commission of Human Rights), 96
ECSC (European Coal and Steel Community), 19–20, 22–24
ECSC Treaty, 19–20
ECtHR. *see* European Court of Human Rights (ECtHR)
EDC (European Defence Community), 20–21, 22
EDC Draft Treaty, 21
EEC (European Economic Community), 22
EEC Treaty, 22, 46
effectiveness doctrine, 76
elections, of ECtHR judges, 66–67
Emre v. Switzerland case, 118–119
enforcement
of ECHR
collective structure of, 65–66
Convention community and, 206
domestic implementation and. *see* domestic law
domestic implementation of, 175–177
supranationality and, 30
of international law, 15, 41–42
Engel case, 75–76
EPC (European Political Community), 21, 22
EPC Draft Statute, 21
erga omnes effect, 153, *see also res interpretata* effect
EU. *see* European Union (EU)
Euratom (European Atomic Energy Community), 22
Euratom Treaty, 22, 24
European Atomic Energy Community (Euratom), 22
European Coal and Steel Community (ECSC), 19–20, 22–24
European Commission of Human Rights (EComHR), 96
European Convention on Human Rights (ECHR)
Articles of. *see* Articles of ECHR
compensation/reparations under, 108
Congress of Europe and, 61–63
constitutional reservations towards, 186–187, 190–194, 203
Council of Europe and, 2, 37, 63–64
direct effect of, 179–180, 183–184
domestic law and, 115–117, *see* domestic law
enforcement of. *see* enforcement
ECJ on, 24–25
vs. EU law, 188–189
implementation of. *see* implementation
interpretations of. *see* interpretations
limitation provisions in, 65, 103–104
negotiations on and drafting of, 61–64
objective nature of, 135–136
Preamble of, 107
purpose of, 62, 67–68, 73–75
restrictions on applicability of, 68–69, 70–72
rights minimalism in, 62, 140
sovereignty and, 62, 82
state-centric and quasi-judicial system of, 64–65
subsidiarity principle and, 86–87, 209–210
supranational adjudication and. *see* supranational adjudication
supranationalization of. *see* supranationalization
supremacy of, 168–170, 184–187, 210–212
European Court of Human Rights (ECtHR). *see also* Rules of Court (of ECtHR)
access to, 88–94, 125
advisory jurisdiction of. *see* advisory jurisdiction of ECtHR
Annex Rules of Court of, 101
applicants to. *see* applicants to ECtHR
assistance by parties to, 101
authority of, 1, 130–131, 201
autonomy of, 206–207
compliance reviews of, 117–120
cooperation and, 98–101
Council of Europe and, 37, 87
domestic courts and, 123–124, 128, 157–159, 208–209
domestic fundamental rights and, 85–86

domestic law and, 7, 91–92, 108–109
Grand Chamber of, 81, 82
infringement procedure of, 120–122
interim measures of, 96–98
interpretations by. *see* interpretations
judges of, 66–67, 81–82
judgments and decisions of. *see* judgments and decisions of ECtHR
judicial integration of. *see* judicial integration of ECtHR
lawmaking function of. *see* lawmaking of ECtHR
legitimacy of, 74, 103
locus standi rules before, 88–91
non-state actors/NGO's and, 80
perception of, 208
post-judgment phase of, 117–122
resistance against, 8–9, 211–212
reviews of. *see* reviews of ECtHR
role of
as Community court, 137–141
as treaty organ of the Convention, 198
as trustee court, 74–75
subsidiarity principle and, 91–92, 102–103, 106–107
supranationalization of. *see* supranationalization
victim requirement and, 89–91
European Court of Justice (ECJ), 24–25
European Defence Community (EDC), 20–21, 22
European Economic Community (EEC), 22
European integration. *see also* European Movement
Schuman Plan of, 18–19
European Movement, 61–63
European Political Community (EPC), 21, 22
European Union (EU)
vs. ECHR, 188–189
law of
direct effect doctrine in, 46–47
scholarship on, 22–24
supranationality in. *see* supranationality
supremacy doctrine and, 49
legal nature of, 26–28
subsidiarity and, 86–87
evolutive/dynamic interpretation, 76–77, 136, 145

Fabris v. France case, 179
Federal Constitutional Court (Germany), 185
federalism, 53–56
in international law
in general, 14–15
institutionalization of, 17–18
Scelle vs. Marc on, 16
of Schuman and Monnet, 18
financial autonomy, 30
follow-up applications, 118–119
formalized dialogues, 127–128
French Court of Cassation, 124, 126
fundamental rights, 140

GAL (global administrative law), 53
general measures, in ECtHR judgements, 112–115, 116–117
Gerards, Janneke, 127
German Basic Law, 185, 187
German Constitutional Court, 184, 189
German law, 185
Ginsburg, Tom, 134
global administrative law (GAL), 53
Golder v. the United Kingdom case, 76, 143–144
Goodwin v. the United Kingdom case, 148–149, 151–152
Gorgülü case, 184
Grand Chamber (of ECtHR)
composition of, 82
re-hearing Chamber judgements, 81
Gross v. Switzerland case, 100–101
Group of Wise Persons, 155

Haider, Dominik, 116–117
Halberstam, Daniel, 55
Handyside v. the United Kingdom case, 105–106
Hay, Peter, 23, 32, 55
Helfer, Laurence R., 43, 152
High Authority (HA, of ECSC), 19–20, 22–23
Hirst saga, 191, 203
homosexuality, 174
Hull, William Isaac, 13, 17–18
human rights
on domestic level, 85–86
interpretation of, as perpetual lawmaking process, 135
Pan-European standard of, 142–147
(re-)imposing of, 152–159
international trends and common grounds in, 147–152
majoritarian methodology for, 143–147
sources for lawmaking of ECtHR, 142
progressive realization of, 140–141
special nature of, 200
Human Rights Directorate (of CoE), 117
human rights protection system
establishment of, 61–67, *see also* European Convention on Human Rights (ECHR)
Council of Europe and, 63–64
European Movement and, 61–63

human trafficking, 149–150
Hutten-Czapska v. Poland case, 119

ICJ Statute, 65, 70–71
ILC (International Law Commission), 108
Ilgar Mammadov v. Azerbaijan case, 121–122
illegitimacy, of children, 77, 179–180
implementation
  freedom of, 164–170
    in general, 164–165
    general duty to secure human rights and, 165–166
    obligation of incorporation and, 166–168
    positive obligations and, 170–173
    proportionality analysis and, 173–175
  use of term, 164
incrementalism, 199–200
independence. *see* autonomy
indirect effect, 45–46, 176–177, *see also* direct effect
individual measures, in ECtHR judgements, 111, 115–116
infringement procedures, 120–122
intergovernmentalism, 25–26
intergovernmental organizations (IOs). *see also* supranational organizations
  CoE as, 37, 63, 198
  notion of regimes and, 36–37
  vs. supranational organizations, 31–32
Interlaken Declaration, 154
international community, 56–57
International Court of Justice (ICJ), 65, 70–71, *see also* Table of Cases
international criminal tribunals, 42
international law
  anthropocentricity of, 15
  community in, 56–57
  domestic law and, 14–15, 48–50
  enforcement of, 15, 41–42
  federalism in
    in general, 14–15
    institutionalization of, 17–18
    Scelle vs. Marc on, 16
  individualistic conceptions of, 16, 17
  supranationality and, 12–14
  supremacy of, 48–50
International Law Commission (ILC), 108
International Prize Court, 12–13
International Seabed Authority, 42
interpretations
  consistent, 45
  of ECHR
    autonomy in, 75–77, 135–137
    consistency and, 178–179
    effectiveness doctrine and, 76
    evolutive/dynamic, 76–77, 136, 145
    procedures for, 122
    variation in, 141
intra-state societies, 14
invocability, 45–48, 58, 183–184, *see also* direct effect
IOs. *see* intergovernmental organizations (IOs)
Ipsen, Hans Peter, 25
Ireland v. the United Kingdom case, 69–70, 138, 140
Irish law, 186
Italian Constitutional Court, 185, 187, 192–193
Italian law, 185, 187, 192–193

Janowiec and Others v. Russia case, 100
judges of ECtHR, 66–67, 81–82
judgment no. 49/2015 (Italian Constitutional Court), 192–193
judgments and decisions of ECtHR
  binding force of, 83, 94–101
  compensation and, 109–110
  compliance reviews of, 117–120
  declaratory nature of, 108–109
  execution of, 117, 118–119
  general measures in, 112–115, 116–117
  individual measures in, 115–116
  just satisfaction and, 109–110
  pilot judgment procedures, 112–113, 114–115, 116–117, 119–120
  remedial measures in, 110–117
judicial integration of ECtHR
  in general, 85–88, 129–131
  compliance reviews and, 117–122
  external judicial review of, 88–108
  remedies and enforcement, 108–117
just satisfaction, 109–110, 119

Karner v. Austria case, 138, 140
Kaufman, Willhelm, 12–14
Keller, Helen, 141, 182, 188, 204, 209
Klabber, Jan, 41
Klass case, 90
Krabbe, Hugo, 13–14, 17
Krasner, Stephen D., 36
Kritsiotis, Dino, 58

Lambrecht, Sarah, 192, 194
lawmaking of ECtHR
  in general, 132–134
  Convention community and, 206–207
  expansive nature of, 134–137
  international trends and common grounds in, 147–152
    beyond consensus, 147–148
    conceptual analysis in, 150–152

examples of, 148–150
interpretative autonomy and, 135–137
majoritarian methodology in, 143–147
comparative approach to, 143–144
conceptual analysis in, 146–147
consensus in, 144–145
progressive realization of human rights and, 140–141
res interpretata effect in
content of, 157–159
legal basis of, 153–157
vs. *res judicata* effect, 94–95, 152–153
scope of, 157
as secondary but standalone function, 137–140
sources of, 142
supranational character of, 161–162
third-party interventions in, 159–160, 162
lawmaking treaties (traités lois), 73–75
lawmaking, use of term, 133–134
legal certainty principle, 179
legal integration of supranationality, 39–51
in general, 39–40
on international level, 40–44
on national level, 44–51
invocability and, 45–48
penetration of domestic law, 44–45
legitimacy
of ECtHR, 74, 103
of international institutions, 53
supranationalization process and, 199–200, 210
Lemmens, Koen, 85
Letsas, George, 136, 147, 152
Lindeiner-Wildau, K. von, 30
Lisbon Treaty, 26
Liszt, Franz von, 12–13, 17
locus standi rules, 88–91
Loizidou v. Turkey case, 70–72, 147–148, 169
Lotus principle, 76

Madsen, Mikael Rask, 65, 107
majoritarian methodology
in lawmaking of ECtHR
comparative approach to, 143–144
conceptual analysis of, 146–147
consensus in, 144–145
Mamatkulov and Askarov v. Turkey case, 97
Marc, Alexandre, 16, 17
Marckx v. Belgium case, 76, 89, 147, 171–172
margin of appreciation doctrine, 105–106, 210
Markin v. Russia case, 138–139
Martens, Judge, 167–168
Martinico, Guiseppe, 188
Mégret, Frédéric, 43, 77
Merger Treaty, 22
Die moderne Staatsidee (Krabbe), 13–14
Monaco, Ricardo, 27
monism, 51–52
Monnet, Jean, 18–19
Moravcsik, Andrew, 190
Müller, Andreas Th., 32, 52
Münch, Fritz, 17

national courts. *see* domestic courts
national law. *see* domestic law
NATO (North Atlantic Treaty Organization), 20
Nietzsche, Friedrich, 12
non-binding force, 126, *see also* binding force
non-state actors/NGO's, 80
normativity, 38
North Atlantic Treaty Organization (NATO), 20

Opuz v. Turkey case, 153–154

Palermo Protocol, 149
Papamichalopoulos and Others v. Greece case, 111
Paulus, Andreas, 57
Permanent Court of International Justice (PCIJ), 13
pilot judgment procedures, 112–113, 114–115, 116–117, 119–120
Pleven Plan, 20
Pleven, René, 20
pluralism, 52
Politis, Nicolas E., 18
Pollicino, Oreste, 188
positive obligations, 170–173
Preamble (of ECHR), 107
precedent doctrine, 136–137
Pretty v. the United Kingdom case, 136–137
Preventive Detention II case, 189
prisoners, disenfranchisement of, 191–192
pro homine principle, 76
proceduralization, of substantive rights, 172–173
proportionality, 104, 173–175
Protocols of ECHR
No. 1, 111
No. 9, 79
No. 11, 60, 79, 81–83, 97, 202, 203
No. 14, 93, 120–122
No. 15, 93
No. 16, 123–124, 128–129, 203

Rantsev v. Cyprus and Russia case, 149–150, 151–152
Rasmussen, Morten, 28
regime, notion of, 36–37
reparations. *see* compensation/reparations
Representation of the People Act (1983, UK), 116, 191

res interpretata effect
  in general, 202
  definitions of, 155–157
  legal basis of, 153–157
  vs. *res judicata* effect, 152–153
  scope and content of, 157–159
res judicata effect, 152–153
reserved domain (*domaine réservé*), 68–69
Ress, Georg, 82
Reuter, Paul, 19
reviews of ECtHR, 101–108
  intensity of, 104–105
  margin of appreciation doctrine and, 105–106
  nature of, 101–103
  proceduralization of, 107
  proportionality analysis and, 103–104
  standard of, 103–106
  weakening of, 106–108
right to a fair trial (Art. 6 ECHR), 76, 105, 171
right to an effective remedy (Art. 13 ECHR), 164–165, 166–168, 175–177, 196
right to individual application (Art. 34 ECHR), 88–91, 92–94, 97, 99–100, 202
rights minimalism, 62, 140
Riker, William, 55
Robertson, Arthur Henry, 23
Rome Treaties (1957), 22, 24
Rules of Court (of ECtHR)
  applicant's rights in, 78
  assistance by parties in, 101
  interim measures in, 96
  pilot judgement procedure in, 112–113
  third party status in, 80
Rules of Procedure (of EComHR), 96
Russian Constitutional Court, 191–192, 203
Russian law, 191–192

S.A.S. *v. France* case, 107
Scelle, Georges, 14–15, 17–18
Scellian theory, 14–15
Schalk and Kopf v. Austria case, 144–145
Schermers, Henry G., 30, 32, 41
Schlochauer, Hans Jürgen, 30
Schroeder, Werner, 32, 52
Schuman Declaration (1950), 18
Schuman Plan, 18–19
Schuman, Robert, 18–19
Scoppola v. Italy (No. 2) case, 150, 151
Scordino and Others v. Italy case, 178
Second Hague Peace Conference (1907), 12
Selmouni v. France case, 92
shared responsibility, 7
Shue, Henry, 171
Simma, Bruno, 73
Single European Act (1986), 25
Slaughter, Anne-Marie, 43
Smith and Grady v. the United Kingdom case, 174
Snow, Alpheus Henry, 13, 17
Solange case, 187
sovereignty
  of Convention states, 210
  ECHR and, 62, 82
  supranationality and, 26–27
Staden, Andreas von, 103
Stiansen, Øyvind, 107, 139
Stockholm compromise, 81–82
Stone Sweet, Alec, 7, 141, 146, 182, 183, 188, 204, 209
subordination principle, 30
subsidiarity
  Brighton Declaration and, 106–107
  Convention community and, 209–210
  ECHR and, 86–87, 209–210
  ECtHR and, 91–92, 102–103, 106–107
  EU and, 86–87
  proportionality and, 104
substantive rights, proceduralization of, 172–173
sui generis notion, 27–28
supranational adjudication
  authority in, 42–44
  ECHR's establishment of, 81
  ECHR's movement towards
    collective enforcement structure and, 65–67
    through early case-law, 67–72
    ECHR as lawmaking treaty and, 73–75
    interpretative techniques and, 75–77
    recognition of broader community and, 79–80
supranational authority
  domestic jurisdiction and, 58
  of ECtHR, 87–88, 96, 103, 110, 129–130, 203
  of international organizations, 42
supranational law, delineation of, 50–51
supranational organizations, 29–32
  in general, 29
  inductive vs. deductive definitions of, 29–30
  relative vs. absolute conceptualizations of, 31–32
  vs. traditional IOs, 31–32
supranationalism
  vs. intergovernmentalism, 25–26
  vs. supranationality, 39
supranationality. *see also* supranationalization
  in general, 24–25
  constitutionalism and, 6, 51–52
  contextualisation of. *see* contextualization of supranationality
  ECSC and, 19–20, 22–24
  European integration and
    acceptance as legal term and, 20–21

banishment to scholarship and, 22
ECSC Treaty and, 19–20
Schuman plan and, 18
framework for. *see* supranationality framework
in EU law
in general, 4–6, 32–33, 35
Community model and, 22–24
EU's legal nature and, 26
supranationalism vs. intergovernmentalism, 25–26
international law origins of
commonalities in the early use of, 17–18
in Congress of Europe resolution, 16
Scellian theory and, 14–15
scholarship of early 20th century on, 12–15
legal integration of. *see* legal integration of supranationality
normativity and, 38
notion of regime and, 36–37
polysemic nature of, 11–12
sovereignty and, 26–27
vs. supranationalism, 39
vs. supranationalization, 39
supranationality framework
beyond EU law, 35–36
beyond IOs law, 36–37
descriptive-analytical value of, 37–38
formal concept of, 38
supranationalization
legitimacy and, 199–200, 210
of ECHR
in general, 1–3, 60–61, 163–164, 180–181, 198–199
driving factors behind, 200–202
horizontal integration of, 3, 201
incrementalism and, 199–200
resistance against, 186–187, 190–194, 202–204
vertical integration of, 3, 188–190, 195–197, 199–200, 202
of ECtHR, 4–6, 60–61, 87–88, 113–117, 129–131, 180–181
vs. supranationality, 39
supra-state societies, 14
supremacy
of ECHR over domestic law, 168–170, 184–187, 210–212
of international law, 48–50
supranationality and, 25, 49
Swiss Federal Supreme Court, 184, 193
Swiss law, 193–194, 203
Swiss National Popular Paty (SVP), 193

Teitgen Report, 166
Teitgen, Pierre-Henri, 63
TFEU (Treaty on the Functioning of the European Union), 128–129
third-party interventions, before ECtHR, 159–160, 162
Tomuschat, Christian, 66
transnational law, vs. supranational law, 50–51
transsexualism, 148–149
Treaty on the Functioning of the European Union (TFEU), 128–129
trustee courts, 74–75
Tulkens, Françoise, 176
Tyrer v. the United Kingdom case, 70, 76, 80, 143, 144
Tzevelekos, Vassilis P., 150–151

United Kingdom Supreme Court, 187
United Nations Interim Administration Mission in Kosovo (UNMIK), 42
United Nations Security Council (UNSC), 42

validity, 45
Van Gend en Loos case, 24, 27–28, 47
Varvara v. Italy case, 192–193
VCLT (Vienna Convention on the Law of Treaties), 143, 147, 150–151
Venzke, Ingo, 74
Verein gegen Tierfabriken Schweiz (no.2) case, 118
Vermeire v. Belgium case, 179–180
victim requirement, 89–91
Vienna Convention on the Law of Treaties (VCLT), 143, 147, 150–151
Vinter and Others v. the United Kingdom case, 144
Voeten, Erik, 107, 139
Volkov case, 112

Wehberg, Hans, 30
Weiler, Joseph H. H., 25
Wemhoff v. Germany case, 135–136
Wildhaber, Luzius, 135
Wouters, Jan, 43

Young, James and Webster v. the United Kingdom case, 80
Yukos v. Russia case, 192

For EU product safety concerns, contact us at Calle de José Abascal, 56–1°,
28003 Madrid, Spain or eugpsr@cambridge.org.

www.ingramcontent.com/pod-product-compliance
Ingram Content Group UK Ltd.
Pitfield, Milton Keynes, MK11 3LW, UK
UKHW020812270926
475880UK00019B/220
9781108830119